INDIAN CONTROVERSIES
Essays on Religion in Politics

By the same author:
Hinduism, Essence and Consequence
Symptoms of Fascism
Institutions in the Janata Phase
Mrs. Gandhi's Second Reign
Religion in Politics
Individuals, Institutions, Processes
These Lethal, Inexorable Laws
The State as Charade
'The Only Fatherland'

INDIAN CONTROVERSIES
Essays on Religion in Politics

ARUN SHOURIE

ISBN 81-900199-2-9

© Arun Shourie 1993

First Published Jan 1993
Second Printing Jan 1993
Third Printing Feb 1993

Published by ASA Publications, A-31 West End, New Delhi-110 021 and
printed at Suman Printers and Stationers, 1/9346-B, West Rohtas Nagar,
Shahdara, Delhi - 110 032.

For Adit
who opened an entire world

for Anita
who filled it

INTRODUCTION

The diabolic use to which Jinnah put religion culminated in dividing India. For three decades after that religion was used mostly by, or at the least most effectively by the secularists—not by those, that is, who were secular but by those who appropriated the label. 'Secular' politicians frightened the minorities—the Muslims in particular—by conjuring miasmas into putting their faith in them. Editorialists of the same kind established their secular credentials by branding others communal.

In the eighties this politics reached its murderous nadir: to out-do the Akalis Mrs Gandhi and her associates stoked Bhindranwale, to get Muslims on his side Rajiv bent the State to fundamentalists among them. On the one side the monsters ran out of hand. On the other, the Hindus began to see in these manoeuvres a replay of the rhetoric and politics of the 1930's and 40's, which had culminated in the Partition. These politicians do not care for us, they began to feel, because we are not organised *as Hindus.* We must acquire the State, they began to feel, *as Hindus.* The double standards in our discourse—in radio and television, in our press in particular, and among our academics—incensed them as much as the genuflections of the State to fundamentalists and terrorists. They began to feel that not only did no one listen to them in their own country, no one was prepared to let them state the facts as they saw them. They began accordingly to see themselves *as Hindus.* That is the reaction our secularists have ignited.

The campaigns of the fundamentalists, the capitulations of the politicians occasioned many controversies. These in turn occasioned much bitterness and vehemence. But they did one good: for the first time in India, at least for the first time in India in this century, Islam too began to be discussed.

The focus of my writing on these matters shifted as one brand of fundamentalism overshadowed another. In the early eighties the focus naturally was Bhindranwale, the attempt of several to misrepresent the teachings of the Gurus, the terrorism in Punjab. Similarly, an earlier book, *Religion in Politics,* which contained several of the essays which are included in this volume had essays for instance on Assam. No one any longer claims that the terrorism in Punjab has anything to do with the teachings of the Sikh Gurus. The fever in Assam too has abated. The issues which have been in the forefront in the last five years are ones which erupted as a result of the campaigns of brokers and 'Sole Spokesmen' who set themselves up in the name of Islam. Accordingly, essays in this collection deal with these, 'Islamic' issues.

But while the focus has shifted, the themes have remained the same: that this misuse of religion must be scotched—otherwise a reaction will set in which no one will be able to control; that the way to scotch it is to establish a polity, to practice a politics which is truly secular, to rid our discourse of double standards; that to bring these things about reformers in all traditions must join hands; that each of us must appropriate all our traditions as equally his own; that he must examine each of them thoroughly and scrupulously—without the slightest self-consciousness of being from this religion or that; that in each tradition there is much that is valuable, but also much that is malignant; that we should together sift one from the other, and build on the good.

Alongwith the themes, the premises too have remained unchanged: the premise that it is the task of those of us who are fortunate enough to be able to get our views to large numbers, it is our special responsibility to lay bare, to persuade, to get our people into the habit of talking things out, of dealing in arguments rather than in the blow and the smear, in data rather than stones; and the premise that reason and argument and evidence *do* make a difference to the outcome. That is why I have used each of these occasions as 'a teaching moment'.

The course these controversies have taken shows that if we do not heed reason in time, if we do not rectify our politics and our ways in response to reason and evidence, society will move to restore balance irrationally—by force of numbers, by counter-violence—and that, as its ways will be haphazard and uneven, the innocent and the weak are the ones who will get clobbered the most. This is the prospect we seem so intent on preparing for ourselves.

There is one slender ray of hope: the results of the campaigns of the fundamentalists and of this cynical use of religion in politics have begun to register even on many who got swept off by them. Sikhs in Punjab and outside see where the rhetoric of Bhindranwale and the guns of the terrorists have landed them. The average Muslim too is beginning to glimpse the costs of the 'victories' the fundamentalist leaders brought him by bending the State. But it is as yet just one tremulous ray. It isn't just that there are designs: how often these days we hear of attempts to forge alliances between Scheduled Castes, Scheduled Tribes, Muslims and other sections. It is that the apparatus of governance, and thereby the decisions which will turn the outcome one way or the other, remain in the hands of precisely the sorts of leaders whose calculations and stratagems have brought us to this pass. So it is only with foreboding that one can contemplate what the complexion of the next collection on these themes will be.

But each one of us can only make his bit of the effort...

October 1992

Post script: This book was already with the binders when news came that the Babri Masjid had been pulled down at Ayodhya. Everyone recoils from destruction. And that was the first reaction to the news. But what the English speaking intelligentsia and the leaders disowned, the Hindus owned up. What the government rushed into doing in the days that followed—arresting L.K. Advani and others, banning the RSS etc., declaring that the mosque would be rebuilt at the very spot, dismissing the BJP governments—and what the English press continued to paste on them, made them own the destruction even more defiantly. The way things are going I would think they will own up to the charge of a conspiracy also even if there was none. "Yes, we acted as Shivaji used to do," I can hear a sect proclaiming. And should the idols be shifted, and the mosque rebuilt at that spot, the destruction of the new structure will become even more an article of faith with the Hindus than the destruction of Mir Baqi's structure had been, in our times specially since the killings by Mulayam Singh's government.

The hand that destroyed the mosque was of course that of the persons who had gathered there. But that hand was impelled by all our familiar perversities.

Politicians pressing their immediate advantage. A government which collects evidence but which, instead of disclosing it, goes on weighing alternatives and eventually puts its trust, not in disclosing the facts to our people, but in cleverness: "Use the Courts to make them do another Srinagar, that will finish them". Courts which go on and on with legalisms... And a totally apologetic, defensive elite.

When Bhindranwale stokes Sikhs into believing that Sikhs are actually slaves in India, that Sikhism has been and forever is irreconcilably different from Hinduism, these worthies say, "When one brother says he is going his own way, what can be done? You have to let him go." When the students in Assam point to the infiltration, they dub them communalists. When Kashmir all but bolts, they see a rationale for that too. When terror and murder by militants compels over two lakh Hindus to leave Kashmir, they tell each other that actually the Governor has encouraged them to clear out so that he can come down all the more heavily on Muslims in the Valley. When but a hundred odd of the three and a half lakh Bangladeshis illegally settled in the very capital of the country are sent back, they heckle the authorities no end. When at last the governments get the two sides to sit down and exchange documents on the *mandir*, the evidence is drowned in all sorts of phony-ness.

It is this which has so distanced the people from the elite. It is this

— more than anything, I would say—which had driven the kar sevaks to that pitch of anger, which had convinced them that, whatever Advani or anyone may say, they were not going to get a hearing in their own country.

And it is because all of us—politicians, civil servants, IB men, editorialists—are so distanced from them that everyone so grossly underestimated the anger which had welled up in the kar sevaks, the anger which converted that congregation into a crowd, that crowd into a mob, and thence into a pack.

No one who sees in the rule of law the only foundation on which a society can rest can reconcile himself to what was done. But to refuse to see the anger which impelled the deed is just as fatal. To condemn the kar sevaks for striking at secularism but to persist with the double-standards and pandering to brokers of bloc votes which impelled them is to confirm them in their conviction. To condemn the Hindus as "savages" one day and to expect them to suddenly heed our appeals to their "great traditions of tolerance" is to play the self-deluding fool. To expect that, after we have day in and day out stuffed eighty per cent of a society with guilt, it will have the will to save itself, is to play the same fool.

The destruction therefore calls to mind once again the sorts of lessons which are the theme of this book. Assume I maintain that I alone have been given the Revelation; that Revelation, I maintain, is in The Book; that as that Book, I say, contains the Revelation, every word in it is true, that it is eternally true, that every word of it is eternally binding; and THAT Book says, "You should surely destroy all the places where the nations you shall dispossess served their gods, upon the high mountains and upon the hills and under every green tree; you shall tear down their altars, and dash in pieces their pillars, and burn their .... (deity) with fire; you shall hew down the graven images of their gods, and destroy their name of that place."

If I insist that as The Book is the essence of my religion I must, that I *will* live by every word of it, I cannot then be surprised that the other fellow, even without the help of The Book, will do the exact same thing to my places of worship, altars and all. I cannot suddenly turn around and say, "But that goes against your traditions of tolerance. That goes against secularism." He will not heed me. When he gets the chance he will do to me what I say is my right and duty to do to him because my God through The Book has bound me to do that to him. The point is not in the passage — that one is not from the Quran or Hadis but from The Bible. The point is in the premise: of my alone having been given the Revelation, of my living by it and not by the laws and mores of the time and place.

Secularism is also a Jealous God, as jealous as Jehovah of the Old Testament, as jealous as Allah of the Quran. For him to prevail, ALL must obey him, all must obey him in every particular. Ayodhya shows how the contrary presumption—that the majority must adhere to secularism but that the minority has the right to live by some other norms—will eventually be blown apart. Similarly, when I insist that on one matter—say, personal law—I shall not abide by secular laws I undermine secularism as such, the very secularism I want to, I NEED to invoke to protect myself, my beliefs, my practices. When I invoke The Book as the justification for not going by the secular laws of the land— for instance, on even such a simple thing as paying alimony—I goad others to disregard those laws too.

What is true of secularism is just as true of the Rule of Law. When I overturn the electoral law so as to nullify a court verdict holding me guilty of corrupt electoral practices; when I prostitute the Constitution to clamp the country in an Emergency, or to dismiss state governments at will; when I overturn the law to overturn a judgement of the Supreme Court regarding an old, indigent woman; when I do not implement its orders on Cauvery, on shifting a grave or two in Varanasi, on clearing out shops in Jaipur, on demolishing illegal additions to a mosque in Calcutta; when I use the courts to stall proceedings against those who have looted the country as in Bofors; when moreover the courts go along with all this, by prevarication if nothing else—I cannot suddenly turn around and shout, "But they must wait for the court verdict." They won't.

The second lesson cuts even closer to the bone. As the passage I began with shows—and the passage is merely one illustration, as will be evident from chapters in this book it can be supplemented with scores and scores literally—there are aspects of the Revelation which are just not compatible with secularism. They are not compatible with living in a multi-religious, closely packed, modernizing society.

It is not enough for me to say, "But I am not executing those decrees. Why are you holding The Book at me?" For I DO invoke The Book —in affirming that my "identity" is distinct and separate for instance, in maintaining that I will live under one set of laws rather than another. Each time I invoke The Book I reinforce the stereotype of me in the other's mind, I draw him to focus on the dogma which I say defines my essence rather than on the fact that I am not really living by that dogma.

Therefore the Revelation has at the least to be reinterpreted, and aspects of it which are incompatible with secularism, with living in a multi-religious society have to be ascribed a new meaning.

There is a third lesson listed in the last chapter which can be recalled here in terms of the Babri Masjid itself.

On all counts, few Muslims had heard of the Babri Masjid five years ago. It may have been at some stage like the *Quwwat ul Islam* mosque in Delhi, a symbol of the triumph of Islam in this land. But that was long, long ago.   Over the last five years, however, it became everything: a symbol of identity—"If I do not stand up for even a mosque, how am I a Muslim?"; a symbol of security—"If we yield on this, what is there to prevent them from swallowing us up altogether?"; a symbol of whether the country is secular at all. And to save this symbol there was the confidence in the old politics: of operating through persons occupying governmental chairs, of operating through progressive historians and the progressive press.

These two factors—this proclivity to see in everything a symbol of Islam, to suddenly conclude that the future of Islam hinges on it, coupled with the confidence in being able to use the State because one can manipulate persons who are holding office—and the collective image Muslims have of Islamic history, of its martyrology lead them to always embrace as their symbol, as their leader, as their standard the leader or position which most stands for intransigence at that moment. Arafat day before yesterday, Saddam Hussain yesterday, the "non-negotiable" position on the structure of the Babri Masjid. The denouement is always the same—Arafat is thrown out of Lebanon, Saddam is defeated. And now the Babri Mosque has been pulverized.

Imagine for a moment what would have happened if Muslims, who as they rightly say have had nothing to do with and therefore no proprietory interest in what Babar did, had said, "Yes, we see that you have believed that this is where Rama was born, that you have gone on trying to regain this spot for 400 years. We will hand over the site to you as a mark of our regard for your sentiments. Join us in shifting this structure to another site. And allay our apprehension that this is not the beginning of your damaging other places of our worship."

The structure would have survived. The gesture would have been the most resonant announcement possible that Muslims esteem the sentiments of non-Muslims also. The Hindus could have been held to a position.

In the event not only is the structure gone, it is gone in the most consequential way : it has not gone by agreement among a few leaders, it has not gone by the verdict of three or four judges, it has been pulverized by very large numbers, and that pulverization has been appropriated by the Hindus—barring, I agree, some of the English speaking among them. The Hindus have thereby been made aware that they are in very large number, and that numbers can do such things.

And the Muslims are put in a real dilemma. If they now follow the government and insist that the mosque be rebuilt on that exact spot, they will be ensuring its destruction, and ever increasing insecurity for themselves. If, on the other hand, they now agree that the structure be rebuilt elsewhere, they will be giving wind to the Hindu militants.

That is the cost of hugging the position or leader that seems most intransigent. It is the cost too of the old politics—of the faith that by manipulating this ruler or that, by getting articles written in some newspapers the "interests" of the "community" can be furthered.

I am not sure that the correct inference will even now be drawn—that the security of every section lies only in, the interests of every section can be advanced only by all of us working together to strengthen institutions, not by that section becoming a vote bank and bolstering this leader or that party in the hope that that leader or party in turn will keep the hordes at bay. In this moment of hurt, one can be impelled to defiance and that in turn can lead one to the opposite resolve: "As I have been pushed to the wall, as I am going to die in any case, I will get ten of them before dying, I will bring the whole thing down." Should any group by that sort of reasoning take to terrorism for instance, that will not be the end of India, but it certainly will be the end of India with Muslims. The same sort of result I fear will follow should Pakistan move to "protect the interests of our brothers", or should Muslim countries shut off oil supplies etc. While the poor Muslim here would have had nothing to do with those decisions, the hardships which will result will be blamed on him—and the consequences will be terrible, for our entire country eventually of course, but for the Muslims immediately.

There are twin lessons for the "secularists" too. No one—no government, no politician—in the end enraged the Hindus as much as the "secularists". It is not just that in this particular instance their efforts to drown the evidence by phony arguments—"Ayodhya was in Afghanistan, says scholar"—were among the main factors which led Hindus to conclude that they would never get a hearing. It is that everything they say and do springs from a superior prejudice. A sheaf of examples can be given from what the English press has been putting out in the aftermath of the destruction. But let us turn to a more durable one.

It is from the Supreme Court itself. For a hundred years westerners, and of course our secularists have denounced Hinduism for what has been an excrescence, for what has to do with an unchanging economic base and has nothing to do with the essence of Hinduism— that is, the rigidities of the caste system. Christianity and Islam have been exalted by contrast on the ground that they do not divide humanity —that the widest possible differentiation between believers and non-believers is an article of those faiths is of course glossed over. Now, the majority judgement in the Mandal case follows this pattern to the dot —it denounces Hinduism for the caste system.

Then it comes time to extend reservations to Muslims, Christians etc. It says that reservations should be extended to them also as there are castes—rigid, endogamous and all—among them too. But this, it says, is so because these religions too have been infected by Hinduism with the virus. The obvious fact that the presence of castes among all religions here itself shows that it is not one religion which has caused castes but an unchanging economic and technological base—that finds no place. The blame is laid at Hinduism.

It is this kind of reflexive slander of which the Hindus have by now had enough. That and the double standards. On the one side therefore the secularists have enraged the Hindus so that by now the latter do not heed them at all, they conclude that they must grab the law in their hands. On the other, by giving Muslims the false impression that they have support among the powerful, the secularists have encouraged them to plummet for that intransigence I spoke of, the one which has brought the current consequences upon the Muslims. The one which has reduced the secularists also to mere heckling.

Much re-examination is therefore in order by the secularists. The essential gene of our country is the religious spirit, and the essence of that spirit is the Hindu ethos—you just have to see the difference between the way Sufis are venerated here and the way they have been set upon elsewhere to see that this is so. By denouncing Hinduism day in and day out, they deny the land itself. They leave the people no sense of self-worth. Will a society bereft of self-worth do anything worth-while? Will a people deprived of self-worth stand by any norms? Do our commentators not see that by the rhetoric they espouse not one leader of our reawakening — Ramakrishna, Vivekananda, Aurobindo, Tilak, Gandhi, Ramana Maharishi — NOT ONE is anything but a Hinduism monger?

Finally, there are four aspects of the destruction of the Babri Masjid which the Hindus have to reflect on — these are things which they have to reverse swiftly, else the consequences will be as harmful for them as they have been for other communities.

While they were propelled to it no doubt by what successive governments, the courts, the secularists were doing and not doing, the fact is that in the end a mob took the law in its own hands. So that this may not become the pattern, all of us must redouble efforts to get the institutions working again. Otherwise there will be mobs of many kinds, and nothing will survive.

Second, sadhus and mahants have been inducted — they have had to be inducted, I am prepared to concede — into what had become in part at least a political question. This must be swiftly reversed lest it lead to the Khomeni-ization of our politics, and to the same results.

Third, while vast numbers among those who gathered at Ayodhya were *bhaktas* of Rama, a number were the sort who would not abide by norms, by civility. Their induction into such a movement, to say nothing of relying on them for any sort of work cannot but disrupt civil society.

Finally, while it is entirely a fact that the State having bent repeatedly to the brokers and Sole Spokesmen of non-Hindus, it was but natural for Hindus to react as Hindus; while it is true also that this they could not have done till an organization, and in our political system a political party rose to espouse their cause; while it is true also that the partisanship of pseudo-secularism could not have been nailed till the Hindus had spoken as Hindus — while all this is true, it is also a fact that this movement has at one level inducted into politics religion narrowly conceived. So that the State may not be bent by others, Hindus had to be awakened as Hindus — true. But it is equally true that any one may enflame any group to a sense of deprivation — as we saw only too recently in the case of Bhindranwale. The mixture is so potent that no one, save perhaps only a Gandhi, can fine-tune the resulting explosion — the inability of leaders like L.K. Advani, of the RSS itself to control the congregation at Ayodhya is as vivid a warning as the genuine anger which had welled up in them. Neither should be ignored. The movement should therefore now be focussed more sharply on ensuring true secularism, and true nationalism rather than on any narrower objectives.

In a word : the Muslims and secularists must look to the recent past and see where the politics of intransigence and the discourse of double standards have landed them and the country ; and the Hindus must look to the future and see where the politics they have been impelled to pursue will lead them and the country.

December 1992

Contents

AYODHYA

WHEN COMMUNALISM BECOMES TERRORISM

FACING THE FUTURE

The Secular Approach

I

On Taking Offence

A chimaera, in Greek mythology was a monster with a lion's head, a goat's trunk, and a serpent's tail, more generally it meant a composite animal. Throughout the ages, painters and writers of fantastic tales have been fond of creating chimaeras. My own favourite brain-child is the momiphant. He is a phenomenon most of us have met in life: a hybrid who combines the delicate frailness of the mimosa, crumbling at a touch when his own feelings are hurt, with the thick-skinned robustness of the elephant trampling over the feelings of others....

Arthur Koestler[1]

'You Hindus have no respect for our Gurus. Don't you remember what your Dayanand said about Guru Nanak? He used to abuse him left, right and centre.'

We hear something like this every second day today — 'Your Dayanand called Guru Nanak a *dambhi* (illiterate), 'Your Jadunath Sarkar called Guru Gobind Singh a *shahi lutera*.'

Question after question leaps to mind. Have you read what Swami Dayanand, or Jadunath Sarkar for that matter, actually wrote? I have yet to come across a person who, though he has internalised the allegation, has actually taken the trouble to read *Satyarthprakash.*

Even if we assume that Swami Dayanand called Guru Nanak a '*dambhi*,' what did he mean by the term? Could the meaning just be, 'Guru Nanak claimed to speak on the authority of the Vedas, but he had not read them, he *could* not have read them, as he did not know Sanskrit' -- an assertion which, howsoever vehemently others may have protested against it, Guru Nanak would have dismissed as irrelevant.

But even if Dayanand had meant something stronger by the term, should we at once take offence? Did Dayanand single out the great and gentle Nanak for such treatment? Quite the contrary. He used much, much harsher language in characterising Hindu sects and saints. Nor did he spare the deities. Indeed, his mission started with a question whose audacity would be enough to ridicule the belief of millions – 'If this *Shivling* cannot protect itself against a common rat,' the young child asked himself on that *Shivratri*, 'how is going to help me?'

Do not all reformers ask such audacious questions? Do not almost all of them speak with equal bluntness? Even the gentle Jesus calls others 'you hypocrites' 'you blind guides,' 'you blind fools,' 'you blind men,' 'you serpents,' 'you brood of vipers.' 'You are like whitewashed tombs,' he tells them, 'which outwardly appear beautiful', but within are full of dead men's bones and all uncleanliness.'[2]

The language of the Gurus too is simple, direct. That is precisely why it is so effective. If the Brahmin is so special, we are asked in the Granth Sahib, why does he not emerge from some other, some special part of the Brahmini? May the Brahmin not take offence on the ground that his mother's vagina is being brought in just to score a debating point? 'Shift your feet,' the devout Muslim tells Guru Nanak. 'You are sleeping with them pointing towards the *Kaba*.' 'Shift them, my friend,'the Guru says, 'to the direction where God is not.' May the Muslim not take offence on the ground that the Guru is refusing to accord the *Kaba* the special status that the Prophet enjoined, that he is placing it no higher than any other place in the world? The Granth Sahib invokes the authority of the Vedas hundreds of times. Its central concept – the *Akaal Purush,* the timeless One, the One without beginning or end, the One without form or attributes – is indistinguishable from the Vedantic Brahma. But Swami Dayanand cites the verse from the Granth,'Even Brahma who constantly read the Vedas died. All the four Vedas are mere fiction. The Vedas can never realise the greatness of a Sadhu.' In a sense, the verse is entirely in consonance with Vedanta – the Upanishads affirm again and again that the Book, howsoever holy, is just a ladder that is to be discarded once one has realised the truth. But given the way we react to his statements without reading them, is it altogether surprising that Dayanand flies into a rage over such verses and takes them as evidence of Guru Nanak being a *naastik* , a reviler of the Vedas?[3] And how should Hindus react to the unambiguous declaration of the Granth Sahib – *Turki Kaane, Hindu Anne,* 'The Muslims are one-eyed, the Hindus blind'? Does it not offend? Can it not incite the faithful?

Guru Nanak condemns the Jains roundly. He accuses them of remaining filthy day and night, of drinking water full of filth, of eating left-overs. 'They spread out their excreta,' he says,'and take into their mouths the stench. It is water they dread....' 'They bring shame upon their parents,' he says, 'Their children weep and run after them.' He admonishes them for not offering oblations to the dead, for being niggardly towards guests, for not performing funeral rites, for not lighting lamps. Where will such persons go after death, he wonders. 'They are not yogis,' he declares,'nor Shaivite monks, nor *qazis*, nor *mullas*. They are the ones damned by God. They wander about as damned....'If they get their hair pulled out, as he says they do, if they do not bathe, as he says they do not, 'let dust be thrown on their heads a hundred times.'[4] May the Jains not object to a portrayal such as this? May they not object to incitement such as that?

Millions worship Durga or Kali. The Granth Sahib, however, portrays them as ones who have forgotten the name of God, who have forsaken prayer, and it says of them:

A *Shakta* is like the son of a prostitute who knows not his father's name.
Without prayer a man goes about like a dog,
He is full of lice, his face is blackened.
Without prayer men carry loads on their heads.
As cattle *Shaktas* carry the weight of horns on their heads.
Without prayer they are driven away like dogs.
So do greedy *Shaktas* find no one to solace them.
Man without prayer destroys himself
The wretched *Shakta* has no family or caste....[5]

'Like the son of a prostitute who knows not his father's name,' 'driven away like dogs,' 'wretched' 'without family or caste', strong words, more than a match for anything Dayanand ever used, and these are the words of two gentle teachers, Guru Nanak and Guru Arjun Dev.

But let us assume that Swami Dayanand was the only one who used blunt words. Should we focus on this trait of his or on

the   general character of his work? For instance, in his mighty
crusade against idolatory, in his crusade to simplify ritual, was he
not closer to the teachings of the Gurus than, say, the practice of
the average Sikh as much as of the average Hindu today?

Even if Swami Dayanand's practice had not been as close to
the teachings of the Gurus as in fact it was, even if he had actually
abused the Gurus, even if he had not just abused them but had
singled them out for abuse, should we take offence? Does abuse
tarnish the sun?

And why do we hold all Hindus responsible for what *one*
reformer—who spoke as harshly about them — said? How are these
words of one reformer more significant, how are they more representative of the Hindus' attitude towards the Sikh Gurus than
the fact that lakhs and lakhs of Hindus revere the Gurus and the
Granth Sahib as much as the Sikhs do?

And how long will we retain this thorn in our hearts? Should
there not be the equivalent of a Statute of Limitations here?

And what is the precise atonement that will remove our grudge?
Or is it that because one Hindu reformer used some distasteful
expressions a hundred years ago, we are sworn to hostility against
all Hindus for ever, and there is nothing they can do to convince
us to the contrary?

Beyond Words

The problem in fact transcends the specific words that a reformer
or a sacred text has used. Even if we agree to purge history as well
as the text of such words, what will we do about the teaching –
the central doctrine, the propositions – that the reformers and the
texts urge? Idols are revered by millions. And yet we know the sort
of words that the Quran uses about idols and idolators, the curses
it pronounces on them, the duty it enjoins on the faithful – the duty
of ensuring 'a wide slaughter in the land' of the infidels. Surely
this is more than just using harsh words against someone. It is more
than intimidation. It is incitement to murder, and wholesale murder
at that. Is the Hindu to take offence and demand that the Quran be
purged of such passages?

Or consider the figure of Jesus. The Quran recognises him
as one of the prophets. But it repeatedly asserts that Jesus was *not*
the Son of God. It also says, for instance, that the one who was

crucified was *not* Jesus but a look-alike. Now, these assertions strike at two notions that are absolutely central to the faith of Christians. Should they take offence and demand that the Quran be purged of these verses? And if *they* ask for this, would *they*, in turn, not be striking at a premise that is just as fundamental to the faith of Muslims as the divinity of Jesus is to that of a Christian, the premise, namely, that every word of the Quran – including, that is, every word asking us to launch *Jihads*, every word denying the divinity of Jesus – is true, that it is of divine origin?

At one stage some Hindu researchers began representing *Rishabha*, the first Tirthankara of the Jains, as an *Avatar* of Vishnu. The Jains took this to be an attempt to swallow Jainism. They retaliated by questioning the divine status of Vishnu himself, and they did so by drawing special attention to what, by the standards that had become current, they said was the 'immoral' behaviour of the *Avatars*. They went so far as to produce new versions of the Ramayana and the Mahabharata, in which the gods revered by the Hindus – Ram, Krishna – were represented as worldly Jain heroes whose deeds were to be weighed in the scales of Jain etnics. Ram survives the change. He does not kill Ravan – Lakshman does that – and so is still reborn in heaven because of his strict adherence to *ahimsa*. But Krishna suffers. As a scholar notes, his deeds of 'treachery and violence' are too numerous to be covered up. After his time on earth, therefore, he is depicted as spending a long, long time in hell. Should the Jains forever hold against the Hindus the latters' attempt to represent their Tirthankara as an *Avatar* of Vishnu? Should the Hindus forever hold the Jains guilty of 'distorting' their epics and vilifying *their* god, Krishna?

Roots

One source of the problem, of course, is that all of us are Koestler's momiphants. We harp on what the *other* man's Guru or scripture says about *our* Guru or scripture, but conveniently forget what *our* Guru and scripture say about persons, texts, beliefs that the other holds sacred.

But there is more. For one thing, if a person who happens to be from another religion shows us up,we are much more liable to pounce on him than if a person from our own religion says the same thing. It isn't just the thing said that matters. Moreover, there

is racialism in   our reaction. Gandhiji used to point to the
asymmetry in the reaction of the Hindus to the slaughter of cows:
how upset you get about the slaughter of cows by Muslims, he
told them, but you say nothing of the slaughter that takes place
daily on behalf of Englishmen.[7] The Muslims react in exactly the
same way. Consider Rodinson's widely   read *Mohammed*. The
Penguin edition is available in bookshops   across   the country. It
relates the teachings of the Prophet to the socio-economic circumstances of the day, as well as to the personal predicaments and
desires of the Prophet. Its central thesis is that Mohammed was an
exceptional man, but one whose career and teaching are best
understood when we see him as a person establishing a State rather
than as person who has any special relationship with God.
Rodinson portrays the exhortations contained in the Quran as being
not revelations from Allah but as mere promptings from the unconscious, and convenient promptings at that. He repeatedly draws
attention to the sequence that precedes the revelation: the
Prophet or his group faces a predicament; the predicament plunges
the Prophet into intense inner turmoil; a revelation dawns in which
Allah says the precise thing that resolves the predicament in the
way most convenient to the Prophet and his dedicated band. For the
faithful the sequence is proof of the special concern that God quite
understandably had for His Messenger. But for Rodinson the sequence suggests that the exhortations are not 'revelations' but
'simply fresh associations produced by the unconscious working
on things which have been seen and heard but forgotten.' The
resulting'ideology', he says, in a typical passage, 'was...built up
from elements imposed on a man by his own situation and adopted
by a society by reason of its situation.'
       In a typical passage he writes, 'It is unlikely that he [the
Prophet] felt for Khadija [his first wife who was fifteen years older
than him] the physical passion which was later to procure him, in
his old age, the young and lovely women of his future harem.'
He writes of the jealousies among the Prophet's wives, of their
collective jealousy of the Coptic concubine, Mariya, of Fatima's for
her step-mother, Aisha, of the Prophet's marriages and the
circumstances – among which was often the helpful revelation – in
which each was contracted. He writes about the Prophet's 'amorous
proclivities later in life,' of 'the troubles of a man mocked for his
lack of male heirs, the frustration of a highly sexed man whose own

moral conscience prevented him from realising his desires, the suppressed fury of a man fundamentally sure of himself, but treated with contempt by practical politicians....' He writes of 'a certain pathological element in his make up.' He dilates on the nature of The Voice that the Prophet heard. He talks of the Prophet 'consummating the [tenth] marriage [to Maymuna] with his usual precipitancy, at the first halt.' He spells out at length how, upon arriving at Medina, when he needed the help of the influential Jewish tribes there, the Prophet first ordained that the faithful adopt the Jewish times of prayer, the Jewish fasts, etc. that while praying they bow not towards the *Kaba* but towards Jerusalem and so on, and how later, once his power had been consolidated, he turned on them and had hundreds of them massacred.[9]

For the devout Muslim the style of the Quran is unparalleled. Indeed, the unequalled excellence and majesty of the verses is taken as proof of its divine origin. But Rodinson says quite casually that the style is typical of the styles of *Kahins* – the soothsayers – of the day, that the style of the later revelations deteriorated and that it is only the piety of the faithful that leads them to regard it so highly.[10]

Here then is what we find in a standard biography.[11] It is available in bookshops all across the country, it is read widely. But you can imagine what would have happened if a brown man, in particular a Hindu, had written anything of the kind – abuse, threats, demands that the book be banned, perhaps a few riots too, would have dogged its heels.

The Book

The next source of the difficulty lies in our not comprehending, in our reluctance to acknowledge, most of all to ourselves, the nature of the texts we revere. In our defensive militancy we insist that The Book is true, that it is excellent, that every word of it is vital, as well as true and excellent, and that it is true and excellent forever.

But in many ways the Books, when they were composed, were hold-alls. Whatever was thought to be valuable at that time was put into them – we thus have medicinal prescriptions, laws to govern inter-personal relations, rules of taxation and inheritance, chants, prayers, chronicles of kings, accounts of places through which the people passed and so on. The only reason many of these things figure in The Book is simply that The Book itself was a hold-all. The Old Testament is full of who slept with whom, who killed whom. None of it has any moral that is of such importance for all eternity that God should have enshrined it in The One Book He was transmitting to us. The fact simply is that at that time The Book was one of the few books around. So the compilers put everything in it — fables, history, morals, law. Today we would put the facts of history in one book, propositions and arguments of ethics in another, provisions of law in a third. And we would not hesitate to revise any one of them as new facts became available or as our norms and opinions changed. We wouldn't feel that we were doing something extraordinary, to say nothing of doing something sacrilegious when we analysed any one of them, picked holes in them, or altered and overhauled them.

But that is not how it was two thousand or a thousand years ago. As a consequence, each advance of knowledge that contradicts a proposition contained in The Book jars us, the attempt of a scholar to examine the text with the tools of critical analysis — tools that we would find perfectly serviceable, were the subject something other than The Book — strikes us as an affront, as a deliberate attempt to denigrate our religion.

Changing Mores

Two factors, specially when they appear together — as they do, for instance, in the case of Islam — complicate the matter further. The first is the special position of the founders and prophets of the religion. These great men exercised an overwhelming, a hypnotic influence over their followers. When he was alive and the slightest doubt arose about what should be done, the followers would rush to the teacher, the prophet, to seek his counsel. When he was gone, it was entirely natural for the followers to recall what he had done in the same or an analogous situation, or to ask what he would have done had he been faced with it now.

What he did or said on small matters as much as on the great ones, on whether we should slaughter the infidels as much as on whether one should have more than one wife, whether one should bed more than one of them in one night, whether one must wash oneself after each intercourse — is therefore set down at great length and with great piety in texts which we have come to regard as sacred. In the Prophet's case, for instance, the words and deeds are set down in the *hadis* collections.

But our ways of looking at things have changed as much since the days of the Prophet as of Moses. What seemed natural and proper then seems an embarrassment today. Therefore if someone so much as reproduces what is written in these texts on a subject – in fact, if he so much as enumerates the kinds of subjects which are dealt with in the texts – we are apt to fly into a rage.

Today monogamy is the norm. In times gone by there was nothing exceptional in having many wives, it might even have been considered a sign of masculinity. Thus,we have Solomon in the *Ecclesiastes* with his 700 wives and 300 concubines. We have the Prophet in the *hadis* and the biographies with nine or eleven or twenty wives and others.[12] Today we look upon polygamy as inequitable and unjust. In the *hadis* we find a young man being urged to get married on the ground that 'the best person of this [Muslim] nation [Muhammed] of all other Muslims, had the largest number of wives.'[13] Today child marriages are taboo, and for a middle-aged man to marry a little girl would be quite unthinkable. But that was not so a thousand years ago. And so we have the *hadis* reporting Aisha's account that the Prophet, then in his fifties, married her when she was six and consummated the marriage when she was nine.[14] Today we frown upon adultery. But Krishna's adventures with the *gopis* are legend. Indeed, they are among the things that endear him to devotees.

Today we prize literacy, and sometimes even think of it as a pre-requisite for wisdom. That was not always the case. Quite the contrary. The fact that the Prophet could not read or write, far from being something to be diffident about, was not just freely acknowledged, it was put forth as proof of the fact that the Quran had come from God, for how could a man who could neither read nor write, it was asked, on his own produce prose and poetry of such majesty, such power?[15]

It isn't just that, time and circumstances having changed, the deeds seem incongruous today and we are offended if someone – especially if he belongs to another religion – so much as recalls them. The change in norms about what is and what is not talked of in polite company, itself leads us to take offence. People were free and open in seventh century Arabia. We have Aisha talking candidly about the Prophet's relations with his wives. Were

someone to so much as reproduce the remarks today, even if this
be to set down the example the faithful should follow, the ideal
conduct being that of the Prophet, a storm would rise.

Indeed, change of an even more trivial kind, change in the way
we talk has the same consequence. In the times recalled by the Old
Testament, in the time of the Prophet, the language people
used was direct, rustic. Today it is 'sophisticated', 'polite'. A *hadis*
will exemplify the resulting difficulty.

> Narrated Ata: I heard Jabir bin Abdullah in a gathering
> saying,'We, the companions of Allah's Apostle, assumed the
> state of *Ihram* [the prohibitions] to perform only Hajj without
> *Umra*.'[16] Jabir added, 'The Prophet arrived [in Mecca] on the
> fourth Dhul-Hijja. And when we arrived [in Mecca], the
> Prophet ordered us to finish the state of *Ihram*, saying, "Finish
> your *Ihram* and go to your wives [for sexual relations]".
> Jabir added, 'The Prophet did not oblige us [to go to our wives]
> but he only made that legal for us. Then he heard that we were
> saying,"When there remain only five days between us and the
> day of Arafat he orders us to finish our *Ihram* by sleeping with
> our wives, in which case we will proceed to Arafat with our
> male organs dribbling with semen"(Jabir pointed out with his
> hand illustrating what he was saying). Allah's Apostle stood
> up and said, "You[people] know that I am the most Allah-
> fearing, the most truthful and the best doer of good deeds
> [pious] from among you. If I had not brought the *Hadi*[the
> animal to be sacrificed]with me, I would have finished the
> *Ihram* as you will do, so finish your *Ihram*. If I had formerly
> known and I came to know lately, I would not have brought
> the *Hadi* with me." So we finished our *Ihram* and listened to
> the Prophet and obeyed him.'[17]

We wouldn't talk and gesture today the way Jabir did , and
certainly not in the presence of a man of God. If we did, no one
would put that down in a holy book. But as it stands, given the
importance that was attached to such questions, the conversation
forms a part of a collection that is revered next only to the Quran
by the devout. If someone so much as reproduces the episode
verbatim we are apt to take offence. 'His only object', we are apt
to allege, 'is to hold our holy books to ridicule.' How different

our reaction is from that of the Prophet. He did not think that it was improper of his followers to raise such doubts or to use such language in his presence. He did not feel that such language or gestures 'lowered his stature' in any way. Nor did he feel that some ordinary person should settle such questions rather than him. And the very purpose of the great compilers like Imam Bukhari in setting such exchanges down was to ensure that we would study them, cite them, propagate them.

The Key

The moral is clear. In examining a religious text or the life and teaching of a religious leader, we must examine the proposition *per se*, the deed *per se*. That the proposition is urged in the Quran rather than the Bible, that the deed is of Krishna rather than of Moses, must make no difference to our assessment of it.

Correspondingly, when we come across a critique of a religious text or of the life and deeds of a religious figure, we must weigh it on its own. That a Hindu or a Muslim has written it must make no difference to our assessment of it.

These two rules are obvious enough. And yet how often it is that accounts of Jinns and spirits seem to us to be superstitious nonsense when we hear them at a gathering of villagers, but how they seem to be veritable 'proofs' of another dimension of reality when we come across them in some text we revere – say the Quran or the *hadis*. How very often is it that when someone of our faith criticises some aspect of our religion the criticism seems to us to be perfectly in order, even scholarly, but how the identical criticism, if it has been made by someone who happens to have been born into a different religion, sends us up the wall. We must grow up. We must discard this defensive militancy. Consider the following law that is laid down in a much revered text:

> If a man has a stubborn and rebellious son, who will not obey the voice of his father or the voice of his mother, and, though they chastise him, will not give heed to them, then his father and his mother shall take hold of him and bring him out to the elders of the city at the gate of the place where he lives, and they shall say to the elders of the city, 'This our son is stubborn and rebellious, he is a glutton and a drunkard.'

Then all the men of the city shall stone him to death with
stones;so you shall purge the evil from your midst; and all [of
our people] shall hear and fear.[18]

Now, would this rule be just if it is in the Quran but unjust if
it is in the Bible, just if it is in Manu but unjust if it is not?
Is retaliation cruel, primitive, barbaric when it is in one text,

... Your eye shall not pity; it shall be life for life, eye for eye,
tooth for tooth, hand for hand, foot for foot...[19]

but   just and fair and humane when it is in another:

O believers, prescribed for you is
retaliation, touching the slain;
freeman for freeman, slave for slave,
female for female. But if aught is pardoned
a man by his brother, let the pursuing
be honourable, and let the payment be
with kindliness...
In retaliation there is life for you,
men possessed of minds...
The holy month for the holy month;
holy things demand retaliation.
Who so commits aggression against you,
do you commit aggression against him,
like as he has committed against you,
and fear you God.[20]

Today we are assured the freedom to practise our religion. Should
we value that or go by the following, typical, provisions of a text
– every word of which is said to be true and excellent, and eternally
so?

You should surely destroy all the places where the nations you
shall dispossess served their gods, upon the high mountains
and upon the hills and under every green tree, you shall tear
down their altars, and dash in pieces their pillars, and burn
their...[deity] with fire; you shall hew down the graven images
of their gods, and destroy their name of that place.[21]

Should we go by the freedom we have today, or by the dictum of the prophet that, should we catch anyone honouring a god other than the one prescribed by him,

> Then you shall bring forth to your gates that man or woman who has done this evil thing, and you shall stone that man or woman to death with stones[22]....?

Would these dicta be wrong if they were edicts of Mohammed Ghaznavi but right if they were proclamations of the Prophet? Would they be impermissible if they were laws of Moses but mandatory if they were laws of Manu or Mohammed?

Today we are free not just to practise our religion but also to peaceably profess it to others. Should we go by this freedom or by the holy text which lays down,

> If your brother, the son of your mother, or your son, or your daughter, or the wife of your bosom, or your friend who is your own soul entices you to serve other gods... you shall not yield to him or listen to him, nor shall your eye pity him, nor shall you spare him, nor shall you conceal him, your hand shall be first against him to put him to death, and afterwards the hands of all the people. You shall stone him to death with stones[23]...?

Is God to be obeyed when he tells us that as for those who fight against Him and His chosen emissary, as for those 'who hasten about the earth to do corruption there' and 'who do not repent before we have subjugated them,'

> They shall be slaughtered, or crucified or their hands or feet shall alternately be struck off, or they shall be banished from the land.[24]....?

Is He to be obeyed when he enjoins that we must, upon encountering those who do not subscribe to the religion that He is laying down in *that particular scripture*,

> Strike off their heads till you have made a great slaughter among them, and of the rest make fast the fetters,[25]

and to be disregarded when He enjoins in a completely different scripture that if 'certain base fellows' in a city preach that we should serve gods other than the one He has specified in *this* scripture(which is naturally not the God specified in the preceding scripture),

> You shall put the inhabitants of that city to the sword, destroying it utterly, all who are in it and its cattle with the edge of the sword. You shall gather all its spoil into the midst of its open square, and burn the city and all its spoil with fire, as a whole burnt offering to the Lord your God, it shall be a heap forever, it shall not be built again[26]...?

Is the holy text of one religion excessive when it provides,

> When you draw near to a city to fight against it, offer terms of peace to it. And if its answer to you is peace and it opens to you, then all the people who are found in it shall do forced labour for you and serve you. But if it makes no peace with you, but makes war against you, then you shall besiege it; and when the Lord your God gives it into your hand you shall put all its males to the sword, but the women and the little ones, the cattle and everything else in the city, all its spoil, you shall take as booty for yourselves, and you shall enjoy the spoils of your enemies, which the Lord your God has given you. Thus you shall do to all the cities which are very far from you,which are not cities of the nations here. But in the cities of these peoples that the Lord your God gives you as your inheritance you shall save alive nothing that breathes, but you shall utterly destroy them....[27]

but a treatise on law of another religion right and just when it enjoins similar conduct? Is one prophet right in the following instance? He orders his followers to wreak vengeance on persons of another group. His followers do so and, as the holy book says, they slaughter every male. They take captive the women of the other people and their little ones and they take as booty all their cattle, their flocks and all their goods. 'All their cities and the places where they dwelt, and all their encampments,' the holy book continues, 'they burnt with fire, and took all the spoil and

all the booty, both of men and of beast.' They bring the booty
and the captives to the great prophet and the priest. The prophet
is livid. 'Have you let all the women live?' he asks. He tells them
that these are the ones who caused them 'to act treacherously'
against the Lord in a particular matter and that is why the plague
came among them. 'Now, therefore,' he orders them, *kill every
male among the little ones, and kill every woman who has known
man by lying with him. But all the young girls who have not known
man by lying with him, keep them alive for yourselves....*' The
subsequent passages tell us that 32,000 little girls are thereby kept
for debauchery and use. And is another equally revered prophet
wrong in the following instance? A few men join his religion, but
later desert him, kill a shepherd and run off with the animals. The
prophet has them caught. He then orders his followers to cut off
their hands and legs and to brand their eyes with heated pieces of
iron. He orders that the cut hands and legs should not be cauterised
so that the men bleed to death. 'And when they asked for water
to drink,' records the Book we revere, 'they were not given water'.[29]

Today a transgression is judged independently of who the
transgressor is and who the victim. Should we abandon this practice
and proceed by the rules of Islamic jurisprudence as much as of
Manu, that the punishment for a crime will depend not only on the
crime *per se* but on who commits it and against whom it is
committed — i.e., on the caste to which the two belong, on whether
one is a believer and the other a non-believer, on whether one is
a free man and the other a slave?

Or consider the texts which assure us that, for instance,
wearing a particular type of beads, smearing oneself with ashes,
putting a particular mark on one's forehead and other parts of
one's body, living in one city, dying in another, reading a text,
having it read to one, having it read to others, falling within the
range of the vision of a realized soul, etc. will absolve us from
the most heinous sins and lift us to states of the most exalted
beatitude. Should we go by the substance of a person's deeds or
by the tokenism that these sacred texts urge? Would the
propositions be valid if the cities in questions were Mecca and
Medina but bogus if they were Mathura and Kashi? Would they
be valid if the Book is an Upanishad but bogus if it is the Quran?

It should be obvious that the deeds, even of great men, must
be evaluated independently of their greatness, that the propositions

of law or of ethics and morality must be evaluated independently of the texts in which they occur. We must judge the prophets as we would judge the ordinary men and women they set out to reform. We must evaluate the sacred texts as we would evaluate any other text.

A Choice

There is, however, a problem. For the fact is that we do indeed have two diametrically opposed traditions in this regard. On the one hand we have the example of the prophets of the Old Testament and of Mohammed, the Messenger of Allah. And on the other, we have the example of the Buddha and of Jesus.

Elisha, as is well known, was a man of God. The Bible tells us that the water parted when he touched it with the mantle of Elijah which he had inherited, that at his bidding unwholesome water became whole-some. He typifies one kind of response:

He went up from there to Bethel[the Bible reports] and while he was going up on the way, some small boys came out of the city and jeered at him saying, 'Go up, you bald head, Go up, you bald head!' And he turned around and when he saw them, he cursed them in the name of the Lord. And two she-bears came out of the woods and tore forty-two of the boys....[31]

This is one way in which a man of God reacts. And that too just to the playful taunts of young children. It was often the pattern of Prophet Mohammed's reaction. After the battle of Badr, instead of following the advice of Umar who wanted all the prisoners to be slaughtered, the Prophet ordered that ransoms should be demanded first and that only those should be killed for whom no one was prepared to pay a ransom. But he was merciless towards two who had disputed his teaching, Uqbab b. Abu Muayt and al Nadr b. al Harith. He ordered that these be slaughtered at once. When one of them screamed, 'But who will take care of my sons, Mohammed?', the Prophet answered,'Hell.' Similarly, he was merciless on returning from Badr. He ordered that Asma bint Marwan who had recited verses against him be got rid of. A follower slaughtered her with his sword as she slept with her children, the youngest, still at the breast, asleep in her very arms.

When he went to the Prophet in the morning and told him, 'Messenger of God, I have killed her,'the Prophet exclaimed, 'You have done a service to Allah and his Messenger.' A few days later the Prophet exhorted his followers to put to death the poet Abu Afak, who was by then over a hundred years old. He too was killed in his sleep. The poet Kab ibn al-Ashraf was killed by treachery with the Prophet's approval and his head was brought back amidst great acclamation to the Prophet's house and flung at his feet. On re-capturing Mecca the Prophet condoned past failings of the populace but, as was his custom, he did not spare those, including some female singers, who had been sarcastic or scornful about him.[32]

The faithful count these executions or murders among the 'military expeditions' of the Prophet and his followers.[33]

This, then, is one sort of example before us. The contrary example is that of the Buddha and Jesus. When someone expressed doubts about their doctrine, they reasoned with him. When someone reviled them or heaped scorn on them, they tried with infinite patience to lead him to the truth they had seen.

We follow the example of the Old Testament prophets and the Messenger of Allah on the false notion that pouncing on those who question any aspect of our religion or our text is a mark of faith. Quite the contrary. Such hypersensitivity shows a *lack of faith*, it shows that we are *nervous* about the doctrine and the text, that we are *not* confident that they will stand scrutiny.

The man of faith can only be delighted when someone sets out to examine his religion and his holy texts. For the examination can only bring out, even more swiftly than would be the case otherwise, their greatness and their unparalleled excellence.

For the humanist, the secularist, the golden rules are thus as follows:

❏ the proposition must stand on its own: the fact that it occurs in one text rather than another makes no difference;

❏ the deed must stand on its own, the fact that it is the deed of one prophet rather than of another, the fact that it is the deed of God rather than of man makes no difference; we must judge God and his prophets the way we would judge one another;

❏ the answer to an argument is a better argument, not abuse or intimidation;

❏ the answer to scorn is wit, not the bludgeon or the knife

The example to follow is that of Buddha and Jesus, not of Elisha and Mohammed.

– May 1986

Notes

1. 'The Lion and the Ostrich,' in *Suicide of a Nation,* Arthur Koestler (ed.), Macmillan, New York,1964.
2. Matthew, 23.
3. Swami Dayanand, *Satyarthaprakash,* Star Press, Allahabad, 1915, pp. 443-6.
4. *Adi Sri Guru Granth Sahib,* Raga Gauri, Mohalla 1, *Sir khohaai piyahi malvaandi juthaa mungi mungi khaai...*
5. *Adi Sri Guru Granth Sahib,* Gauri, Mohalla 5, *Bin simran jaise sarap arjari....*
6. The example is taken from Padmanabh S. Jaini, 'The disappearance of Buddhism and the survival of Jainism,'in *Studies in the History of Buddhism,* A.K. Narain (ed.), BR Publishing Corporation, Delhi,1980.
7. For instance, *Young India,* 29 May, 1924.
8. Maxime Rodinson, *Mohammed,* Penguin Press, London, 1971, pp. 77-8, 237.
9. *Ibid,* pp. 51,55-6,121,125,158-9,170-2,187,208-14,255, to cite just a few examples.
10. *Ibid,* pp. 92-4.
11. Rodinson's biography is just one of the available ones. Much stronger examples can be gleaned from the earlier biographies or essays of Muir, Mcdonald and scores of others.
12. Ali Dashti, *Twenty-three Years, A Study in the Prophetic Career of Muhammad,* George Allen and Unwin, 1985, p.120ff, gives one count, this one reaching twenty.
13. *Sahih al-Bukhari,* LXII. 5-7.
14. For instance, *Sahih al-Bukhari,* LXII.64,65,88.
15. Thus the *Hadis* freely report the Prophet, upon being asked by Allah to recite, saying twice, 'I am not lettered': cf. *Sahih Muslim,* LXXIV. 301-8.
16. Hajj without Umra: the lesser pilgrimage in which one dispenses with the sacrifice.
17. *Sahih al-Bukhari,* XCII.464.

18. Bible, Deuteronomy, 21.18.
19. *Ibid.*, 19.21(see also *Ibid.*, 19.11-13).
20. Quran, 2.173-5, 190.
21. Bible, Deuteronomy,12.2-3.
22. *Ibid.*, 17.2-7.
23. *Ibid.*, 13.6-11.
24. Quran, 5.37-8.
25. *Ibid.*, 47.4-5.
26. Bible, Deuteronomy, 13.12-16.
27. *Ibid.*, 20.10-18.(Compare the chapter on *Jihad* in the great
    compilation of Sheikh Burhann'd-din Ali on Muslim law, *The
    Hedaya.*)
28. Bible, Numbers, 31.1-54.
29. *Sahih al-Bukhari*, 82.794-7; *Sahih Muslim*, 4130-7.
30. Scores and scores of passages in the Upanishads are marred by this
    tokenism. For some examples see Arun Shourie, *Hinduism, Essence
    and Consequence,* Vikas, Delhi,1979, pp.114-128, 216-7.
31. Bible,Kings, 2.23-4.
32. On these incidents see Ibn Ishaq, *The Life of Muhammad*,
    A.Guillaume   (tr.),Oxford,Karachi,1978, pp. 308,364-9, 550-1, 675-
    8;   or Maxime Rodinson, *Mohammed, op.cit.*: pp.167-8,171-2,176-
    7, 261-2.
33. For instance, *Sahih al-Bukhari*, LIX.297-301,369-372.

II

Secularism: True and Counterfeit

We are regressing back to our religious identities – more and more of us are once again looking upon ourselves as 'Sikhs' or 'Muslims' or 'Hindus' rather than as Indians. Each is thus distancing himself from the other – the 'Us' from the 'Them.'

Sikh fundamentalism has already taken its toll in blood. In recent months the Government has anointed Muslim fundamentalists as the sole spokesmen of Muslims. And by now so great is the resentment among Hindus that it would take a Swami Dayanand-in-arms just four or five years to inflame them as they have never been inflamed before.

Every issue today appears as a 'Hindu v. Sikh,' a 'Hindu v. Muslim' issue. Whether a run-down building is a mosque or the birthplace of Lord Ram, whether a 75- years-old woman should get alimony or not, whether a procession should proceed along one route or another – none of these remains the specific, often trivial question that it is. Each becomes a matter of honour, a trial of strength, a prelude to some eventual but great calamity or victory. And as the question no longer concerns the specific issue, as it is now a question of 'who is to prevail – Hindus or Muslims', it seems entirely natural and fully justified to employ all possible means to resolve it in one's favour.

The last few years show what happens once communities set off on this course:

❑ The malady multiplies like cancer;
❑ The longer a ground for separateness is allowed to persist – reservations linked to castes are an example, different personal laws for different religious groups are another – the more deeply each group comes to believe that its security, indeed its identity, consists in the external marks of separateness;
❑ The longer these last, the more accustomed and also more

adept does each group become at exploiting these marks for wresting advantage. Soon enough, operating through these channels is the only way that the members of the group know. Every proposal to reform or integrate the laws now appears to them to be a conspiracy to deprive them of the only instrument they have of securing at least a few advantages for at least a few among themselves;

❑ More than the group or the community, its leaders develop an interest that is even more deeply vested in these contours. They are seldom men of religion themselves, and certainly not men of God, but they use religion to whip up the laity;

❑ Among them the extremists come to set the standard of fidelity to the cause. The moderates are forever panting to keep up with the rhetoric, the demands of the extremists. The moderates are forever telling everyone that the demands had better be conceded, and conceded through them, the moderates, as the alternative is to have the extremists prevail;

❑ Anxious to avoid hard choices society makes-believe, '*This* concession will allay the laity, it will finally give the moderates the strength they need.' In fact each concession – specially as it is made after that momentary show of firmness – vindicates the extremists, it shows once again that this society will not heed you till you grab it by the scruff, but the moment you do so, it will capitulate wholesale, and will itself fabricate rationalisations for having done so;

❑ Pusillanimity towards one group inspires other groups. The way Mrs. Gandhi dithered in dealing with Bhindranwale gave an impetus to self-styled leaders of Dalits; the new capitulation on Muslim personal law will stoke the Akalis to revive their demand for a separate personal law for the Sikhs;

❑ It isn't just that capitulating to the militant communalism of one group provides the spur to other groups. The State itself then finds it that much less defensible to resist similar demands from other groups. Should the State, having caved in to the Muslim fundamentalists, later insist that it will not allow Sikhs to decide the personal laws under which they will live, its refusal is broadcast by the extremists as proof positive of dis-crimination against the Sikhs;

❑ Finally, each action by one group ignites reaction in other groups. The net result of the Bhindranwales is that a powerful reaction is building up throughout Hindu society. 'We won't be pushed around in our own country,' one hears that said in all corners of the country today.

So close are we to a precipice. And what is our response? It is to do something that day – *anything* – that will help us just get through that day. That and to keep chanting, 'Secularism, Secularism'.

Indian Secularism

Our laws do not discriminate between citizens on grounds of religion. This is a great advance. It is one of the most precious legacies of our freedom struggle, and one of the best results of the spread of modern, liberal ideas in India.

Apart from this our secularism consists mainly in

❏ chanting verses from scriptures of different religions at State functions;

❏ covering each issue with a syrup of cliches; 'Islam is the religion of peace,' 'Islam alone assures the fullest equality and dignity to women,' are the ones we have heard in the latest round;

❏ allowing institutions and groups of some religions what we would readily, and rightly, deny to others: we would not allow, and thank God for that, usurpers to do in a Hindu shrine what the extremists were allowed to do in the Golden Temple; we would not allow, and thank the Lord for that, the leader of a Hindu sect to exploit his followers the way we allow the Syedna to exploit and hold in thrall the Bohras;

❏ allowing institutions or groups that dress themselves up in religion a latitude that we readily, and rightly, deny secular institutions and groups: no governing body would be allowed to condone the usurpation and misuse of the premises under its charge the way the Shiromani Gurdwara Prabandhak Committee has been allowed the abet what has been done in and from the Golden Temple;

❏ giving 'secular' speeches while making deals with every communalist – with the Akalis in Punjab, the Shahi Imam in Delhi, with this odd Baba or that in U.P., with the Muslim

League in Kerala – who controls, or is rumoured to control
the vote banks;
❑ branding others 'communal', just as for decades to establish
one's progressive credentials, it was enough – it was also
necessary it would seem – to brand others 'reactionary';
❑ being ostentatiously anti-religion in public while
practising the rituals and observing the superstitions in private,
this being often accomplished by a division of labour: the man
ostentatiously disregards tradition in public while his wife is
put to going through the *paaths*, *havans* and *pooja* at home,
he declaims rationalism in public while she shows the
horoscopes in private. 'You know these women..' he says,
should a visitor turn up unexpectedly.

How things have changed in the last fifty years. During the
freedom struggle, if you looked upon a Muslim as being someone
apart, as being someone other than just a human being like yourself,
the 'progressive' was bound to brand you 'communal.' Today
unless you look upon the Muslim as separate, that is, *unless* you
see him as a Muslim rather than as just a human being like
yourself, the 'progressive' brands you 'communal'. Fifty years
ago when a Hindu scholar by his deep study perceived and wrote
about *The Essential Unity of All Religions* – the title of Bhagwan
Das' famous work – that was looked upon as humanist scholarship
at its best. Today when a scholar points to the identity of what
is taught in the Granth Sahib and what is taught in, say, the Hindu
Bhakti tradition, it is taken as proof positive of a deep conspiracy
to swallow Sikhism.
    There is the schizophrenia. We chant, 'Hinduism, Islam, Chris-
tianity are our common heritage.' But when a scholar proceeds in
that belief – when a Hindu scholar, for instance, examines the *hadis*
with the same tools as he does Puranas – we shout, 'Communal'.
    And there are the double standards. It is progressive to demand
that the Government appoint trustees to manage the Vishwanath,
Tirupati, Nathdwara, Guruvayur temples. But it is communal to
demand that it do so in the case of a Gurdwara, even when the
SGPC has run away from its responsibility under the law. It is
progressive to denounce, say, the RSS for holding *shakhas*. But
it is communal to so much as draw attention to the fact that the
official budget of the SGPC – a body constituted under our secular

laws, elections to which are held under the supervision of (and
at the expenses of) our secular Government – has 'training in
arms' as one of the heads of expenditure. It is progressive to heap
scorn upon ill-informed pamphlets published by some *math*. But
it is communal to document the poison being spread from the
Damadmi Taksal. It is progressive to denounce a Hindu *swami* for
trying to influence his followers on a secular matter. But it is rank
communalism to point out that the obligation to obey *hukamnamas*
and *fatwas* has no place in a secular State. All this has roots in at
least three things.

The first is our ignorance of our traditions. Far from having
a knowledge of all our traditions, far from Hindus having studied
the Quran, etc. rare is the Hindu who has studied – just studied,
to say little of having thought over, and to say nothing at all of
trying to live by – the Upanishads or even the Gita, rare the
Muslim who has studied the Quran, the Sikh who has studied the
Granth Sahib. The Western educated Indian has merely
internalized the sophisticated, indeed subversive slander of Western scholars about his texts, beliefs, practices. Much of this scholarship was associated with – much of it directly arose from – the
need to justify the notion that the East had to be 'civilized' by
missionary activity, by imperial conquest. We have not studied
even this body of work in detail. But we *have* internalised three
general notions from it: that by and large our tradition is of little
worth (how often we hear it echoed, 'The tradition is pessimistic,
it is life-denying'); that our present condition – in particular,
the backwardness of 20th century India – originates in this
tradition; finally, that we are not one stream but an artificial
geographical construct, that the Sikhs, Muslims, Hindus, etc.,
are inherently, irreconcilably separate.

Ignorant of the facts, we think of one another in stereotypes,
we see one another through our prejudices. And we are by turn unnecessarily apologetic towards the foreigner, and unnecessarily
defensive-aggressive towards our fellow countrymen.

The second reason for our schizophrenia, our double standards,
is that on these issues, as on other public issues, we are not prepared
to take the trouble to go into specifics. The superficial generalisation, the angry slogan and – our favourite – the abusive label
is enough for us. Therefore, every issue naturally becomes a
'Hindu v. Muslim,' a 'Progressive v. Reactionary' issue. This

is all the more so because many of the 'religious' issues that arise
– the route of the *Pankhon ka* procession and the *Ganesh Chaturthi*
procession in Hyderabad and the behaviour of the processionists
– have been stoked up in the first place, not because they are in
any way central to the religion, but to proclaim power: the power
of the group *vis-a-vis* other groups, the power of one leader *vis-a-vis* other leaders within the group. No group of citizens makes
it its business to educate people to the fact that these processions
have nothing to do with religion, that no text ordains processions,
that they are just displays of power. Nor does any group take the
trouble to chart out alternative routes the procession could take,
routes that would be no less 'sacred' but would provide less of an
occasion for the riots that follow the processionists. The
processions are allowed, the killings and arson follow, year after
year – and Hindu-Muslim animosity is deepened.

But the most important source of what passes for secularism
today is that we just don't want to take the steps that the situation
demands. For three long years, as the killings in the Punjab
proceeded, as perceptions of Hindus and Sikhs about each other
were poisoned, the Government proclaimed, 'We will not enter
the Gurdwaras as we do not want to hurt the sentiments of the
Sikhs.' The outcome on Muslim personal law has been no
different: 'The community alone must decide for itself.' But why
not the country? Now, in a given situation it may or may not be
expedient to act. But we should at least be clear on where the
principle lies, and whether all we are doing is to dress up dithering
as principle.

Modernisation and paranoia

Why are we retreating to religious identities? Having retreated
to them, why does each group feel insecure? The cause is not the
other, rival religious group, but modernisation itself.

Modernisation opens up new opportunities. It also dislocates
and entails hardships. As we can take advantage of the opportunities
– for instance, funds and jobs flowing from the State – and as
we can fortify ourselves against the dislocations most readily as
groups, we rush to persons who speak the same language, who
are from the same region, who belong to the same caste or religion
as us. It is around these contours 'they' have been distinguished

from ' us' the longest. Pushed around now, but also tempted by the new possibilities, we rush back to the identities that we have known the longest, identities that are therefore the most deeply ingrained.

But modernisation even as it hurls us back to these identities, blurs these traditional contours. We may revert to the caste group to grab at the development funds reaching our region. But at the same time,and in part because of the same factors, mobility between regions as well as occupations increases, entirely new occupations which do not fit the old categories come into being; differentiations within an occupation become finer; thus, while in the old, 'unchanging' mode, one occupation differed so obviously from another, now – what with a much larger number of occupations, as well as finer gradations within an occupation – they are arranged not along a discrete hierarchy but more or less along a continuum. Thus, while on the one side we are hurled back to our caste group, the contours that demarcate this caste from others become hazier by the year.

The case of religion is no different. Faced with uncertainty, I nestle closer to my religious group. But the new opportunities and hardships throw up new questions every day that the Book, the Church, the example and words of the Teacher of a thousand years ago, are just not able to answer. The primary uncertainties into which modernisation plunges me are therefore compounded. I rush to the only group I know for security, for answers, for acting in concert, only to find that the very basis of the group is being eroded, to find that the only answers that the group and the authorities within the group know do not see me through. I am seized now not just by uncertainty but by the 'fear of freedom'.

Moreover, there are many in the group who in their own interest are spurred to , and who are well equipped to inflame this new sense of insecurity. Over the centuries the only channels through which the members know how at act are the ones carved out by the leaders of their group. Even more than the laity the leaders, too, acquire an interest in these contours of separateness. Their dominance *rests upon* this identity, this self-perception of the group as being different from other groups. As the edges are blurred, as they are knocked around, these leaders are the first to be seized by the uncertainties. They see that the very basis of their hegemony is being shaken. They project their paranoia on to the community. While what is happening is merely that one set of demarcations is getting hazier, while all that is happening is perhaps that one set of demarcations is being replaced by demarcations along other earth-faults, they cry, 'Islam is in danger,' 'The *Panth* is in danger,' 'Hinduism is in danger'. And the group, conditioned over the centuries to think that its essence consists in the externals that differentiate it from other groups – that it consists in the equivalent in the psyche of each us of the five 'K's – believes that this indeed is so. Modernisation itself provides the 'reasons' for paranoia, the 'evidence' which 'justifies' it. With freer ways the members of the group become negligent in their observances – beards are clipped, the prayers are not said in time, the festivals become mere holidays that are spent in the purely secular pursuit of leisure. Each of us by his own volition slips into 'Western' ways. The cumulative result of these separate, individual decisions, however, appears to be – and is made out to be – that the *Panth* is in danger. The result flows from *our* decisions, *our* actions, but we attribute it to '*the other*', indeed to the deliberate design of '*the other*'. Modernisation is the corrosive. But that is too abstract a notion. Paranoia needs a specific, personified devil. We therefore blame it all on the other – 'the Hindu,' 'the Muslim,' 'the Sikh' – who is out to swallow 'my *Dharma*,' 'my *Panth*,' 'my *Qaum*.'

Again modernisation provides a 'reason' to confirm this surmise. At the best of times we are only too ready to believe that the others are out to do us in; after all, this is such a reassuring notion – it 'explains' why, in spite of our manifest virtue and our exemplary effort, we are not more 'successful' than we are. But now, as everyone steps out of his tradition-ordained niche, as it becomes equally legitimate for anyone to pursue any activity, each in fact becomes the rival of all. Because of centuries of conditioning, each looks upon the other not as another human being – in fact, a human being who is being buffetted around by the same forces – but as 'a Hindu,' 'a Musalman.' It is 'the Hindu,' thus, 'the Musalman' who appears to be snatching the bread from my hands, as well as the one who is out to swallow my *Panth*.

All is thus set for a defensive militancy. The experience of each group in dealing with the State spurs its militancy. The State is both preoccupied and enfeebled. As a consequence it does not heed a demand so long as the group is civil. But the moment the group takes to the streets, the moment it threatens to take to arms,

the State caves in. And so each round reinforces the lesson:
'Militancy pays'.

What Must Be Done?

Thus we are not up against an ephemeral rash, the problem is
not just one or two madmen who have seen an opportunity in
religion for advancing themselves. The problem has to do with the
structure of our society and the transition to modernisation. It will
accordingly be with us for decades, and the troubles it has caused
us are but a preview of the havoc that, unattended, it is certain
to cause. What then must be done?

Each of us is free to pursue his religion. In addition, our laws
do not discriminate between individuals on grounds of religion.
These are the corner-stones of a secular State. But in view of recent
events, as the preceding discussion shows, we must go further. The
State must be scrupulously fair. It must also be absolutely firm.
When, confronted by a Bhindranwale, it flounders, it breeds
terrorists. In the same way, when following the massacre of 2700
Sikhs in the capital, it does not bring the guilty to book, it breeds
terrorists.

The group or institution of one religion must not be allowed
to do what groups or institutions of other religions are denied.
No religious group or institution must be allowed what a non-
religious group or institution is denied. Fairness as well as
firmness must inform the policies of the State in all matters, small
as well as big. We often postpone doing the right thing for 'The
Great Issue' to arise. But just as for the individual the only way
to gain strength for 'The Great Issue' is to acquire it by acting on
the 'small' issues as they arise, the only way for the State to keep
its apparatus in order, as well as to have that reputation of being
just and competent which it needs to tackle 'The Great Issue,' is
to tackle the 'small' issues promptly, competently and fairly. A
State which does not enforce the Public Nuisances Act to regulate
loudspeakers that blare from places of worship, which does not
prevent religious groups from grabbing Government land, disables
itself. It will not be able to act when the nemesis of this pattern
of behaviour will confront it in the shape of 'The Great Issue'.

Apart from these specifics, we must move further on two
general principles. First, in a secular State no religious organisation

must have the authority to decree what is to be done on a secular matter. *Fatwas, hukamnamas* and the like have no place in a secular State. Furthermore, given the authority 'religious' leaders claim for themselves on 'religious' matters, we must circumscribe the ambit of what is a religious matter, limiting it to purely self-regarding actions, and even among these to actions of a spiritual kind. 'But that was our personal fight,' a leader of the extremists in Punjab said recently in talking about the Bhindranwale-Nirankari killings, 'Why did he [a journalist], why did the Government step in?' But killing others, even if it be from purely religious zeal, is not a self-regarding action.

'But my religion makes no distinction between the secular and the religious, between *Miri* and *Piri*,' we are told. That claim can be made on behalf of almost all religions. For instance, Hinduism no less than Islam decreed a complete code, a code covering all aspects of life. And this was natural. At that time there was no State as we know it today. Those who were founding the religion or organising it were also founding the State. The Prophet's case is the most obvious one. It was as natural for him to be not just the religious teacher but also the legislator as it was for a rishi like Manu. Moreover, as in those days of heteronomy the only sanction that man would listen to was that of God, it was as natural for the Prophet to decree the laws in the name of Allah as for Manu to decree them in the name of Brahma. When they were yet weak, Christians hearkened to the words of Jesus, 'Give unto Caesar what is Caesar's' but soon enough Christianity became the State religion and the distinction was obscured. The *Syllabus of Errors* that Pope Pius IX put out in 1870, to cite just one of the scores of examples that come to mind, once again affirmed the overriding authority of the Church on *all* matters – secular, intellectual, spiritual, private as much as public.

Hence, it makes little sense to insist that I will heed the *fatwas,* the *hukumnamas* because my religion makes no distinction between the secular and the religious. If I claim that latitude for myself, I cannot deny it to the other as my religion is not the only one which has disregarded this distinction. Now that the State is in place all must obey it, and not the text or practice of our respective religion. If the traditions or doctrines of religion prescribe duties that are not compatible with the principles of a secular State – for instance, if our religion ordains, as Islam does, that we must either convert the one who adheres to some other religion or slay him – *those* duties must be jettisoned and not the principles of a secular State.

The next thing to remember, indeed to internalise, is the following: the security and prosperity of the minorities as much as of the Hindus lies, not in building fortresses around our parochial groups, but in all of us joining together to ensure that the institutions of parliamentary democracy work. The individual must be the unit of account, not the group and most certainly not the religious group. Many leaders from Sir Syed Ahmed through Jinnah and down to the little Jinnahs of our day, have stoked the fear that, should the individual be the unit of account, the majority will swamp the minorities. But this is to attribute to the majority a cohesion that it does not possess, at least not at the beginning of the process. It is entirely possible at that stage to encourage the values which will lead members of it to see themselves as individuals, as human beings, as citizens rather than as members of a religious group. But once you start treating minorities as a group, even if this be in response to their apprehensions, you ensure a reaction, you ensure that members of the majority too will begin to see themselves as members of a religious group rather than as citizens.

Apart from the reaction it foments, treating minorities or the majority as groups has several specific drawbacks. The State begins to buy peace, the politicians begin to buy votes by pandering to those who today control the groups. This affects the nature of political life, of the State itself. It results in the kind of political chicanery and opportunism that led Congress politicians to have foreigners enrolled in the electoral lists in Assam, and, as happened in Assam, in the end it robs the entire State of legitimacy. In the ensuing avalanche the minorities are reduced to a state of helplessness which would never have been theirs had we put our faith in the rule of law, in building institutions rather than in circumventing these to grab advantages by striking deals with this politician or that.

Moreover, the concessions that are made ostensibly to the group are gobbled up by the better-off, the better-organised within the group. These sections become the brokers. Their power in turn rests on the fact that the State deals with the group only through them. They thus acquire an interest in keeping their group backward and ignorant, in keeping it dependent on themselves. They prevent most assiduously the emergence of other leaders within the group. The manipulations of some of the 'leaders' of Harijans illustrates the point, as much as those of Jinnah. Furthermore, they acquire an interest in fomenting in the group the feeling that it is separate, that it is being discriminated against, that it is in fact in imminent danger of being swallowed up. The end of this process is Bhindranwale.

This way of looking at things – that is, of thinking in terms of groups rather than individuals – perpetuates the tyranny of the leaders of the group on its members – of the Syedna on the Bohras – and of some sections of the group on other sections in it – of Muslim men on Muslim women, of landowning Thakurs on landless Harijans. Indeed, it gives the oppressing leaders and sections a shield. The moment anyone from outside the group speaks on behalf of the oppressed, he is denounced for 'interfering' in the 'internal affairs' of the group. 'The community – the *sangat,* the *umma* – alone has a right to decide these matters,' the leaders shout. But 'the community' is unorganised, it is powerless in the face of the leaders and usurpers within it, it is in their thrall.

The principal losers are the members of the group itself. It is that much more difficult for them to throw off the domination of the very ones whose power and prosperity depend on this backwardness. The members of the majority lose too. Even in the best of circumstances all of us distance ourselves from the victim. Look at our reaction to the morning's news: 'Four shot down by Punjab terrorists.' But he was a policemen, we tell ourselves, the other was the local secretary of the Congress, and all that is in Punjab, not here. We ward off insecurity by this distancing. This is our normal reaction in ordinary circumstances. When in addition the rhetoric and actions of the group itself proclaim its members to be separate from us, the distancing is that much easier. Indeed, it is automatic. Potential help to those who are beleaguered in that group is cut off, of course. But the rest of us too are disabled. Having become accustomed to ignoring oppression inflicted on others we become that much less sensitive to injustice among ourselves, and are therefore that much less able to resist oppression.

The   point is not to have atomised, unorganised individuals facing a leviathan in the hands of Hitler or Stalin. There ought to be limits on the collective also, in particular on the State. The State must deal with the individual *qua* individual. It must recognise the many-facetedness of each individual who, in turn, must associate with others in many different kinds of organisations, each of which specialises in enabling him to develop different dimensions of his potential. In addition to recognising the individual in his many-facetedness, the collective − whether this be in the form of a particular group or the State − must respect as inviolate a sphere of autonomy of the individual. Safeguarding this sphere and enlarging it must be one of the principal objectives of each of the different kinds of associations. Religious millenarianisms invariably become as much of a rationalisation for crushing this sphere of autonomy as do the secular millenarianisms of the Hitlers and Stalins.

Religious Millenarianism

That there is but one truth and only one way to it; that God has revealed it to 'us' the 'Chosen People,' and to 'us' alone, that it is contained in our Book, and in our Book alone; that as God Himself dictated or revealed it to 'us' every word of the Book is eternally true, eternally excellent and eternally binding; that the Book itself is beyond the comprehension of most of even the believers, and *a fortiori* beyond that of the non-believers; that therefore we must heed the Church, the Priest; that adherence to the faith is the overriding, peremptory duty, as is the duty of making others see this light; that as this is the only truth, as it alone will lead us to the millenium, as it will do so surely, for its own good mankind must be awakened to it; that therefore no cost is too great for holding on to it, no means are impermissible for converting others to it.

Such millenarianist claims of religions, such millenarianist beliefs, in religions must by replaced by tentativeness, by openness and receptivity. For certainty is the *sine qua non* of intolerance, bigotry, of dividing human beings into 'them' versus 'us'. Doubt is what will bring us together. It is the spur to tolerance as well as to pressing on with enquiry.

To dispel our parochial certainties we have to do two things:

we have to learn, and we have to examine.

'The new "discoveries" and "inventions" of modern science are already contained in the Vedas'; 'All knowledge is contained in the Quran – there is nothing worth knowing which is not in it, what is not in it is not worth knowing'; 'Sikhs are and have always been different from Hindus'; 'Sikhism is closer to Islam than to Hinduism'; 'The Shariat is divinely ordained, therefore to seek to amend it is to strike at Islam'; 'Ninety percent of the sacrifices in the independence struggle were made by the Sikhs.' Such assertions are being repeated day in and day out, they are being internalised by frighteningly large numbers. Unless we have read and thought over the Granth Sahib, the Quran, the *hadis*, the Hindu scriptures, unless we have thorough knowledge of our history and ways of living, we cannot even begin to deal with these assertions, to say nothing of arresting the poison in them.

We must discover what is common in the scriptures, and what the irreducible differences are. Each of us, for instance, preens himself on the uniqueness, on the singular excellence of his scriptures. But, to take just one instance, when we see that legend after legend, narrative after narrative, and proposition after proposition in the Quran can be traced to Jewish and Christian doctrines of the time, that the Prophet was often at pains to affirm that he was merely reminding the people of the teaching that God had already conveyed to them through the earlier prophets, we are less apt to think ourselves unique, and singularly excellent.[1]

Similarly, when we study the catholic and inclusive Granth Sahib and remember that, in addition to the compositions of the Gurus, it incorporates those of sixteen Hindu mystics and Sufi saints – from Jaidev and Namdev and Parmanand and Ravidas and Mira and Surdas to Kabir and Farid – we glimpse what the spirit was that impelled the Gurus. It is on seeing that the legend of Krishna's birth – a king is warned that a child born at such and such a time will kill him, he decrees that all infants be killed; this special infant is carried across a river, and is then brought up by a poor couple – is common to so many traditions that we think less of our uniqueness and more of what the common human needs have been and how different groups have ever so often come up with identical notions to meet them.

The *insistence* on uniqueness must be taken as proof of the opposite. The fact is that the more a tradition borrowed from another, the more determined it became to deny any link with it, the more hysterical became its insistence that the Book, the notions were uniquely its own, that they were the originals that it had received directly from God. How apposite is what Freud says about one of the reasons for the Christians' hostility towards the Jews:

> We must not forget that all the people who now excel in the practice of anti-semitism became Christians only in relatively recent times, sometimes, forced to it by bloody conversion. One might say they all are 'badly christened'; under the thin veneer of Christianity they have remained what their ancestors were, barbarically polytheistic. They have not yet overcome their grudge against the new religion which was forced on them, and they have projected it on to the source from which Christianity came to them. The fact that the Gospels tell a story which is enacted among Jews, and in truth treats only of Jews has facilitated such a projection. The hatred for Judaism is at bottom hatred for Christianity...[2]

Is this not at least a part of the explanation for the subsequent hatred of Muslims for both the Jews and the Christians?[3] And if we substitute 'Muslims' or 'Sikhs' for 'Christians' in the foregoing, would we not glimpse one of the reasons for the hostility of these for the Hindus in our own time? May a part of the explanation not lie in the fact that the one Book that the devout Sikh is exhorted to revere is saturated with accounts of Hindu deities and heroes? May a part of the explanation for the rage of the Indian Muslim not lie in the fact that deep down he realises that his *practice* – from the worship of saints to the faith in paid-for amulets to the language he speaks – is closer to the *practice* of the Hindu or the Sikh than to the teaching of Islam?

Hunting down the origins, locating the similarities, is doubly important for another reason. Those who in their scriptures, their beliefs, their practice are tied together in such symbiotic relationships are precisely the ones who have become mortal enemies later on. Nothing punctures the claim to uniqueness, nothing puts the self-image of being the 'Chosen' in perspective as much as the knowledge that in fact what we profess to be so unique and excellent about ourselves is not just shared with but is in fact derived from precisely those whom we proclaim to be the misguided, the inferior, the ones whom God has damned.

The differences must be studied as closely as the similarities. Which of them is worth breaking one another's heads over? Are they not akin to the dispute Lenin parodied, the dispute over whether the Devil is green or yellow? Would the Buddha have attached any importance to the issues over which the Hinayanists and the Mahayanists split?

We must of course go beyond studying these similarities and differences. We must study religions in relation to the great questions they set out tackle. Is any one of them able to explain the persistence of evil and suffering in the face of an omnipotent, omniscient, all-merciful God? Does each of them not assert that not a leaf moves but at His command, and yet also insist that the wrong an individual does originates solely from him – i.e., the individual – and he must suffer for it? Does each of them not peddle the same soporifics? If the faithful win, that is proof that God is with them. If they lose, as they so often do, it is just that God is testing their faith in Him! None of them explains why the All-powerful, All-knowing, Creator-Ruler-Destroyer should be so concerned that a few of us here on this small speck of an earth, in this one among a million galaxies, in this one corner of a universe that is millions of light years across do or do not have faith in Him.

Apart from learning about our doctrines, we should learn about our churches and our priests. How do people become 'Swami so-and-so', 'Bhagwan so-and-so' among the Hindus? How do they become 'Baba so-and-so', and 'Sant so-and-so' among the Sikhs? So many of us turn to the Shahi Imam of the Jama Masjid in Delhi. Has he acquired the honour by virtue of his piety or learning? Or is it another one of those inherited posts? How many of these religious heads owe their current post, as the Syedna does, to the decisions of sundry magistrates? Even more than the manner of ascending to or acquiring the status or post, what is their social practice? If a 'religious' head is acquiring petrol pumps from politicians in return for delivering block votes or if, like the head of the *math* in Bodh Gaya, he is into amassing real estate, should that not alter our predisposition to revere all and sundry among them? What is the mark of a man of God, the office he occupies or the service he renders? As Jesus said to his disciples when a dispute arose among them at the Last Supper as to which of them was to be regarded as the greatest, 'For which is the great, one who sits at table, or one who serves? Is it not the one who sits at table? But I am among you as one who serves.'

Examine the Book

There was a time when the only way to justify a rule was to assert that it had been ordained directly by God. Thus we have Manu claiming that his statutes have been created by Brahma Himself, we have Moses bringing the Tablets down from the mountain, we have the Bible ascribing everything to God and His Son, we have the Prophet claiming that the Quran which was revealed to him by Allah through the angel Gabriel was a reproduction of the original which is lying in heaven. Divine ordination was the necessary sanction. (It was not always the sufficient one as is evident from the fact that ever so often physical force, and a great deal of it, had to be used to make people head the decrees.)

Now, this sanction could be enforced only by insisting that every word that had come down from Brahma, or God, or Allah was true, eternal, excellent. Hence the claims on behalf of the Bible and the Quran among the *ahl al kitab*. As invariably happens, once the respective churches were founded, what had been claimed on behalf of the Book – literal inerrancy, eternal infallibility – was soon claimed on behalf of the churches, the *ulema*, and the Pope. These claims both for the respective books and the priests survive to this day, and are at the root of intolerance and reaction, as well as of heteronomy among followers.

We must therefore examine the claims to infallibility that are made on behalf of religion and are believed by the faithful.[4] What did the religions and the texts prophesy, and how did things turn out in fact? The world for instance, was to have ended and the Second Coming was to have taken place within the lifetime of some of Jesus' companions. That this did not happen became, as Schopenhauer noted, an embarrassment even to Peter and Paul. Similarly, every statement of fact in the Book – about the cosmos, geography of the earth, history (including the history of the Books themselves), medicine – should be tabulated and set against what we know today. Several things will become clear at once. First, it will be clear that in the light of what we now know, we just cannot maintain any longer that every word of the books or the traditions is literally true. The assertions about creation in the Bible and the Quran, about conception, illness, and medicine in the *hadis* so patently reflect the state of knowledge at that time that even clerical scholars now say that the accounts of creation in the Bible, for instance, are not to be taken literally, that they reflect not the literal truth but are just a manner of speaking.

Second, the internal evidence of the Books themselves shows that 'every word' in them just cannot be true. The Bible gives two accounts of the creation; the accounts differ. It attributes its 'books' to Moses, Isiah, etc, but, as Tom Paine argued, on its own showing several of the events narrated in each of them took place long after – in some cases hundreds of year after – the supposed author had died. At one place (*Mark*, 2.26) David enters the house of God and eats the leaves of offering under the high priest Abiathar. At another (I *Samuel*, 21.1, etc) this occurs not under Abiathar but his father, Ahimelach. In one place *Matthew* (27.9) attributes a prophecy to Jeremiah and in another (11.12) to Zachariah. In the New Testament the genealogy of Jesus is given in two places – once in the Gospel according to Matthew, and once in the Gospel according to Luke. Both give the names beginning from David down to Joseph, the husband of the Virgin Mary, the mother of Jesus. On Matthew's reckoning David is followed seriatim by twenty-five heirs – whom he lists – before we get to Joseph. On Luke's by forty. And apart from the first and the last names in the series – i.e., the names David and Joseph – our authors have not one name in common. It isn't that the names of who succeeded whom are common and that it is just that in a few places the order is different. *Not one name in one list so much as occurs in the other.* Moreover, as Paine asked, what is the point of listing the twenty-five or the forty? Jesus, being the Son of God, and having been born to a virgin, was not in any case the son of Joseph.

One fact after another about that all-important event – the crucifixion of Jesus – is different in the different Gospels.

In *Matthew* (26. 14-16), Judas promises to the priests that he will identify Jesus for them in return for the thirty pieces of silver that they actually give him, in *Mark* (14. 10-11) and *Luke* (22.3) for the money they promise to give him. In *Luke* (22.3) Satan enters Judas at this stage itself, i.e., before the Last Supper. In *John*

(14.27) he does so at the Last Supper.

Accounts of the Last Supper differ a great deal. To continue with Judas, for instance, in *Mark* and *Luke,* Jesus tells his twelve disciples in a general way that one of them will betray him, one who is at the table with him, who is eating with him and dipping bread in the same dish with him (*Mark*, 14.17 - 21). In *Matthew* he is a bit more specific but not entirely so; when like the others Judas asks him, 'Is it I Master?,' Jesus answers, 'You have said so' (*Luke,* 26.25). But in *John,* Jesus identifies Judas clearly and specifically. When the disciples ask who is it among them who will betray him, Jesus says, 'It is he to whom I shall give this morsel when I have dipped it.' And John adds, 'So when he had dipped the morsel, he gave it to Judas, the son of Simon Iscariot' (*John*, 14.21-6).

In *Mark, Luke* and *John* we hear no more about Judas. But in *Matthew* (27.3-5) Judas repents when he sees the result of his betrayal and returns the silver pieces. But it is too late. And, penitent, he hangs himself.

The exchanges with Pilate too differ. Matthew (27.11-14) and Mark (15.1–5) state that after answering Pilate's question, 'Are you the king of the Jews?' with the ambiguous 'You have said so,' Jesus does not answer any further questions at all. Luke too reports him responding to that question in the same way, but he says nothing about Jesus answering other questions or remaining silent. On the other hand, John (18.33-8, 19.10-11) reports lively exchanges between the two.

In *Matthew, Mark* and *John* the 'trial' takes place only in the presence of Pilate. In *Luke*, however , Pilate finding that Jesus has done no wrong, sends him to Herod, from whose jurisdiction Jesus hails and who happens to be in Jerusalem.(Herod too finds that Jesus has done no wrong and sends him back to Pilate.)

In *Matthew* (27.32), *Mark* (15.21) and *Luke* (23.26), Simon of Cyrene is compelled to carry the cross on which Jesus is to be crucified. In *John* (19.17) Jesus is made to carry it himself.

Each gives a different account of the words that were put above Jesus's head, specifying the charge. *Mark* and *Luke* do not specify who writes them and puts them there. From *Matthew* (27.37) it seems the soldiers do so. In *John* (19.19) Pilate himself writes them out and puts them on the cross.

John tells us nothing about the attitude of the two thieves who are crucified along with Jesus, one to his left, one to his right. *Matthew* (27.44) and *Mark* (15.32) report both of them as reviling him. But in *Luke* (15.32) one thief reviles Jesus and the other one rebukes the former for doing so.

The accounts differ as much on the last words of Jesus. *Matthew* (27.46-50) and *Mark* (15.33-08) both report Jesus as crying out in a loud voice, 'My God, my God, why hast thou forsaken me?' And after crying out once again, breathing his last. The words do not occur in *Luke* and *John* at all.

Instead *Luke* (23.34) reports Jesus as saying first, 'Father, forgive them, for they know not what they do.' 'Next (23.39-41), he reports one of the thieves reviling Jesus, the second rebuking the first for doing so and entreating Jesus, 'Jesus, remember me when you come in your kingly power,' and Jesus assuring him, 'Truly, I say to you, today you will be with me in Paradise.' It is after all this that *Luke* (23.44-54) reports Jesus as crying out in a loud voice. But the words Jesus cries out are not the same as in the account given by *Matthew* and *Mark*. Instead, in *Luke* Jesus cries, 'Father, into thy hands I commit my spirit.' And with this he breathes his last.

In *John* we have nothing at all of the above. Instead, upon noticing his mother and a loved disciple, he tells Mary, 'Woman, behold your son,' and to the disciple he says, 'Behold your mother.' After this Jesus 'knowing that all was now finished,' says, 'I thirst.' As in the other accounts a sponge with vinegar is put to his mouth, and , taking it, he says, 'It is finished,' bows his head and gives up the spirit.

The hour at which Jesus is eventually crucified is different in the narratives. The events that transpire in the skies and on earth are different. The accounts of the resurrection differ just as much. They differ again in regard to Jesus appearing before the disciples after his resurrection – in *Matthew* the disciples encounter him in a mountain in Galilee, in *Luke* they do so in a house in Jerusalem, in *John* in yet another setting. While in the Gospels of Matthew, John and Mark, Jesus would seem to fall out of sight after the resurrection till he appears to the eleven disciples (on the mountain in Galillee or in the house in Jerusalem), according to the Gospel of Luke he travels in disguise with two of them to a village some seven and a half miles from Jerusalem and eats with them, and only then disappears from sight. He appears not to the eleven, but first to the two. And so on.[5]

Over the last three hundred years considerations such as these have led even devout scholars to conclude that the authors were not as concerned in each instance to record what had actually happened, but to recreate the overall situation in a way that would reinforce the central message of faith. They now hold that it is not 'the literal inerrancy' that we must look for in, say, the Bible, but the integrity of the overall mind-set of faith which the authors create through the dramatic situations they construct.

There is much to be said for this view, as there can be no doubt at all about the enormous impact that each of the four Gospels has on the reader, non-Christian and Christian alike. The contradictions or differences in regard to specific details are as nothing when set against this impact. But, while it is entirely correct to acknowledge that the overall impact of the narratives, is what was the concern of the narrators, in urging that we focus on the overall impact rather than on the precise details, on 'the atmosphere' that the words create rather than on the words themselves, we are clearly discarding the position that every single word of the text is the truth, the whole truth and nothing but the truth. By focusing on the overall impact than on 'the literal inerrancy' we are saying in effect that the authors of the Gospels are not to be looked upon as chronologists listing what transpired but as dramatists, each concerned with making the particular event he is portraying most effective, with making the particular speech that is being delivered at that moment most evocative, without bothering about whether what he is setting down conforms to or contradicts what other dramatists have written about that scene or speech, or what in fact happened.

The next fact that stands out, however, forces us to move beyond this realisation too. Often the Books treat of the same events. Now, each is sacred. Each is said to be from God. Every word in each is said to be true, and eternally so. What is one to do then when they differ with each other in their accounts of the same event? A single example will have to suffice. Jesus is mentioned in 15 *Suras* of the Quran. Ninety-three verses deal directly with him. The annunciation of the Virgin and the birth of Jesus are differentiated at one place (*Quran*, 19.17) — an angel appears and informs the Virgin that God has decided to make a sign of her (i.e., that He has decided to perform an extraordinary thing, a miracle through her so that people realise His greatness) by having her, a virgin, bear a son who shall be perfect, etc. At other places (*Quran*, 21.9, 66.12) the two events are telescoped into one so that God is represented as both telling her and putting the child in her. Mary subsequently gives birth to Jesus near the trunk of a palm tree (*Quran*, 19.22. -34). The Quran informs us again and again _that Jesus, while a prophet, was not the son of God (for instance, 3.51-5; 4.169; 5.19-21; 5.76-9; 19.35-6; 43. 57-65). In the Gospels Jesus does not reveal the nature of his mission to his companions till after a long period of preparation. In the Quran (3.41, 19.30) he proclaims it from the cradle itself. Most important, the Quran reports that Jesus was not crucified at all, that the man who was crucified was just a look-alike (*Quran*, 4.154-9). As Jesus was not killed, there was no occasion for subsequent events like the resurrection etc.

The devout Christian is liable to find the 'reasons' that the Quran gives for concluding, for instance, that Jesus was not the Son of God, to be just as unconvincing as the devout Muslim is liable to find puerile the 'reasons' that one may extract from the Bible for the proposition that he *was* the Son of God. The Quran says, for instance, that it is wrong to attribute a son to God as the latter has no consort (6.101; 112.3). But, surely, a Being who can endow a virgin with a son so as to make a sign of her so that men believe in Him, i.e., in Allah, a Being who can create the entire cosmos, including time and space, out of nothing, should be able to create a son out of nothing too. How can His not having a consort be an impediment? Similarly, the Quran says that it is a sin to ascribe a son to God, 'when it beseemeth not for the God of Mercy to beget a son' (19.91-3). But why is it *seemly* for God to have prophets, apostles, messengers (on whom He lavishes extraordinary, paternal care to the point of always rushing to get them out of their personal predicaments), and *unseemly* for Him to have a son? Why is it *seemly* for God to have evil and suffering among His creations and *unseemly* to have a son among them?

Are the 'reasons' of the Quran as much as the Bible not something else altogether? The Bible must affirm that Jesus *is* the Son of God so as to exalt him to his unique position, a position so unique that a religion can be founded after him. *For exactly the same reason,* the Quran must insist that he was *not* the Son of God, *for the same reason* it must deny the central event of Christian martyrology, namely, that Christ was crucified. If it accepts these affirmations it cannot create for Mohammed the unique position it must, if it is to found an entire religion on the latter.

The Prophet of course did say that Jesus will come again, but it is unlikely that Christians would adopt his account of the Second Coming. The Prophet said that Jesus would descend once again ('soon' in one tradition, 'at the last hour' in others), that he will be 'a just judge' and 'will break crosses, kill swine, abolish the *Jizya,* and leave the young she-camels so that collectors of *zakat* will not be employed for them,' that 'he will marry, have children, and remain forty-five years, after which he will die and and be buried along with me in my grave. Then Jesus son of Mary and I will arise from one grave between Abu Bakar and Umar' (*Mishkat,* 24.6). Furthermore, on the Day of Judgment, we are told, Jesus will be a witness *against* the Christians. He will testify to the grave sin they have committed by putting him and Mary at par with God.[6]

All this strikes at the very roots of the message conveyed in tne New Testament. Both sets of accounts are equally revered, equally authentic. But in view of diametrically opposing assertions such as these, they cannot both be literally and simultaneously true. And the examples can be multiplied many times over.

The Secular Approach to the Book

The Book is thus a ladder, not a fence – a scaffolding, not a prison. The believer who merely chants, 'Every word of it is true,' is forgoing the benefits that one may derive from the Book just as much as the ostentatious non-believer who just keeps shouting, 'It is all a fable.' Neither is reliving the experience that the texts enshrine, neither is letting the texts address him. We should approach the text with an open mind, a receptive one, and instead of making the Book an object either of superstitious reverence or of exhibitionist 'taking apart,' we should appropriate it, reading it creatively, meditating on it creatively, looking at a passage this way today and that way tomorrow.

The humanist and secular attitude to all texts can only be as follows:

❏ Every Book is man-made;
❏ Each of the books we revere has much that is valuable, but also much that is dated, and much that is just not tenable;
❏ Each of us has the right – and, in the poisoned air of today, the duty – to study and interpret each Book;
❏ Our surest guide in doing so is direct experience and not the diktat of some intermediary; in particular, most of us have a greater capacity to understand and interpret the texts than the professional priests and theologians, and an infinitely greater capacity to do so than the politicians who hector us in the name of religion.

Because of the nature of the Hindu tradition, because of the special position that the mystic – to whom books are nothing, and direct perception everything – has had in it, and also because of the work of the great reformers of that tradition – Vivekananda, Dayanand, Aurobindo, Gandhi and others – these propositions are well accepted in relation to the Hindu texts. The humanist and secularist must extend them to the other texts too.

It is only when we acquire this freedom in relation to a Book that we can benefit from it. It is only when we acquire this freedom in relation to all the Books that we will be enriched by what is valuable in each. It is only when we appropriate all the Books in this way that each Book, instead of dividing us, will become our common heritage. It is only in this way that we will learn to, and acquire the self-confidence to, differentiate the external, the adventitious which divides us from the essential that can benefit us all.

But a word of caution is necessary. Ever so often we go about contriving 'the essential unity of all religions' by picking seemingly similar passages from the different texts. Thus a Vinoba publishes an entire book, *The Essence of the Quran*, bowdlerising all the blood-curdling cries for *Jihad,* sanitising out every verse that enjoins eternal, uncompromising hostility to the non-believers.[7]

Such selectivity, even when it is inspired by the highest motives, won't work. The faithful, after all, will read the Quran and not the well-meaning compiler's *Essence of the Quran.* And the others, were they to go by the *Essence,* would be misled as to the mind, the world view that the text forms.

In contrast to the honey-and-syrup school of selectivity, I would urge that in reading, interpreting, appropriating the texts,

❑ we go by the entire text, and not by the isolated verse;
❑ we go by the primary text and not the commentaries;
❑ we go by the plain, manifest meaning of the text and the passage, and not by the convoluted construction put on it by theologians and priests;
❑ we go not by the effect that an isolated passage is liable to have on the believer, but by the mind-set, the world-view that is liable to result from the text as a whole; and
❑ finally, that we go by the entire corpus of texts revered in that tradition and not by just this single volume or that.

It is by proceeding thus that we will, as Sri Aurobindo would say, break out of 'ecclesiastical tyranny.' It is by acquiring this freedom towards the Book that we will break the rival millenari- anist claims of the religions. Once the millenarianist claim is undermined, a religion will not be able to demand total, unreason- ing obedience. And once it cannot demand that, it will be much less able to set us at one another's throats.

The Church and the Priest

After comparing what the Books say about the universe, about the geography and evolution of the earth, about history in one place with what they say in another, after comparing what one sacred Book says about the matter with what another equally sacred one says, after comparing what all of them say with what we now know about the matter, the programme of secular education should catalogue the positions that have been enunciated, indeed enforced in the name of religion by the religious establishments. A *Syllabus of Errors* to match that of Pope Pius IX should be prepared setting out what was insisted upon and enforced about the solar system from the times of Giordano Bruno, Copernicus, Galileo, what was insisted upon about the evolution of man a century ago; setting out what is being enforced today, say on the matter of contraception; setting out assertions such as the one that it is sacrilegious to use anesthetics to alleviate the pains of the mother in childbirth − the scripture having decreed, 'In sorrow shall thou bring forth children' (*Genesis*, 3.16) – while it *is* permissible to use them while operating on men (as the Lord Himself had put Adam into deep sleep before extracting the rib); setting out notions such as the one that there are witches and it is one's bounden duty to exterminate them – the scripture having enjoined, 'Thou shalt not suffer a witch to live' (*Exodus*, 22.18) – and the propositions certified by the Council of Trent that original sin is transmitted through procreation, that ordination leaves an indelible mark on the soul.[8]

The catalogue must also list the considerations on account of which the custodians of religious truth have propagated, and tenaciously held onto, such notions. The position of the Vatican on contraception is a case in point. 'It amounts to thwarting God's will,' say successive encyclicals and five successive Popes. Surely that can't be the reason. After all, they have officially sanctioned surgery, including heart transplants, to say nothing of spectacles and hearing – aids. The reason is to be found in the authoritarian nature of the organisation: such an organisation *must keep a hand in the most intimate activities of those under its sway,* for only by making them heed it in an activity that personal can it establish the notion that is the *sine qua non* of its authority – the notion that there is no inviolate sphere of autonomy for the individual. *This* is the reason why successive Councils and Popes, having altered, amended even shed so much, hold on to the archaic view on this singular matter. And then there is the 'reason' that they just cannot acknowledge that the Pope and Church have erred for so long in the face of so much well-intentioned counsel to the contrary. The authority of the Church rests on the proposition that the Pope is infallible. And the reason on account of which he is infallible is that, being the successor to Peter, he is at all times being directly guided by the Holy Spirit. With five Popes having affirmed over half a century that contraception violates 'natural law,' 'the will of God,' to now acknowledge that the correct position is the opposite would strike at the very basis of the claim to Papal infallibility and hence at the very basis of the authority of the Church. The minority of the Papal Commission on birth control (the minority whose position the Pope adopted, rejecting the position arrived at by the majority of the Commission he had himself appointed) put the matter squarely:

What weighs more heavily, however, is that this change [in the Church's position on birth control] would involve a heavy blow to the doctrine of the assistance of the Holy Spirit promised the Church to lead the faithful on the right way toward their salvation... For the Church to have erred so gravely in its grave responsibility of leading souls would be seriously suggesting that the assistance of the Holy Spirit was lacking to her.

Indeed it would amount to saying that the Holy Spirit had been guiding the enemies of the Pope and his Church, that is Protestants and the like. As has been well put,

If contraception were declared not intrinsically evil, in honesty it would have to be that the Holy Spirit in 1930 (in reference to the encyclical, *Casti Connubii*), in 1951 (in reference to the address of Pius XII to midwives) and 1958 (in reference to his address to the Society of Haematologists), assisted the Protestant Churches, and that for half a century did not protect Pius XI, Pius XII and a large part of the Catholic hierarchy against a very grave error, one most pernicious to souls, for it would have suggested that they condemned most imprudently, under the pain of eternal punishment, thousands upon thousands of human acts which were now approved. Indeed, it can be neither denied nor ignored that these acts would be approved for the same fundamental reasons which Protestants alleged and which they [Popes and bishops] condemned or at least did not approve.[9]

Saving face may be an exclusively Eastern preoccupation, but saving authority by saving face seems to be a Western concern too. A *Syllabus of Errors* of this kind will establish that the infallibility which cannot now be claimed for the Book can be claimed even less for the Church and the Priest, that the Book is just an aid – a ladder to be used, up to a stage, and then discarded – and that to benefit from the aid, direct experience, direct experimentation is what is necessary, the intermediation of the Church and the priest is not. It will teach us that each of the techniques, each of the assertions of the Book, of the Churches and Priests, must be examined on its merits. In no case must their veto, their embargo or their certificate be accepted without scrutiny.

Relativity

The Book is said to contain, not just truths, but eternal truths. It is on the basis of this claim that the laws it enunciates or which are derived from it, the institutions and practices it sets up or that flow from it are said to be excellent for all time. It is on this, too – and on the supplementary claim that they are the legatees of the founder and his companions – that the claim of the church, the priest, the politician parading-as-priest to unquestioning obedience rests.

Generations of scholars have shown how institutions and laws, far from being eternal verities, are very much the products of time and circumstance. The Laws of Manu, for instance, clearly bear the impress of the distribution of power among different castes at that time. The laws and institutions of early Islam too can be seen to flow directly from the needs of a desert, in part nomadic society, of an unruly and feuding society attempting to create a State.

Several of the formulations, revelations, rules of law can in fact be traced directly to the personal circumstances of the founders and leaders of the religions. The correspondence has been often written about in the case of the Prophet. The formulations about the Jews, for instance, changed drastically during the Prophet's years in Medina. When he arrived with his small band of followers he needed the assistance of the Jewish tribes which were influential and powerful in and around Medina at that time. To this period as to the earlier period in Mecca, when the Prophet faced difficulties from all sides, we owe the revelations urging, 'Thy religion to thee and to me mine.' At this period the Prophet urged that his followers adopt the Jewish holidays as their holidays, the Jewish times of prayer as their times of prayer, etc. The original direction in which the faithful had to bow while praying was fixed not as Mecca but Jerusalem. Once the Prophet's power was consolidated in Medina, however, the nature of the revelations about the Jews and other non-believers changed abruptly. The revelations took on an increasingly intolerant character.

Other than this many specific provisions of law also had to do with the personal and intimate predicaments of the Prophet. Thus, for instance, the rule that there must be four eye-witnesses to 'the fact of adultery' originated in the revelation that followed the scandal about the Prophet's favourite wife, Aisha. Similarly, the modification of the earlier revelations about whether one could or could not marry the wife of one's adopted son, whether one could or could not consummate the marriage before the period of *iddat* was over, all these arose directly from the exigencies of the Prophet's personal life. A single example will suffice. As more than one wife was allowed, there were rules by which the husband had to rotate among them. However, after a delicate chain of events Allah revealed to the Prophet:

> You (O Mohammed) can postpone (the turn of) whom you will of them (your wives) and you may receive any of them whom you will and there is no blame on you if you invite one whose turn you had set aside (temporarily) (*Quran*, 33.51).

On hearing of the revelation, Aisha was quick to tell the Prophet 'I feel that your Lord hastens in fulfilling your wishes and desires.' Naturally, out of the great affection and regard they bore for the Prophet and also because of the awe they had for the power and wrath of Allah, Aisha and everyone else complied with this as with all other revelations concerning the great authority and privileged position of the Prophet. This was not always, however, without some heart-burning. For instance, when a companion asked Aisha what she said when Allah made the aforegoing revelation to the Prophet, she replied, 'I used to say to him, "If I could deny you the permission (to go to your other wives) I would not allow your favour to be bestowed on any other person" (*Sahih al-Bukhari*, 60.311,312).

Several notions that go beyond mere rules of law etc., are even more obviously utilitarian. Consider a typical account of Paradise. We are assured that the inhabitants are immortal, that they are forever young. No illness afflicts them. They eat and drink, 'but they do not pass water or void excrement,'nor do they spit or suffer catarrh. Instead, they 'belch and sweat,'and this serves the purpose. The sweat however is musk. Everyone is affluent, living as they all do under a 'tent of a single hollowed pearl' which is sixty miles wide.

All have wives. These are 'large-eyed maidens,' each sixty cubits tall and so delicate that 'the marrow of their shanks glimmers through the flesh.'

There are rivers there, of course, including the Nile and the Euphrates. There is also a street to which the inhabitants come every Friday. The north wind scatters fragrance on their faces and clothes and adds to their beauty and loveliness.

There are feasts as one would expect, beginning with the one on the Day of Resurrection at which the entire earth becomes one giant piece of bread and is seasoned with fish, plus the liver of fish and ox (*Sahih Muslim,* 6710-11, 6793-6807).

Now, are such accounts reportage? Are they not instead compensatory prophecies? In promising these things in such abundance on the other shore, is the author not compensating for his not being able to provide them for the faithful in the here-and-now? Are such descriptions, whether in the Quran or the Bible or the Puranas, not mere devices to use our instincts of fear and greed to lure adherents and to get them to do things that the church needs done? Recall Plato's dictum in *The Republic* that 'cheerful views of the next world must be enforced by the State not because they (are) true, but to make soldiers more willing to die in battle. [10] Are the accounts then reportage or are they the necessary auxiliaries of the exhortations to *Jihad*?

God that is Allah

The influence of time, circumstance, need can be seen not just in peripheral notions like Paradise, or in sundry provisions of law but in the central concepts too. Consider as an example the be-all and end-all of the Old Testament and the Quran, that is God or Allah Himself. What is His central, His exclusive concern, indeed His preoccupation? It is that we acknowledge two things – namely,that He is great and that He alone is great.

'I am the Lord your God,' He tells us through Moses,'... You shall have no other gods besides Me. You shall not make for yourself a graven image or any likeness of anything that is in heaven above, or that is in the earth beneath, or that is in the water under the earth; *for I the Lord your God am a jealous God* visiting the iniquity of the fathers upon the children to the third and fourth generation of those who hate me, but showing steadfast love to thousands of those who love me and keep my commandments...' (*Deuteronomy*, 5.6-10). The refrain recurs several times in the Old Testament. Even Jesus in the New Testament says at one point,

'Truly, I say to you, all sins will be forgiven the sons of men, and whatever blasphemies they utter; but whoever blasphemes the Holy Spirit never has forgiveness, but is guilty of an eternal sin...' (*Mark,* 3.28-30).

In the Quran this concern of God becomes a preoccupation, indeed an obsession. 'For God hath said,' we are told, 'take not to yourselves two Gods – for He is one God: Me, therefore! yea, Me revere,' 'All in the Heavens and in the Earth is His! His due unceasing service! Will ye then fear any other than God?' (*Quran,* 16.53-4).

The purpose of almost everything He does is to ensure that we recognise and acknowledge His power. Thus, for instance, He says that he creates the heavens, earth, clouds, lightning, plants, beasts and everything else as 'signs' so that we, His creatures may see that He is All Powerful, that He alone is the creator, that He has no associates, no equals, no offspring and as a manifestation too of His munificence so that we may partake of His creation (2.157-60; 6-99). He rescues the Israelites from drowning so that those who are to come afterwards may know the things He can do (10.90-2). 'I have not created djinn and men,' He declares, 'but that they should worship Me; I require not sustenance from them, neither I require that they feed Me' (51-6) – that is, Allah is self-sufficient, needing neither food nor any other kind of sustenance from us, yet He creates us; He does so for one purpose, for one purpose alone: so that He may be worshipped. Indeed, He clearly states that nothing is of greater concern to Him than this:

O ye to whom the scriptures have been given [He declares] believe in what We have sent down confirmatory of the Scripture which is in your hands, ere We efface your features, and twist your head round backward, or curse you as we cursed the sabbath-breakers; and the command of God was carried into effect.
Verily, God will not forgive the union of other gods with Himself: But other than this He will forgive to whom He pleaseth...(4. 50-5).

His punishment for our not believing in Him, and only in Him, is swift, certain, terrible, it is 'a severe chastisement' (3.3). 'We will cast a dread into hearts of the infidels,' He says, 'because they have joined gods with God without warranty sent down; their abode shall be the fire; and wretched shall be the mansion of the evil doers' (3.144). 'But who so shall charge Our signs with falsehood, on them shall fall a punishment for their wicked doings' (6.49). 'If thou didst.see,' He reminds us, 'when the angels cause infidels to die: They smite their faces and their back... Their state is like that of the people of the Pharaoh and of those before them who believed not in the signs of God. Therefore God seized upon them in their sin, (8.52-4; 7.170-8 similar).

He goes to the most extraordinary lengths to remind us of His power and glory. Thus, for instance, He visits afflictions on a people to humble them; next He sends them a prophet so that they may believe in him; and when they don't believe in the prophet (and this too, it must be remembered, happens by His decree) He wreaks the most terrible vengeance on them. A single passage will suffice to give us a glimpse of His obsession in the mater and of the extraordinary lengths to which He goes to have that obsession prevail:

Nor did We ever send a Prophet to any city without affliciting its people with adversity and trouble, that haply they might humble them...
Then changed We their ill for good, until they waxed wealthy and said, 'Of old did troubles and blessing befall our fathers'. Therefore did We seize upon them suddenly when they were unaware...
But *if that the people of these cities had believed and feared Us,* We would surely have laid open to them blessings out of the Heaven and the Earth: but they treated Our signs as lies, and *We took vengeance on them for their deeds...*
Were the people therefore of these cities secure that Our wrath would not *light upon them by night while they were slumbering?...* Were the people of those cities secure that our wrath would not *light on them in broad day, while they were disporting themselves?...*
Did they therefore deem themselves secure from the deep counsel [i.e, the stratagem] of God? *But none deem themselves secure from the deep counsel of God, save those who perish. Is it not proved to them who inherit this land after its ancient occupants, that if We please We can smite them for their sins*

and put a seal upon their hearts, that they hearken not?
We will tell thee the stories of these cities. Their apostles came
to them with clear proofs of their mission; but they would not
believe in what they had before treated as imposture – *Thus
does God seal up the hearts of the unbelievers.* And We found
not of their covenant in most of them; but We found most of
them to be perverse (7.92-100).

What would we say of a man whose sole concern was that we
acknowledge that he is powerful, that he is excellent, that he alone
is powerful, that he alone is excellent? What would we say of a
man with whom this was an obsession, who incited others to kill
us, burn us, torture us (for there is passage after passage exhorting
that this be done) if we failed to pander to this obsession of his?
But those are exactly what Allah's concerns and commands are
in the Quran. Like the God of the Old Testament, Allah
deliberately creates a distinction between virtuous deeds and sin;
next, He deliberately creates man in such a way that he *will*
transgress, that he *will* sin; while He exhorts everyone to forgive
trespasses, He insists that *He* will not forgive one trespass – and that
is the failure to acknowledge that He is great, that He alone is
great. We can only conclude with Schopenhauer that He
deliberately creates the world to watch it suffer forever.[11]
Clearly, this is a peculiar conception of God. Self -sufficient in
all respects, why is He so concerned that this puny little man, on
this puny little earth, in this puny little solar system, in this little
bit of the universe acknowledge His greatness? And even if this is
an obsession with Him, surely He – all powerful, omniscient, as He
is – can find an easier way of having man acknowledge His
greatness? Why does He not instil the veneration directly rather
than by adopting these circuitous and painful routes – of springing
His wrath by night, while the poor man is slumbering, and
springing it in broad day, while he is disporting?
In fact, to say of such accounts of God that they are 'peculiar'
is hardly appropriate. 'Blasphemous' seems more to the point. How
right was Thomas Paine when on reading what was said to have
been ordained by God, he exclaimed, '...There is no authority for
believing that the inhuman and horrid butcheries of men, women
and children, told in these books [he was talking of the Bible, but
the words apply to many other scriptures just as well] were done,

as those books say they were at the command of God. It is a duty incumbent on every true Deist, that he vindicate the moral justice of God against the calumnies of the Bible.'[12]

Clearly, then, such accounts of God cannot be taken as reportage. It is hard to convince oneself that the authors have 'seen' God and found Him to be so singularly obsessed with our opinion of Him. The accounts make sense in only one way. They portray not God but *what it is in our conduct that we want to rationalise,* they portray *what we want our conduct to be* that is, they show *the role-model that we are putting before ourselves.* In brief, whatever the nature of the real God, God as we know him from these Books is a product of our needs, of the environment and circumstances in which the books were written.

Consider the 'God' thus portrayed as *a parable for the nascent State.* The obsession with being recognised as powerful, with being supreme, with being the only one to whom the people owe allgeiance, with being the only one for whom the faithful 'kill and are killed,' as the Quran says (9.113), at once falls into place and with it the central character of the Quran, its *leitmotiv.* Is God really all that intolerant of other gods or do *we* make Him that intolerant so that *we* may in His name be as intolerant of other humans? Are the accounts of miracles necessary so that God may prove Himself to puny men, or so that men believe in the Prophet-who-parts-the-sea or the Prophet -who-splits-the-moon – and in the State he establishes?

The Books thus deal with relatives, with things born of time and place, not with eternal verities. Once we have documented this for concept after concept,[13] and once this fact percolates into the common mind, we will see that the Book, the religion that flows from it and the priest and politician who strut about in its name are not things over which we should be breaking one another's heads.

Examine Every Cliche

'The trouble with us Hindus,' the Hindu says, ' is that we are divided – Arya Samajis v. Sanatanis, Vaishnavites v. Shaivites. Look at the Muslims, on the other hand, and the Sikhs.' 'The trouble with us Muslims,' the Muslim says, 'is that we are always fighting each other – Shias v. Sunnis v. Ahmediyas... Look at what

is happening between Iraq and Iran. Just see how the Arabs have
never been able to get together to fix Israel. Look at the Hindus
on the other hand, and the Sikhs – united to a man.' 'The trouble
with us Sikhs,' says the Sikh, 'is that we are always at each other's
throats – Jat Sikhs v. non-Jat Sikhs, Amritdharis v. non-
Amritdharis, Akalis v. non-Akalis, Sikhs in Punjab v. Sikhs outside
Punjab. On the other hand, look at the Hindus, the Musalmans'...

We know more about ourselves, about our group, and so the
internal differences within our group are what strike us. We know
little about the other group, and so each crisis further reinforces
our stereotype of it, till in the end that other group is one,
undifferentiated *howwaa,* one dark, menacing, enveloping cloud.

'The Hindus do not have a sense of history,' says a
Western publication. 'The word in Hindi for "yesterday" and for
"tomorrow" is the same, *"kal."'* But is the word the same in, say,
Malayalam or Tamil or Telugu? Or is it that only those who speak
Hindi are Hindus? And what about the Sikhs in Punjab or the
Muslims in U.P.? Speaking Punjabi or Hindustani, they also use
'*kal*' to denote both 'yesterday' and 'tomorrow.' Is the absence
of a sense of time then confined to Hindus or does it cover them
also?

'Hindus and Muslims can never be one. One bows to the east,
the other to the west. One eats pork, the other kills cows.' But what
of the Hindus who do not eat pork, who are, say, vegetarians? Are
they for that reason closer to the Muslims than those that do? And
could eating beef have been so central to being a Muslim in seventh
century Arabia, where cows were not all that abundant? And if such
externals determine whether we will be close to one another or
not, are we to conclude that the Jew and the Muslim will always
be friends because both are circumcised?

'Sikhism is closer to Islam,' says Khushwant Singh. 'Both
are monotheistic. Both abhor idolatry.' But the *Akal Purush* of the
Granth Sahib is an inclusive concept, it incorporates, it welcomes
others – witness the thousands and thousands of times that other
Hindu deities are venerated and invoked in the Granth Sahib –
while Jehovah of the Old Testament and Allah of the Quran
exclude, repel others. As for idolatory, Khushwant Singh himself
notes how the Granth Sahib is now venerated, prayed to, looked
after like an idol. He attributes this to 'the influx of Hindus into
the Sikh fold.' Even so, he insists on the distinction. 'Despite these

customs,' he concludes, 'the Granth is even today not like the idol
in a Hindu temple nor the statue of the Virgin in a Catholic
cathedral. It is the means and not the object of worship.'[14] But *that*
is precisely what the idol is supposed to be for the Hindus – an
aid like a *mantra* or anything else. As for popular practice,
unfortunately that is quite the same among both Sikhs and Hindus.

Cliches of this kind, stereotypes of this kind, divide us. Some
fall for them and then give currency to them out of no more than
slipshod scholarship, superficiality, a breezy penchant for the
sweeping generalisation. In other cases – much of the writing
of British scholars on Sikhism around the turn of the century is a
case in point – the generalisation is set forth as part of a design.
The title of the then Lt. Governor, M.Macauliffe's work tells its
tale, *A Lecture on the Sikh Religion and its Advantages to the
State*.[15] He is candid about the impetus of the new approach:

At former [census] enumerations village Sikhs in their
ignorance generally recorded themselves as Hindus, as indeed
they virtually were. With the experience gained by time, a
sharp line of demarcation has now been drawn between Sikhs
and Hindus...

The cliches, the stereotypes were part of conscious policy by
which to further imperialist interests. The Sikhs, as David Petrie,
the then Assistant Director of Criminal Intelligence, put it were
'encouraged to regard themselves as a totally distinct and separate
nation.'

Whether their origin is a cavalier superficiality or design, the
stereotypes do great harm. Each of them should be examined
threadbare. By seeing through the cliches we will be that much
better equipped to tackle the genuine differences.

What is true of differences between our traditions is equally
true of what needs to be done to strengthen each tradition itself.
Each of them has many strengths, each has many lacunae. But
the only way to forge ahead is to identify correctly the real
deficiencies. If we keep addressing problems that aren't there – or
if, conditioned by thinking in stereotypes and cliches, we continue
to ascribe the problems to the wrong cause – the real deficiencies
will remain to plague us. A single example will suffice.

A Typical Generalisation

'Hinduism is life-denying, other-worldly, fatalist. The Hindu
scriptures are fatalist through and through. The Hindus resign
themselves to "fate" as they believe in the theory of Karma, in the
notion that their present condition is predetermined by acts in the
past. On the other hand, Islam is activist, life-affirming.' Few
generalisations are as common as these.

Is the Hindu peasant, sweating his guts out in the noonday sun
to wrest a meal from nature, 'life-denying'? Is he concerned with
the 'other-world' or with *this*? Is the Hindu merchant, scurrying
around like any other merchant to make a quick buck, 'life-
denying'? Are his pursuits not very much of this world? The Gita
is as close to being a scripture for the Hindus as any. It is perhaps
the most commonly resorted-to text among the Hindus. What is
the dialogue all about? What is Krishna asking Arjuna to do? To
deny life, to go off into the forest and await summons to the other
world? Is the whole and singular message not, 'Rise and fight'?
And how does the dialogue end? What is the culmination? Does
Arjuna trundle off to contemplate the other world? Does he not
on the contrary declare, 'Destroyed is delusion...I am firm, with
doubts gone,' – and then does he not fight?

Similarly, if the 'theory of Karma' has so powerful a hold on
my psyche as to lead me to resign myself to my present lot in the
belief that all efforts are bound to be futile as the present
is already predetermined by my deeds *in the past*, why does that
very 'theory' not spur me *to act today* in the certain conviction
that what I do today will determine my condition in the future?
Does scripture determine life? Or does life determine the meaning
I read into the scripture?

Consider the question from another point of view, that of
Islamic scriptures.

The Quran, as we know, is just as full of preordination as any
other scripture. 'God's behest is a fixed decree,' we are told (*Quran*,
33.38). 'Say,' Allah exhorts the faithful, 'Nothing can befall us but
what God has destined for us' (9.51). 'We never destroyed a city
whose term was not pre-fixed,' says Allah. 'No people can
forestall or retard its destiny' (15.4, 5). 'No mischance chanceth
either on earth or in your own persons,' He tells us, 'but ere we
fixed them, it is in the Book [of eternal decrees]' (57.23).

Will a person die or not at a particular moment, will he heed the message or not – every outcome is already determined by Allah's decree. Thus, for instance, we are told that even if a person fearing death, decides to refrain from *Jihad* and to stay at home, 'they who were decreed to be slain would have gone forth to the places where they lie...'! (3.148). The fact they shirk *Jihad* too is the result of God's decree: they do so, we are told, because 'God was averse to their marching forth, and made them laggards...' (9.40.9). As they stay behind, though it be in accordance with what Allah has decreed, evil befalls them.

From the point of view of Allah and therefore of the Quran, the most important fact about a person is whether or not he is a believer. Everything else is secondary, everything else follows from whether he believes or not. If the outcome of this all-important question is preordained, then preordination must be taken to be as central to the Quran as to any other scripture. Now, how is it that some come to believe the message that Allah has sent and thus ascend to Paradise, etc. and that some, in spite of the numerous signs that Allah places in their path to remind them of His greatness, fail to believe? Is this upto a person's effort, or is it preordained by Allah?

Allah bestows this favour on whomsoever He wishes, the Quran tells us again and again (3.73, 74; 5.54; 57.21; 62.4, for instance). He is the one 'who brings low and raises up' (3.25). 'He turns astray whom He wishes' (6.39; 12.5; 14.4; 16.93; 35.6).' 'He aideth whom He will...,' we are told (30.4). 'Thus God misleadeth whom He will, and whom He will doth He guide aright...' (84.34; 7.67-7 is similar). 'We have placed veils over their hearts,' Allah says, 'that they may not understand, and a dullness into their ears' (18.57). Accordingly, the Quran speaks of 'he whom God knowingly has sent astray, whose hearing and whose heart He has sealed, and on whose eyes He has set a blindfold...' (45.23); it speaks of 'these are they whom God hath cursed, hath cursed, and made deaf, and blinded their eyes...'(47.24, 25).

It isn't just that Allah ordains who will see the light and who will not. Once He does so, there is nothing that either they or anyone else, even a Prophet, can do to help them. So firm is the preordination.

'As to the infidels,' Allah tells the Prophet, 'alike is to them whether thou warn them or warn them not – they will not believe.

Their hearts and their ears hath God sealed up and over their eyes
is a covering...Diseased are their hearts. And that disease hath
God increased to them...God shall mock at them, and keep them
long in their rebellion, wandering in perplexity...They are like
one who kindleth a fire and when it hath thrown its light on all
around him...God taketh away their light and leaveth them in
darkness – they cannot see. Deaf, dumb, blind. Therefore they shall
not retrace their steps from error...' (2.5-17). Indeed, every new
revelation, far from setting them right, confirms them in their
unbelief (9.125-8). And so, 'whom God sends astray shall have
neither surety nor guide' (17.97; 18.17; 39.29, 37; 7.186; 13.33).
'Had we pleased,' Allah declares, 'We had certainly given to
every soul its guidance. But true shall be the word which hath gone
forth from Me – I will surely fill hell with Djinn and men together,
(32.13). The decree that consigns them to ignorance is as
irrevocable as the torment that must follow it is certain:

> Verily, We have sent down the warning, and verily, We will
> be its guardians;
> and already have We sent Apostles, before thee, among the
> sects of the ancients;
> But never came Apostles to them whom they did not deride.
> *In like manner will We put into the hearts of the sinners of*
> *Mecca to do the same.*
> *They will not believe in him though the example of those of old*
> *hath gone before.*

So final and unalterable is Allah's ordainment that

> Even were We to open above them a gate in heaven, yet
> all the while they were mounting up to it,
> They would surely say: It is only that our eyes are drunken; nay
> we are a people enchanted...   (*Quran*, 15.10-15)

'Verily,' the Quran says, 'this is no other than a warning to
all creatures; To him among you who willeth to walk in a straight
path: *But will it ye shall not, unless as God willeth it, the Lord*
of worlds' (81.27). Such is the predeterminism of the Quran. The
hadis if anything are even more graphically and emphatically
predeterminist.

Allah decrees everything that a man will do or believe, and His decrees are final; the *hadis* report the Prophet saying repeatedly, 'The pen has dried after writing what you will surely encounter' (*Sahih al-Bukhari,* 67. Ch. 1). '...O Allah! the Prophet says, 'No one can withhold what You give, and none can give what You withhold, and the fortune of a man of means is nothing before you' (*Bukhari,* 67.612). Allah decrees the fortune of a man when he is still in the womb, and do what the man may, the decreed fortune comes to prevail in the nick of time:

Verily your creation is in this wise. The constituents of one of you are collected for forty days in his mother's womb in the form of blood, after which it becomes a clot of blood, in another period of forty days. Then it becomes a lump of flesh and forty days later Allah sends his angel to it with instructions concerning four things, so the angel writes down his livelihood, his death, his deeds, his fortune and misfortune.

'Then his document of destiny is rolled,' the Prophet tells us, 'and there is no addition to or subtraction from it.' And whatever the creature may do or contrive, in the end what has been written will prevail: 'By him besides whom there is no God,' says the Prophet on oath,

that one amongst you acts like the people deserving Paradise until between him and Paradise there remains but the distance of a cubit, when suddenly the writing of destiny overcomes him and he begins to act like the denizens of Hell and thus enters Hell, and another one acts in the way of the denizens of Hell, until there remains between him and Hell a distance of a cubit that the writing of destiny overcomes him and then he begins to act like the people of Paradise and enters Paradise (*Sahih-al-Bukhari,* 67.593, 603-4; *Sahih Muslim,* 6390-7).

The decree operates from the greatest to the smallest deeds, from whether or not you will acquire understanding and knowledge to whether or not you will commit adultery. 'Verily, Allah has fixed the very portion of adultery which a man will indulge in and which he of necessity must commit,' the Prophet affirms, whether this be adultery with his tongue, his eyes or his genitals. And 'there would be no escape from it,' the Prophet stresses. The deeds, as well as their practical consequences follow immediately. Thus, for instance, illnesses must be borne patiently, as they have been ordained by Allah, as has the manner in which and the time at which they are to end. Similarly, it doesn't matter whether you do *azl* (*coitus interruptus*) or not, the Prophet tells his followers, because whether a child will be conceived or not has already been ordained by Allah.[16]

Thus, the Quran and *hadis* have as much predeterminism, as much fatalism in them as any other scripture. And yet the stereotype is repeated day in and day out: 'Hinduism is life — denying, fatalist; Islam is life — affirming, activist.'

Towards Conclusions

Passages and examples of this kind can be multiplied many times over. The few that have been cited however will be enough to show how careful we must be before we let fly the sweeping generalisation. The passages illustrate two further points, and so it will pay us to stay with them awhile.

First of all, it is easy to see how the world-view that emerges from the doctrine sketched above — and we know that Islam is not the only religion that has elements of it — leads, step by inexorable step, to heartlessness and worse.

The people charge prophets with falsehood in accordance with God's decree, says the Quran. Therefore the prophet must wait patiently for the appointed time when the non-believers will see the error of their ways. He should not pine for a sign from Allah so that he may with its aid convince them; after all, 'if God please, He would surely bring them, one and all, to the guidance' (6.35). 'If thou art anxious for their guidance,' Allah counsels His messenger, 'know that God will not guide him whom He would lead astray, neither shall they have any helpers' (16.38, 39). Do not waste your breath on them, Allah counsels:

> Just now is Our sentence against most of them; therefore, they shall not believe. On their necks have We placed chains which reach the chin, and forced up are their heads.
> Before them have We set a barrier and behind them a barrier, and We have shrouded them in a veil, so that they shall not

see. Alike is it to them if thou warn them or warn them not;
they will not believe (36.6-9).

In fact, Allah tells the Prophet, leave them to their torment,
waste no grief on them:

And what has been sent down to thee from thy Lord will
surely increase many of them in insolence and unbelief; *so
grieve not for the people of the unbelievers* (5.72).

As their unbelief, indeed their persistent, obstinate unbelief
has been decreed by Allah, it is but right that we should not treat
the believers and the non-believers equally:

Shall he, the evil of whose deeds are so tricked out to him that
he deemeth them good, be treated like him who seeth things
aright? Verily, God misleadeth whom He will, and guideth
whom He will.
Spend not thy soul in sighs for them: God knoweth their doings
(35.9).

It is not enough of course to spare no thought or grief for them,
to 'Leave them to their forging' (6.139), 'They demand thee to
hasten the chastisement that Allah has decreed' (22.45-6). Therefore, the Quran enjoins, when they persist in their unbelief, and,
they surely will for God has decreed it, 'Kill them wherever ye
shall find them and eject them from whatever place they have
ejected you' (2.186). Fight them 'and let them find in you a
harshness' (9.125), make sure that 'wheresoever they are come
upon they are slaughtered all' (23.60-4). 'When you encounter the
infidels,' Allahs tells the Prophet and the faithful, 'strike off their
heads till ye have made a great slaughter among them, and of the
rest make fast the fetters...' (47.4-5).
    The lesson for us is as follows. By itself, as we know, preo-
rdainment can result in heartlessness, even cruelty. And so the
secularist must hunt it down. But when it is combined – as it is
in Islam, though not only in Islam – with millenarianism, it
inevitably does so. The secularist must then expose and contend
with it all the more resolutely.

Think for Yourselves

The examples help us in yet another way. They lead us to an essential element of the secular outlook, namely, that we must think for ourselves, and not swallow the scriptures. The point will be evident from the confusions into which the predeterminism of the Quran, no less than that of other traditions and texts, lands the believer.

Recall that Allah is the author of everything, of every person, deed, fortune, misfortune, whatever. He creates man. He determines his growth, his fortune, the things that will help and those that will hinder him (56.57-75). He is the author of every act, whatever it be: 'It is God who has created you and all that you have done' (37.196). 'And that unto thy Lord is the term of all things. And that it is He who causeth to laugh and to weep, and that He causeth to die and maketh alive...' (53.43-55). He is the one who created the soul and 'balanced it', 'and breathed into it its wickedness and its piety' (91.7-8).

Recall in particular that *it is Allah Himself who decides and ensures that some will not believe, that they will sin.* 'Seeth thou not,' He asks, 'that We send the Satans against the infidels to urge them to sin?' (19.86).

Recall also that *it is because of this decision of Allah that the errors, lapses, sins occur.* 'Verily,' we are told again and again, 'they against whom the decree of thy Lord is pronounced shall not believe, even though every kind of sign comes to them, till they behold the dolorous treatment...' (10.96-9). It is only because Allah has so willed that they persist in their unbelief and then suffer for it. To continue the preceding verse, 'But if thy Lord had pleased, verily all who are in the earth would have believed together. What! wilt thou compel men to become believers? No soul can believe but by the permission of God: and He shall lay His wrath on those who will not understand.'

Nor is it that evil and suffering occur without Allah's knowledge, behind His back so to say. 'No leaf falls but He knows it,' we are told, 'There is no seed in the darkness of the earth, no green shoot or dry but it is inscribed in the perspicuous Book' (6.59). 'No female conceives or brings forth,' we are reminded, 'without His knowledge' (35.11) 'He well knew you when He produced you out of the earth,' we are told, 'and when you were embryos in your mother's womb' (53.33). Allah knows 'that which his [i.e. man's] soul suggests to him, Allah is closer to him than the jugular vein' (1.16). So, He decrees everything, He knows what is happening as well as what is to happen. And He is all powerful to make it happen or to stop it from happening.

The question naturally arises: why does the all-knowing, omnipotent, merciful God deliberately decide to mislead millions and then punish them for being misled?

Those who are cursed to suffer ask the question directly in the Quran on more than one occasion (e.g., 6.149-51; 16.35-45). They correctly say that if they are idolators then they are so by the decree of God. Why must they be made to suffer for obeying the decree of God?

The answers are evasive, contradictory, manifestly unsatisfactory. 'Even so the people before them cried lies until they tasted Our might,' Allah says in response to the query. Instead of providing an answer, Allah merely asks the believers to put down the question: 'Say: "Have you any knowledge to bring forth for us? You follow only surmise, merely conjecturing." Say: "To God belongs the arguments conclusive, for had He willed, He would have guided you all..."' (6.149-50). But that precisely was the question: *why* did He not guide us all? When ten *suras* later the idolators are again reported as affirming 'If God had willed we would not have served, apart from Him, anything, nor we nor our fathers, nor would we have forbidden, apart from Him, anything,' the response is the same: 'So did those before them.' The message has been sent to every nation by Him, Allah says, 'Then some of them God guided, and some were justly disposed to error' (16.35-44). But the question is: *why was it just in their case that they should have been disposed to error?*

Having affirmed again and again that everything happens because Allah has so decreed, having affirmed again and again that it is Allah who lays down the provisions of man, his deeds and actions, his fortune and misfortune to the smallest detail, the Quran, exactly like other texts, has Allah disown the authorship of the evil that men do: *They*, that is, the men whose every deed and action has been preordained by God, are the authors of the disorder for which they are justly punished, says the Quran (2.15-17). Although on its own showing God has unalterably pre-fixed everything they will ever do, and what the outcome of that deed will be, it asserts that He is not the one who wrongs them, they wrong themselves (16.35-8).

Suddenly, from being the author of everything, God becomes the author of good alone:

> Whatever good betideth thee is from God, and whatever betideth thee of evil is from thyself; and We have sent thee to mankind as an apostle... (4.79,81)

In one breath He is the one who initiates every deed, He is the one who determines every outcome. In the next, there is a sharp division of labour: 'Nor happeneth to you any mishap, *but it is your own handiwork;* and yet He forgiveth many things' (42.29). 'But in the tournaments of Hell shall the wicked remain forever; It shall not be mitigated to them, and they shall be mute for despair therein. For it is not We who have treated them unjustly but *it was they who were unjust to themselves*' (43.74-6).

At one moment, God is the one who creates the soul and 'balances it,' and 'breathes into it its wickedness and its piety.' At the next what happens thereafter becomes the responsibility of man: 'Blessed now is he who hath kept it pure and undone is he who hath corrupted it' (91.7-10).

This is patently self-serving. Pressed further the 'explanations' become circular. Allah turns their hearts aside, He consigns them to unbelief and sin, we are told, *'because they are a people devoid of understanding'* (9.128). But why have they been left without understanding? And who but Allah left them in that condition?

'Surely the worst of beasts in God's sight,' we are informed, 'are those that are deaf and dumb and do not understand. If God had known any good in them He would have made them hear, and if He had made them hear they would have turned away, swerving aside' (8.20). But He, Allah, is the one who originally determined whether there would by any good in them or not. How is it that He first decrees that there should be no good in them, then, on not seeing any good in them, He blurs their vision and blocks their hearing, He deliberately misleads them, and finally punishes them for being misled? Is that just? Is that what we would expect to flow from Allah's compassion, His mercy?

Passage after passage is equivocal, in fact evasive. 'Verily, God will not change His gifts to man, *till they change what is in themselves'* (13.12). But how are men to 'change what is in themselves' when God is the one who lays down what shall be in them, when He preordains every deed, and does so unalterably? The words of the very verse testify to the difficulty. Exhorting men to change what is in them, it adds the caveat, 'And when God willeth evil unto men, there is none who can turn it away' — presumably the 'none' includes the person in whom evil has been willed, the one who has been exhorted to change what is in him — 'nor have they any protector beside 'Him' (13.12).

'O man!,' asks the Quran, 'what hath misled thee against thy generous Lord, Who hath created thee and moulded thee and shaped thee aright? In the form which pleased Him hath He fashioned thee. Even so; but ye treat the Judgment as a lie' (82.6-9). But if He has created us and moulded us, and if He has fashioned us in the form which pleased Him, *who but He* could have misled us into distrusting the Judgment?

As usual, the *hadis* do not carry the matter any further. Everything you will do, to the smallest details, everything that will happen to you, to the smallest details, the Prophet affirms again and again in them, has already been decreed by God. And that decree is final, forever unalterable. If that is so, asks a companion, shall we not depend on this? Shall we not abandon deliberate effort, exertion? 'No,' says the Prophet, 'But carry on your deeds, for everyone finds it easy to do such deeds [as will lead him to his preordained place]' (*Sahih al–Bukhari,* 77.602; *Sahih Muslim,* 6398-405). But surely that is not a satisfactory reason: why should one do something *merely because it is easy, especially if the place preordained for one is Hell and this deed, though 'easy,' is bound to hasten one to that?*

The *hadis* report the Prophet recounting an argument between Moses and Adam. Moses is blaming Adam for violating God's command and thereby bringing misery on mankind. Adam asks, 'What is your opinion, how long would the Torah have been written before I was created?' 'Forty years before,' says Moses. Whereupon Adam asks, 'Did you not see these words: "Adam committed an error and he was enticed to (do so)?"' Moses acknowledges that he did see the words. And so Adam counters as anyone would, 'Do you then blame me for an act which Allah had ordained for me forty years before He created me?'

'This is how Adam worsted Moses in the argument,' the Prophet concludes (*Bukhari,* 77.611; *Muslim,* 6409-15).

I take it that by this the Prophet signals his approval of Adam's disclaimer. And yet he invariably justifies Allah's punishments. He is indeed zealous in executing them himself.

There is no explanation of why it is that Allah decrees one thing for 'X' and another for 'Y' caprice seems all: 'And your Lord decides as He desires...,' 'And your Lord decides *as he likes*...,' 'And then the Lord decides *as he likes*..., 'is all that the Prophet tells us.' (*Muslim,* 6393-6).

And circularities abound here as they do in the Quran. When an infant dies and the indomitable Aisha says that he must be destined for Paradise as he had not committed any sin, the Prophet corrects her. 'Aisha,' he says, 'peradventure, it may be otherwise for God created for Paradise those who are fit for it while they are yet in their father's loins, and created for Hell those who are to go to Hell. He created them for Hell while they are yet in their father's loins' (*Muslim,* 6435-7).

Nor are the Quran and the *hadis* exceptional in the confusions to which their accounts of predestination *vis-a-vis* free will, of an omnipotent, all-knowing, all merciful God *vis-a-vis* the persistence of evil and suffering lead. The Bible's answer to the question of Job is as evasive, contradictory, inadequate, as are the explanations that one may infer from the Upanishads and the Gita.

And the persistence of evil, of suffering is but one of the questions on which the scriptures, the churches, the priests, to say nothing of politicians posing as priests, fail us.

The first step to secularism, to humanism, therefore, is to think for oneself.

Conclusion

To fashion a fair and firm State; a State and society in which the individual is all, an individual with an inviolate sphere of autonomy that neither the State nor anyone acting in the name of religion nor any other collectivity can breach; a State and society in which we learn to look upon one another as human beings, in which the habit of partitioning our fellow-men between 'them' and 'us' is shed; a State and society in which a man of God is known not by the externals − by his appearance, by the rituals he observes,

by the religious office he holds – but by the service he renders
to his fellow-men; a State and society in which each of us
recognises all our traditions as the common heritage of us all;
a State and society in which we shed the dross in religion and
perceive the unity and truth to which the mystics of all traditions
have borne testimony; a State and society in which we learn, in
which we examine, in which we begin to think for ourselves –
fashioning such a State and society is a programme worthy of those
who aspire to humanism and secularism.

The *sine qua non* for such a programme is that all of us
accept a limitation on means. We must accept the right of everyone
to his own opinion and belief as well as the right of everyone
to influence others to adopt his opinion and belief, but simultaneously each of us must vow that he will influence others by
persuasion alone or not at all.

And the hallmark of the humanist and the secularist in regard
to the ideals he will pursue and the means by which he will pursue
them is not, 'I will be secular, I will be a humanist, only when all
the others also conduct themselves as secularists and humanists.'
Our conduct must be principled,   whatever the conduct of others.
'For,' as Jesus said, 'if you love those who love you, what reward
have you?'

–March 1986

Notes

1. The similarities between the Bible and the Quran have been
   enumerated many times over. See, for instance, Henry Preserved
   Smith, *The Bible and Islam*, Scribner's, New York, 1897; W. St.
   Clair-Tisdall, *The Sources of Islam*, translated and abridged by
   William Muir, T & T. Clark, Edinburgh, 1901; Richard Bell, *The
   Origin of Islam in its Christian Environment*, Macmillan, London,
   1926; Charles Cuttler Torrey, *The Jewish Foundation of Islam*,
   1933, Ktav Publishing House, New York, 1967; Abraham I.
   Katsh, *Judaism in Islam*, New York University Press, 1954. So
   great and numerous were the similarities that the 'Israeliyat' odour
   of the revelations became a matter of serious concern and contention, of accusation and counter-accusation, even in the Prophet's

time itself. Several of the notions and traditions were so obviously of Jewish origin that it was alleged that two of the informants – Kab al-Ahbar and Wahb b. Munabbih – were deliberately trying to subvert Islam by smuggling Jewish notions into it; on how the charge is handled see, C.H.A. Juynboll, *The Authenticity of the Tradition Literature*, E.J. Brill, Netherlands, 1969.

2. Sigmund Freud, *Moses and Monotheism*, 1939, Vintage Books, New York, 1967, pp. 116-17.

3. And how right Freud is when he says, '...The founding of Mohammedan religion seems to me to be an abbreviated repetition of the Jewish one, in imitation of which it made its appearance', *Ibid*, p. 118.

4. In the following I shall choose almost all my examples from the Bible and the Quran. I shall do so in part because the reader is more likely to be familiar with the Hindu texts than with these and will be able on his own to recall corresponding examples from the former. And in part because, even though were I to write the book today, I would write a substantially different one, I have already used material from the Upanishads, Brahma Sutras and the Gita to urge similar propositions in *Hinduism, Essence and Consequence* (Vikas, 1979). But I shall do so primarily because I want to help break the taboo that has reined in India for the last two hundred years against a Hindu discussing Islam, or a Muslim discussing Hindusim. All the religions that prevail in Inda today are our common heritage. Each of us must appropriate all of them. As long as the taboo lasts we will continue to be ill-informed about each other, to talk irrationally about and at each other. Breaking the taboo is the first step to sane, informed, rational dialogue, and a paper on *secularism* of all things seems to me to be an excellent occasion to do so.

5. One spirited enumeration of all this in the case of the Bible is of course Thomas Paine's classic, *The Age of Reason*.

6. For synoptic accounts of this see the entry under 'Jesus Christ' in Hughes' *Dictionary of Islam*, under 'Isa' in *The Encyclopedia of Islam*, and in Geoffery Parrinder, *Jesus in the Quran*, Oxford University Press, New York, 1977.

7. Vinoba, *The Essence of the Quran*, Sarva Seva Sangh Prakashan, Varanasi, 1962.

8. Bertrand Russell's *Religion and Science*, as well as White's *Warfare of Science with Theology* and Locky's *History of Rationalism in Europe*, which he often cites, recount what are in retrospect hilarious notions, but on the strength of which men were for centuries cabined, persecuted, tortured, and burned to death.

9. On this typical question see the courageous writings of the Catholic theologian Hans Kung, for instance, his, *Infallible?*, Collins, London, 1971, from which the foregoing statements are quoted, and *The Church Maintained in Truth*, Seabury Press, New York, 1980. On reading these and on reflecting upon the harassment to which scholars like Kung are subjected to this day, one realises how fortunate are those whose religion does not have a church.

10. Bertrand Russell, 'An Outline of Intellectual Rubbish' in, *Unpopular Essays*, 1950.

11. Cf. Schopenhauer, 'On Religion,' in *Essays and Aphorisms*, Penguin Classics, 1981, pp. 183-5. The Old Testament and the Quran are obviously not the only scriptures which present a God with this as His singular concern. In the *Janma Saakhis*, for instance, God summons Guru Nanak often. Each time the Guru appears before him, God orders, '*Nanaka, Meri sift kar*' – 'Nanak, praise Me.'

12. Thomas Paine, *The Age of Reason*, Paris 1794; reprint Prometheus Books, New York, 1984, p. 84.

13. And God-that-is-Allah is just one example. Scores and scores of scholars have used scores and scores of different examples to draw our attention to the correspondence. Two justly famous works which argue the point from completely dis-similar perspectives deserve special mention, Marx and Engels' *The Holy Family* and Toynbee's *Study of History*. The parts of the latter relevant to our discussion are summarised in Toynbee's *An Historian's Approach to Religion*, Oxford, London, 1956.

14. Khuswant Singh, *A History of the Sikhs*, Volume 1, *1469-1839*, Princeton, 1963, Appendix 2, and elsewhere.

15. Government Central Printing Office, Simla, 1903.

16. For these and other examples see, *Sahih al-Bukhari*, 67.599, 600, 609, 612; *Sahih Muslim*, 6406-7, 6421-2.

III

The Imam's Stenographers!

One says, 'The .... is of the firm view that the *status quo* as it existed in respect of all places of worship on the 15th August 1947 should not now be altered and any controversy over any place of worship, such as the Somnath temple, should be foreclosed. To achieve these objectives, statutory measures should be taken.'

The other says, 'The .... stands by the position that the status of all religious monuments and places of worship, as on August 15, 1947, shall be maintained.'

One says, 'The .... is committed to finding a negotiated settlement of this (the Ram Janamabhoomi – Babri Masjid) issue which fully respects the sentiments of both communities involved. If such a settlement cannot be reached, all parties must respect the order and verdict of the court. The . . . is for the construction of the Temple without dismantling the mosque.'

The other says, 'The Ram Janmabhoomi-Babri Masjid dispute must be resolved either through a negotiated settlement or by due processes of law. The ... will make sustained efforts to solve the problem on the above lines.'

One says, 'A composite Rapid Action Force charged with the special task of quelling communal riots and specially constituted, trained and equipped for the purpose will be set up'

The other says 'Communal riots shall continue to be put down strongly by effective prohibition of incitement to communal passions, and by pursuing appropriate recruitment policies in the police services. A special anti-riot force shall be created so as to ensure totally impartial conduct from them.'

One says, 'Statutory provision will be made for speedy and adequate compensation to victims of communal riots.'

The other says, 'Full compensation will be provided to victims of communal and caste riots.'

One says , 'It shall make special efforts for careful selection and placement of officers in communally sensitive districts; holding district level officials responsible for preventing and containing riots; and severe punishment to government personnel found guilty of abetting communal offences.'

The other says, 'Action will be taken against officers who fail to control riots.'

One says, 'Socially and educationally backward minorities will be included in the beneficiaries entitled to reservations and other measures intended for the Backward Classes (OBCs). Muslims engaged in occupations such as scavenging will get the benefits available to those sections – while efforts will be made to abolish these occupations.'

The other says, 'Reservations already announced by . . . for the socially and educationally backward among the minorities under the Mandal Commission shall be implemented.'

One says, 'Maximum assistance will be provided for promoting and accelerating the pace of education among the minorities (1) by direct assistance and other concessions to trusts, social service organisations and other minority educational institutions engaged in this cause, and (2) by expanding scholarship and other assistance to individual minority students.'

The other says, 'The ... considers the education of the minorities, both religious and linguistic, to be a national responsi-bility and will take vigorous steps to see that the constraints on their educational progress are removed as speedily as possible through planned and concerted action.' To this end it promises, *inter alia*, 'encouragement for establishment of technical and polytechnic institutions by minorities.'

One says, 'Every effort will be made to provide due representation to the minorities in jobs under the Government and in the public and private sectors. The drive launched in 1986-89 for the recruitment of minorities to the police, the para-military forces and the armed forces will be renewed.'

The other says, 'Concrete steps will be taken to ensure adequate employment opportunities and jobs for minorities,' and adds the specific commitment of 'assuring representation for minorities on various recruitment committees and boards.'

One says, 'Special assistance on concessional terms will be provided to cooperatives organised by minority groups.'

The other says, 'it will set up 'Minority Financial Corporations.'

One says, 'Educational institutions of minority communities will continue to receive full Constitutional and legal protection.'

The other says, 'Minority character of the institutions guaranteed by the Constitution shall be respected.'

One says, 'The Waqf Act, 1954 will be reviewed, and suitable amendments adopted, to make it more effective and beneficial.'

The other says, 'Waqf properties shall be brought under Public Premises (Eviction) Act, properties belonging to Waqf and other religious endowments shall be exempted from the Rent Control Act as a means to augment their income to fulfill their commitments.'

One says, 'The Minorities Commission will be provided statutory status and given the necessary powers to carry out its duties effectively.'

The other says, 'The Minorities Commission will be given statutory status. The Bihar Government has already conferred legal status on its Minorities Commission by an ordinance and a Bill is to be adopted soon.'

. *One says*, 'The ... will adhere to its established principle of desisting from alteration in personal laws until an unequivocal demand is made by the section of people governed by the concerned laws.'

The other says, 'Complete non-interference will be observed in their personal laws, their cultural advancement and fulfilment of their distinctive cultural identities.'

Who and Why

As you would have guessed the 'one' is the Congress-I in its manifesto, and 'the other' is the National Front in its manifesto.

Nor is the reason for this embarrassing identity any mystery.

Both have been wooing Syed Bukhari, the Imam of Delhi's Jama Masjid. He asked each of them to prove fidelity by adopting his list of demands. Each has done so. The Imam's men, to establish his primacy as the Sole Spokesman, have been proclaiming his triumph: 'See, how the Imam Sahib has got both sides to concede whatever he asked for.'

Triumphant, he has upped the ante: the Muslims to be fielded must be cleared by him, he has insisted. V P Singh, being the more desperate one, has agreed to that in terms – Arif's revolt is the visible testimony. The Congress is executing one of its balancing acts – it is keeping up the appearance of independence in public even as in private it mollifies the Imam in Delhi, the Muslim League in Kerala. The difference in the outcome will be no more than the difference in the manifestos. The Congress(I)'s formulations as we saw are more prolix, and on a point or two a bit better camouflaged, but that is all. In the selection of candidates too the same difference will be seen: V P Singh will let it be known openly that he has selected the candidates the Imam espoused; the Congress(I) will adopt the candidates the Imam and the like approve but present them as ones it has selected on its own. Not just the Sole Spokesman, therefore, but the Sole Broker.

This is secularism! That you should kow-tow to the Imam.

That jobs – in the government, in the public sector, and in the private sector – should be distributed on the basis of religion.

That appointments to recruitment boards should be made on the basis of religion.

That financial corporations and cooperatives should be set up on the basis of religion.

That recruitment to the police, to para-military forces, to the army should be on the basis of religion.

Secularism or Opportunism?

How desperate our secularists have become !

Each time it has sought to trample on the fundamental rights of the people, the Congress has invoked Part IV of the Constitution – that is the Directive Principles of State Policy. 'They embody the charter of socio-economic emancipation,' it has proclaimed. 'They have over-riding significance,' it has proclaimed. 'Bourgeois rights will not be allowed to come in their way,' it has proclaimed.

Well, the relevant Directive Principle – Article 44 of the Constitution – lays down, 'The State shall endeavour to secure for the citizens a uniform civil code throughout the territory of India.'

But the Congress – the same Congress which has been proclaiming the over-riding primacy of Directive Principles – proclaims in its manifesto, 'The Congress will adhere to its established principle of desisting from alteration in personal laws until an unequivocal demand is made by the section of people governed by the concerned laws.'

The National Front manifesto while talking of women proclaims, 'Women shall be assured of equal rights in family property. Review shall be made of all legislations which discriminate against women and all laws concerning marriage, divorce, maintenance, custody, adoption and inheritance'. But when it comes to the code of personal law which discriminates on each of these matters – 'marriage, divorce, maintenance, custody, adoption and inheritances' – against women the most, that is Islamic law as it has been frozen in India, the same manifesto proclaims, 'Complete non-interference will be observed in their personal laws....'

The essence of secularism is that for all dealings of the State the individual shall be the unit. The essence of each of these promises is that the group – identified by religion, by caste – shall be the unit.

The essence of secularism is that no religious organisation shall be allowed to do what a non-religious organisation is prohibited from doing. Here while secular organisations must adhere to Rent Control laws, properties owned by organisations of a religion shall be exempt from them.

The essence of secularism is that the organisations of no religion shall be allowed what is prohibited to the organisations of other religions. But here institutions owned by minorities will be exempt from labour and other laws applying to institutions owned by Hindus!

Secularism, indeed!

Nor are these politicians and Imams alone to blame. The progressive intellectuals are to this day cheering them on. And not only among the non-Muslims. I remember meeting Muslim intellectuals and social workers in Jaipur. They had been struck dumb by the riots. So many of them protested that the Imam in Delhi was not representative of Muslims or their opinions. In fact, in private they used the harshest language to denounce him. Several of them said how revolted they were each time his visage appeared on the television – it was being projected very often those days. They held the press responsible for creating – some accused it of deliberately creating – the impression that the Imam was the spokesman of Muslims just so that Hindus would come to hate and fear Muslims. They must these days be reading about these political parties trooping to the Imam, they must be reading about his dictating terms to them in return for delivering Muslim votes. Not one of them has spoken up. The image that the Imam is the Sole Spokesman and Sole Broker of the Muslims will therefore be reinforced. The reaction will be that much more severe. And our friends, silent when they should be making themselves heard, will again grieve and wail, and blame the press.

I Despair

All this comes on top of promises by both these parties to do similar things on the basis of caste — reservations of jobs in government, the public sector, the private sector, a separate Backward Classes Development Corporation, the lot. If these promises get to be implemented, four consequences are inevitable: another brake on modernisation of the economy; disruption of the State apparatus; vastly sharpened animosities between communities and castes; and, I use the words with care, an irreversible descent towards the further dismemberment of the country.

The measures will also bring ruin upon the minorities. The bending of the State on a mere alimony case, on the banning of a mere book which few would have read fuelled Hindu reaction to an extent that today all are apprehensive. When jobs are reserved for Muslims solely because they are Muslims, when financial institutions are set up from which only Muslims can borrow and from which they can borrow solely because they are Muslims, when members are seen to be sitting on selection boards not because they are competent to do so but solely because they are Muslims — the reaction among Hindus *qua* Hindus will be a lethal avalanche.

And these things have a dynamic of their own. Competitive wooing by these parties which proclaim their secularism so insistently has led to the adoption of such ruinous demands by these 'national' parties. But can that be the end? The moment you set up the financial corporation, the Chief Broker, on the pain of withdrawing his testimonial, will demand that only the ones he approves must be appointed in it. And then that loans should go only to...

Each step shall make the next inevitable. Each step shall reinforce the hold of these brokers over the community. They are the most reactionary elements in the community. Their hold over the community depends on fomenting fear and insecurity in the community. It depends on fanning a sense of separateness in the community. It depends on keeping the community gullible and ignorant.

And here we are providing them the means to do all this.

In no country would measures so manifestly ruinous, so clearly the steps to division, be even contemplated. Here they are the major planks of major political parties. How will we save our poor country from ruin? How will we save it from being dismembered? I despair....

– 21 April 1991

IV

Listening to Each Other

"We are viewed through stereotypes" – it was an articulate intellectual, a Muslim by birth, speaking in Jaipur. I happened to be in the city to deliver some lectures. The thoughtfulness of gracious hosts had enabled me to meet thirty thinkers, social workers and professionals. Apart from four or five, each had been born Muslim, each was a devout Muslim, each an Indian.

And each – Muslim and Hindu alike – had been shaken to the core by the recent riots. It was the second bout within a year. And on all counts it had been ghastly, as all these things are. The two bouts had had an even more shattering impact on the residents of this city than such horrors do elsewhere as Jaipur had not had Hindu-Muslim riots in living memory. Amity had been a point of pride in the city. And now...

"In fact," it was said then, and the point was elaborated later, "most cannot think of Muslims beyond just five or ten cliches. That Muslims cheer for Pakistan at cricket matches. That Muslims are fundamentalists. That Muslims marry four wives, that they do not go in for family planning, and that therefore their numbers will soon overwhelm Hindus in India. That they live under a separate personal law by which they not only exploit women etc., they also perpetuate their separateness. That they are hogging favours and concessions from one government after another. . . ."

None of these would bear scrutiny, I was told. No one bothered to examine the facts on these matters, but everyone had internalised the cliches and now saw Muslims only through them, I was told.

That is an important point. For the "Them" versus "Us" psychology has two roots: that we see another group as a monolith, when it is no more a monolith than our own; and that we see that monolith through spectacles such as these cliches.

The Hindu, acutely aware of the differences between Vaishnavas and Shaivites, between Arya Samajis and Sanatanis, between this caste and that, thinks of his community as splintered. But he sees the Muslims as one solid, granite boulder that is about to come hurtling down on him. The Muslim on the other hand sees Shias fighting Sunnies, Sunnies crushing Ahmediyas, he sees Arabs arraigned against Arabs, he recalls West Pakistani Muslims disemboweling East Pakistani Muslims, and he knows that the Muslims are not one block. To him it is the Hindus who appear as that solid boulder which is about to hurtle down and . . .

Such perceptions in turn as well as the hold that stereotypes have acquired have a common origin: we know more about our own little group, and therefore know how splintered, and therefore less-to-be-feared it is, and know little about the other group, and therefore imagine it to be the terror it is not.

And the terror persists and grows because we do not subject it to the scrutiny of facts.

"Muslims have hogged the favours" – a friend who was at the meeting, and who had himself been a senior civil servant, took up this presumption later. Of the 250-odd IAS officers in Rajasthan, he said, there was only one Muslim, of the 175 or so IPS officers only one was Muslim. Which were the favours which had been hogged, he asked. Not in anger; in sorrow at the way our people were being torn asunder by such presumptions.

Muslims too must be seeing Hindus through stereotypes of the same kind. The lesson thus is: we should believe no cliche or stereotype about another, we should certainly not purvey it till we have examined the facts on the matter.

But Why?

But I would draw a further lesson. It is not just that each community should assess whether what it believes of the other has any basis in fact. Each must also examine why the other has acquired that particular image of it.

The model I think is what Gandhiji wrote about Katherine Mayo's *Mother India.* He showed at length how prejudiced and false the book was and how for that reason no American or Englishman would benefit from reading it. But, he said, it was a book that every Indian could read with some degree of profit – for we could glean from even so prejudiced a work many of the things about ourselves that we needed to set right.

Thus, to continue the example of hogging favours for instance, while Hindus must pinpoint which are the favours that Muslims *qua* Muslims have received, the latter must examine how it is that, even though they have not received any special favours, the Hindus have come to believe that the Muslims have received undue advantages.

Facts will dissolve Hindu presumptions. And reflection will show Muslims how costly the politics of the Shahi Imam, of the Shahabuddins has been. These leaders made the State bend on Shah Bano, on Rushdie's book, they published journals and maps proclaiming how important the Muslim votes were and how they would as a block determine the outcome in so many constituencies. They made politicians and through them the State bend on such matters. Their successes in doing so were hailed as victories for Muslims *qua* Muslims, if not for Islam.

The "victories" brought no benefit to the ordinary Muslim. In fact, their only effect as far as Muslim laity was concerned was to establish the Imam in Delhi, to establish Shahabuddin as the leaders of the community, as its sole spokesmen.

But these very "victories" − chimaerical though they were − had another effect, an effect the consequences of which are now proving so onerous, the precise effect which persons like me forecast and for forecasting which we were branded "communal". In brief, these successes in bending the State engendered the perception that Muslims were extorting favours from governments.

Just as the Hindus must therefore examine whether their stereotypes about Muslims are at all grounded in fact, Muslims must assess the consequences of the politics of Imam Bukhari, of Shahabuddin, of Owaisi etc.

"But why do you fellows think that these two or three speak for all Muslims?"

Hindus must see the point of that question. At the same time, articulate Muslims must assess whether it is not their silence which is responsible for giving currency to the belief that these three or four do in fact speak for all Muslims.

The point of course transcends this kind of politics and this kind of political leader. It touches every specific.

Thus, to continue with the example, the Hindus must examine the facts about the numbers of Muslims in various services etc. to see whether their presumption has any basis. On the other hand, the Muslims must examine whether their low representation in

these services is the result of   discrimination or the result of
Muslim children not getting the sort of education which would
equip them for these jobs. They will see too that the remedy is
not reservations, but what a philanthropist has done in UP – he has
made the quantum of assistance to Muslim schools proportionate to
the results of the students, specially of girl students, in competitive
examinations, and thereby ensured a dramatic improvement in their
scores, and thereby in their ability to do well in professions.

Media

"Everyone blames the politicians for the riots. In fact, no one is
more responsible for them than the media": that charge was shared
by most who were present. They alluded to specific news reports
which, they said, had inflamed the Hindus to attack Muslims, but
which, they said, had not the slightest basis in fact. Almost
everyone present named one paper in particular, though some added
that other papers in the state had been no better.

"The press does not project our point of view," it was said,
"and we have no minority press." "You refuse to publish what we
say on the ground that you have to check it out," it was said, "But
a Minister or a Chief Minister has but to ring you up and you publish
as fact whatever he says." And so on.

So traumatic had been their experience with the press that the
Muslims, it was said, had boycoted the principal paper. So
traumatic had it been, it was said, that if any independent person
or group would undertake to publish an independent and objective
paper, funds would be available from persons of all communities.

What should the aggrieved do in such circumstances?

The first thing is what my friends were counselling us to do
about communities: we should not see the press any more than we
should see a community as a monolith: it is *not*.

The second thing too is what my friends were counselling us
in regard to Shahabuddin etc – a local newspaper is no more the
sole spokesman of the press than Imam Bukhari, let us say, is of
the Muslims.

When the local paper is printing what we think are patently
false stories we should not conclude that the entire press is so
inclined. Even it we assume that the local papers, or even all the
papers in a region, will not heed the facts when these are brought

to their attention, we should reach the facts – as well as particulars about what the local papers are doing – to papers outside the region. Assuming – without examination – that the local papers in Rajasthan or in UP refused to publish the correct version, I cannot imagine that papers in Delhi, let us say, would have refused to do so had the facts been brought to their attention.

It is entirely possible that we may not be able to reach the facts to papers outside the region in the midst of a maelstrom. We should in that case do so at the first opportunity.

But *specific* facts – the news-report which was published, the actual facts about the incident, the efforts to apprise the paper of the facts, the reaction of the paper – these, and not just the general grievance.

Perhaps because of the traumas which every one present had been through, and also because so many of them had been busy with urgent work like rehabilitation, facts of this kind had not yet been brought to the attention of, say, the papers in Delhi.

Nor are papers outside the region the only ones whom the aggrieved may approach. The Press Council, the Editors Guild – there are a number of such organisations whose duty it is, and which are always ready, to examine such instances. They too should have been approached by now.

For when we do not approach them we not only fortify the one who errs and embolden him for the future, we internalize the grievance and make-believe that no remedy is available. The grievance then festers. Correspondingly, the institution, by not being invoked, does not acquire the sinews which would make it an effective remedy in the future.

Relief

Apart from the role of the press, the thing that came up for the severest censure was ironically what was meant to be succour: that is, the relief that had been provided by the state government.

It had been tardy – policemen had refused to register FIRs, it was said, the authorities had demurred at claims. It had been inadequate. And, worst, it had been, it was said, discriminatory: more had been given to Hindu victims than to Muslim victims.

I have on occasion heard the exact opposite in regard to riots in Bihar and UP: that Muslims had been given more than Hindus.

Why should even this little thing be beyond our capacity to mend?

A life is a life. The same amount must be paid by the state to the survivors who have lost a relative. Where is the need for ambiguity, for extended analysis?

It is lack of candour which gives rise to suspicion. Not only should it be mandatory therefore to pay identical amounts for life and limb, governments must be bound by law to publish the names of victims, their addresses and the relief which has been provided to the survivors.

There is of course the long-standing premise that publishing the names of victims will foment further trouble. It is on this premise, for instance, that news-papers take to circumlocution: "Mobs killed three of a particular religious community. . . ." Such circumlocution does not engender restraint, it enflames rumours. And every group believes the worst of them. The premise should therefore be reviewed even in reporting violence as it is occurring. In any case, as far as relief is concerned the matter is much simpler. Governments can be required to publish the particulars of persons who have been provided relief and the quantum of such relief, say, three months after the tragedy. There will be no danger of the mandatory disclosure fuelling the fire as it burns; on the other hand, it will obviate presumptions of discrimination on the one side, and restrain governments that may actually be inclined to discriminate, on the other.

Compensation for losses of property because of arson etc. naturally provides greater room for discretion. But here also the remedy is obvious. Instead of clutching on to this function as some exclusive preserve of government, governments should associate honourable persons from both communities in the task of identifying the victims and determining the compensation.

The Pre-requisites

But these are specifics. To realise them in practice we must attend to the point with which we started – our preconceptions.

I remember going to Assam in 1982-83. The Assamese were convinced that they were being belaboured by the BSF and the CRPF because they were Assamese and these forces were non-Assamese. But the BSF and CRPF were doing in Assam exactly what they were doing elsewhere.

The Assamese were convinced that the central government was not listening to them, that Mrs Gandhi in particular was not listening to them because they were Assamese and these latter were non-Assamese. But Mrs Gandhi and her government were not listening to any one else either.

They were convinced that the rest of India was exploiting them in particular by not paying them an adequate royalty on crude. But was it paying Bihar a price any more just for coal and iron-ore? Was Assam itself paying Bihar a price any more just for these materials?

When we suffer, when we are discriminated against we must see that we are not being singled out, that what is befalling us on that particular occasion is the general lot of others on other occasions. And we will be able to set things right not by wresting this or that for our particular group on this particular occasion but by joining hands with all who strive to improve the general state of affairs.

The anti-dote to discrimination in government recruitment is not a quota for our caste or religion. It is to prevent politicians from mutilating the Services Selection Boards. The anti-dote to a biased provincial constabulary is not a quota for our caste or religion in the force, nor another force which will degenerate just as soon given our ways. It is to prevent politicians from mutilating the existing force. The anti-dote to a paper which purveys falsehood is not a "minority press". It is to convey the truth to other papers, to bring the paper to book through institutions whose job it is to watch over all papers.

That is about our perception of the State. The second is about our relying on it.

Nothing is in a worse condition in our society than the State. And yet it is on the State that we rely for everything, even for talking with each other.

On the State, on politicians, with results that we then bemoan.

That problem is endemic, of course. But here is a good place to begin: at every level, in every crisis, on every problem communities should talk to each other directly, and not through politicians and officers of State.

And talk everything that is in their heart about the other.

– 29 December 1990

V

Arguments in Jaipur

"But when the Constitution provides for Article 370 why do these people want it abolished? Were the framers of the Constitution not wise men? Did they not know what the country needed? In what way have the circumstances changed since then?" – it was an articulate and prominent Muslim leader.

I was back in Jaipur. I had been to the city about a year ago, soon after the riots of 1989. The thoughtfulness of a friend had enabled me to meet thirty or so intellectuals, social workers, government servants and religious leaders who happened to be Muslims. The number this time was a bit larger, and there were more lawyers than there had been on the last occasion. And the backdrop to our meeting too was more relaxed : we had met last year in the wake of the riots; this time the *Ekta Yatra* was of course much in everyone's mind, but it was still far away in Maharashtra, its rumble distant and muffled.

The title itself of Article 370 in the Constitution, I pointed out, is "*temporary* provisions with respect to the State of Jammu and Kashmir". It was included to give the people of Kashmir a little time to get accustomed to the ways of the rest of the country; more than enough time has passed; far from being a provision enabling the Kashmiris to get acclimatized to the ways of the country, the Article is being made the argument for perpetual separateness. Moreover, are we not invoking the Constitution as an argument of convenience? Is it something we are prepared to abide by in all respects, I asked. What about Article 44 which urges the State to strive for a common civil code?

"But were the provisions for Reservations not temporary? Have they not been extended from time to time?" But that proves the opposite : by going on extending such temporary provisions we have fanned a leadership which thrives by fomenting separateness in the group, by sowing insecurity in it. And the continuance

of Article 370 has led to demands for similar provisions in regard
to other regions – Mizoram has already been granted that status;
how can it be withheld from Punjab? And it has not benefited the
common Kashmiri at all: a corrupt oligarchy has fattened under its
cover.

"But the Kashmiris have not asked for its being abolished.
Why should the demand be raised by persons outside the state? We
– Muslims of Rajasthan, of UP – we are of course not concerned,
Article 370 does not affect us. But I am just inquiring. The
Deorala Sati took place. We said it is an internal matter of the
Hindus. We never demanded that the culprits be punished or
anything. Why did you raise a hue and cry over Shah Bano? How
were the Hindus harmed whether a Muslim paid his wife alimony
or not?''

Wrong on every single count. The fervour with which the
arguments were being pressed showed that Muslims outside are just
as concerned, and why should they not be? Assume that the
abolition of Article 370 will harm the country: why should
Muslims outside Kashmir not be concerned and stop the people
from pressing on a course which will harm the country?
Correspondingly, assume the opposite. Assume that the continuance of the Article harms the country: why should persons outside
Kashmir not be concerned, why should they not press for its
deletion? Are we not one country? Should what happens in one part
not concern each and every one of us equally? If the Muslims
had remained silent on the murder in Deorala, they were not being
magnanimous. They were being negligent, and cruelly so of their
duty as citizens.

It was a difference in our premises, I will not say
perspectives, which was to come up again and again. The gentleman
was articulating the view, which is widely held, that the affairs of
a community, of a region should be left as they are till the people
of that community or region say they want to alter them. I believe
this to be a premise that harms both – the members of the particular
group, and the country. Reformers within the group remain beleaguered: by definition they are few, a tiny minority; the community
or region is in the thrall of ways which and persons whom the
reformers are trying to modify and replace; as long as we hold to
the dictum that the group or region alone has the right to decide
such matters we consign the members of that group to stagnation:

that premise places a veto in the hands of the very persons whose
domain rests on things continuing as they are. The country too
is harmed as these leaders seek to perpetuate their dominion by
feeding the sense of separateness of the group, and by frightening
it into the belief that it is in imminent danger of being smothered
by the rest of the country. All our traditions are our common
heritage, all regions are part of the country: each of us has not just
the right but the duty to consider every tradition and every region
as our own and to urge what ought to be done in the interests of
the country as a whole.

In the Beholder's Eye

"But the demand is being made at the wrong time, by the wrong
mouth. The time is wrong as the country is already tense because
of the Babri Masjid - Ayodhya controversy. And the mouth is
wrong – *yeh log to hamaari tapti laashon par apni rotiyan sekte
hain*: these are persons who bake their *roties* on the pyre of our
corpses."

What with the threat from terrorists in five states, what with
Kashmir having almost bolted beyond the reach of the country just
a year ago there has seldom been a moment when it was more
necessary than it is today to shake the country out of its stupor –
that was the minor point. The "wrong mouth" and the "*tapti
laashon par. . .*" expression pointed to two things which embitter
relations much more.

Confronted with a proposition, we do not assess it on its
merits, we judge it by the mouth from which it has come. Once we
have judged that mouth to be the "wrong" one, we reject out of
hand everything that the person says. This precludes dialogue, it
rules reason out of court. Name-calling and piling suspicion on
suspicion about "the real motives" of the other person are
naturally all that ensue. There is just nothing the other person can
do which does not become further proof of his diabolic intent.

An example came a moment later. "But don't you see the
pictures they have put on the *Ekta Yatra rath*?," a friend asked.
"Who is this Subramaniam Bharati? We don't even know, no one
in North India knows. There is a Hindu. There is a Sikh Guru.
Could they not have had a Muslim's portrait also?" Now, there
is another way to look at the pictures: of these two pictures one

is of a person from the South, one of a person from the North; one of a Hindu, one of a non-Hindu; one of a great nationalist, the other of the very person – Guru Tegh Bahadur – who sacrificed his life to save the very kind – Kashmiri Hindus – who have been rendered homeless today. And the fact if it be true that no one in North India knows who Subramania Bharati is – is that not reason itself for putting his picture up? And the declaration "We don't even know who he is" – would that not become another argument in the hands of some Tamil chauvinist to proclaim that the North does not look upon the Tamils as part of India?

I was arguing thus, and saying that whatever we may think of the *yatra*, the symbols had clearly been chosen with care, and I was pointing as examples of this to the brothers of Bhagat Singh and Rajguru and the sons of Abdul Hamid having been chosen to flag-off the march, when a friend interjected, "But why did they not also invite the relatives of Ashafaqullah – did he not also die as heroically as Bhagat Singh and Rajguru? And we will not go into the inducements by which the sons of Hamid might have been enticed to participate in the ceremony."

It was the old premise – of "the wrong mouth" – again. If the person we have judged to be the wrong one succeeds in getting the sons of Hamid to the function, we assume he has "enticed" them by inducements "into which we will not go". If he fails to get the relatives of Ashafaqullah, we conclude he has not done so because that hero was Muslim. Was it that the BJP organizers had tried to get the relatives of Ashafaqullah and failed, or that they had not tried at all? If the former, had they failed because no relatives are around or because the relatives had refused to participate? Even if the sole object of the BJP organizers had been to reap political advantage, as they had concluded that one way to do so was to get some Muslims to flag-off the march – a fact that was evident even on this reckoning from their having got Hamid's sons over – why would they have excluded the relatives of some well known Muslim hero? None of us present knew the answer. But some were clearly prepared to proceed on one assumption as the deed was being done by the "wrong" person.

Now, this is nothing peculiar to Muslims. There are Hindus who proceed in exactly the same way. Having concluded that Muslims are "in their heart of hearts" Pakistanis, they too interpret anything and everything the latter do with the jaundiced eye.

The consequences are before us. We should reverse the presumptions. Instead of rejecting out of hand a proposition because it comes from "the wrong mouth", we should assess it on its merits. As for the person, we should, instead of imagining "the real motive" behind what he is saying or doing, take him at his word, and hold him to it. And then there is the effect our language has. Rithambara's vituperations on the one side and the poetic flourishes on the other – "persons who bake their *roties* on the pyre of our corpses". In either form the language becomes an issue in itself, it becomes yet another reason to take what were mere assumptions to be facts. The lesson is obvious.

Religion as Cover

We were but to begin dispersing that the next lesson was brought home. A fine gentleman who had till recently held high positions in government pressed the copy of a memorandum and photographs. Together they charged the Collector of Ajmer with having unleashed wanton destruction of old structures around the Dargah of the venerated Moiuddin Chisti, with in fact having caused the destruction of walls etc. which were a part of the Dargah itself. The memorandum charged the Collector with having done all this even as she had left unauthorized structures of Hindus intact.

It so happened that we were all in Ajmer just two days later to pay our homage at the Dargah and to seek the Saint's intercession. On the way to the Dargah we were set right by a venerable social worker and her charming husband. Each is respected in the city, each has been a part of its recent history, each is devoted to the city, to its residents, and to its tradition. "Do not believe these *Khadims* (literally, 'those who serve' – in this case families who claim descent from those who attended on the *Gharib-Nawaz*)," they said, "All priests, whether the *Pandas* in Pushkar or these *Khadims* here, are alike. Our young Collector has not touched the Dargah at all. Not a bit of the Dargah's property either. Only the encroachments on government land have been removed."

The husband said that in view of the allegations he had

inspected the entire perimeter of the Dargah. Nothing but nothing of the Dargah had been touched. On the contrary, the long approach to the Dargah which had become well-nigh impassable had now been restored to being the wide road it had been meant to be. Not just unauthorized extensions of shops and canopies which obscured even the majestic *Buland Darwaza* from view had been removed, the electric poles had been taken out too so that they may not impede the pilgrims; the wires had been affixed along the walls. The houses far from being damaged had been white-washed at government expense. And so on.

The transformation is to be seen to be believed. Everyone present remarked on how vast was the improvement which the clearing up had brought about: how the road had become impassable because of the encroachments, how the devotees approaching the shrine could not see even the entrance to the Dargah, to say nothing of the Dargah because of the coverings the shopkeepers used to spread over the portions they had usurped; how what had been done was strictly in accordance with the Master Plan; how it was but the first step in implementing that Plan; how the last person to have done anything of the kind was T N Chaturvedi when he was the Collector in Ajmer and how he had not been allowed to complete the job of clearing and sprucing up the area; how the lady had stood up to the stones which shopkeepers and agents of the *Khadims* had hurled at her; how she had spurned the bags of money which were sought to be given to her; how they hoped she would be allowed time enough to complete the task. . .

And on the other side was the memorandum with its photographs. It was being circulated to members of Parliament, to the press: two papers in Ahmedabad and Pune had already picked up the canard, it was said.

Now, the point is not, it most emphatically is NOT, "Muslims misuse religion to cover up encroachments." The social worker and her husband who first put us wise to the facts happen to be devout Muslims. The shopkeepers who had occupied the road etc. are Hindus as well as Muslims. The point is a different one altogether.

I was reminded of the canards which were put out when Jagmohan had begun to clean up the environs of Vaishno Devi. Those in charge had not been using the offerings of the devotees for either the shrine or the pilgrims. The entire 14 kilometre route

to the place had become a tortuous stretch of filth and stench. But
when Jagmohan initiated steps to set things right – and with the
funds the pilgrims used to offer at the shrine itself – the canards
flew. Memoranda were put out. The High Court was moved. All
in the name of piety and religion.

"He is an Arya Samaji and is working out his scorn for idol-
worship." "His object is entirely political : he wants to deprive Dr.
Karan Singh of his base and the funds." "The government is
usurping control of the affairs of a Hindu shrine." And much
more.

Jagmohan moved with speed. For once happily, Delhi was
preoccupied, and the controllers of the shrine happened not to
have at that moment access to the levers of power there, and so
no one impeded him. And in his counter-affidavit he documented
what the controllers of the shrine had been doing with the funds as
well as the staff of the shrine. That and the growing enthusiasm
of the devotees for the improvements silenced the controllers.
They withdrew the writs.

By now the improvements are a show-piece. The number of
pilgrims has QUADRUPLED. There is more for each pilgrim, as
well as more for the upkeep of the shrine.

The lesson is manifest. These are not Hindu-Muslim
questions. Encroachments are encroachments. Usurpation and
misuse of property and premises are usurpation and misuse.
Must violations of secular laws not be put down just because they
are done in the shadow of religion or by persons who in other
capacities happen to hold religious office? Clearly, the violations
must be put down and they must be put down with an even hand:
for instance if there are structures of Hindus which offend the
Master Plan of Ajmer and the Collector were to leave them
standing she would undo much of the good work she has begun.
Is putting such violations down not an elementary principle of
secularism? And would so many of our problems even arise if
we were to act on just this elementary principle?

– 5 January 1992

VI

Climbing Out of Despair

As a sequel to Hindu-Muslim riots about 230 persons were locked up under the Terrorist and Disruptive Activities Act in Rajasthan in November 1989 and March 1990. In spite of two years having passed most of them continue to languish in jails. As about 120 of them happened to be Muslims, about 95 to be Sikhs and only 15 or so happened to be Hindus, the Muslims in the state have come to believe that the state government has let the detenues rot because they have happened to be Muslims.

Several factors have compounded this surmise: while Muslims had suffered more in the riots, far more Muslims happened to have been locked up than Hindus; all of them have been locked up under the Terrorist and Disruptive Activities Act and the Explosives Act even though the Home Minister of Rajasthan had informed the State Assembly in March 1991 that no arms or explosives had been found on 178 of the 228 detenues; the pattern of releases too has seemed to have weighed heavily in favour of non-Muslims; while some Hindus have been enabled to secure their release *via* the High Court instead of the Court which has been specially set up for handling cases under TADA, the latter has dealt with bail applications of Muslims with a heavy hand – when the applications were first moved, the Court held that as the charges had yet to be framed the applications could not be entertained; after these had been framed, the Court held that *prima facie* the charges were so grave that bail could not be allowed. The fact that, though a Congress government was in office when the arrests were first made, for most of the period a BJP-led coalition has been in office has reinforced the presumption in the Muslim mind that the prisoners are being kept on in jails merely because they are Muslims.

Repeated efforts were made at all levels to move the state administration to dispose of the cases. When all of them had been exhausted, Muslim social workers as well as Congressmen approached the Centre. The matter was raised in Parliament. It was taken up in meetings that central leaders had with the Rajasthan government. In the event, these efforts were taken as an affront – "It has become a prestige issue with the government," those taking up the case were warned.

While a few have been released, most continue to languish in jails. And with nothing in prospect – not even the investigations, to say nothing of the cases seem to be proceeding. Within the Rajasthan Muslim community therefore the instance is well on the way to becoming what the Jodhpur detenues case had become in the psyche of the Sikhs.

What has happened is what happens every day in India: persons have been rounded up; no one in government has had either the time to examine the facts or the courage in the absence of incriminating facts to discharge the detenues. We have seen this happen not just in an instance like the Jodhpur detenues – one in which large numbers were involved, one in which what was done to them had become a chip in the bargaining between militants and the State. We have seen it happen even in cases in which no more than an unknown individual has been involved – a scientist picked up on the suspicion that he was carrying "secrets" abroad when all he was carrying was his Ph.D. thesis. In that case too, and in similar ones, years passed and no one in government had either the courage or the time to see that justice was done. That is the thing – a very difficult one, no doubt – which those who empathise with the victims must remember and hammer home all the time : that what is being visited upon the victims is the fate that befalls every one who is unlucky enough to fall into the nets of our courts and governments, that it has little to do with the victim being the member of this community or that.

The lesson which governments must act on is of course the opposite: the lesson namely that, given what the atmosphere is in India today, no victim, no one belonging to any community or caste or region is liable to put the forgoing construction on what is being visited upon him; he is certain to believe that he is being put to those troubles because he is a Muslim, an Assamese or Tamil, or a Harijan. What should therefore be anger at a paralysed institution – the non-functioning Special Court, for instance – is bound to become anger at, and repudiation of the

whole, a turning away from India as it is. Quite apart from the
inhumanity involved in having persons rot like this, here is the
most urgent of reasons for governments not to stand on prestige,
not to neglect such cases : if there is no evidence against the
detenues they must be released forthwith; if evidence in fact exists
of their involvement, it must be made public and the cases must
be proceeded with on a day to day basis. A state like Rajasthan,
after all, is not yet in the position of Punjab or Kashmir that no
evidence will be available, that no witness will come forward to
testify to the facts.

A Pervasive Despair

The case of the TADA detenues is but an instance of a despair
which is becoming general among the Muslims. They see what the
politics of Shahabuddin and Imam Bukhari, and the "successes"
they totted up – on Shah Bano, on Rushdie – have spawned : a deep
and pervasive reaction among the Hindus. They see too that there
now exists a national political party which is trying consciously to
embody this reaction. They see finally that the reaction is bound
to get more and more militant as time goes by. They see the
growing swell in the country for ties with a country like Israel.
They see that with the collapse of the communist bloc the West
is bound to turn upon pan-Islamism, and that this is bound to stoke
further the reaction within India which has begun.

The picture is even more gloomy on the other side : the
Muslims can no longer rely on those – the left, the Janata Dal type,
even the Congress – to whom they have looked for protection
and advancement. They see that the interest of each of these in
them has been only to the extent to which he could garner their
votes etc. They see that that particular brand of politics – of
barter – has its limits: if Muslims under encouragement from
these elements continue to act as a vote bank then the Hindus too
will organise themselves as a vote bank. Worse, these erstwhile
champions of their cause are discredited, and they are in disarray:
the left exemplifies the discredited, the Congress the ones in
disarray, the Janata Dal exemplifies both. The disability this
imposes on the Muslims is indeed substantial: the jostling between
Hari Deo Joshi, and Nawal Kishore Sharma, and Nathu Ram
Mirdha, and Ashok Gehlot, and many others in the Rajasthan

unit of the Congress, exacerbated as it now is by the organisational
elections, has meant that no one in the party has had any time to
take up the detenues case for instance, even when it would have
been so handy a ram with which to batter the BJP government of
the state.

There is an even darker cloud : modernization itself. Because
of their continued dependence on *madrasaas*, because of the
higher drop-out rates which result from poverty, because of the
threats which the industries in which so many Muslims are
concentrated face today, the Muslims see how ill-equipped they are
to hold their own in the world today.

A Fateful Choice

They face a fateful choice. They can agitate to secure protection
for the traditional occupations in which so many of them are
concentrated – brassware in Moradabad and the rest. They can
agitate that as they are not liable to get an even share of facilities
in open competition, separate institutions and facilities should be
set up for them. And the quickest way to get such things is for
them to get behind their traditional leaders – behind those, that
is, who have already established themselves as the brokers of
Muslims.

The moment is doubly dangerous. For not only are Muslims
– made anxious by these ominous clouds – liable to retreat into
demanding these things, to such leaders, there are many on the
other side who will be only too anxious to concede such demands,
to continue to barter with such leaders so as to win Muslim votes.
The manifestoes under which the Congress and the Janata Dal
fought the last elections are textbook examples of this : what with
their promises of extending caste-based reservations to Muslims,
of providing additional assistance to educational institutions
run for and by Muslims, of providing "special assistance on
concessional terms" to cooperatives set up by and for them, of
setting up separate "Minority Financial Corporations".

Should Muslims, on their own or upon being beguiled by our
"secular" politicians, choose this route, they will be compound-
ing their difficulties no end. Whatever protection may be
announced today for traditional industries, it will have to be
abandoned soon enough – it will not be possible to maintain the

brassware industry in Moradabad in its present form any more
than it is to maintain jute in West Bengal, or sisal in Tanzania for
that matter. Similarly, the moment separate facilities are set up
for Muslims, their access to general facilities will become that
much less. And the special facilities will become the fiefdoms
of the current brokers – the Imam Bukharis will insist on having,
and will be readily given vetoes over appointments in and over
the functioning of these institutions, be they for finance or
education. That is, these institutions will fall to the very persons
whose politics, to say nothing of whose perspective, has brought
Muslims to their present despair. And the more the hold of these
leaders is fortified, the more will reaction be stoked.

The way out therefore is the exact opposite of what the
Muslims, anxious as they are today, are inclined to adopt. It is
not to retreat into a ghetto demanding special treatment for
themselves on the ground that they are in a ghetto. It is not
to try and sweep back the flood of technological change. It is
to join all others in the country to strengthen the institutions
and mores by which alone parliamentary democracy can function.
It is to say "Yes" to modernization. Accordingly, they must
assess political parties and leaders not by the superficials with
which these latter have beguiled them – the *Iftaar* parties of Mrs.
Gandhi, the *khula* payjama and fur cap of VP Singh, the cap and
"They call me Mulla Singh" of Mulayam Singh. Nor by the
special, that is separate concessions these parties and leaders
promise them. But by the extent to which their conduct
strengthens or weakens our institutions. And by the extent to which
they equip the ordinary Muslim for modernization – they should
opt, that is, not for the government or leader who gives a subsidy
to carpet weavers to continue as they are, but for the one who
gets new designs to them, who organizes better marketing for
them, who enables those incredibly nimble and adept craftsmen
to switch from carpets and brass inlay work to electronics.

Beyond These

"You say this and that. But in the end it amounts to a whitewash
of that other point of view. Not once in three hours have you said
what we would have liked to hear" – it was an earnest, dedicated
young lady coaxing me at the end of the arguments in Jaipur. "As

I sat listening through those three hours," said my friend, "I noticed how we are unable to put forth in the form of logical arguments what we know are the facts. On the other hand, you put forward all the logical arguments but you don't see what is in our hearts."

Although the first remark had been half to tease me, and though the second was by no stretch a complaint, the two led me to reflect. For the remarks might as well have been made by any group in India today – by the Kashmiris, by the Assamese, by Harijans, by OBCs. But that fact itself contains the answer. *Every* group today feels beleaguered, it feels it is being taken advantage of, being sat upon. *Every* group wants to be treated as being special, at least as being specially vulnerable. But that now includes the majority itself – that is, Hindus *qua* Hindus. They too want to hear soothing things, things which will confirm them in the apprehension that they are being had. Even before this had come to pass, but most certainly now the country cannot withstand special treatments for every group.

The only way is to establish a truly secular polity – where the individual is the unit in all dealings of the State, and not a group; where secular laws are enforced strictly; where they are enforced uniformly for all; where no one is allowed to do in the name of religion what a secular body is not allowed to do.

And to prepare the way for such a polity we can begin with three things here and now.

We should meet in small groups and large, in ones and twos and pour out everything that is in our hearts. We should go on doing so – not till we have convinced each other, that is not necessary, and it may not be something we can aspire to immediately. We should continue doing so instead till each of us thoroughly learns the arguments and facts which have led the other to hold the beliefs he holds today.

Second, we should look around and see, all the propaganda to the contrary notwithstanding, how similar the lives of our people are.

Finally, we should re-establish social relations. Once again, this should not be left to leaders, nor should it be attempted at the level of general categories – "Hindus" and "Muslims". At a seminar organized by the *Maya* Group of publications in Allahabad recently, Saed Naqvi put forward the really telling idea.

He asked the audience to shun the hypotheses and arguments which had been urged upon it for five hours. Instead, he said, every Hindu in the audience should vow to make just one Muslim his friend, every Muslim should vow to make one Hindu his friend. And such a friend that he would not think of finalising the date or time of the marriage of his child without taking counsel of the other. And you will see, he said, the transformation that will come about − as we begin to realise that each of us is just like the other. Quite the way to begin.

− *5 January 1992*

The Pattern

VII

The Gloss-over School

Few things have harmed public discourse in India as much as the dread that so-called liberals have had of speaking the whole truth.

And this dread has been greatest in regard to four subjects: the communalism of leaders who have enflamed the Muslims first and the Sikhs now as a religious community; the doings within India of the so-called leftists; certain domestic policies or programmes – for instance, the working of public sector firms – which have come to be associated with 'progressivism'; and the nature of leftist regimes as well as their doings abroad.

It is not commitment or affection for the left or, say, the Muslim that has brought about this silence. It is dread, the fear that someone will brand us 'communal' or 'reactionary'. The dread has been reinforced by the fact that in India there is a great supply of calumners. And that too-for a reason: the surest way to establish one's secular credentials has been to go about calling others 'communal', the surest way to ensconce oneself as a 'progressive' has been to brand others 'reactionary'. And as it is the so-called left and the so-called secularists who have perfected the smear-technology, the two subjects towards which our 'liberals' have shut their eyes most zealously are the communalism of the Shahabuddins and Bhindranwales and everything that has even faintly smelt of the left.

It is only when the left or the communalists have themselves disowned their earlier words or deeds either because of disastrous consequences or because of factional fights within their establishments – the Stalinist purges, the time-for-violent-revolution-is-now-line of the CPI in the early fifties, Jinnah after the break up of the country – that the 'liberal' has plucked up enough courage to talk about these matters. And then too in apologetic tones – 'But that was an aberration,' 'But that is all over and done with,' 'But the mistake has been acknowledged,' 'But why rake those mistakes up now?'

The consequences have been pernicious. In economic policy, for instance, liberalisation was delayed a decade and a half in part because Indian intellectuals, afraid of being charged as being the mouthpieces of Western capitalism, of the World Bank or IMF or multi-nationals, did not speak out about the consequences of the licence-quota *raj*, they did not speak out about the real condition, the recalcitrant – in some cases the incorrigible – condition of many of our public sector enterprises. Similarly, as the intellectuals have been reluctant to talk about leaders like Sir Syed Ahmed Khan, Iqbal, Jinnah – leaders and ideologues the very premise of whose politics was the dismemberment of India – our people are not as alert as they ought to be to the dangers inherent in the politics of such leaders; if our intellectuals had documented and broadcast even the rhetoric alone, the bare presuppositions of the Iqbals and the Jinnahs, our people would have been able that much more readily to recognise the beast each time it has raised its head.

But it isn't just the people in general who are harmed, the communities who fall prey to such leaders, religious minorities who fall for the Owaisies, young men and women who fall for the Charu Majumdars, are harmed just as much. We do not speak the whole truth about the Akali *jathedars* and thereby harm the Sikhs. We do not speak the whole truth about the progenitor of the two-nation theory, of the 'Muslims should keep aloof' theory, Sir Syed Ahmed Khan, and thereby help perpetuate the backwardness, and thereby the disadvantages, of the Muslims.

Thus silence retards reform. If large numbers were writing and talking about the communalism of these leaders, for instance, the reformers within these communities would not be as isolated, indeed as beleaguered as they are today. Worst of all, not speaking the whole truth becomes a habit. Concealing one's convictions, glossing over the evidence, deception, become almost an ingredient of public discourse. And this entails maladies that go far beyond the specific issues – communalism, supposedly progressive economic policies – that may have first occasioned the silence.

An Illustration

As an illustration of the types of things our 'liberals' do not talk about, I shall take the writings and speeches of Sir Syed Ahmed Khan. Sir Syed is a good illustration for several reasons:

❏ His image in the public mind today is almost wholly a result of this selective, this assiduous silence, reinforced now by governmental hagiographic propaganda.

❏ The propositions he injected into public discourse were the precise ones – in sequence, and word for word – which Jinnah picked up once he decided that his future lay in playing the communal card.

❏ The propositions are again and again picked up by leader after leader who reckons that the way to national importance is by becoming the leader of one community, and the way to the latter is the religion-in-danger shriek; as such leaders keep erupting – Bhindranwale one day, Shahabuddin the next – the reader will at once see the contemporary relevance of Sir Syed's propositions.

❏ The propositions will also serve to show how deep the two-nation malaise had gone and consequently how great were the difficulties that Mahatma Gandhi and others had to contend with. Recalling the propositions themselves, and the fact that they had been drilled into the people by such influential men as Sir Syed for a century, will also put in perspective the simplistic analyses – that of Maulana Azad, for instance – which seem to suggest that cataclysms like Partition would have been avoided had one or two ministers been included in the UP ministry, or had Pandit Nehru not said something at a press conference. The cancer of such propositions acquires a momentum of its own, and unless they have been scotched at their first appearance, societies cannot avoid the terrible recoil of consequences. Indeed, the leaders who invoke them become prisoners themselves. It has been argued – most recently by Ayesha Jalal in *The Sole Spokesman* – that Jinnah, for instance, was not really serious in his demand for Pakistan, that it was for him just a bargaining ploy. Such an argument only strengthens the point: serious or not, once Jinnah set off on the communal road in 1934 even he could not turn back except at the cost of ruling himself out of the political scene altogether.

Sir Syed Ahmed Khan

We have been brought up to think of Sir Syed as 'a great moderniser', 'a great nationalist', as 'one of the builders of modern India'. Official hagiographies never tire of repeating his remark that Hindus and Muslims are as the two eyes of a bride.

He was indeed the first to stress the importance of modern education for Muslims. His views on many social questions – vaccination, codification of laws, laws being applicable to all, including Eurasians, equally – were indeed progressive. And in advocating these he fought the traditionalists long and hard.

All this is true. But, as we shall see, it is only a part – and as far as consequences for the country go, it is only a small part – of the truth.

Sir Syed's writings and his political work were premised on the following propositions:

❏ the Muslims of India are a separate nation;
❏ they have fallen on bad days;
❏ to recover their position they should ally themselves with the British, and take to Western education.

In order to fulfil these objectives Sir Syed went to great pains to affirm that:

❏ British rule is the best thing that has happened to India, that it is particularly beneficial to the Muslims, that it should last forever;
❏ Muslims should accordingly be assiduously loyal to the British government in India;
❏ Muslims must completely shun any and every activity that may even be suspected by the British to be against the interests of the Empire, that they must in particular shun the Congress;
❏ Every proposal which seeks to democratise governance spells woe for the Muslims and must never be allowed to prevail;
❏ If the Congress or the British persist in pushing these proposals the Muslims will fight with the help of the Turks and Pathans if necessary.

As the attitude of the British was in his view the key to the advancement of Muslim interests, Sir Syed spent a lot of his energies in convincing the British that Muslims were the most loyal of subjects, that they had proven this by the services they rendered the Empire during the 1857 uprising. To buttress this image, Sir Syed indulged in embarassing theological gymnastics, asserting, for instance, that

❏ Muslims are enjoined by the Quran and the Prophet to be loyal to the ruler;

❏ India under the British, though no longer the *Dar ul Islam*, is not the *Dar ul Harb* in which Muslims are enjoined by Allah to fight for the victory of Islam;

❏ Muslims are taught by the Quran that the people who are most likely to be their friends are the Christians in contrast to the Kafirs.

Sir Syed was not content with stating these propositions. He served the British, rising to be a member twice of the Viceroy's Council. He set up the Anglo-Oriental College as well the Indian Patriotic Association for purposes which we shall just see.

Given the image we have been fed, the propositions sound improbable, to say the least. And so it is best to let Sir Syed speak for himself.

Representative Statements

Sir Syed has been written about a great deal – a study lists about fifteen biographies alone – and his writings and speeches too survive in great volume. For ease of reference I shall recall passages only from one representative collection. This is *Writings and Speeches of Sir Syed Ahmed Khan* (Nachiketa, 1972) edited by one of his biographers, Shan Mohammad. Page numbers appearing after each passage refer to this collection.

1. The proposition that Muslims are a separate nation is the bedrock of his speeches and writings. Scores of passages can be recalled (e.g., 106, 159, 180-1, 184-5, 204, 208, 241).

This expression and idea are used exactly as Jinnah was to use them later – i.e., to assert that as the Hindus and Muslims are eternally different, it is inevitable that if the two were left on their own one would sit upon the other. In the light of the repeated assertions to this effect, the attempt of apologists to put a gloss on his meaning – by "nation" Sir Syed only meant community' (e.g., 265-8) – is worse than pathetic.

Sir Syed spent much time and energy in making the Muslims aware that they are a separate nation with a glorious past and a distinct future. Recalling the objects for which he has founded the Anglo-Oriental College he says:

The second thing which I wish to see established in our people is national feeling and sympathy; and this cannot be created unless the boys of our nation read together. At this moment, when all of us Mohammedans have come together the assembly itself has an effect on our hearts, and an involuntary emotion gives birth to the thought –'Our Nation!' 'Our Nation!'– but when we separate the effect vanishes. This is not merely my assertion; I trust that all here will acknowledge its truth. If you will reflect on the principles of religion, you will see the reason why our Prophet ordered all the dwellers in one neighbourhood to meet five times a day for prayers in the mosque, and why the whole town had to meet together on Fridays in the city mosque, and in Eid all the people of the district had to assemble. The reason was that the effect of the gathering should influence all, and create a national feeling among those present, and show them the glory of the nation. These outward shows have a great effect on the human mind. They create unity and draw a picture of the nation on the heart. These thoughts will not grow up in the minds of men unless they are forced on their attention. Hence, it is necessary for the good training and education of Mohammedans that they should be collected together into one place to receive it; that they may live together and eat together, and learn to love one another....(200-1)

2. He often referred to the Hindus as the other nation that inhabited India. But often enough he maintained that the Hindus in fact consisted of several, separate nations. India, in contrast, for instance, to England, 'is peopled with different nations. Consider the Hindus alone. The Hindus of our Province, the Bengalis of the East, and the Mahrattas of the Deccan, do not form one nation....' (208)

'I have no animosity against the Congresswallahs,' he writes to the *Pioneer*, 'that I should undertake the work of trying to have them arrested by the criminal courts. Their opinions and ours are

different. We believe that what they want is very harmful for
Mohammedans, for Rajputs, for the other nations of the Hindus, and
specially for the peace of the country....'(249)

When he came to be widely criticised for driving a wedge
between the two communities so as to secure advantages for one of
them from the British, he on occasions referred to Hindus and
Muslims as being the two eyes of a bride, to the Muslims having
adopted India as their home, to their having left behind and
forgotten the cultures from which they had come (159-60, 162-3).
There is even the expression once that the two are one nation(160).

But expressions such as these seem to be rhetorical glosses to
the bedrock of his beliefs. And even as he put out these palliatives
he said that they should not be taken to mean that Hindus and
Muslims should join for political action. Castigating Badruddin
Tyabji for joining the Congress and assuming its presidentship at
the Madras session, Sir Syed in a typical passage writes:

> I ask my friend honestly to say whether out of two such nations
> whose aims and objects are different, but who happen to agree
> in some small points, a 'National' Congress can be created? No.
> In the name of God — No. I thank my friend for inducing the
> twelve Standing Committees to sanction the rule 'that any
> subject to which the Mussalman delegates object, unani-
> mously or nearly unanimously, must be excluded from all
> discussion in the Congress.' But I again object to the word
> 'delegate', and would suggest that instead of that word be
> substituted 'Mussalman taking part in the Congress.' But if this
> principle which he has laid down in his letter and on which he
> acted when President, be fully carried out, I wonder what there
> will be left for the Congress to discuss. Those questions on
> which Hindus and Mohammedans can unite, and on which they
> ought to unite, and concerning which it is my earnest desire
> that they should unite, are social questions. We are both
> desirous that peace should reign in the country, that we two
> nations should live in a brotherly manner, that we should help
> and sympathise with one another, that we should bring pressure
> to bear, each on his own people, to prevent the arising of
> religious quarrels, that we should improve our social condition,
> and that we should try to remove that animosity which is every
> day increasing between the two communities. The questions on

which we can agree are purely social. If the Congress had been made for these objects, then I would myself have been its President, and relieved my friend from the troubles which he incurred. But the Congress is a political Congress, and there is not one of its fundamental principles, and especially that one for which it was in reality founded, to which Mohammedans are not opposed.

We may be right or we may be wrong; but there is no Mohammedan, from the shoemaker to the Rais who would like that the ring of slavery should be put on us by that other nation with whom we live. Although in the present time we have fallen to a very low position, and there is every probability we shall sink daily lower (especially when even our friend Badruddin Tyabji thinks it an honour to be President of the Congress), and certainly we shall be contented with our destiny, yet we cannot consent to work for our own fall. . . . (241-2)

So: two nations, whose interests and objects are irremediably opposed.

3. Among the two, the Muslims, Sir Syed felt, have fallen on terrible days. The Muslim Empire is gone. The kings are gone. The great families are in ruin. 'The oriental poet has well said,' Sir Syed recalls, 'There is no misfortune sent from Heaven, which ere it descended to earth, did not seek for its resting place the dwelling of Mohammedans!' (35). 'I perfectly admit the kindly feeling towards Mohammedans which pervades the whole book,' writes Sir Syed about Hunter's *Indian Musalmans*, 'and for this I heartily thank the talented author. At the same time,' he adds, 'I regret deeply that his good intentions should have been so grievously frustrated by the manner in which he has written, and that he has used his "power of the pen" in a way calculated still more to embitter the minds of Englishmen against the already little-loved Moslems' (67).

4. As Hindus and Muslims are two eternally separate nations, as one cannot exist but by riding over the other, the governance of India must continue in the hands of the British. 'In whose hands shall the Administration and Empire of India rest?,' Sir Syed asks, and replies:

Now, suppose that all the English and the whole English army were to leave India, taking with them all their cannon and their splendid weapons and everything, then who would be rulers of India? Is it possible that under these circumstances two nations – the Mohammedans and the Hindus – could sit on the same throne and remain equal in power? Most certainly not. It is necessary that one of them should conquer the other and thrust it down. To hope that both could remain equal is to desire the impossible and the inconceivable. At the same time you must remember that although the number of Mohammedans is less than that of the Hindus, and although they contain far fewer people who have received a high English education, yet they must not be thought insignificant or weak. Probably they would be by themselves enough to maintain their own position. But suppose they were not. Then our Mussalman brothers, the Pathans, would come out as a swarm of locusts from their mountain valleys, and make rivers of blood to flow from their frontier on the north to the extreme end of Bengal. This thing – who after the departure of the English would be conquerors – would rest on the will of God. But until one nation had conquered the other and made it obedient, peace cannot reign in the land. This conclusion is based on proofs so absolute that no one can deny it. . . . . (184-5)

Contrary interests and mutual hostility are just one set of reasons that require that the British continue to rule India. There are others also. Should the British withdraw from India, Sir Syed says, one of the other European powers – the French, German, Portuguese or Russians – will attack India; neither Hindus nor Muslims will be able to defend the country and the rule of these other European nations will be much harsher (185-6). 'It is therefore necessary,' Sir Syed says, 'that for the peace of India and for the progress of everything in India the English Government should remain for many years – in fact forever' (185-6).

5. As the objectives of the two nations are irreconcilably opposed, and as the Hindus outnumber the Muslims four to one, all proposals for democratisation of the legislatures, of the executive, must be resolutely fought and defeated. In a typical passage he says:

Lord Ripon had a very good heart and kind disposition and every qualification for a Governor. But, unfortunately, his hand

was weak. His ideas were radical. But, that time the Local
Board and Municipality Bills were brought forward, and the
intention of them was that everybody should be appointed by
election. Gentlemen, I am not a Conservative, I am a great
Liberal. But to forget the prosperity of one's nation is not a sign
of wisdom. The only person who was opposed to the system of
election was myself. If I am not bragging too much, I may, I
think, say that it was on account of my speech that Lord Ripon
changed his opinion and made one-third of the members
appointed and two-thirds elected. Now just consider the result
of election. In no town are Hindus and Mohammedans equal.
Can these Mohammedans suppress the Hindus and become the
masters of our 'Self-Government'? In Calcutta an old, bearded
Mohammedan of noble family met me and said that a terrible
calamity had befallen them. In his town there were eighteen
elected members, not one of whom was a Mohammedan; all
were Hindus. Now, he wanted Government to appoint some
Mohammedans; and he hoped Government would appoint him.
This is the state of things in all cities. In Aligarh also, were
there not a special rule, it would be impossible for any Mohammedan, except my friend Maulvi Mahomed Yusuf, to be
elected; and at last he, too, would have to rely on being
appointed by Government. Then how can we walk along a road
for which neither we nor the country is prepared?. . . (216)

Elections are to be opposed, he says, not only because Hindus
outnumber Muslims, but also because Muslims are not equal to the
Hindus in that they are not fit enough for attaining such posts
through elections, nor are Muslims likely to take time off from their
businesses etc. to attend to the work:

The second demand of the National Congress is that the people
should elect a section of the Viceroy's Council. . . .

Now, let us suppose the Viceroy's Council made in this manner.
And let us suppose first of all that we have universal suffrage,
as in America, and that everybody, *chamars* and all, have
votes. And first suppose that all the Mohammedan electors vote
for a Mohammedan member and all Hindu electors for a Hindu
member, and now count how many votes the Mohammedan

members have and how many the Hindu. It is certain the Hindu members will have four times as many because their population is four times as numerous. Therefore, we can prove by mathematics that there will be four votes for the Hindu to every one vote for the Mohammedan. And now how can the Mohammedan guard his interests? It would be like a game of dice, in which one man had four dice and the other only one. In the second place, suppose that the electorate be limited. Some method of qualification must be made; for example, that people with a certain income shall be electors. Now, I ask you, O Mohammedans! Weep at your condition! Have you such wealth that you can compete with the Hindus?. . . . (209-10)

Now, we will suppose a third kind of election. Suppose a rule to be made that a suitable number of Mohammedans and a suitable number of Hindus are to be chosen. I am aghast when I think on what grounds this number is likely to be determined. Of necessity proportion to total population will be taken. So there will be one member for us to every four for the Hindus. *NO* other condition can be laid down. Then they will have four votes and we shall have one. Now I will make a fourth supposition. Leaving aside the question as to the suitability of members with regard to population, let us suppose that a rule is laid down that half the members are to be Mohammedan and half Hindu, and that the Mohammedans and Hindus are each to elect their own men. Now, I ask you to pardon me for saying something which I say with a sore heart. In the whole nation there is no person who is equal to the Hindus in fitness for the work. . . . (210-11)

And show me the man who, when elected, will leave his business and undertake the expense of living in Calcutta and Shimla, leaving alone trouble of the journeys. Tell me who there is of our nation in the Punjab, Oudh, and North-Western Provinces, who will leave his business, incur these expenses, and attend the Viceroy's Council for the sake of his countrymen. When this is the condition of your nation, is it expedient for you to take part in this business on the absurd supposition that the demands of the Congress would, if granted, be beneficial for the country? Spurn such foolish notions....(211)

For the same reasons competitive examinations for posts in
government must be fought: Indians are not one nation; the
different nations in India are not at par, Muslims being unable to
compete on equal terms with Hindus; competition would place
posts in the hands of persons – the Bengalis, those from the lower
social strata – who are not fit to rule. The arguments and invective
are worth reading at some length:

What is the result of competitive examination in England? You
know that men of all social positions, sons of Dukes and Earls,
of *darzies* and people of low rank, are equally allowed to pass
this examination. Men both of high and low family come to
India in the Civil Service. And it is the universal belief that it
is not expedient for Government to bring the men of low rank;
and that the men of good social position treat Indian gentlemen
with becoming politeness, maintain the prestige of the British
race, and impress on the hearts of the people a sense of British
justice; and are useful both to Government and to the country.
But those who come from England, come from a country so far
removed from our eyes that we do not know whether they are
the sons of Lords and Dukes or of *darzies*, and, therefore, if
those who govern us are of humble rank, we cannot perceive
the fact. But as regards Indians, the case is different. Men of
good family would never like to trust their lives and property
to people of low rank with whose humble origin they are well
acquainted (Cheers). . . . (207-8)

The third case is that of a country in which there are different
nationalities which are on an equal footing as regards the competition, whether they take advantage of it or not. Now, I ask
you, have Mohammedans attained to such a position as regards
higher English education, which is necessary for higher appointments, as to put them on a level with Hindus or not? Most
certainly not. Now, take Mohammedans and the Hindus of our
Province together, and ask whether they are able to compete
with the Bengalis or not? Most certainly not. When this is the
case, how can competitive examination be introduced into our
country? (Cheers). Think for a moment what would be the
result if all appointments were given by competitive examina-

tion. Over all races, not only over Mohammedans but over Rajas of high position and the brave Rajputs who have not forgotten the swords of their ancestors, would be placed as ruler a Bengali who at sight of a table knife would crawl under his chair (Uproarious cheers and laughter). There would remain no part of the country in which we should see at the tables of justice and authority any face except those of Bengalis. I am delighted to see the Bengalis making progress, but the question is – What would be the result on the administration of the country? Do you think that the Rajput and the fiery Pathan, who are not afraid of being hanged or of encountering the swords of the police or the bayonets of the army, could remain in peace under the Bengalis? (Cheers). This would be the outcome of the proposal if accepted. Therefore if any of you – men of good position, *Raises*, men of the middle classes, men of noble family to whom God has given sentiments of honour – if you accept that the country should groan under the yoke of Bengali rule and its people lick the Bengali shoes, then, in the name of God jump into the train, sit down, and be off to Madras, be off to Madras! (Loud cheers and laughter). . . . (208-9)

6. Sir Syed pressed the argument further. It isn't just that proposals like representation, elections etc. would ruin the Muslims. The proposals are 'monstrous' (186), 'unrealisable and impossible' (211), they are 'sheer nonsense' (211), for other reasons too.

First of all, as a conquered people we have no right, Sir Syed says, to representative government or to being put in sensitive posts; the Empire has to be maintained, and the rulers cannot trust Indians with confidential matters:

When it has been settled that the English Government is necessary, then it is useful for India that its rule should be established on the firmest possible basis. And it is desirable for government that for its stability it should maintain an army of such a size as it may think expedient, with a proper equipment of officers; and that it should in every district appoint officials in whom it can place complete confidence, in order that if a conspiracy arises in any place they may apply the remedy. I ask you, is it the duty of Government or not to appoint European officers in its Empire to stop conspiracies and rebellions? Be just, and examine your hearts, and tell me if it is not a natural law that people should confide more in men of their own nation. If any Englishman tells you anything which is true, you remain doubtful. But when a man of your nation, or your family, tells you a thing privately in your house, you believe it at once. What reason can you then give why Government, in the administration of so big an empire, should not appoint as custodians of secrets and as givers of every kind of information, men of her own nationality, but must leave all these matters to you, and say: "Do what you like"? These things which I have said are such necessary matters of State administration that, whatever nation may be holding the Empire, they cannot be left out of sight. It is the business of a good and just Government, after having secured the above mentioned essentials, to give honour to the people of the land over which it rules, and to give them as high appointments as it can. But, in reality, there are certain appointments to which we can claim no right; we cannot claim the post of head executive authority in any *zila*. There are hundreds of secrets which Government cannot disclose. If Government appoint us to such responsible and confidential posts, it is her favour. . . . (189-90)

And again:

O brothers! I have fought the Government in the harshest language about these points. The time is, however, coming when my brothers, Pathans, Syeds, Hashimi and Koreishi, whose blood smells of the blood of Abraham, will appear in glittering uniform as Colonels and Majors in the army. But we must wait for that time. Government will most certainly attend to it; provided you do not give rise to suspicions of disloyalty. O brothers! Government, too, is under some difficulties as regards this last charge I have brought against her. Until she can trust us as she can her white soldiers she cannot do it. But we ought to give proof that whatever we were in former days, that time has gone, and that now we are as well-disposed to her as Highlanders of Scotland. And then we should claim this from Government. . . . (215)

Not just that. Decisions in Government require knowledge of

the subjects. Indians do not have it. So they should not ask for, nor should they be given a say in crucial matters like determining provisions of the Budget. Sir Syed takes the example of expenditures on the armed forces.

The Empire has to be maintained on the firmest possible basis, he says (189-90, 206). This requires an army. Indians know nothing about modern weapons and formations. Hence they should not ask for and should not be given the right to deliberate over allocations for the armed forces:

I come now to some other proposals of the Congress. We have now a very charming suggestion. These people wish to have the Budget of India submitted to them for sanction. Leave aside political expenses; but ask our opinion about the expenses of the army. Why on earth has Government made so big an army? Why have you put Governors in Bombay and Madras? Pack them off at once. I am also of the opinion that their ideas should certainly be carried out. I only ask them to say who, not only of them but of the whole people of India, can tell me about the new kinds of cannon which have been invented – which is the mouth and which the butt end? Can anyone tell me the expense of firing a shot? Does anyone understand the condition of the army? One who has seen the battlefield, the hail-shower of shots, the falling of the brave soldiers one over another, may know what equipments are needed for an army. If then, under these circumstances, a Mohammedan were on this Council, or a Bengali – one of the nation which in learning is the crown of all Indian nations, which has raised itself by the might of learning from a low to a high position – how could he give any advice? How ridiculous then for those who have never seen a battlefield, or even the mouth of a cannon, to want to prepare the Budget for the army?. . . (214)

Now, the Muslims, Sir Syed says repeatedly, will understand all this, not these 'Bengalis', because we Muslims have ourselves ruled an Empire and these Bengalis have never done so:

The English have conquered India and all of us along with it. And just as we made the country obedient and our slave, so the English have done with us. Is it then consonant with the principles of Empire that they should ask us whether they should fight Burma or not? Is it consistent with any principle of Empire? In the times of the Mohammedan Empire, would it have been consistent with the principles of rule that, when the Emperor was about to make war on a Province of India, he should have asked his subject-peoples whether he should conquer that country or not? Whom should he have asked? Should he have asked those whom he had conquered and had made slaves, and whose brothers he also wanted to make his slaves? Our nation has itself wielded Empire, and people of our nation are even now ruling. Is there any principle of Empire by which rule over foreign races may be maintained in this manner?. . . (187)

And again:

The aspirations of our friends the Bengalis have made such progress that they want to scale a height to which it is beyond their powers to attain. But if I am not in error, I believe that the Bengalis have never at any period held sway over a particle of land. They are altogether ignorant of the method by which a foreign race can maintain its rule over other races. Therefore, reflect on the doings of your ancestors, and be not unjust to the British Government to whom God has given the rule of India; and look honestly and see what is necessary for it to do to maintain its Empire and its hold on the country. You can appreciate these matters; but they cannot who have never held a country in their hands nor won a victory. O, my brother Mussalmans! I again remind you that you have ruled nations, and have for centuries held different countries in your grasp. For seven hundred years in India you have had Imperial sway. You know what it is to rule. Be not unjust to that nation which is ruling over you, and think also on this: how upright is her rule. Of such benevolence as the English Government shows to the foreign nations under her, there is no example in the history of the world. See what freedom she has given in her laws and how careful she is to protect the rights of her subjects. . . . (191)

7. The last passage takes us to one of the principal premises of Sir Syed's worldview – namely, that 'the British rule in India is the

most wonderful phenomenon the world has ever seen' (125).

Pre-British India was just 'mitigated slavery', he says, in which the people groaned under the 'tyranny and oppression' of 'despotic governments' conducted on the 'arbitrary will. . . . caprices, or . . passions' of rulers marked for their 'vice, tyranny and self-seeking'.

It was then that God willed to set things right:

After this long period of what was but mitigated slavery, it was ordained by a higher power than any on earth, that the destinies of India should be placed in the hands of an enlightened nation, whose principles of government were in accordance with those of intellect, justice, and reason. Yes, my friends, the great God above, He who is equally the God of the Jew, the Hindu, the Christian, and the Mohammedan, placed the British over the people of India – gave them rational laws (and no religious laws revealed to us by God can be at variance with rational laws), gave you, up to the year 1858, the Government of the East India Company. The rule of that now defunct body of merchant princes was one eminent for justice and moderation, both in temporal and religious matters. The only point in which it failed to satisfy the wants of the age latterly, was the fact of its not being a regal Government, a necessity which had gradually forced itself more prominently into notice as time rolled on, when the once solitary factory on the banks of the Ganges had grown into an Empire half as large as Europe, with a population of nearly two hundred millions. . . . (117)

And this lacuna the Proclamation of Queen Victoria as the Empress of India had at last removed.

'. . .it is [the Muslims'] happy fortune,' he writes, three years after 1857, 'to live beneath the shadow of a great and righteous Government, ever ready to be gracious unto their obedient and dutiful subjects, by extending to them protection and patronage' (37-8).

'Without doubt Government is itself anxious for the progress of the people in India,' he writes, opposing the Congress proposals for reform. 'If the present state of things be compared with that at the commencement of British Rule then the advancement that the British Government has given to the people of India is really astonishing, and it is still inclined in the same way to give them further advancement, and is giving what it thinks expedient, and will continue to give. . . .' (104)

Writing precisely at a time when British rule was turning racialist, Sir Syed assures us repeatedly that Her Most Gracious Majesty, Queen Victoria wishes all her subjects irrespective of their religion, tribe or colour to be treated equally (114-5).

Even as British rule had destroyed education in India, Sir Syed proclaims, 'It will not be out of place to express in a public manner the profound gratitude which we feel for the great attention which the English Government in India has paid to the education of our countrymen. It is, indeed, only doing justice to our feelings when we say that never before in the history of the world has one nation so striven to raise the moral and intellectual state of another' (123). 'We should be thankful,' he says, 'to our government that besides protection, it has also given us such help in the educational sphere. There happens to be no government which would have done so much for the education of its subjects' (172).

'The British rule in India,' he says,

is the most wonderful phenomenon the world has ever seen. That a race living in a distant region, differing from us in language, in manners, in religion – in short, in all that distinguishes the inhabitants of one country from those of another – should triumph over the barriers which nature has placed in its way, and unite under one sceptre the various peoples of this vast continent, is in itself wonderful enough. But that they, who have thus become the masters of the soil, should rule its inhabitants, not with those feelings and motives which inspired the conquerors of the ancient world, but should make it the first principle of their government to advance the happiness of the millions of a subject race, by establishing peace, by administering justice, by spreading education, by introducing the comforts of life which modern civilisation has bestowed upon mankind, is to us a manifestation of the hand of Providence, and an assurance of long life to the union of India with England. . . . (125-6)

The amendment in the Criminal Procedure Code, he says, is actuated by considerations of a higher order than even administrative expediency. I allude to those noble principles of freedom, justice, and humanity which have their home nowhere as much as in the bosoms of the nation which first came forward to release the slave from his thraldom; which first announced to the people of India that in matters of constitutional rights, distinctions of race and creed should have no place in the eye of the law. Never in the history of the world has a nation been called upon to act up to its principles more than the British in India. The removal of disabilities under which certain sections of the community laboured in England in regard to constitutional rights sinks almost into insignificance in comparison to what England has already done in India. The history of Indian legislation is the history of steady progress, of well-considered reforms, of a gradual and cautious development of the noble principle that between British subjects the distinctions of race, colour or creed shall make no difference in legal rights; that whilst, on the one hand, the British rule enforces submission, and expects loyalty and devotion from the people of India; on the other hand, it accords to them rights and privileges of equality with the dominant race. My Lord, I am convinced that it is on account of these noble principles, remarkable alike for their justice and their wisdom, that the British rule has founded itself upon the hearts and affections of the people − a foundation far more firm than any which the military achievements of ancient conquerors could furnish for the domination of one race over another. . . . (169)

The British Government is sensitive and responsive to public needs, to public opinion, he says. He therefore opposes the ways of the Congress as,

taking all these things into account I cannot but think that there is no requirement of the country that cannot be brought to the notice of Government. And nothing can prevent our expressing our views on the subject and being heard by Government. So that whatever comfort we can experience under any Government, we have under the British Government (Cheers) (206-7).

8. Apart from its general beneficence, the British Government, Sir Syed reminds his co-religionists repeatedly, is particularly well disposed towards the Muslims. Thus he writes:

> The actuating and promoting influences of the Rebellion have been deeply probed by the Authorities, and the result of the most careful and searching enquiries has not led our enlightened and benevolent Rulers to endorse the hastily formed opinions put forth by our detractors. When therefore the Government are on the side of the Mohammedans, wherefore should they feel any concern at the reports, that have been circulated to their prejudice, by the newspapers, and the authors of the works above alluded to?. . . . (237)

Writing about the 1857 uprising he says:

> When I say that Government are on the side of the Mohammedans, I do not say so unadvisedly, for the most conclusive evidence of the fact may be seen in the rewards which, with a liberal hand, have been bestowed upon all loyal Mohammedans, in the shape of titles, endowments of land, pensions and promotions. This being the case it cannot be said that Mohammedans have nothing to be proud of, or no reason to be grateful. And yet the loyalty and good services of Mohammedans are rarely alluded to in the newspapers, while the writers on the Mutiny seem to have ignored them altogether. . . . (37)

In the Address presented to the Viceroy on behalf of the Foundation Committee of the Anglo-Oriental College, he says:

> We, the Mussulman subjects of Her Imperial Majesty, consider ourselves more particularly bound in gratitude to the Government of India for its having of late years shown so strong a disposition to advance the cause of education amongst our community, and for issuing directions to the provincial Governments to adopt special measures to supply our intellectual needs. That we have not availed ourselves so fully as we might of the education offered by the State, is due to a variety of causes. . . . (124)

On the other side the Hindus , in particular the Bengalis, are getting together, Sir Syed reminds Muslims. For this reason too, he counsels Muslims to make common cause with the Government and the 'Christians' – a word he often uses as a synonym for the British rulers. In a typical exhortation he puts the case thus:

I do not think the Bengali politics useful for my brother Mussalmans. Our Hindu brothers of these Provinces are leaving us and are joining the Bengalis. Then we ought to unite with that nation with whom we can unite. No Mohammedan can say that the English are not "people of the Book." No Mohammedan can deny this: that God has said that no people of other religions can be friends of Mohammedans except the Christians. He who has read the Koran and believes it, he can know that our nation cannot expect friendship and affection from any other people. ('Thou shalt surely find the most violent of all men in enmity against the true believers to be the Jews and the idolators: and thou shalt surely find those among them to be the most inclinable to entertain friendship for the true believers, who say "we are Christians."' Koran, Chap. V.) At this time our nation is in a bad state as regards education and wealth, but God has given us the light of religion, and the Koran is present for our guidance, which has ordained them and us to be friends. Now God has made them rulers over us. Therefore we should cultivate friendship with them, and should adopt that method by which their rule may remain permanent and firm in India, and may not pass into the hands of the Bengalis. This is our true friendship with our Christian rulers, and we should not join those people who wish to see us thrown into a ditch. If we join the political movement of the Bengalis our nation will reap loss, for we do not want to become subjects of the Hindus instead of the subjects of the "people of the Book." And as far as we can we should remain faithful to the English Government. By this my meaning is not that I am inclined towards their religion. Perhaps no one has written such severe books as I have against their religion, of which I am an enemy. But whatever their religion, God has called men of that religion our friends. We ought not on account of their religion but because of the order of God to be friendly and faithful to them. If our Hindu brothers of these Provinces, and the Bengalis of

Bengal, and the Brahmans of Bombay, and the Hindu Madrasis
of Madras wish to separate themselves from us, let them go, and
trouble yourself about it not one whit. We can mix with the
English in a social way. We can eat with them, they can eat with
us. Whatever hope we have of progress is from them. The
Bengalis can in no way assist our progress. And when the
Koran itself directs us to be friends with them, then there is no
reason why we should not be their friends. But it is necessary
for us to act as God has said. Besides this, God has made them
rulers over us. Our Prophet has said that if God places over you
a black negro slave as ruler you must obey him. See, there is
here in the meeting a European, Mr. Beck. He is not black. He
is very white (Laughter). Then why should we not be obedient
and faithful to those white-faced men whom God has put over
us and why should we disobey the order of God?. . . (192-3)

9. He resorts to this passage of the Quran repeatedly to urge that
Muslims are liable to find the Christians to be their best friends;
on occasion he seems to suggest that they will find the Christians
alone to be their friends.

Dispelling 'unfounded reports' three years after the 1857
uprising he writes:

Among such unfounded reports was this: that the Mohammedans are, by the tenets of their religion, necessarily hostile
to the professors of the Gospel of Christ; whereas indeed the
very reverse of this is the fact, for Mohammedanism admits that
there is no sect upon earth but the Christians with whom its
people may maintain amity and friendship.
"Thou shalt surely find the most violent of all men in enmity
against the true believers to be the Jews and the idolators, and
thou shalt surely find those among them to be the most
inclinable to entertain friendship for the true believers, who
say, 'we are Christians.' This cometh to pass because there are
priests and monks among them and because they are not elated
with pride". . . . (39)

And he cites incidents such as the decision of some of the
Prophet's followers to seek refuge in Ethiopia, the promise of Allah
upon seeing the Muslims depressed at the defeat of the (Christian)

Greeks by the Persians, that He would now grant victory to the
former – Sir Syed cites such incidents to prove that amity between
Christians and Muslims is what has been ordained by God and what
has indeed prevailed through the ages (39-40, 42, 81).

As for the English, it isn't just that they are Christians. Sir Syed
recalls history:

> Gentlemen – Our desire that there should exist sympathy
> between the Mohammedan and the English nation is by no
> means an odd one. There never has been a time when there
> might have happened any occurrence between the Moham-
> medans and the English nation which could lead to any ground
> for unpleasant feeling or enmity between ourselves and the
> English people, or which could inspire them with a revengeful
> feeling, or which could make us feel any way jealous of their
> increasing prosperity. The English people mostly held aloof
> even of the Crusades which happened at a time which was
> productive of all sorts of ill-feeling. . . . (177)

It isn't just that God has ordained friendship, and that such
friendship has prevailed through history; God Himself has now
willed that the rulership of India should be taken over by the
British:

> You can gain nothing this way. God has made them your rulers.
> This is the will of God. We should be content with the will of
> God. And, in obedience to the will of God you should remain
> friendly and faithful to them. Do not do this: bring false
> accusations against them and give birth to enmity. This is
> neither wisdom nor in accordance with our holy religion.
> Therefore the method we ought to adopt is this, that we should
> hold ourselves aloof from this political uproar and reflect on
> our condition, that we are behindhand in education and are
> deficient in wealth. Then we should try to improve the
> education of our nation. Now our condition is this, that the
> Hindus, if they wish, can ruin us in an hour. The internal trade
> is entirely in their hands.... (194)

10. This being his view, Sir Syed goes very, very far in reading
meanings into events in Islamic history; in confining fundamental

institutions like the Caliphate to a narrow pen; in overturning concepts fundamental to Islamic conduct like *Dar-ul-Islam* and *Dar-ul-Harb*; he goes very far in reading meaning into verses of the Quran itself.

Each of these exercises has two objectives, and two alone: to convince the Muslims that they must serve and strengthen British rule in India; and to convince the British rulers that the Muslims are indeed loyal to, that they cannot but be loyal to, that they are indeed serving British rule in India.

There was the apprehension among Britishers, specially after the rise of Shah Waliullah's Wahabi movement, that the Muslims would rather obey some Muslim ruler elsewhere — for instance, the Caliph — than the British Government. Sir Syed argues strenuously that under Islam the Caliph is just the Sultan of the country over which he rules, that Muslims who are not directly under his rule are not obliged by religion to be loyal to him or to obey him in any way.

This is specially so in the case of Muslims in India, he says, because the British government has allowed them full freedom to practise their faith, and to propagate it. In a typical passage on the matter he says:

We, the Mohammedans of India, are the subjects of the British Government under whose protection we live. The Government has given us peace and allowed us all freedom in religious matters. Although our English rulers profess the faith of Christ yet the Government presents no difficulties to a Christian who comes to Mohammedanism, as it does not prevent Mohammedans becoming Christians. The Christian Missionaries have nothing to do with the Government. As they are wandering about preaching their religion so are hundreds of Mohammedans delivering public sermons on Islam. If a Mohammedan becomes a Christian, there is, on the other hand, always some Christian converted to Islam. So that the English Government has given to us Mohammedans who live as subjects under their protection, enough liberties in matters of faith. Over and above that, under the English Government our lives and property are safe and we enjoy all the rights concerning matrimony, divorce, inheritance and wills, gifts and endowments which Mohammedan law allows us, even when Christian Judges have to decide upon them, because Christian Judges are obliged to decide according to the law of Islam; so it is our religious duty to remain faithful to and well-wishers of the English Government and not to do or say anything practically or theoretically inconsistent with our loyalty and goodwill to that Government. . . . (256-7)

The same Sir Syed who warns the Congress and its sympathisers that should they press their proposals for representation, for democratisation, 'then our Musalman brothers, the Pathans, would come out as a swarm of locusts from their mountain valleys, and make rivers of blood to flow from their frontier on the north to the extreme end of Bengal', (185; similarly, 215, 220) – the same Sir Syed argues emphatically that in a war between a Muslim country and the British government the Muslims are bound by their religion to remain loyal to the latter. He writes:

The true and sound principle of the faith of Islam is that those Mohammedans who live under the protection of a non-Mohammedan sovereign as his subjects are not allowed by their religion to intrigue or to spread rebellion at any time against him. Further, in the event of a war between non-Mohammedan and Mohammedan sovereigns, the Mohammedan subjects living under the protection of the former are strictly prohibited by their religion to side with the latter or to assist him in any way. Moreover, it should be borne in mind that the wars of the present day, though they are waged between Mohammedans themselves or between non-Mohammedans, or between Mohammedans and non-Mohammedans, cannot be taken as the wars of religion or Crusades, because they are not undertaken with religious motives; but they are entirely based upon political matters and have nothing to do with Islamic or religious wars. . . . (254)

True, Islam asks that the faithful rest not till they have converted the *Dar-ul-Har*b, the Land of War, into the *Dar-ul-Islam,* the Land of Islam, the faith which is synonymous with peace, but in fact war is not to be waged, Sir Syed says, as India is in the twilight zone in which Islam does not require its followers to wage war:

It is a great mistake to suppose that the country can only be either a *Dar-ul-Islam* or a *Dar-ul-Harb* in the primary signification of the words, and that there is no intermediate position. A true *Dar-ul-Islam* is a country which under no circumstances can be termed a *Dar-ul-Harb*, and *vice versa*. There are, however, certain countries which, with reference to certain circumstances, can be termed *Dar-ul-Islam* and with reference to others *Dar-ul-Harb*. Such a country is India at the present moment. . . . (79-80)

It isn't just in circumstances such as those prevalent in India that the faithful are not required to wage *Jihad*; Sir Syed asserts repeatedly that they are required *not* to wage war. *Jihad* is just not conceivable, he says:

And, further a *Jihad*, according to the principles of Mohammedan faith, really cannot take place under the present regime! The reason is that the Mohammedans are living under the protection of their European rulers, and the protected cannot make a Crusade against their protectors.

The British have obtained domination in Hindoostan by two models *viz.*, by conquest and by cession. In either case, the Mohammedans have, as a natural consequence, become their subjects, and enjoy peace and protection under their administration, while the Government reposes confidence in their loyalty and submission. How then could the Mohammedans rise against the Government in a *Jihad*, when the very first condition of a religious war is that there should not subsist the relations of protected and protectors between the Crusaders, and those against whom the Crusade is undertaken? This point is distinctly laid down and enforced in the book of *Alumgeeree*, in which the author says that there are two indispensable requisites to a *Jihad* – first, that there be no *ummun* or protection, and secondly, that there be no treaty or engagement between the parties. . . (44)

In the *Hedaya* it is written that *Mustemun*, i.e. protected, is a term applied to those who live in peace and security under a Government professing a different creed. This is precisely the case with us who abide under the protecting arm of the British. Again, it is stated in the *Hedaya* and *Alumgeeree* that when a Mohammedan enjoys protection and security under the rule of a nation not of his own faith, it is in highest degree infamous if, from a professedly religious motive, he commits any outrage upon the person or property of those by whom he is governed. Our law provides that when we on our own motion desire to elect a King to reign over us, he must be a professor of our faith, and be taken from the tribe of Koreish. But if any man raises himself to supreme power by force of arms, it is by no means a *sine qua non* that he should be a believer in the Prophet and this of course implies that Mohammedans are enjoined to obey faithfully the ruler under whose dominion they may happen to dwell, be his creed what it may. In two of our religious books, entitled *"Tatarkhanee"* and *"Mooltugil"*, it is also written, that it is not at all essential that the King of the country in which Mohammedans reside, and by whom they are protected, should be Mohammedan.

The precedent for this is found in the *Touret*, or Book of Moses, where it is recorded, that Joseph served Potiphar, King of Egypt, and was obedient and faithful to him in all things, although Potiphar was not a Jew – (see Genesis ch. XXXIX). In like manner the Mohamedans dwell in obedience to the laws and Government of the British, who extend to them the canopy of their protection; and this obedience is nothing more than the proper and bounden duty of their Mohammedan subjects, as inculcated and enforced by the precepts of our religion. . . . (45)

The test is that under the British Muslims have full freedom to practise and preach their faith:

It is evident that as long as Musalmans can preach the unity of God in perfect peace, no Musalman can, according to his religion, wage war against the rulers of that country, of whatever creed they be. Next to the Holy Koran, the most authoritative and favourite works of the Wahabis are *'Bokhari'* and *'Muslim'*, and both of them say: "When our Prophet, Mohammed, marched against any infidel people to wage holy war upon them, he stopped the commencement of hostilities till morning, in order to find out whether the *azan* (call for prayer)

was being called in the adjacent country. If so, he never fought
with its inhabitants.'' His motive for this was, that from hearing
the *azan* he (the Prophet) could at once ascertain whether the
Moslems of the place could discharge their religious duties and
ceremonies openly and without molestation. Now, we Mohammedans of India live in this country with every sort of religious
liberty; we discharge the duties of our faith with perfect
freedom; we read our *azans* as loud as we wish; we can preach
our faith on the public roads and thoroughfares as freely as
Christian missionaries preach theirs; we fearlessly write and
publish our answers to the charges laid against Islam by the
Christian clergy, and even publish works against the Christian
faith; and last, though not least, we make converts of Christians
to Islam without fear of prohibition. . . . (81)

But, as usual, Sir Syed stretches the point to an extreme.
He argues that even if the British were to abandon their neutrality
in matters of religion, the faithful would not be obliged to wage,
they would not be even justified in waging war against the
Government:

Now, although it is well known that the Government has not
hitherto opposed any obstacle to the free use and observance of
the ordinances of their religions by their subjects, and also that
it will not do so in the time to come, for the Queen in her
Proclamation has graciously given a guarantee to that effect;
yet, allowing for the sake of argument, that this neutrality were
violated, still even then the Mohammedans would not be
justified in rebelling against the Government. All that they
could do under such circumstances would be to expatriate
themselves.
In one of the commentaries on the Alkoran, called *Tufseer
Ahmudee*, it is written that if any person is debarred the
privilege of worshipping God in conformity with his education
and belief, by reason of the arbitrary edicts of tyrants or Kaffirs,
he is perfectly justified in withdrawing into another country,
under the Government of which he may be permitted that
liberty of conscience, which was despotically denied to him in
the land of his birth or adoption. . . . (46)

But, then, what about all those who rose against British rule during 1857? Were they wrong in assuming or being told that they were waging a religious war? Most certainly, says Sir Syed again and again. They were a handful of '*badmaashes*', he says, they were just murderers and traitors, he says.

As he puts it:

Be it known however that I am no advocate of those Moham-medans who behaved undutifully, and joined in the Rebellion; on the contrary I hold their conduct in utter abhorrence, as being in the highest degree criminal, and wholly inexcusable; because at that momentous crisis it was imperatively their duty, a duty enjoined by the precepts of our religion, to identify themselves heartily with the Christians and to espouse their cause; seeing that they have, like ourselves, been favoured with a revelation from Heaven, and believe in the Prophets, and hold scared the word of God in His holy book, which is also an object of faith with us. It was therefore needful and proper, that where the blood of Christians was spilt, there should also have mingled with it that of Mohammedans; and those who shrunk from manifesting such devotedness, and sided with the rebels wilfully disobeyed the injunctions of religion, besides proving themselves ungrateful to their salt, and thereby incur-ring the severe displeasure of Government, a fact that is patent to every peasant. . . . (36)

And those who aroused the people by virtue of being Moulvies, he says, were not men of religion at all:

Among the scum of the people who were upheaved to the surface amidst the convulsions into which the country was thrown, it is remarkable how many there were who were styled Moulvies; and yet they were merely ignorant and besotted scoundrels; who had no just claim to the appellation, which may have been given to them by courtesy only, because some of their ancestors may have been Moulvies. The fellows were alluded to in the public prints as really what they professed to be, and having assumed high-sounding and inflated names to give themselves the prestige of learned Moulvies and holy Fuqeers, it was natural that the authorities should be misled into

the belief that men of note and influence were implicated in
the rebellion, as its promoters and leaders. The fact is,
however, that not one of these individuals was looked up to as
a Pastor or spiritual guide; on the contrary, they were of no
repute whatever, and were heartily despised by all good
Mohammedans, who had penetrated the character of these low-
bred pseudo-Moulvies. Those who were really learned and
pious Moulvies and Durveshes kept aloof, and did not pollute
themselves by the smallest degree of complicity in the rebellion, which they utterly denounced and condemned as infamous
and criminal in the extreme. With one solitary exception I do
not find that any learned and influential Moulvie took an active
part in the rebellion. I know not what possessed him to act in
the way he did, but his understanding must have been warped;
and we know that "to err is human". . . . (42-3)

'Is it then not astounding', Sir Syed asks,

is it not incredible, that the gentlemen who have enlightened
the world with their sapient views on the recent events, should
promulgate *ex-cathedra*, the dictum, that those abandoned,
merciless, treacherous, and low-lived wretches, who in demo-
niacal fury committed every species of revolting barbarity
during the rebellion against the children of the Book, let alone
Kaffirs, were actuated thereto by a zeal for the Mohammedan
religion, and were fulfilling its behests, when it has been
clearly shown that such brutal conduct is utterly and undenia-
bly at variance with, and altogether repugnant to, the tenets of
that faith! May the Lord defend us from such monstrous
calumnies. . . . (47)

But wasn't the uprising sparked by the use of pork grease in the
cartridges? Were the rebels not right in taking that to be a religious
cause? Did the British not lead the soldiers to unwittingly violate
Islam? Not at all, says Sir Syed. His gymnastics are truly worth
attention:

Now it is pretty generally known and acknowledged, that the
greased cartridges were the origin and cause of the mutinies;
it may therefore be pertinently asked, what harm could rest to

the religion of Mohammedans by biting those cartridges? It is written in our Scriptures that we may eat food with the children of the Book, and we cannot lawfully reject any animal food provided by them. It may be that hog's lard was used in the cartridges. What then? Could that have excluded us from the pale of salvation! It is written, that what things are not obviously unclean or vile, may be accepted as clean and pure; and it is absurd to say, that by the mere act of biting a cartridge, in the composition of which the fat of an unclean animal had been used, a Mohammedan must necessarily become an outcast from his faith! It would be a sin certainly, but one of a venial complexion when compared with those atrocities which have rendered infamous the memory of the events of the rebellion. "This day are ye allowed to eat such things as are good, and the food of those to whom the Scriptures were given is also allowed as lawful unto you, and your food is allowed as lawful unto them." (*Alkoran Soorut Amayda*, v. b.–Sales's Trans. Ch. V.)

In the *Abou Daood* it is stated upon the authority of Ibn Abbas, that we may partake of food upon which the blessing of God has been invoked; that is to say, we may eat the flesh of animals which have been slaughtered in the name of God, but not of those which have been sacrificed before idols. In other words, animals slaughtered by men of a nation to whom the light of revealed religion has been vouchsafed may be lawful food for us, and what we may kill is lawful food for them.

It is universally known, that our creed forbids the use of swine's flesh, and of wine, while Christians use both; yet our Prophet has said, that we may lawfully make use of vessels in which swine's flesh may have been dressed, or out of which wine may have been drunk, after cleansing them with water. It is recorded in *Abou Daood*, that Ubbee Salba Khushanee said to the Prophet, that he lived in the neighbourhood of other children of the Book, who were accustomed to feed upon the unclean animal, and he begged to be informed, for his own guidance, whether he could bring to his own use the vessels (i.e., vessels of clay) in which food of this nature had been boiled, or out of which wine had been imbibed. The Prophet answered that he might use such vessels after washing them, if others were not procurable. . . . (52-3)

It is only because they have stayed in India long and thereby 'adopted many of the usages peculiar to the Hindoos', says Sir Syed, that the Muslims have forgotten these teachings and have become hesitant, for instance, to eat food prepared by Christians (57-8).

But did not Shah Waliullah, the founder of the Wahabi movement, proclaim it as the religious duty of Muslims to rise in arms against the British? 'No,' says Sir Syed. Shah Waliullah advocated *Jihad* only against rulers who interfered with Islam, which the British do not. But whatever he taught, did the Wahabis not in fact wage *Jihad* against the British? Not at all, says Sir Syed: '. . . The Indian Wahabi *Jihad*. . . was intended solely for the conquest of the Sikhs; and that, even although the band of mutineers at Mulka and Sittana may have given trouble to Government after 1857, the frontier colony, composed as it was of Hindus as well as Mohammedans, was scarcely one which could be designated as a *Jihadi* community' (77).

11. Far from Muslims being hostile to British rule, far from their being jealous of the British for taking over the Empire which they – the Muslims – held, Sir Syed says, the Muslims fully realise that God has willed that rulership pass from them to the British. They accordingly welcome the assumption of power by the British. He puts the proposition with characteristic vigour:

> It is quite true that we have enjoyed the sovereignty of India for centuries, and it is also quite true that we can on no account forget the glories of our forefathers, but at the same time if any one is inclined to think that we Mohammedans are any way jealous of the English nation or the English Government, because of their having secured for themselves the sovereignty of India which was once enjoyed by our forefathers, then he is far from the fact and this thought of his is utterly groundless and unreasonable. The time when the British Rule established itself in India was a time when India was already left a poor widow and she stood in need of another husband, which husband she herself chose in the English nation in order to fulfil the commandment of the Gospel that "the twain shall be one flesh." But at this time, it would be almost needless to point out, how far the English nation has fulfilled that sacred promise. We contributed to the establishment of the British

Rule in India for the sake of our own prosperity. In the matter of the establishment of the British sovereignty in India we and the English nation are joined together like the two blades of a pair of scissors; no one could say which of the two blades contributed most towards it. Thus to entertain any idea that we Mohammedans look at the English Rule with an eye of disgust and disagreeableness would be utterly unsound and far from the truth. The English nation came into this conquered country of ours like a friend, not like a foe. It is our earnest desire that the English Rule in India should last not only for a long, long time but that it should be everlasting and eternal. This desire of ours is not for the sake of the English nation itself, but for the sake of our own country; it is not for the sake of flattering the English people but it is for the prosperity and welfare of our own country. Thus there is no reason to suppose that there should be no sympathy between them and ourselves. Gentlemen – by sympathy I do not mean political sympathy; political sympathy has no intrinsic value in itself just as the plated ware can boast of none over the copper one. The political sympathy produces no real effect on the minds of either party; one party knows it to be a copper ware while the other takes it for a plated one. What I mean by sympathy is true brotherly and friendly sympathy. . . . (177-8)

Again and again Sir Syed returns to this theme, that is to assure the British that the Muslims welcome the establishment of British rule and that they remain its most loyal supporters. Three years after the 1857 uprising, Sir Syed published his famous tract, *The Loyal Mohammedans of India*. Stating his object Sir Syed says that in view of the calumnies which were being entertained about the Muslims, that they had risen against the British,

It has appeared to me advisable to publish a series of narratives, setting forth the loyal acts done by this class of people, more especially by those in the service of Government, so far as they have come to my knowledge; and to each case will be appended a notice of the mode in which a gracious Government has been pleased to testify their recognition of those services in order that the fame of the discriminating justice and princely munificence of our paternal Government may be spread among all

classes of their subjects, and that the gratitude of Mohammedans may be thereby excited, and that they may be led to
emulate each other in the performance of all good and just
actions, being fully assured that it is their happy fortune to live
beneath the shadow of a great and righteous Government, ever
ready to be gracious unto their obedient and dutiful subjects,
by extending to them protection and patronage. . . . (37-8)

He has examined the evidence, he says, and 'one glorious fact'
stands out:

Some of the acts of the horrible Drama have already been
exposed, but as day by day all the particulars are gradually
brought to light, then, when the naked truth stands revealed,
then will this one glorious fact stand out in prominent relief,
and become patent to the universe that if in Hindoostan there
was one class of people above another, who, from the principles
of their religion, from habits and associations, and from kindred
disposition, were fast bound with Christians, in their dread hour
of trial and danger, in the bonds of amity and friendship, those
people were the *Mohammedans*, and they alone! – and then will
be effectually silenced the tongue of slander now so loud in
their condemnation. . . . (35)

And yet what are facts? The very opposite indeed of what the
mistaken popular opinion would show them to be; for I really
do not see that any class besides the Mohammedans displayed
so much single-minded and earnest devotion to the interests of
Government, or so willingly sacrificed reputation and status,
life and property, in their cause. It is an easy thing to make
empty professions of loyalty and service, and to write an
occasional bulletin of news, false or true, but it is to the
Mohammedans alone that the credit belongs of having stood
the staunch and unshaken friends of the Government amidst
that fearful tornado that devastated the country, and shook the
Empire to its centre; and who were ever ready heart and hand,
to render their aid to the utmost extremity, or cheerfully to
perish in the attempt, regardless of home and kindred, of life
and its enjoyments. . . . (36)

Accordingly, when the Congress begins its petitions, and we must remember that at that time Congress was nothing but a body of loyal petitioners, Sir Syed inveighs against it. He tells the British again and again, 'My nation, the Muslims, are not with the Congress.' (e.g., 103, 182-3). Indeed, his explanation for coming out so vehemently against the Congress is that some in it have made the 'false accusation' that 'my nation', the Muslims, are in sympathy with its demands (e.g., 106, 108).

12. Just as on the one hand he tries to convince the British that Muslims are loyal to British rule in India, on the other hand he exhorts the Muslims to be so very loyal that the British, far from having reason to doubt their loyalty, are not able to entertain even a suspicion about it. And he often holds up his own loyalty as an example to them:

> Here am I, a servant of Government speaking out plainly to you in this public meeting. My attachment to Government was proved, as many of you know, in the eventful year of the Mutiny. It is my firm conviction, one which I have invariably expressed both in public and in private, that the greater the confidence of the people of India in the Government, the more solid the foundation upon which the present Government rests, and the more mutual friendship is cultivated between your rulers and yourselves, the greater will be the future benefit to your country. Be loyal in your hearts, place every reliance upon your rulers, speak out openly, honestly, and respectfully all your grievances, hopes, and fears, and you may be quite sure that such a course of conduct will place you in the enjoyment of all your legitimate rights; and that this is compatible, nay, synonymous with true loyalty to the State, will be upheld by all whose opinion is worth having. . . . (120; see also, 211-2)

Inculcating such loyalty is among the principal objectives of founding the Anglo-Oriental College, he tells the Viceroy and his co-religionists:

> To make these facts clear to the minds of our countrymen; to educate them; so that they may be able to appreciate these

blessings; to dispel those illusory traditions of the past which have hindered our progress; to remove those prejudices which have hitherto exercised a baneful influence on our race; to reconcile oriental learning with Western literature and science; to inspire in the dreamy minds of the people of the East the practical energy which belongs to those of the West; to make the Mussalmans of India worthy and useful subjects of the British Crown; to inspire in them that loyalty which springs, not from servile submission to a foreign rule, but from genuine appreciation of the blessings of good government, – these are the objects which the founders of the College have prominently in view. . . . (126)

The Government will be wrong if it harbours suspicions about Muslims, he says, but Muslims must remember that it has reasonable ground for doing so:

We ought to consider carefully our circumstances and the circumstances of Government. If Government entertains unfavourable sentiments towards our community, then I say with the utmost force that these sentiments are entirely wrong. At the same time if we are just, we must admit that such sentiments would be by no means unnatural. I repeat it. If Government entertains these bad sentiments it is a sign of incompetence and folly. But I say this, we ought to consider whether Government can entertain such thoughts or not. Has she any excuse for such suspicions or not? I reply that she certainly has. Think for a moment who you are. What is this nation of ours? We are those who ruled India for six or seven hundred years (Cheers). From our hands the country was taken by Government into its own. Is it not natural then for Government to entertain such thoughts? Is Government so foolish as to suppose that in seventy years we have forgotten all our grandeur and our Empire? Although, should Government entertain such notions, she is certainly wrong, yet we must remember she has ample excuse. We do not live on fish; nor are we afraid of using a knife and fork lest we should cut our fingers (Cheers). Our nation is of the blood of those who made not only Arabia, but Asia and Europe, to tremble. It is our nation which conquered with its sword the whole of India, although its peoples were all of one religion (Cheers). I say again that if Government entertains suspicions of us it is wrong. But do her the justice to admit that there is a reasonable ground for such suspicions. Can a wise ruler forget what the state of things was so short a time ago? He can never forget it. If then the Mohammedans also join in these monstrous and unreasonable schemes, which are impossible of fulfilment, and which are disastrous for the country and for our nation, what will be the result? . . . . (212-3)

And so,

Our course of action should be such as to convince Government of the wrongness of her suspicions regarding us, if she entertains any. We should cultivate mutual affection. . . . (213)

13. It is but to be expected, then, that Sir Syed spends an enormous amount of his energy during the latter part of his life in fighting the Congress, even though the Congress is then in nothing but the incipient, loyally petitioning stage.

Everything about the Congress programme will ruin the Muslims, he says (132, 243). It will benefit only the Bengalis, Brahmins and Maharattas, he says (219).

The government is itself keen to usher in reforms, what it has already given the Indian people is 'astonishing'. It is sensitive to public opinion as well as the needs of the people (205-6). Therefore, there is no need for the Congress programme.

Worse, far from accomplishing anything, the Congress programme will delay reforms as 'the Sepoy Mutiny' of 1857 did, he proclaims repeatedly.

'If that Mutiny had not occurred,' he says, 'then hundreds of our young men of a soldierly temper would have been Volunteers; the Arms Act would not have been passed; many among us would have been Captains and Colonels, and Generals in the army; and we would have said to Government: "Do not trouble your European officers and British soldiers. See – we, and we alone, will advance beyond the Frontier, and will give the Russians a practical lesson how to advance and how to give fight" ' (104).

Moreover, apart from its being undesirable, the Congress programme just cannot succeed any more than the 'the Sepoy Mutiny'

(103-4). The Government will crush the Congress (211-2), and it will be more than justified in doing so (103, 105) as the programme and the proposals of the Congress are spreading disaffection among the people towards British rule, as they are endangering the peace, as they are sowing hostility between Hindus and Muslims (103-5, 212, 264).

He comes down heavily against Muslims who have begun to support the Congress, to attend its meetings. He pastes motives on them as well as on those who have persuaded them to join the Congress. He accuses the former of ignorance, of running after applause, after quick returns, of being 'induced to go [to the Congress meetings] either by pressure, or by folly, or by love of notoriety, or by poverty' (181, 182). The Hindus who have persuaded them to join he accuses of 'wrongly tampering with our nation', of putting pressure on them, of 'offering the temptation of money' (181-2). Some indeed, he charges, have a deeper, baser motive: 'Some Hindus – I do not speak of all the Hindus but only of some – think that by joining the Congress and by increasing the power of the Hindus they will perhaps be able to suppress those Mohammedan religious rites which are opposed to their own, and, by all uniting, annihilate them' (183).

He puts the blame as usual on the Hindus in general, and on the Bengalis in particular for thus way-laying the unsuspecting Muslims. And not just the Muslims. After characterising an attribution by Hume to him of a rumour, Sir Syed exclaims, 'I am at a loss to conceive how English gentlemen have adopted those qualities which Lord Macaulay has so eloquently described as characteristic of the Bengali' (251). He concludes:

I am grieved that Mr Hume should have thought me capable of such ideas – ideas which he would hardly attribute to the meanest and guiltiest of mankind. I can only account for it by remembering that he is also an old man, and that through his close intimacy with Bengalis his method of thought may well have been distorted into this most un-English character. . . . (252)

He therefore exhorts the Muslims to stay away from the Congress, to fight it, to join hands instead with the British rulers. Sometimes he urges this in the interests of the general peace and well-being of the country, disclaiming with vigour any parochial motive:

> That the Government will show special favour to those who oppose the Congress party is too ridiculous an opinion to be entertained by any man in his right sense, and if any one has joined the opposition with that end in view, that man, I do not hesitate to say, is a mean, contemptible wretch. Our desire to see the British Government firmly established in India is based upon our conviction that its strength and continuance are essential to the peace and well-being of the country, and the support we accord to our present rulers is entirely the outcome of our love for our own fellow countrymen. . . . (25)

At others he holds out to Muslims the advantages they will gain by helping put the Congress down:

> Therefore the method we ought to adopt is this, that we should hold ourselves aloof from this political uproar and reflect on our condition that we are behind hand in education and are deficient in wealth. Then we should try to improve the education of our nation. Now our condition is this, that the Hindus, if they wish, can ruin us in an hour. The internal trade is entirely in their hands. . . . (194)

> Never imagine that Government will put difficulties in your way in trade. But the acquisition of all these things depends on education. When you shall have fully acquired education, and true education shall have made its home in your hearts, then you will know what rights you can legitimately demand of the British Government. And the result of this will be that you will also obtain honourable position in the Government, and will acquire wealth in the higher ranks of trade. But to make friendship with the Bengalis in their mischievous political proposals, and join in them, can bring only harm. If my nation follows my advice they will draw benefit from trade and education. Otherwise, remember that Government will keep a very sharp eye on you because you are very quarrelsome, very brave, great soldiers and great fighters. . . . (194-5)

O brothers! I have fought the Government in the harshest language about these points. The time is, however, coming when my brothers, Pathans, Syeds, Hashimi and Koreishi, whose blood smells of the blood of Abraham, will appear in glittering uniform as Colonels and Majors in the army. But we must wait for that time. Government will most certainly attend to it; provided you do not give rise to suspicions of disloyalty. O brothers! Government, too, is under some difficulties as regards this last charge I have brought against her. Until she can trust us as she can her white soldiers she cannot do it. But we ought to give proof that, whatever we were in former days, that time has gone, and that now we are as well-disposed to her as the Highlanders of Scotland. And then we should claim this from Government. . . . (215)

On the other hand if Muslims join in demanding reforms, he says, *they* are the ones who will end up suffering more, not the Hindus:

Leaving this aside, it is not expedient that Mohammedans should take part in proceedings like that of the Congress, which holds meetings in various places in which people accuse Government before crowds of common men of withholding their rights from her subjects, and the result of which can only be that ignorant and foolish men will believe Government to be tyrannical or at least unjust. They will suffer greater misfortunes from doing so than the Hindus and the Bengalis. What took place in the Mutiny? The Hindus began it; the Mohammedans with their eager disposition rushed into it. The Hindus having bathed in the Ganges became as they were before. But the Mohammedans and all their noble families were ruined. This is the result which will befall Mohammedans from taking part in political agitation. . . . (243)

14. He proclaims therefore that 'the more anti-Congress associations be formed, whether Hindu or Mohammedan, the better' (248). He himself establishes 'The Indian Patriotic Association' to further the following objects:

(a) To publish and circulate pamphlets and other papers for

information of members of Parliament, English journals, and the people of Great Britain, in which those misstatements will be pointed out by which the supporters of the Indian National Congress have wrongfully attempted to convince the English people that all the nations of India and the Indian Chiefs and Rulers agree with the aims and objects of the National Congress.

(b) To inform members of Parliament and the newspapers of Great Britain and its people by the same means of the opinions of Mohammedans in general, of the Islamia Anjumans, and of those Hindus, and their Societies, which are opposed to the objects of the National Congress.

(c) To strive to preserve peace in India; and to strengthen the British rule; and to remove those bad feelings from the hearts of the Indian People, which the supporters of the Congress are stirring up throughout the country; and by which great dissatisfaction is being raised among the people against the British Government. . . . (107)

Looking forward to the continuing growth of the Anglo-Oriental College he says:

I am assured that you, who upon this occasion represent the British rule, have sympathies with our labours. And to me this assurance is very valuable, and a source of great happiness. At my time of life, it is a great comfort to me to feel that the undertaking which has been for many years, and is now, the sole object of my life, has roused on one hand the energies of my own countrymen, and on the other, it has won the sympathy of our British fellow-subjects, and the support of our rulers; so that when the few years I may still be spared are over, and when I shall be no longer amongst you, the College will still prosper and succeed in educating my countrymen to have the same affection for their country, the same feelings of loyalty for the British rule, the same appreciation of its blessings, the same sincerity of friendship with our British fellow-subjects as have been the ruling feeling of my life. (Cheers). . . (129)

15. And he warns Hindus in general and 'Congress-*wallahs*' in particular that should they persist in pressing their proposals,

proposals which are certain to reduce the Muslims to subjugation, the Muslims will take to arms, that the Pathans will come down upon them, that there will be a civil war:

> We also like a civil war. But not a civil war without arms; we like it with arms. If Government wants to give over the internal rule of the country from its own hands into those of the people of India, then we will present a petition that, before doing so, she pass a law of competitive examination, namely, that that nation which passes first in this competition be given the rule of the country; but that in this competition we be allowed to use the pen of our ancestors, which is in truth the true pen for writing the decrees of sovereignty. Then he who passes first in this shall rule the country. If my friends the Bengalis pass first, then indeed we will pick up their shoes and put them on our heads; but without such a civil war we do not want to subject our nation to be trodden under their feet. Let my Hindu fellow-countrymen and Bengali brothers understand well that my chief wish is that all the nations of India should live in peace and friendship with one another; but that friendship can last so long only as one does not try to put another in subjection. The Bengalis and also the educated Hindus of this Province have tried on this game, and hope that we Moham-medans will join them: "'tis imagination, 'tis impossible, 'tis madness.". . . . (220)

Conclusions

Contrast the propositions, and the prose and rhetoric urging them, with the image that we have been fed.

Nor has there been any difficulty in getting at the facts. Sir Syed's writings are available in plenty. Several Britishers wrote glowing accounts of him – eulogising him for his loyalty to the Empire and for the great services he rendered it. And several accounts of him have been published in Pakistan; in them he is eulogised as the progenitor of the two-nation theory and hence of the course which led eventually to Pakistan. Moreover, the littlest effort is all that is needed to show up the propositions around which Jinnah forged his politics as the isomorphs of what Sir Syed sowed – two irreconcilable nations, the British must continue till they can decree a solution congenial to the Muslims, the vehement denunciation of every proposal for democratisation, the threat of civil war.... The two were different, of course – Sir Syed was the Westerniser, Jinnah was the Westerner. But Jinnah's were but the *fleurs du mal* of seeds planted by Sir Syed.

All this is obvious. And yet we shut our eyes and mouths lest someone call us 'communal'. This is cowardice, not liberalism. And it foments illiberalism by the currency that it gives to leaders who would destroy the liberal society.

For liberalism to survive, we must at the least:

❏ Examine all the evidence;
❏ Examine it in minute detail; and
❏ Speak the whole truth.

And to do the latter we must deafen ourselves to abuse. We must not, as Mao would say, remain silent, we must not be evasive 'to save our skin', to avoid 'reprimands'. We must instead, as Mao said after the Lushan Conference, 'thicken our scalps, and bear it.'

– July 1989

VIII

The Pistol Jinnah Forged

'India is just a geographical entity, a mere composite of cultures, religions, nations. ' 'We are a separate nation and must have special rights as such.' 'Politics is for Religion, Religion is for Politics.' We hear these slogans every day. Often our leaders proclaim them merely because they have already exhausted the milder ones.

But, once introduced, the notions spread at lightning speed, and they acquire a life of their own: you cannot inflame followers over the years, and then switch them off one day. And these slogans and propositions have a logic of their own too – to the point of devouring the leaders and movements that proclaim them.

For instance, in his *A History of the Sikhs* Khushwant Singh recalls that the expression 'The Sikhs are a separate nation' was first used just forty years ago, in 1944, by Master Tara Singh. Even in the sixties just a couple of 'intellectuals' were using it. By 1973 it became the basic postulate of the Anandpur Sahib Resolution. In 1981 Longowal piloted a Resolution saying that the Sikhs are a separate nation and as such they must have special rights. Within a year, along with the assertions about Sikhs having been reduced to slavery, it became the basis of both Bhindranwale's speeches as well as the Akali *Dharmyudh*. An 'Accord' has now been signed. Commending it to his flock in Anandpur Sahib, Longowal had this to say: 'This[the Accord] is a victory for the *Panth*. This is an agreement signed not once but on each page. This is as good as a treaty between two countries. Not since the era of Maharaja Ranjit Singh has such an agreement taken place between Punjab and Hindustan.' And within weeks he was gunned down by the very persons who had been inflamed by that kind of rhetoric.

There are many differences between the 1940s and today, and

we will revert to the crucial one in a moment. The rhetoric of those days, the steps by which Jinnah and Muslim League advanced from one proposition to the next, do not therefore constitute a parallel. But they do provide a benchmark. All of us − Sikhs, Hindus, whatever, leaders as well as followers − should recall that terrible descent and internalise the lessons from it. For, as has been well said, those who fail to learn from history are condemned to repeat it.

Jinnah's Steps

As is well known, Jinnah had left India and settled down in England in 1930, convinced that there was little that he could do here. He returned in 1935 in response to the requests of several Muslim leaders and set about galvanising the Muslim League for the 1937 elections. The League did not do as well as its leaders had hoped: it got only 108 out of a total of 1,585 seats; even out of the 482 seats reserved exclusively for Muslims, its share came to less than a quarter.

Jinnah now set about to 'unify' the Muslims 'under one Allah, and behind one flag, one slogan, one leader,' to 'organise' the League so that it would become their sole spokesman, and, finally, to centralise authority within the League entirely in himself.

1. Henceforth his proposition was to be that the entity 'India' was an artificial construct, that it was a mere geographical entity, that the country as it existed was something 'artificial', something that was being maintained solely by the force of British arms. 'The present artificial unity of India dates back only to the British conquest,' he told the Muslim League Session at Lahore in March 1940 (the Session at which the 'Pakistan Resolution' was adopted) 'and is maintained by the British bayonet....'[1] 'It must be realised that India was never a country or a nation,' he told the League's 29th Session.'India's problem is international in this subcontinent and differences − cultural, social, political and economic − are so fundamental that they cannot be covered up, concealed or confused, but must by handled by all as realists....'[2] 'I have explained in great detail the fundamental and vital differences between the Hindus and the Muslims,' he told the League Legislators' Convention in Delhi. 'There never has been, for all these centuries, either social or political unity between these two

major nations. The Indian unity that we talk of up to today is held
by the British Government, and they have – by their ultimate
sanction of the police and the army – maintained peace and
law and order in this country....'[3]

2. The significant point about the Muslims, he began saying, was
not that they were a quarter of the population of the country, that
they were a minority.'It has always been taken for granted
mistakenly that the Muslims are a minority,'he told the Lahore
Session, 'and of course we have got used to it for a long time that
these settled notions sometimes are very difficult to remove. The
Musalmans are not a minority. The Muslamans are a nation by any
definition....' 'The Musalmans are not a minority, as it is
commonly known and understood....Musalmans are a nation
according to any definition of a nation, and they must have their
homelands, their territory and their State....'[4]

3. He maintained now that the Muslims and Hindus were not just
two different nations but two completely and irrevocably
opposed civilizations and therefore 'to yoke together two such
nations under a single State, one as a numerical minority and the
other as a majority, must lead to growing discontent and the final
destruction of any fabric that may be so built up for the
Government of such a State.'Meetings of the League would
henceforth be decorated by banners and posters proclaiming his
assertion:

> We are a nation of a hundred million, and what is more, we
> are a nation with our own distinctive culture and civilization,
> language and literature, art and architecture, names and no-
> menclature, sense of value and proportion, legal laws and
> moral codes, customs and calendar, history and tradition,
> aptitudes and ambitions, in short, we have our own distinctive
> outlook on life and of life. By all canons of International Law
> we are a nation.[5]

Language? Names and nomenclature? Sense of value and
proportion? Aptitudes? Ambitions? A 'nation' based on these? And
were they in fact different from the corresponding ones of the
Hindus? Assertion, incessant repetition were the argument.

The 'proofs' that were offered were often circular. The
Hindus and Muslims have never got along, they cannot get along

ever because they are fundamentally and irretrievable different. How do we know that they are fundamentally and irretrievably different? From the very fact, for one thing, said Jinnah, that they do not get along.[6]

4. As the Muslims were now taken to be a nation, and not a minority, he started saying, they must have a share in the apparatus of the State that was not merely proportionate to their share in the population — for that, remember, was no longer the significant fact about the Muslims — but one that would assure them a sense of security and honour. And the precise share that would assure them this sense of security and honour kept rising, of course.

Since the Minto-Morley Reforms of 1909 the Muslims had had separate electorates. Now Jinnah said that this was not sufficient at all. The Muslims — being a separate, and therefore an equal nation — must have complete parity with the Hindus. And they must have this parity not just, say, in the Viceroy's Council but in every part of the apparatus. Speaking in Madras in April 1941 at the 28th Session of the Muslim League, for instance, he declared that the only way in which the British could secure Muslim (i.e. the League's, i.e. Jinnah's) cooperation in the War effort was, first, to give 'a definite and categorical assurance to the Muslims of India that no interim or final Constitution will be adopted by the British Government without the consent and approval of Muslim India'; and, second, that the British Government be 'ready and willing to associate Muslim leadership as an equal partner in the Government, both at the Centre and in the Provinces. In all Provinces,'he said, 'Muslim leadership must be fully treated as an equal and with an equal share in the authority and control of the Government, Central and Provincial.' If the Congress came in, he said, Muslim representation must be equal to that of the Hindus in the Executive Council. 'Otherwise they (i.e. the Muslims, i.e. the League, i.e. his nominees) should have the majority of the additional numbers, as it is obvious that the main burden and responsibility will be borne by the Muslims in that case.' In the Provinces where Section 93 operated, he said, non-official advisers should be appointed, adding, 'The number should be fixed after discussion and the majority of the non-official advisers should be representatives of Muslims....'[7]

5. Soon enough, of course, even parity was not enough. He had

been maintaining, as we shall see, that the Congress represented merely the Hindus, but at least that it represented the Hindus. As he gathered speed, he began saying that the Congress represented the upper caste Hindus only. Thus, he now said, bodies such as the Executive Council and later the Interim Government must have representatives, not just of the League and the Congress but also – and separately – of the Scheduled Castes, of Sikhs, of Christians, of Parsis, etc. But as those latter representatives, though separate, were liable to side with the Congress in its quest of freedom for a united India, two further conditions must be satisfied in effect. First, the Muslim League, representing a separate nation, must have 50 per cent of the seats, and the remaining 50 per cent must be distributed among the rest – the high caste Hindus represented by the Congress, the Scheduled Castes, Sikhs, Christians, Parsis, etc; and, second, Jinnah, while having the exclusive right to nominate Muslims, of course, must also be consulted on who would represent the non-Congress groups in the latter lot.[8]

And all this followed straight from the twin propositions: the Muslims are a separate nation, a beleaguered one, and therefore things must be so arranged that they can have a sense of security and dignity.

Notice that this sense of dignity and security could not be assured by merely having 50 per cent of the appointments in hand. Jinnah demanded an equal share in the authority 'and control of the Government.' In practice this meant *a veto*. This was justified on the grounds that the Muslims – a separate nation – were in imminent and perpetual danger, and that mere representation in the offices of State could never be sufficient guarantee against the danger. Moreover, the scope of the subjects over which the Muslims (i.e. the Muslim League, i.e. Jinnah) must have a veto grew longer and longer. At first it seemed to be confined to 'communal subjects' – that is to subjects, e.g. laws, that directly affected one community or another. It was soon put out that in fact the condition of communities was affected not so much by 'communal subjects' strictly construed as by what was decided about a broad range of national matters. The veto thus had to cover all national matters. Finally, as the interests of the Muslims were liable to be affected more by what shape the new Constitution took than by anything else, the Muslims (i.e. the

League, i.e. Jinnah) must have a veto on every aspect of the new Constitution.[9] This soon became the credo of Muslim League resolutions, alongwith the threat that if a Constitution was brought into being without their consent 'the Musalmans would be forced to resort to every measure and method to resist it with all the power at their command,' that the resistance 'by Muslim India with all its might' 'will inevitably result in strife, bloodshed and misery the   responsibility of which will   rest   on   the British Government   alone.'[10]

A separate nation. Therefore, parity. A beleaguered   nation. Therefore, veto.   A   veto on communal affairs. Therefore   on national   affairs. Therefore   on the Constitution. Therefore on whether India would   stay as one country or not.

6. The last step flowed in a straight line from the first. For within three years of beginning his campaign Jinnah began saying that there just was no constitutional arrangement which would ensure for the Muslims that sense of security and dignity which was their due. There were two reasons for this, he said. First, the Hindus were 'a permanent   majority' in the country; second, the only significant thing about a Hindu was that he was a Hindu – 'It is plain,'he said, 'that you cannot get away from being a Hindu if you are a Hindu.'[11] Since Hindus would always act as Hindus – i.e., not as human beings, not as citizens but only as the members of the one bigoted, aggressive religion – and as their numbers ensured them 'a permanent majority,'no Constitution could safeguard the Muslims within a united India.

A joint Constituent Assembly would not do because, by whatever formula its members were elected, the majority of Hindus in the electorate or the electoral college would ensure that in the Assembly the Muslims were outnumbered, and so the Assembly would start with a   presumption in favour of a united India. Assuring the right to secede under such a scheme too would not do.'The alleged power of the minority in the matter of secession in the document,' he said while dismissing the Cripps proposals, 'is illusory, as Hindu India will dominate the decision in favour of one all-india Union in all the provinces, and the Muslims in Bengal and the Punjab will be at the mercy of the Hindu minority in those provinces, who will exert themselves to the fullest extent and length for keeping the Musalmans tied to the chariot wheel of Hindudom. Thus the Musalmans will be doomed to subjection in all the provinces.'[12]

A federation would not do as, whatever the distribution of powers to begin with, 'once the units accept the basis of federal Central Government, it follows that it will inevitably and out of sheer necessity resolve itself into an all powerful central authority, and the units will be compelled to grant and delegate more and more powers to the Centre, which also can hold these units as connecting links – more or less like country councils or glorified municipalities or feudatory states under the central authority.' As a result, 'any scheme...(or)any proposal which has for its basis any conception or idea of Central Government, federal or confederal' was unacceptable, 'for it is bound to lead in the long run to the emasculation of the entire Muslim nation – socially, educationally, culturally, economically and politically – and to the establishment of Hindu majority Raj in this subcontinent.'[13]

In Jinnah's reckoning, the trouble with every solution proposed was that it gave weight to numbers – universal adult franchise, joint electorates, in fact democracy in any shape or form were equally evil for this reason. 'Muslim India cannot accept any Constitution which must necessarily result in a Hindu majority Government,'he declared. 'Hindus and Muslims brought together under a democratic system forced upon the minorities, can only mean Hindu Raj. Democracy of the kind with which the Congress High Command is enamoured would mean the complete destruction of what is most precious in Islam.'[14] A Constitution for a united India and democracy were 'two carrots,'Jinnah said, that the British were 'dangling before donkeys' – the 'leadership of Hindu India' being the 'donkey'.[15] Both were unacceptable, indeed *inconceivable*, and this too followed from his two-nation theory. 'Democracy,'he said, 'means, to begin with, majority rule. Majority rule in a single society is understandable, although even there it has failed. Representative Government in a single nation, harmonious and homogeneous, in one society, is understandable; but you have only got to apply your mind a few minutes: can such a system ever work or succeed when you have two different nations, more than two different nations?'[16]

The Congress declarations for democracy, he said, were a ruse; his own declarations *against* democracy, on the other hand, were actually a commitment to a higher form of democracy. 'We have   made it clear that there cannot be any room for democracy when you have a nation working on these lines,' he declared in Delhi in 1943.

> Not only have we evidence, but we have suffered and experienced that. When you talk of democracy, you mean Hindu Raj, to dominate over the Muslims, a totally different nation, different in culture, different in everything. You yourself are working for Hindu Nationalism and Hindu Raj. Ladies and gentlemen,we learned democracy 1,300 years ago. It is in our blood, and it is as far away from the Hindu society as are the Arctic regions. You tell us that we are not democratic. It is we who have learned the lesson of equality and brotherhood of man. Among you, one caste will not take a cup of water from another. Is this democracy? Is this honesty? We are for democracy. But not the democracy of your conception, which will turn the whole of India into a Gandhi Ashram. One society and one nation will, by its permanent majority, destroy another nation or society in permanent minority − all that is dear to the minority.[17]

7. Thus, there was just no constitutional arrangement that could assure security and dignity to the Muslims in a united India. Partition alone would do that, he said, and so Pakistan must be the cornerstone of whatever was discussed or proposed. The creation of Pakistan, he further maintained, was not a device to divide India, but a device − indeed, the only device − to obtain freedom from the British, to ensure peace and Hindu-Muslim unity; it was, in fact, he said, in the interests of the Hindus themselves that he was advocating it.[18]

8. Once Partition was at hand, a few said that it was the League's 'last demand.' Not so, said the candid Suhrawardy who had organised the League for the killings in Bengal. 'Is Pakistan our last demand?,' he asked the League Legislators' Convention in Delhi in April 1946, and responded, 'I will not attempt to give an answer. But that is our latest demand. I would like the Congress to recall that we in the past asked for much less, and we were prepared to accept the superior number of Hindus in a democratic Constitution, but they turned down every one of our modest demands. Now there is nothing left for us except to demand

separation.... 'He said that there were many Hindus who looked
to the League for emancipation. What the Muslims wanted was
only two corners in India at the present moment. 'If you wage war
against us,' he said, 'I am not prepared to forecast the future.'[19]

Jinnah of course made the future too a matter of principle.
The right to intervene in the affairs of what would remain India too
flowed directly from the propositions that the Muslims were a
separate nation, that the League was their sole spokesman and
protector, and that Pakistan was being created for their advancement and protection. He told the same convention in his
concluding address, 'We are not going to start with quarrels. We
shall have enough to do, and they will have enough to do, but if they
begin it and our minorities are ill-treated, Pakistan cannot
remain a passive spectator. If Britain in Gladstone's time could
intervene in Armenia in the name of the protection of minorities,
why should it not be right for us to do so in the case of our
minorities in Hindustan – if they are oppressed?'[20]

Jinnah's Devices

But that takes us into the future. We should retrace our steps. By
what devices did Jinnah enflame the sense of total and incompatible separateness, the psychosis among Muslims? His propaganda consisted of five assertions:

❑   What is significant about a Hindu is that he is a Hindu, not that
    he is another human being or another citizen, for he shall
    always act as a Hindu and not as a human being or a citizen;
❑   The Hindus are already organised into a murderous monolith;
    the Hindu Mahasabha, etc. are themselves strong, but they are
    just the tip;
❑   The Congressmen are nothing but Hindu Mahasabha-ites in dis-
    guise;
❑   Everything that the Congress does has one, singular and
    exclusive, objective – that is, to fulfil the Hindu dream of
    annihilating the Muslims;
❑   The Hindus are already subjecting the Muslims to
    unspeakable atrocities, suppression, discrimination; you can
    imagine what will happen when they acquire absolute power
    in a united India.

The assertions were repeated day in and day out – as self-evident truths that required no proof. One harangue was like the other, one occasion as good an opportunity to repeat the allegations as any other.

1. 'The Congress press may clamour as much as it likes,' he told the League Session in Patna in December 1938.

They may bring out their morning, afternoon, evening and night editions; the Congress leaders may shout as much as they like that the Congress is a national body. But I say it is not true. The Congress is nothing but a Hindu body. That is the truth and the Congress leaders know it. The presence of the few Muslims, the few misled and misguided ones, and the few who are there with ulterior motives, does not, cannot, make it a national body. I challenge anybody to deny that the Congress is not mainly a Hindu body. I ask, does the Congress represent the Muslims? (Repeated shouts of 'No,No.') I ask, does the Congress represent the Christians? ('No.') I ask, does the Congress represent the Scheduled Castes? ('No.') I ask, does the Congress represent the non-Brahmins? ('No.') I say the Congress does not even represent all the Hindus. What about the Hindu Mahasabha? What about the Liberal Federation? The Congress, no doubt, is the largest single party in the country. But it is nothing more than that. It may arrogate to itself whatever titles it likes; the Congress High Command in the intoxication of power, like persons who are drunk, may make any claims it pleases them to make. But such claims cannot alter the true character of the Congress. It remains what it is – mainly a Hindu body.[21]

'The Congress, I may tell you,' he told the Session in Madras in 1941,'is nothing more, nothing less than the solid body of Hindus behind it – and other offshoots and the little bodies and little *bachchas*, like the Hindu Mahasabha and the All-India Hindu League, Liberal Federation and other small little bits. They are all one. I do not say they are one in the sense that they necessarily approve of the action of the Congress; but really, if anybody really represents Hindu India, it is Congress.'[22]

2. The only difference between the two, he insisted, was that
'the Congress masquerades under the name of nationalism, whereas
the Hindu Mahasabha does not mince words.'[23] The one and
exclusive objective of the Congress, he said, was to establish
Hindu Raj, to subjugate the Muslims. 'One thing has been
demonstrated beyond doubt,' he said in December 1938, 'namely
that the Congress High Command wanted the Musalmans to
be a mere understudy of the Congress, mere footpages of the
Congress leaders, to be used, governed and brought to heel when
they had served the purpose of the Congress. The Congress
leaders wanted them to submit unconditionally to Hindu Raj. That
game has now been fully exposed....' 'I say the whole idea
behind the Congress leaders' move is once again to deceive the
Muslims,' he said in the same speech. '...If they get a majority, they
will accept the Federation with utmost glee; and then they will
begin to pursue their nefarious scheme of destroying the Muslim
culture and organisation, and to build up the Congress organisation,
as the one and only totalitarian organisation, on the Fascist
pattern. Then they will be able to establish their ideal of Hindu
Raj in Hindustan.'[24] His explanation for opposing the Quit India
Movement was similar: 'So far as we are concerned, it is not a
question of non-cooperation,' he said, 'It is a question of defence
against the attitude the Congress has taken up since 1937,
to dominate Musalmans and to establish, by hook or by crook,
Hindu Raj and Hindu Government. We are defending ourselves
against that monstrosity, those machinations and those designs....'[25]
3. By his reckoning, *every* single thing that the Congress did
was aimed solely at suppressing the Muslims, at establishing Hindu
Raj. If at any moment the Congress made no special effort to reach
out to the Muslims, the charge was that it did not care for them.
If it tried to reach out to them through a 'mass-contact' programme,
the charge was that it was trying to divide them. *Bande Mataram*,
the efforts to propagate Hindustani, the Wardha Education
Scheme, literally *everything* had one aim — to finish off the
Muslims. His description of 'Gandhi's institutions' was typical:
The Gandhi Ashram at Sevagram, Wardha, has been created 'to
serve as the Vatican of Gandhism and the capital of Congress';
Gandhi Harijan Seva Sangh, 'to consolidate the Depressed Class
as integral parts of Hinduism and to prevent their conversion to

Islam or Christianity'; Gandhi Hindi Prachar Sangha, 'to propagate Sanskritised Hindi as the State and national language of India and to displace Urdu from its place of primacy and popularity'; Gandhi Nagri Prachar Sabha, 'to propagate the idea that all Indian languages should be written in Devanagari script and to displace Urdu script'; Gandhi Wardha Talim Sangha, 'to propagate Gandhian principles of religion, spiritualism, national economy and nationalism through a State-controlled system of compulsory primary education. Under the Wardha scheme, the entire system of education of the country was sought to be made subservient to the propagation of Gandhism (which was only a new form of Hinduism to the exclusion of all other religions)', etc.[26]

When the Congress started agitations in states like Hyderabad, he said it was doing so to dislocate the Muslim rulers of these states.[27] When it demanded universal adult franchise and joint electorates, he said it was doing so to swamp the Muslims.[28] In accepting the British parliamentary model, he said, '...the High Command was actuated by the ambition to perpetuate the rule of a communally minded majority party....'[29] Its demand that the Government must not interfere in the working of the popularly elected ministries 'was only meant to confirm the tyranny of monopolist rule and to suppress the claims of the minority.'[30]

Its individual disobedience movement 'ostensibly for freedom of speech, is really meant to coerce the British Government to concede the Congress demands regarding the future Constitution of India, which are really and virtually for a transfer of sovereign powers to the Hindus and thus delegate the Muslim nation of 100 millions and the Indian minorities to the status of mere subjects of Hindu Raj throughout the country.'[31] The Quit India Movement too was 'in pursuance of their objective of establishing Congress Hindu domination in India,' '[it] is directed not only to coerce the British Government into handing over power to Hindu oligarchy, and thus disabling them from carrying out their moral obligations and pledges given to the Musalmans and other sections of the peoples of India from time to time, but also to force the Musalmans to submit and surrender to Congress terms and dictation....'[32]

Indeed, the very demand for freedom for a united India, he said again and again, was just a euphemism for establishing the domination of Hindus over Muslims. 'Is it possible to expect us

unless we are unconscious – and we were unconscious before
the War, but now we are fully conscious,' he asked the League
Session at Karachi in December 1943, 'to expect Muslim India to
agree to Akhand Hindustan and Hindu Raj in this subcontinent?
(Shouts of "It is not possible.") But that is the proposal, and they
have not given up their dreams. On the other hand, there is the talk
of independence. I ask, "Whose independence?" I warn you, and
I have repeatedly warned you, they mean the independence
of Hindu India and the slavery of Muslim India. Now, what do we
say? We say , "Pakistan".'[33]

In this way, having inflamed the Muslims, Jinnah wrought
spectacles through which they would see.

4. The other side of this coin – about the Congress being nothing
but a Hindu organisation whose sole objective was to establish
Hindu Raj – was that the Muslim League represented the Muslims,
that it alone represented them. With a single-mindedness rare
among our politicians he ensured that the League was recognised
as such and that he, in turn, was recognised as the League. The
British were in any case eager to accept both his claims as a
counter-weight to the Congress. The War buttressed their
inclination with reason. As Jinnah put it to the Lahore Session
of the League in 1940,

After the War was declared, the Viceroy naturally wanted
help from the Muslim League. It was only then that he
realised that the Muslim League was a power. For it will
be remembered that up to the time of the declaration of War,
the Viceroy never thought of me, but of Gandhi and Gandhi
alone. I have been the leader of an important party in the
Legislature for a considerable time, larger than the one I have
the honour to lead at present, the Muslim League Party in the
Central Legislature. Yet, the Viceroy never thought of me
before. Therefore,when I got this invitation from the Viceroy
along with Mr. Gandhi, I wondered within myself why I was
so suddenly promoted, and then I concluded that the answer
was the 'All-India Muslim League,' whose President I happen
to be. I believe that was the worst shock that the Congress
High Command received, because it challenged their sole
authority to speak on behalf of India. And it is quite clear
from the attitude of Mr. Gandhi and the High Command that

they have not yet recovered from that shock. My point is that
I want you to recognise   the value, the importance, the
significance of organising ourselves, I will not say anything
more on the subject.[34]

And he berated Gandhiji and the Congress for not accepting
him as the League, and the League as the Muslims' sole representative:

Why does not Mr. Gandhi agree – and I have suggested this
to him more than once, and I repeat it again from this platform
– why does not Mr. Gandhi honestly now acknowledge that the
Congress is a Hindu Congress, that he does not represent
anybody except the solid body of a Hindu people?   Why
should not Mr. Gandhi be proud to say, 'I am a Hindu, the
Congress has solid Hindu backing?' I am not ashamed of saying
that I am a Musalman. I am right I hope, and I think even a blind
man must have been convinced by now, that the Muslim
League has the solid backing of the Musalmans of India. Why
then all this camouflage?   Why all   these   machinations?
...Why not come as a Hindu leader proudly representing your
people and let me meet you proudly representing the Musalmans?....[35]

Gandhiji saw the mischief in all this, and always met Jinnah
as an Indian meeting an Indian, as a person dedicated to emanci-
pating his fellow men meeting a person similarly dedicated. But
Jinnah never wavered from his goal of being the equal leader, of
another nation. When, in the face of communal killings, on the
prodding of Pandit Nehru and Mountbatten, and in spite of his
strong disinclination to go anywhere near the thing (after all, the
killings had resulted from Jinnah's 'Direct Action,' and while
Jinnah and his colleagues were pressing on with this programme,
he, Gandhi, had been risking his life to save both Muslims and
Hindus) when in spite of this disinclination, Gandhiji joined
Mountbatten and Jinnah in signing a joint appeal for communal
peace, *Dawn* was at once exultant, perverse and vicious:

There is novelty in the manner of the dramatic appeal which
the leaders of India's two nations have signed, but there

is hardly anything in it which the Qaid-a-Azam has not said
before without anybody's prompting....
The next step should follow without much delay and in
the logical sequence. We stress the word 'logical' advisedly
because the very fact of the Viceroy having chosen the
Qaid-i-Azam and Mr. Gandhi for the purpose of an appeal
of this kind being conveyed to the public is tantamount to
a *recognition that two voices and not one must speak in this
context. Why is it necessary that the two should make such an
appeal if it is not recognised that there are two peoples, two
nations, who would respect their own respective leader only*?

It added:

Mr. Gandhi has been *persuaded* by the Viceroy to denounce
violence 'for all time' as a means to the attainment of
political ends, but the Mahatma's political heir and successor
remains still unpersuaded.[36]

Jinnah's object in signing the appeal was only to sign something as
an equal of Mountbatten and Gandhiji. As Pyarelal records:

To expect the League to throw away the only 'pistol' which
Jinnah had claimed they had forged, would have been
wishful thinking. But Gandhiji reasoned with himself that
even if the Muslim League was not sincere, the joint appeal
having been issued at Mountbatten's instance, made by
implication the Viceroy party to it and put upon him the
burden of its full implementation, which he would not fail to
discharge. This implication, the Viceroy has since stated, he did
not accept, though he told Gandhiji that he would do
everything in his power to help bring about communal peace.
Be that as it may, Gandhiji felt this was not enough. But
neither then nor with subsequent pleading could he induce
the Viceroy to change. The peace appeal, consequently,
remained a dead letter and Gandhiji expressed his disappoint-
ment over it more than once.[37]

5. As he was the League and as League was the the sole
spokesman, the sole representative of the Muslims, the Muslims
who did not toe Jinnah's line could be only one of two kinds:

either fools or knaves. Thus, for instance, he said that Muslims who were with the Congress had been 'deceived by the high-sounding but insincere promises of the Congress, or have betrayed the Muslim cause by deserting the community and joining hands with its avowed opponents, in order to serve their own selfish ends,'[38] they were 'dupes of the Congress', 'betrayers',[39] 'careerists',[40] 'traitors, cranks, supermen or lunatics',[41] 'quisling Muslims.'[42] Their conduct was an even greater obstacle than 'the network of Congress and Mahasabha wiles' – 'But the conduct of these dupes of the Congress and these betrayers well nigh dishearten(s) me,' he declared, 'and I sometimes ask myself if a community which can still produce so many foolish or treacherous men is worth striving for, praying for and weeping for. Yet, gentlemen, we must not, we cannot, we will not yield to despair....'[43]

It wasn't just that any Muslim who was with the Congress betrayed Islam, but any Muslim who opposed him did so. His outburst against Fazlul Haq at the League Session in Delhi in April 1943 was typical:

They [the Muslims of Bengal] were persecuted and the Chief Minister, who I am ashamed to say was a Musalman. (Cries of 'shame, shame')... Ladies and gentlemen, if I were to give you an account of to what extent this Ministry headed by Fazlul Haq stooped – no decent human being could ever stoop to the foul methods he adopted.... This tyranny, this persecution, this manoeuvering, these machinations in utter disregard of elementary principles of justice and fairplay, were resorted to by an organised government headed by Mr. Fazlul Haq. Thus we have gone through the crucible in Bengal and today Fazlul Haq is no more, and I hope for the rest of his life he will be no more. He often said that if he was a hindrance, he was willing to go. But he never went. I say with all due deliberation and with all responsibility that he was not only a hindrance but a curse to the politics of Bengal. He was a curse to the Musalmans because he betrayed us; he was a curse to the Hindus because he served them as a puppet and their creature. He has met his Waterloo. Let him now remain in St. Helena and repent for the rest of his life, and pray to God that

He may forgive his sins. Bengal has therefore shown that there is no room for duplicity.... It is now the voice of the League, the voice of the people, it is now the authority of the *Millat* that you have to bow to, though you may be the tallest poppy in the Muslim world.[44]

Thus the Muslim League was the sole spokesman for the Muslims. He was the Muslim League. He spoke for the *Millat*. Those who did not agree with him were traitors and worse. Therefore, for instance, he insisted in 1937 that there could be no negotiations regarding Ministry formation, election of Speaker, etc. except through him. When he felt in July 1941 that the Premiers of Punjab, Assam and Sindh had been invited to join the National Defence Council without reference to him, he made them resign. Later he insisted that the League alone had the right to nominate Muslim members to the Executive Council, and later still to the Interim Government.

Two nations. Congress represents a part of one. The League is the sole and exclusive representative of the other. Hence, not just parity, but veto. On everything.

Scare-mongering

Behind all this was scare-mongering of the most blatant and vicious kind. The wildest allegation would be made about atrocities and injustices perpetrated by 'the Hindu Congress'. The offer of the Congress to have a British Chief Justice examine them would be contemptuously refused, and instead blatantly exaggerated 'Reports' – like the notorious Pirpur Report of 1938 – would be released.

6. And there were tactics – to go on escalating the demands, to press for a set of demands, to grab what was conceded and then begin a barrage focusing on what remained, to adopt what Pandit Nehru characterised as 'the permanently negative attitude' to all proposals except his own.

7. And there were operating rules. Ally with any one who will serve your purpose, Jinnah told his followers:

I had a talk with some friends of the North-West Frontier Province. I am told that in that Province our co-religionists

– credulous Pathans as they are – have been told that the Congress is for the good of the people, that the Muslim League is the supporter of Imperialism and an ally of Imperialism. I say there cannot be a greater falsehood than the allegation that the Muslim League is an ally of Imperialism. Inside the legislature or outside the legislature, have I on any single occasion supported Imperialism, not to speak of proving myself an ally of Imperialism? (Shouts of 'No, No.')
I am sure that even if there were a few Muslims who had thought in the past that the Muslims might gain their ends through an alliance with British Imperialism, they have now been thoroughly disillusioned. I say the Muslim League is not going to be an ally of anyone, but would be the ally of even the Devil if need be in the interest of Muslims.
It is not because we are in love with Imperialism; but in politics one has to play one's game as on a chess board....[45]

But trust no one, he told them:

I think it is a wise rule for everyone not to trust anybody too much. Sometimes we are led to trust people; but when we find, in actual experience that our trust has been betrayed, surely that ought to be sufficient lesson for any man not to continue his trust in those who have betrayed him.[46]

8. Following such rules he was always fishing for allies who, though untrustworthy, could be used to counter the Congress demand for freedom for a united India. Speaking in Madras, he incited the 'Dravidistanis':

In this subcontinent you have two different societies, the Muslim society and the Hindu society – and particularly in this land, there is another nation, that is the Dravidian.
This land is really Dravidistan, and imagine its 3 per cent of Brahmin high castes, by skilful maneuvering and by skilful methods of electioneering, 3 per cent of them should secure a majority. Is this democracy or is this a farce? Therefore, I have the fullest sympathy and give my fullest support to the non-Brahmins, and I say to them: the only way for you to come into your own is to live your own life, according to your

culture, according to your language – thank God that Hindi did not go far here – according to your own history – go ahead. I have every sympathy and shall do all to help, and you can establish Dravidistan where the 7 per cent Muslim population will stretch its hands of friendship and will live with you on lines of security, justice and fair play.[47]

Next, the Scheduled Castes were separate too and the Congress, representing only the high caste Hindus, had no right to represent them in the Executive Council or the Interim Government.

Next, the Adivasis. They too are a separate nation, it was proclaimed. Feroze Khan Noon and others proposed that a separate area should be carved out for them in Bihar which would then on its own want to federate with Pakistan, as the Adivasis were closer to Islam than to Hinduism. 'For the 47 lakhs of Bihar Muslims', Noon wrote in April 1947,

there are two courses open: (a) they can move into Western Bengal involving exchange of population, (b) they can move either to the North of the Ganges where their population is 22 per cent or to the South where their population is about 11 per cent. Inside Bihar, or Western Bengal, they can be given an area which will be federated with Pakistan. I am inclined to think that Adibasi tribesmen of Bihar Province will want to federate with Muslim Bengal and not Hindu Bihar. If a plebiseite of Adibasis were held, their verdict would be clear. If they had separate electorate [sic] today, they and the Muslims would form a majority in the Bihar Legislature. Jamshedpur with Tata (Iron) Works is in the Adibasi country and all the mineral resources of this tract are being exploited for the benefit of Akhand Hindustan. Adibasis, who eat beef and bury their dead, are as far apart from caste Hinduism as Islam or Christianity.[48]

The overtures to the Sikhs and how they eventually came to be rejected are by now well known.

9. To pursue his objective Jinnah said that he would if necessary not just ally with the Devil but that he would use *all possible means*. 'No settlement with the majority is possible,' he declared at

the commencement of his campaign, 'as no Hindu leader speaking with any authority shows any concern or genuine desire for it. An honourable settlement can only be achieved among equals; and unless the two parties learn to respect and fear each other, there is no solid ground for any settlement. Offers for peace by the weaker party always mean a confession of weakness, and an invitation to aggression. Appeals to patriotism, justice and fair play and for good will fall flat. It does not require political wisdom to realise that all settlements and safeguards will be a scrap of paper unless they were backed up by power. Politics means power, and not relying only on cries of justice or fair play or goodwill.'[49]

Soon enough the Muslim League leaders were saying, 'If Pakistan was not to be had on demand, we will have it by force.'[50] Jinnah would repeat the refrain at every opportunity:

Our formula, [he declared in Delhi] gives the Hindus three-fourths of this subcontinent... whereas, if the Congress demand is accepted, it is clear as daylight that we shall be thrown under the yoke not only of Hindu Raj but this present Congress Junta' will still have the temerity to harp that they alone represent India, and that they are the sole successors to step in and establish the Congress Raj in place of the British Raj – a position which is impossible and intolerable.

Muslim India will never agree to its realisation, and will be bound, and will have no other course open but to resist it by every means possible.
The British are threatened that if they don't surrender to the Congress demand there will be bloodshed, for which preparations are going on: that they will paralyse British trade, and they further threaten that the same will be the result if they favour Pakistan.
If, unfortunately, the British are stampeded by the threat of bloodshed, which is more a bluff than a reality, *this time Muslim India is not going to remain passive or neutral. It is going to play its part and face all danger.* Mr. Nehru is greatly mistaken that there might be trouble, as he says, but not very much. He is still living in the atmosphere of 'Anand Bhavan'.[51]

Others were quick to take the cue and spell out what was meant by the League 'playing its part'. Khan Abdul Qayum Khan said that during his journey to Delhi for the convention Muslim students had asked him when 'marching orders would be given by the Qaid-i-Azam,'that if the British acceded to the Congress proposals 'I hope that the Muslim nation will gather together and strike swiftly, so that a Central Government may never be established,'that 'If the British force the setting up of a Government of the *Akhand* Hindustan type, and if they decide that there should be one Constituent Assembly, then the Muslims will have no other alternative but to take to the sword and rebel against it.'

Shaukat Hayat Khan said,'I represent the martial clans of Pakistan who do not believe in words but in action.' 'They will fight to death,'he said, 'if any attempt is made to subject their nation to the domination of anyone else. I speak for the Punjab soldier, and I say that three-quarter million demobilised soldiers in the Punjab are pledged to achieve Pakistan....' Turning to Jinnah he said, 'You, Sir, are holding us back, and we beg of you to give the word of command. Let us prove to the doubting how we can and how we mean to defend our Pakistan.'

Feroze Khan Noon threatened that they might turn to Russia for support and that 'If Britain sells our freedom to gain the trade of *Akhand* Hindustan, if the British force on us an *Akhand* Government, the destruction and havoc which Muslims will cause, will put to shame the deeds of Halaku Khan and Chengiz Khan, and the responsibility for this will be Britain's....'[52]

This logic reached its predictable goal in July 1946, when the League passed its 'Direct Action' Resolution:

The Council of the all-India Muslim League is convinced that now the time has come for the Muslim Nation to resort to Direct Action to achieve Pakistan to assert their rights, to vindicate their honour and to get rid of the present British slavery and the contemplated future caste-Hindu Domination.

Concluding the Session Jinnah declared, 'Today we have said goodbye to constitutions and constitutional methods,' and now 'we also have a pistol.'

Within a month the League commenced its 'Direct Action' by organising the terrible Calcutta killings and those in Noakhali, and then in Punjab and the NWFP.

Two nations. Two eternally incompatible nations. The right of one nation to have its way by all possible means. The forging of a pistol. The Direct Action. One straight line.

A Crucial Difference, but on Three Conditions

There are, of course, crucial differences between the position in the 1940s, and the position now. The principal one among these is that at that time the apparatus of the State was in the hands of the British – in the hands, that is, of the very power that had assiduously and for half a century fanned divisions between Hindus and Muslims, the power for whom the independence movement led by Gandhiji was the Enemy Number One, the power that had decided that if it could no longer hold on to India it would at least break it up.

That the State apparatus was in hands sympathetic to his aim provided invaluable help to Jinnah. In day-to-day negotiations British officials, determined to thwart Gandhi and his men, would keep him posted about the position that the Congress was adopting, about what its private offers were, about the division of opinion among its senior leaders. And Jinnah could always be certain that however tortuous the course the Government might adopt, it would ultimately settle for the position that would further his aim another notch. By the time he started preparing the League for 'Direct Action,'and specially when he commenced it from August 1946, the fact that the army, police and bureaucracy were in the hands of the British proved decisive. Wavell, to take just one instance, refused to use his influence to have Suhrawardy put down the Calcutta and Noakhali killings by using the provincial police, and refused equally to send central forces for the purpose. 'The Provinces are autonomous,' he said. And when the 'Direct Action' reached NWFP, the effect of the partisanship of the Governor, Olaf Caroe, on the one hand, and the 'helplessness' of Mountbatten on the other hand, was identical. The League thus could continue its work till all were convinced that Hindus and Muslims were indeed mortal enemies, that indeed they could not live together.

Moreover, the final outcome depended in a sense on the formal decision of the British – that is, of the Cabinet, of the Parliament in London. The British were to depart-by-agreement, they were not, for instance, being pushed out by military defeat. They were therefore not just an essential party in the negotiations. They were the referee too. Jinnah knew that he would not get Pakistan once the British left. That is why he was insistent that they must partition the country *before* leaving. 'Quit India,' Gandhiji said. 'Divide and Quit,' said Jinnah, and refused to deal with or through anyone but the British. 'But I would like to request Jinnah Saheb, implore him, to have direct talks with us, at least now,' Gandhiji told his prayer meeting on 4 June 1947, the day after the Working Committee conveyed its acceptance of the Partition Plan to the Viceroy. 'Whatever has happened is all right, but now let us sit together and decide about the future. Let him forget about the Viceroy now, and let him invite us to come to any understanding he wishes to have, so that it is in the interest of all of us.'[53] The appeal was repeated the next day, the day after that, and the day after that too. But Jinnah knew that his advantage lay in the referee.

Today the final decisions depend on a government and Parliament elected by us. And the apparatus of governance is in hands that do not start with a predilection for dividing the country. This can be a decisive difference, but only on three conditions. First, the country must have the patience, the quiet determination to stay the course, to see wars of attrition to the end. Second, those who man the apparatus must accord overriding priority to maintaining the unity of the country; neither their attention nor their resolve must waver for a moment. And, third, the apparatus itself must be made fighting fit. Neither a disembodied resolve, however strong, nor mere goodwill, however intense, can keep the country together.

Quite the contrary. That terrible decade, 1937-47, shows how things change in just ten years. In 1936 the League, even among the Muslims, was but one of a number of the smaller contending parties. By 1946 Partition had become inevitable. The decade shows how potent religion-as-poison can be. It shows how a person who is himself not religious – Jinnah's fondness for pork and ham was well-known, he could barely speak the Urdu he said was endangered – can in fact come to embody the passions and resentments of a religiously inflamed community. It shows how the resentments can be inflamed into hatred, how they can become real and potent even when the grounds for resentment are fabricated.

The decade shows that to combat the danger one must act in time – i.e. one must discern the *potential* inherent in a move, an event, and act to forestall it. To wait till its effects have matured, till all the data is in, is to consign oneself to certain defeat. It shows too that among the best indicators of what leaders or groups are up to are the declarations of the leaders themselves. Such groups make no secret of their aim. The speeches of the leaders, the resolutions, and even more so the pamphlet-literature, the speeches of the second-rung leaders, all proclaim the goal, and what the group is going to do to attain it. The point is to study the speeches and resolutions diligently, and to take them seriously.

'Taking them seriously' means to recognise that *a new situation has arisen,* that a group and its leaders have declared war on the country. You cannot go on minding your personal affairs as of old, pursuing your personal businesses and careers as of old, and expect that, in spite of everyone going on in the old way, the new situation will somehow be overcome. To overcome the challenge the country must acquire the ability to defeat the Jinnahs in the field of their choice – that is, the field of power. It must fashion an answer to the 'pistol' that the Jinnah forges.

How apathetic ninety per cent of us are. How we cavil and complain at the little inconveniences to which we are put by the efforts of others and the State to meet the new situation. How we ignore the information that stares us in the face, how we wish the danger away, how we make believe that we have contained it by meeting the demands half-way, by appeasing the Jinnahs, that we have warded it off by the convoluted formulation, by clever words.

The Peril of Clever Words

Partly on account of the actual power that the Muslim League was acquiring among the Muslims, and partly in the hope that just one more concession would satiate Jinnah, the Congress kept making one concession after another.

It had always maintained that its goal was freedom for a united

India; that the British must go first because, as long as they were around, not only did they foment the League, but the League too felt no need to be reasonable for it knew that it could always get from the British what it did not from the Congress.

But soon enough the Congress started its slide from concession to concession.

Five features stand out in the sequence.

First, the Congress and its leaders had put themselves in a situation, as much psychological as real, in which at each turn they felt that the onus for finding a solution, for devising some new formula, was on them. Second, as at each step the previous formula had not placated Jinnah, the new one had necessarily to bend a bit further towards his position; at each step, in view of what had been conceded earlier, the latest concession seemed just an extension of what had already been granted earlier, a mere terminological amplification, and was often presented as such. Third, at each step one principle was said to inevitably imply the next – non-violence *implied* that we would not coerce anyone who wanted to leave the Union, to stay against his will; non-coercion *implied* that we were committed to Partition-with-self determination; Partition-with-self-determination *implied* that we were committed to Partition *per se*, and so on. Fourth, at each step the arguments were virtually identical – 'we have to be practical'; 'there is no other way out'; 'if we do not agree to this now, what will the world say of us; on the other hand, if we agree to this, Jinnah will be put on the spot, *he* will have to prove his *bona fides* by working this formula rather than going on asking for more and more'; 'but what is all the fuss about, we accepted the principle long ago, this is just an application of it.' Fifth, at each step clever words were there to camouflage what was being done – to camouflage it from others, of course, but most of all from ourselves.

It is a long and sorry tale. The slide began with convoluted formulations. In April 1942 the Working Committee said that it 'cannot think in terms of compelling any territorial unit to remain in an Indian Union against their declared and established will. While recognizing this principle, the Committee feel that every effort should be made to create a common and cooperative national life. Acceptance of this principle inevitably involves that no changes should be made which would result in fresh problems being created and compulsion being exercised on other substantial groups within that area. Each territorial unit should have the fullest autonomy within a Union consistently with a strong national state.' For autonomy within a Union *as well as* for self-determination. For self-determination to the point of secession *as well as* for a cooperative national life.... Congressmen convinced themselves that this was nothing but the age-old Congress commitment to democracy. Congress leaders tried to convince Jinnah that he should not ask for more as, by such formulation, the Congress had in any case conceded the *principle* of Pakistan.

But why not concede the reality then, Jinnah countered.

By such steps the Congress accepted the principle of parity one day, the Cabinet Mission's Plan with its groupings of Provinces, its Sections, its weak Centre the next; a veto on communal matters for the League one day, a veto on all national affairs the next; the 'administrative partition' of Punjab and Bengal one day, the complete Partition of the country the next; referendum in the NWFP without any intimidation one day, 'referendum' in spite of intimidation the next; a referendum on the question whether the NWFP would join Pakistan or India or would remain independent one day, a 'referendum' with the key question missing the next.

Throughout, Jinnah maintained what Pandit Nehru correctly characterised his 'permanently negative attitude', and throughout the Congress leaders kept feeling that the onus for finding yet another formula that might at last be acceptable to him lay upon them.

The Muslim League's 'Direct Action' – the killings in Calcutta and Noakhali, the retaliation in Bihar, the murders in Punjab and then in the NWFP – completely unnerved the Congress leaders. And there was the eight-month experience of trying to work the Interim Government. Jinnah had first agreed that the League would join the Government, then, pressing the advantage further, kept it out. He then had Liaqat Ali and others join it with the Muslim League leaders declaring explicitly that – whatever the objectives for which or principles on which the Interim Government had been formed – their men were going in to wreck it from within, to use it for achieving Pakistan. 'We are going into the Interim Government to get a foothold to fight for our cherished goal of Pakistan.... The Interim Government is one of the fronts of "Direct Action",' said one. 'The League's participation in the new Government...only means that the struggle for Pakistan will now be carried on within as well as without the Government,' said another.[54]

League Ministers began packing their departments with their sympathisers. And Liaqat Ali used his stranglehold over the finance portfolio to well-nigh paralyse the Government.

The British Government prepared a plan for partitioning the country. On 2 June 1947 the Viceroy called the principal leaders – Pandit Nehru, Sardar Patel and Acharya Kripalani from the Congress, Jinnah, Liaqat Ali and Rab Nishtar for the League, plus Baldev Singh – for a meeting and obtained their concurrence. The Congress leaders in turn undertook to persuade the Working Committee and this they did successfully that very afternoon. The Committee sent its acceptance in writing that very day in the form of a letter to Acharya Kripalani, the Congress President.[55] The Plan was announced on 3 June.

And so when the All India Congress Committee met on 14 and 15 June 1947 to accept or reject the Plan to partition India, it had before it, not just the formal Resolution of the Working Committee endorsing the Plan, but also the knowledge that the Plan had been announced only *after* the leaders and the Working Committee had given their prior consent.

The speeches that our leaders made at the Session tear one's heart. Here were patriots of the first water, men and women who had sacrificed all for the country. But they were now tired, exhausted, beaten. The British had the State, Jinnah had the pistol. And they had only words. The speeches show how Jinnah's 'Direct Action' had completely unnerved the Congress leaders, how by paralysing the Interim Government Jinnah had broken their patience, their will itself. All they wanted now was to get it over with, and to put on as brave a face as possible while doing so.

Pandit Pant moved the Resolution. Maulana Azad seconded it. The Resolution was full of the usual poetry:

The Congress has consistently upheld that the unity of India must be maintained. Ever since its inception, more than 60 years ago, the National Congress has laboured for the realisation of a free and united India, and millions of our people have suffered in this great cause. Not only the labours and sacrifices of the past two generations but the long course of India's history and tradition bear witness to this essential unity. Geography and the mountains and the seas fashioned India as she is and no human agency can change that shape or come in the way of her final destiny. Economic circumstances and the insistent demands of international affairs make the unity of India still more necessary. The picture of India we have learnt to cherish will remain in our minds and hearts

The AICC earnestly trusts that when present passions have subsided, India's problems will be viewed in their proper perspective and the false doctrine of two nations in India will be discredited and discarded by all.

Acharya Kripalani, speaking as the President of the Congress, said:

These ghastly experiences have no doubt affected my approach to the question. Some members have accused us that we have taken this decision out of fear. I must admit the truth of this charge, but not in the sense in which it is made. The fear is not for the lives lost or of the widows' wale or the orphans' cry or of the many houses burnt. The fear is that if we go on like this, retaliating and heaping indignities upon each other, we shall progressively reduce ourselves to a state of cannibalism and worse. In every fresh communal fight the most brutal and degraded acts of the previous fight become the norm. So we keep on degrading each other and all in the name of religion. I am a Hindu and am proud of the fact. But this is because Hinduism for me has stood for toleration, for truth and for non-violence, or at any rate for the clean violence of the brave. If it no more stands for these ideals and if in order to defend it people have to indulge in crimes worse than cannibalism then I must hang down my head in shame. And I may tell you that often I have felt and said that in these days one is ashamed to call onself an Indian.

He recalled that he had been with Gandhiji for 30 years, that even when he differed with him he had deferred to Gandhiji's political instinct, and went on:

Today also I feel that he with his supreme fearlessness is correct and my stand is defective. Why then am I not with him? It is because I feel that he has as yet found no way of tackling the problem on a mass basis. When he taught us non-violent non-cooperation, he showed us a definite method which we had at least mechanically followed. Today he himself is groping in the dark. He was in Noakhali. His efforts eased the situation. Now he is in Bihar. The situation is again eased. But this does not solve in any way the flare-up in the Punjab. He says he is solving the problem of Hindu-Muslim unity for the whole of India in Bihar. Maybe. But it is difficult to see how that is being done. There are no definite steps, as in non-violent non-cooperation, that lead to the desired goal.

And then unfortunately for us today, though he can enunciate policies, they have in the main to be carried out by others and these others are not converted to his way of thinking.

The Acharya said he had already shown how the communal rioting could be stopped:

The Government in Bihar should have given a warning to the Government of Bengal that if the Hindus who were living in Bengal were cruelly treated, the Bihar Government with the best will in the world would not be able to protect the lives of the Muslims resident in Bihar. This would have meant that the issue had been raised to the international plane where organised governments deal with each other. The issue would have been taken out of the hands of the excited mob fury that knows no morality, no law, no restraint. Mob is fury always blind. International violence has at least some system and method about it.

That was his practical suggestion. He said that they should 'bend all our energies to the goal of unification which we have missed in order to achieve our freedom quickly. This can best be done by making India a strong, happy, democratic and socialist State where all citizens, irrespective of religion or caste, shall have equal opportunities of development. Such an India can win back the seceding children to its lap.'

He reminded the audience that the Working Committee had already sent its acceptance in writing and that too *before* the Plan was announced. The AICC, he said, had met now either to ratify or to reject the commitment which had been made by the Working Committee. He explained that the Resolution accepted the possibility of certain parts of India seceding from the Indian Union, but that, he reminded them, was already implied in the declared policy of the Congress.

Pandit Pant said that the Resolution was 'the only way to achieve freedom and liberty for the country.' It would assure an Indian Union, a strong Centre, which, in turn, would ensure progress and help their country take its 'rightful place in the world.' The Congress had worked hard and sacrificed everything for the sake of unity, he said, but there was a limit beyond which it could not go. Their choice today was between accepting the statement of 3 June or committing suicide. Concluding, he said, 'it was better to accept the statement of June 3' rather than 'fritter away' energy 'trying to keep unwilling people in the Union.'

Maulana Azad affirmed that he 'did not think that the present decision was the right decision, but the Congress had no alternative. The choice before the Congress was not which plan to accept and which to reject, but whether the present state of indecision and drift should continue. There was the unfortunate problem of internal disorder and strife and there was 'the obstinacy of the Muslim League.' That is why, he said, they had opted for 'an immediate settlement.' 'The Congress stood by the ideal of a United India,' he said, 'but it was also committed to the principle of self-determination and was against coercing any unwilling areas to join the Union.'

Whatever be the result of the referendum, or whatever the Punjab and Bengal legislatures may decide just now, he was sure, he said, that those provinces which now sought to cut themselves away from India would in the very near future hurry back to the Union. 'The division is only of the map of the country,' he said, 'and not in the hearts of the people and I am sure it is going to be a short-lived partition.'

A few speakers, from Purushottamdas Tandon to Maulana Hafizur Rahman and Ansar Harwani, opposed the Resolution, characterising it as a 'surrender' and worse. Some were loftily enigmatic. Ram Manohar Lohia advised the AICC to remain

neutral. While the Resolution was bad, he said, they themselves
were responsible for the acceptance of the Plan of 3 June. They
could not blame the leaders as they themselves were weak and
the   leaders were therefore forced to accept the   Government's
proposals. Therefore, they could not vote against it. On the other
hand, as they had objections to it, they could not support it either.

Gandhiji had consistently maintained that, as long as the British
were around, neither side would make the adjustments necessary
to win over the other as each would think that it could bargain
with the British instead, that therefore the British must leave first,
that if rivers of blood must flow before we learnt to settle
our   differences among ourselves, well, flow they must.

But   the   others did not have his patience. Day by day
they turned their backs on him. It was June 1946. They had been
negotiating with the Cabinet Mission. Gandhiji saw mischief in
the crucial paragraph 19 of the statement. He and Sardar Patel met
the Mission members. Gandhiji's doubts were confirmed but on
the ride back Sardar Patel tried to press him into accepting what
the Sardar thought was their categorical assurance on the matter.
The Sardar wanted Gandhiji to give a ' yes' or 'no' immediately.
He said they had promised to send their reply that afternoon.
Eventually, that being his day of silence, Gandhiji   scribbled,
'There is   no question of my feelings being hurt. I am against
deciding the issue today but you are free to decide as you wish.'

They met the Viceroy and the Cabinet Mission again that
evening. Gandhiji's doubts hardened. He wrote to Cripps that night
informing him that he would advise the Working Committee not
to accept the Plan with its ambiguities.

The end is best described in Pyarelal's words:

At 8 A.M. Bapu went to attend the Working Committee
meeting. He asked me to read out the note which he had written
to Cripps last night. He then addressed them very briefly, 'I
admit defeat, you are not bound to act on my unsupported
suspicion. You should follow my intuition only if it appeals to
your reason. Otherwise you should take an independent course.
I shall now leave with your permission. You should follow the
dictates of your reason.' A hush fell over the gathering. Nobody
spoke for sometime. The Maulana Sahib with his unfailing
alertness at once took in the situation. 'What do you desire?

Is there any need to detain Bapu any further?,' he asked.
Everybody was silent. Everybody understood. In that hour
of decision they had no need for Bapu. They decided to
drop the pilot. Bapu returned to his residence. The Working
Committee again met at noon and addressed a letter to the
Cabinet Mission, rejecting the proposal for the formation of
the Interim Government at the Centre and accepting the long
term plan with its own interpretation of the disputed clauses.
In spite of that they made Bapu attend the afternoon session
of the Working Committee. At noon the Cabinet Mission
invited the members of the Working Committee to meet them.
Bapu not being a member was not sent for and did not go. On
their return nobody told Bapu a word about what had happened
at the meeting.[56]

Within a month Jinnah passed his 'Direct Action' resolution,
and within a month of that the great killings in Calcutta and
Noakhali started. Gandhiji left for Noakhali. The leaders would
visit him periodically for advice. They did so in late December
1946 too. Gandhiji warned them against accepting the *ex post*
interpretation that the British Government was putting on the
'Groupings'. The AICC rejected his advice and decided to adopt
the British Government's construction. 'When the news was
broadcast it was received at night,' Nirmal Kumar Bose was to
record later, 'and conveyed by a messenger to Gandhiji's camp.
When the present author communicated the news, he distinctly
remembers that Gandhi said to him, "*Yeh to mera khatma ho gaya*
(this is my end)."'[57]
   The League commenced 'Direct Action' next in Punjab. About
2,000 Hindus and Sikhs were killed, another 1,000 were seriously
injured. The Congress leaders were appropriately unnerved.
Gandhiji was in Bihar. Without so much as informing him, the
Congress Working Committee passed a Resolution demanding
that Punjab and Bengal be partitioned. The Resolution showed
that the Congress had no answer to and no stomach for Jinnah's
'Direct Action,' though Panditji and others said that this resolve
to partition the two provinces would bring Jinnah to his senses
and make him give up his proposal to divide India.
   Gandhiji read about the Resolution only in the newspapers.
He was heart-broken. 'I think I did not know the reason behind

the Working Committee resolution,' he wrote to Panditji. 'I cannot understand it,' he wrote to Sardar Patel.[58]

That was in March 1947. Two more months passed, two months that showed even more clearly to Gandhiji that neither the country nor the Congress had time for him any longer. The fear of chaos has seized the Congress leaders, he told his associates in Bihar, and it is this which is driving them to agree to Partition.[59] 'The Congress has practically decided to accept Partition,' he told Dr. Mahmud just before leaving Patna for the crucial Working Committee meeting, 'but I have been a fighter all my life. I am going to Delhi to fight a losing battle.' In Delhi, he was rent by doubts. Mistaking the hands of his watch on 1 June, he awakened earlier than usual. 'As there was still half an hour before prayer,' Pyarelal records, 'he remained lying in bed and began to muse in a low voice:

> The purity of my striving will be put to the test only now. Today I find myself all alone. Even the Sardar and Jawaharlal think that my reading of the situation is wrong and peace is sure to return if Partition is agreed upon....They do not like my telling the Viceroy that even if there is to be Partition, it should not be through British intervention or under the British Rule.... They wonder if I have not deteriorated with age.... Nevertheless I must speak as I feel if I am to be a true and loyal friend to the Congress and to the British people, as I claim to be.... regardless of whether my advice is heeded or not. I see clearly that we are setting about this business the wrong way. We may not feel the full effect immediately, but I can see clearly that the future of independence gained at this price is going to be dark. I pray that God may not keep me alive to witness it....

'With a final effort,' Pyarelal records, he concluded,

> I shall perhaps not be alive to witness it, but should the evil I apprehend overtake India and her independence be imperilled, let posterity know what agony this old soul went through thinking of it. Let it not be said that Gandhi was party to India's vivisection. But everybody is today impatient for independence. Therefore there is no other help.

'Using a well-known Gujarati metaphor,'says Pyarelal, 'he likened independence-cum-Partition to a "wooden loaf". If they [Congress leaders] eat it, they die of colic; if they leave it, they starve.'[60]

Two days later, during his morning walk, he told Rajendra Prasad, 'Of late I have noticed that I very easily get irritated. That means I cannot now live for long . But my faith in God is daily becoming deeper and deeper. He alone is my true friend and companion. He never deserts even the least of His creatures.'

'In all probability the final seal will be set on the Partition Plan during the day,' Pyarelal records Gandhiji saying as he lay in his bath that day. 'But though I may be alone in holding this view, I repeat that the division of India can only do harm to the country's future. The slavery of 150 years is going to end, but from the look of things it does not seem as if independence will last as long. It hurts me to think that I can see nothing but evil in the Partition Plan. Maybe that just as God blinded my vision, so that I mistook the non-violence of the weak – which I now see is a misnomer and contradiction in terms – for true non-violence, he has again stricken me with blindness. If it should prove to be so, nobody would be happier than I.'[61]

But the die had been cast. The impatience of his colleagues and the indifference of his people had taken the matter out of his hands. 'But now we must accept what is an accomplished fact,' he told his prayer meeting on 4 June. The Partition is already an accomplished fact, he told them again the next day, separate Constituent Assemblies have already been formed. 'The division is now a *fait accompli*,' he repeated two days later. The Working Committee was their authorised representative. It had issued a *hundi* on their behalf. They must honour it, though they may replace the Working Committe after doing so. 'I must confess that I am not happy about this decision,' he told them, 'but many things happen in the world that are not to our liking; and yet we have to put up with them. We have to put up with this thing in the same manner.' He was helpless, he told them. 'If you do not approve of the decision of the Working Committee you can frankly say so at the next AICC meeting. I have no intention to attend the session. I will attend if I am invited. But who is going to listen to my solitary voice? After all, you are the people. You can convey it to the Congress in a civil manner whether or not you approve of what it has done.'[62]

14 June arrived. Gandhiji was disconsolate, torn. Talking to Manu Gandhi early that morning, he spoke of the great love that Pandit Nehru and the Sardar bore for him, and said, 'He [Jawaharlal] would be heart-broken if I hesitated to attend the AICC. He has made me a captive of his love.'[63] And so he went to address the session. His heart was not in it. He had not come to plead for the leaders of the Working Committee, he said.'Who will listen to my pleading? But the President [Acharya Kripalani] said that I should at least show my face here. Hence I have come to show my face and speak a few words.'[64]

'You will no doubt agree that no one could be as much hurt by the division of the country as I am,'he said,'and I don't think that anyone can be as unhappy today as I am. But what has happened has happened.' The Working Committee, he reminded them, acted on behalf of the Congress. 'If you reject it [the Working Committee Resolution] the world will call you irresponsible.' The leaders had accepted the Partition 'because there was no other way. They now see it clearly that the country is already divided into two camps.'

'The decision that has been arrived at,' he told the members in plain words, 'has been reached with your complicity and yet you complain of the Working Committee which has men of such great calibre.' It was easy to criticise the leaders, he said, but the critics should think out what they would do if they were in the leaders' place. 'I criticise them, of course, but afterwards what? Shall I assume the burdens that they are carrying? Shall I become a Nehru or a Sardar or a Rajendra Prasad? Even if you should put me in their place I do not know what I should be able to do.'

'You have a perfect right to do so [to reject the Working Committee's Resolution] if you feel that you have the strength,' he told the members. 'But I do not find that strength in us today. If you had it I would also be with you and if I felt strong enough myself I would, alone, take up the flag of revolt. But today, I do not see the condition of doing so.'

He therefore advised them to accept the Resolution without changing it in any way and set their minds to what was to be done in the future. 'We have to draw something good out of this bad thing,'he said. 'I am not the one to be upset by defeat....We should draw out gold and diamonds even from mud.'

Pandit   Nehru, the *Register* records, was   'outspoken.''India's heart has   been   broken,' he said, 'but her essential unity   has   not been destroyed. How will you repair the broken heart? It can be only on the basis of a programme for a partition.' The Register continues:

Pandit Nehru expressed his horror and disgust at the riots in the Punjab, Bengal and elsewhere and said that they   were no isolated incidents. They were planned attacks. It seemed the administration had broken down and there was no authority left in the country to enforce order.

After giving a resume of the events that led to the June 3 Statement, Pandit Nehru said that it would be a futile controversy to go into the merits of Dominion Status versus Independence. The most urgent task at present was to arrest the swift drift towards anarchy and chaos. Disruptive forces were at work and the most important disruptive force was that of the Muslim League. Their first task should be the establishment of a strong Central Government to rule the country firmly and to assure the individual's liberty of life. All other questions were of secondary importance. Asserting that there was no question of any surrender to the Muslim League and that what he and his colleagues had agreed to was that the issue of Partition should be referred to the   people for a verdict. Pandit Nehru said that there was nothing novel in the plan for Partition. The House would   remember   Mr.   C. Rajagopalachari's formula on the basis of which Mahatma Gandhi carried on negotiations with Mr Jinnah. At that time, he and his colleagues were in Ahmednagar Fort. They discussed the question in prison. While they disagreed with the approach to the whole question, there was no disagreement on the formula. It must be realised that it was not possible to coerce even with swords, unwilling parts to remain under the Indian domain. Had they been forced to stay in the Union, no progress and planning would be possible. They must take the warning from   China. Continued internal strife and turmoil would bring the progress of a nation to a standstill.

In arriving at a decision, they must look at the international context as well. The picture of the world today was one of destruction and impoverishment which, by itself, might present an immediate war. But one could never say what would happen in the future.

The Congress, Pandit Nehru declared, could not afford to act in an irresponsible manner by passing high-sounding resolutions. A responsible body must not think in terms of today only; for there was tomorrow and a day after that. It would be ridiculous to suggest that the British should do everything before they quit the country.

The riots in Rawalpindi, Multan, Amritsar, Calcutta, Noakhali, Bihar and elsewhere, Pandit Nehru said, presented the situation in a different light. To suggest that the Congress Working Committee took fright and therefore 'surrendered' was wrong. But it was correct to say that they were very much disturbed at the prevailing madness. Homesteads were burnt, women and children were murdered. Why, he asked, were all these tragic and brutal things happening? They could have checked them by resorting to the sword and lathi. But would that solve the problem? Some people from the Punjab had said that the Congress had let them down. What was he to do? Should he send an army? He was sad and bitter and India's heart was broken. The victims in Rawalpindi said that they were being killed in order that the League might rule. The wound, he said, must be healed. With whatever they were able to salvage, they must plan out a programme on the basis of Partition.

The Congress Working Committee passed a resolution in favour of the partition of the Punjab into two administrative provinces. Partition was better than murder of innocent citizens. After the resolution was passed, the Committee received numerous complaints from Bengal that Bengal also should be divided. The underlying principle in the case of the Punjab and Bengal was one and the same.

Deploring the disturbances in the country, Pandit Nehru reiterated that government authority had almost collapsed. The British were no longer interested because they were leaving. The acceptance of Dominion Status was without prejudice to the Republic Resolution adopted by the Constituent Assembly. But the composition of the present government was such that no agreement could work and no convention could be established and the Viceroy, therefore, suggested the June 3 Statement and the Congress accepted it.

Pandit Nehru said that all talk of Pakistan and Hindustan was due to a misunderstanding. Both from the practical and legal point of view, India as an entity continued to exist except that certain provinces and parts of certain provinces now sought to secede. The seceding areas were free to have any relations they liked with foreign powers. The Government of India was intact and there should be no further confusion of Hindustan and Pakistan and people should not allow such ideas to grow.

Sardar Patel gave 'a vigorous speech,' the *Register* records:

His experience in the Interim Government had convinced him, he said, that it was just as well that the State Paper had gone. Had they accepted the State Paper the whole of India would have gone the Pakistan way. Today they had 75 to 80 per cent of India which they could develop according to their genius and make it strong. The League could develop the rest of the country....

Nobody liked the division of India, he said, and his heart was heavy. But there were stark realities of which they should take notice. The choice was whether there should be just one division or many divisions. The fight today was not against the British. They had no desire to stay on in India and if they wished to stay they desired to do so only with India's consent. The earlier May 16 Plan had no doubt given them a united India. The Congress had agreed to it in spite of its shortcomings. But the Plan could not be executed if one or the other party withheld cooperation. Thus the State Paper had been in the nature of an imposed award. But the position today was different. The Congress must face facts. It could not give way to emotionalism and sentimentality. They must coolly assess the pros and cons and arrive at a deliberate decision. Sardar Patel denied that the Working Committee accepted the Plan out of fear. They had never known fear. He deeply regretted the many massacres that had happened. In one family of 30, there were only two survivors. Many were maimed and disabled for life. They had gone through all that. But he was afraid of one thing and that was that all their toils and hard work these many years should not go to waste or prove unfruitful. They worked for independence and they should see as large a part of this country as possible become free and strong. Otherwise, there would be neither 'Akhand Hindustan' nor Pakistan. Further, taking any course other than the one which the Working Committee had suggested, would not only be injurious, but would also make the Congress the laughing stock of the world. Here was a chance for India to attain her independence. Was she going to throw it away? It would be incorrect to say: 'First, let the British go away. Then all questions could be solved.' How were they to be solved and what would happen afterwards?

His nine months in office, Sardar Patel said, had completely disillusioned him of the supposed merits of the State Paper. He had noticed that Muslim officials right from the top down to the *chaprasis*, except for a few honourable exceptions, were all for the Muslim League. There should be no mistake about it. Mutual recriminations and allegations were the order of the day. The May 16 Plan was gone and he was glad. That Plan left much room for conflict and bickerings. The Congress was opposed to Pakistan, but yet the Resolution before the House accepted Partition. Whether the AICC liked it or not, there was already Pakistan in action both in the Punjab and in Bengal. In the circumstances, he would prefer the real Pakistan because then they would have some sense of responsibility.[65]

The Resolution was eventually put to vote; 157 votes were cast for it, 29 against. 'The House then adjourned for tea,' the *Register* records, 'after which the Resolution on Indian States was taken up.'

Notice how the never-to-be-accepted had become the inevitable, how Jinnah had forced the Congress leaders to speak his very words, how they had neither Jinnah's stomach for violence nor the Mahatma's patience for riding it out. Notice how the best and the most dedicated of leaders made even this last step out to be just a logical extension – 'There is nothing novel in the plan for Partition,' Panditji said – of what had been accepted earlier, how helpless the Congress leaders were because the State apparatus was in the hands of the British, and 'the pistol' was in the hands of Jinnah.

What will others say of us? Communal rioting can be stopped by being made an international matter? We will be reduced to cannibalism and worse? This is the way for India to get the seceding children back into its lap? We have to accept everything because whatever has happened has been done by the prior consent of our leaders? We should not fritter away our energies? What is being divided is just the map of the country and not the hearts of the people? India's heart has been broken but its essential unity has not been destroyed? The way to repair the broken heart is to partition the country? Partition is not a novel thing? The Congress is not giving in to coercion, it is just acting 'after realising the present situation'?

Words as soporifics.

Of course, the country was not partitioned because of what was said or not said at this meeting. The meeting was just a wake. The country broke because of what had not been done in the preceding decades to forestall Jinnah and his men. One must act in time. And that is doubly so because, once done, these things can rarely be undone. Expressing his anguish at what was being done as well as his perennial faith that every wrong could be rectified, Gandhiji told his prayer meeting, 'I had already said that they should not worry about anarchy. I am, after all, a gambler. But who would listen to me? You do not listen to me. The Muslims have given me up. Nor can I fully convince the Congress of my point of view. I tried my best to bring the Congress round to accept the proposal of May 16. But now we must accept what is an accomplished fact. The wonderful thing about it is that we can undo it anytime we want.'[66] Acharya Kripalani talked of bringing the 'seceding children' back. The Maulana forecast that it was certain to be a short-lived Partition.

But these were just words. Everyone was just putting on a brave face. Jinnah had no time for those who wanted Pakistan to be an Islamic State. Yet it ended that way. And predictably so. For these things have a logic of their own. He gave assurances upon assurances that minorities would be well treated . But we know what happened to the Hindus, in facts to all Bengalis – Muslims as well as Hindus – in East Pakistan, and what is happening to the Ahmediyas in Pakistan today. Nor did the creation of Pakistan emancipate the Muslims in Pakistan or India, as Jinnah had insisted it would. Yet what had been done could not be undone.

Hence, one must act in time. But *who* must act?

The Vital Lesson

Why don't you lead a crusade to stop the Partition, Gandhiji
was asked repeatedly in those weeks. You used to say that the
vivisection   of India would be your vivisection, that India could
be divided only over your dead body. Why don't you go on a fast
unto death now?

I feel no compulsion from within to do so, Gandhiji said. The
Congress is the national organisation and I am its servant, he said.
It has accepted the division. Would fasting against it now not
amount to insisting that it must do everything only after consulting
me? 'If the Congress is seized with madness, should I also go
mad? Should I die in order to prove that I alone was right ?' In
any case, the Partition is already a *fait accompli:* separate
Constituent Assemblies have already been formed. 'Should I now
die to nullify them? I am not going to die that way....'And so on.[67]

But the main reason he pointed to was different: the people
are no longer with me; in accepting the division of the country
the Congress is indeed reflecting public opinion; in such circumstances there is little that a leader can do.

'You should not feel sorry in your heart that India is being
divided into two,' he told his prayer gathering on 4 June. 'The
demand has been granted because you asked for it....''Lately I
have been receiving a large number of letters attacking me,' he
said on 9 June.'A friend points out how ineffective were my words
when I said that vivisection of the country would be the vivisection
of my body and calls me strongly to oppose the partition of the
country. But I do not think I am in any way to blame in this matter.
When I said that the country should not be divided I was confident
that I had the support of the masses. But when the popular view
is contrary to mine, should I force my view on the people? I have
repeatedly said that we should not compromise with falsehood and
wickedness . And today I can say with confidence that if all the
non-Muslims were with me, I would not let India be divided .
But I must admit that today the general opinion is not with me,
and so I must step aside and stay back....'[68]

In the crucial meeting of the AICC, as we have seen, he frankly
told the delegates that the decision had been taken with their

complicity, that no one would listen to his pleading, that in view of the situation neither they nor he could now stand in the way of Partition.

In the months following the meeting too, many kept returning to the question. His answer was always the same: there is a limit to what a leader can do, he cannot go far beyond what the people themselves are prepared to suffer for, to put in.

In was August 1947. The people were killing each other. The country was hurtling towards independence and Partition. The massacres had brought Gandhiji back to Calcutta. Was his support of the Working Committee's Resolution, N.K. Bose asked him, not aimed at protecting the leaders who had already decided to accept the Partition?

'It may bear that interpretation,' Gandhiji replied, 'but it is not true. With whom was I going to carry on the fight? Don't you realise that, as a result of one year of communal riots, the people of India have all become communal? They can see nothing beyond the communal question. They are tired and frightened. The Congress has only represented this feeling of the whole nation. How can I then oppose it?'

But if he knew that Partition was wrong why did he not make the Congress alter its decision? Only the future could say whether he had been right or wrong in supporting the decision, Gandhiji replied, 'I felt that the situation was not ripe for my opposition.'

'Could you not have *created* a situation?,' Bose asked him. 'You have done so on many an occasion.'

'I have never created a situation in my life,' Gandhiji said. 'I have one qualification which many of you do not possess. I can almost instinctively feel what is stirring the heart of the masses. And when I feel that the forces of good are dimly stirring within, I depend upon them and build up a programme. And they respond. People say that I had created a situation; but I had done nothing except giving a shape to what was already there. Today I see no sign of such a healthy feeling.'[69]

That is the significant lesson for us. If *we* do not alert ourselves to the declarations and programmes of the Jinnahs, if *we* do not locate and read the pamphlets of poison and hate they put out, if *we* do not bother to heed the evil that is in them, if *we* do not equip ourselves to forestall the evil they portend, if *we* are

not prepared to suffer for the goal, if *we*   have become 'tired
and frightened,' even a Gandhi cannot help us.

– August 1984

Notes

1. M.A.Jinnah, Presidential Address to the 27th Session of the Muslim
   League, Lahore, March 1940, in *Foundations of Pakistan, All-
   India Muslim League Documents, 1906-1947*, Volume II, p. 338,
   Syed   Sharifuddin Pirzada (Editor), National Publishing House,
   Karachi, 1970   (henceforth, *Pirzada* II).
2. *Ibid.*, p. 388.
3. *Ibid.*, p. 508.
4. *Ibid.*, pp. 337-8, for instance.
5. *Ibid.*, p. 505.
6. *Ibid.*, pp 338-416.
7. *Ibid.*, pp. 365-6.
8. See, for instance, negotiations about representation at the   Simla
   Conference   and in the Interim Government, Pyarelal, *The   Last
   Phase*, Volume I, Book I, pp.131, 264, Navjivan, Ahmedabad,1965.
9. On the last see, for instance, *Pirzada II*, pp. 334, 365.
10. As examples of the refrain see, for instance, the League's
    resolutions of 1940, 1941, 1943, *Pirzada II*, pp. 340, 373, 435.
11. *Ibid.*, p. 335.
12. See Jinnah 's Presidential Address to the 29th Session of the
    League, April 1942, *Pirzada II*, pp. 383-9.
13. *Ibid.*, pp. 426-7.
14. *Ibid.*, p. 338, see also 332-3.
15. *Ibid.*, p. 361.
16. *Ibid.*, pp. 361-2.
17. *Ibid.*, p. 415.
18. See, for instance, *ibid.*, 356-7, 380-2, 401, 418-19, 455.
19. *Ibid.*, pp. 514-15.
20. *Ibid.*, p. 524.
21. *Ibid.*, pp. 304-5.
22. *Ibid.*, p. 364.
23. *Ibid.*, p. 268; see also p. 294.
24. *Ibid*, pp. 304. 308.
25. *Ibid.*, p. 460.
26. *Ibid.*, pp. 412-13.

27. *Ibid.*, pp. 307-8, 319.
28. *Ibid.*, p. 353.
29. *Ibid.*, p. 355.
30. *Ibid.*, p. 355.
31. Cf. Muslim League Resolution of April 1941, *ibid.*,p. 373.
32. Muslim League Working Committee Resolution, August 1942, *ibid.*, pp. 395-96.
33. *Ibid.*, p. 455.
34. *Ibid.*, p. 329.
35. *Ibid.*, p. 333.
36. Pyarelal, *The Last Phase*, Volume II, pp. 87-8 (italics added).
37. *Ibid.*, p. 88.
38. *Ibid.*, p.286.
39. *Ibid.*, p. 287.
40. *Ibid.*, p.303.
41. *Ibid.*, p. 428.
42. *Ibid.*, p. 549.
43. *Ibid.*, pp. 286-7.
44. *Ibid.*, p. 405.
45. *Ibid.*, p. 309.
46. *Ibid.*, p. 330.
47. *Ibid.*, p. 362.
48. In *Divide Bihar*, Muslim Students Federation, April 1947,quoted in Pyarelal, *The Last Phase*, Volume I, Book II, Navjivan, Ahmedabad, 1966, pp. 316-18.
49. *Pirzada* II, p. 269.
50. For instance, *ibid.*, p. 483.
51. *Ibid.*, pp. 509-10.
52. On all this, see *Pirzada II*, pp. 519-22.
53. *Collected Works*, Volume LXXXVIII, p. 76. See also pp. 85, 93-100.
54. Cf. Pyarelal, *The Last Phase*, Volume I, Book I, Navjivan, Ahmedabad, 1966, pp. 269, 274.
55. On all this, see, for instance, Pyarelal, *The Last Phase*, Volume II, Navjivan, Ahmedabad, 1958, pp. 212-16.
56. Pyarelal, *The Last Phase*, Volume I, Book I, Navjivan, Ahmedabad, 1965, pp. 227-8.
57. N.K. Bose, *Studies in Gandhism*, Navjivan, Ahmedabad, 1972,pp.272-3.
58. Pyarelal, *The Last Phase*, Volume II, *op. cit.*, pp. 3, 10-11, 34-5.
59. *Ibid.*, p. 200.
60. Pyarelal, *The Last Phase*, Volume II, *op. cit.* 1958,pp. 210-11.
61. *Ibid.*, p. 215.
62. On all this see his addresses at the prayer meetings on June 4 to 7,

1947, *Collected Works,* Volume LXXXVIII, pp. 75-6, 84, 97-9.

63. *Ibid.,* p. 150.

64. The following is based on *Collected Works,* Volume LXXXVIII, pp. 153-7.

65. As noted earlier the preceding account of speeches at the meeting is taken, in large parts verbatim, from *The Indian Annual Register,* 1947, Volume I, pp. 122-37. See also Pyarelal, *The Last Phase,* Volume II, Navjivan, Ahmedabad, 1958, pp. 242-57; and N.K. Bose, *Studies in Gandhism,* Navjivan, Ahmedabad, 1972, pp.276-291.

66. Address at prayer meeting, 4 June, 1947, *Collected Works,* Volume LXXXVII, pp.75-6.

67. *Collected Works* , Volume LXXXVIII, pp. 75-6, 83-5, 98-140.

68. *Collected Works,* Volume LXXXVIII, pp. 117-18.

69. N.K. Bose, *Lectures on Gandhism,* Navjivan, Ahmedabad, 1971, pp. 111-12.

A Grievous Blunder

IX

'Your Wives are Your Field . . .'

❑ 18 June, Beemapally, near Trivandrum. By orders of the Jamaat, Sulekha Beevi to be flogged 101 times and her head shaven on a charge of adultery and drinking.

❑ 1 November, Perumathura, near Trivandrum: Shahbanat, a divorced young woman with two children, removed forcibly from her home on the charge of adultery, shaven and beaten by her former husband and the Jammat men till she became unconscious.

❑ 13 November, Calicut: All India Muslim Personal Law Board announces its decision to set up Shariat courts in different parts of the country.

❑ 15 November, Indore: Shah Bano asks the Supreme Court to 'withdraw' the verdict it had given in her favour.

❑ 20 November, Bombay: Over a hundred thousand Muslims demonstrate against the Supreme Court's verdict on the Shah Bano case.

❑ 21 November, Ahmednagar: A mob of 10,000 stones 40-odd reformists and forces them to call off a state-wide campaign in support of the Court's judgement.

❑ 24 November, Patna: A dozen are injured as a procession against the Shah Bano verdict turns violent.

A simple decision on whether a 70-year-old woman should get the Rs 25 as maintenance that the magistrate had decreed, or the Rs 500 that Section 125 of the Cr. P.C. specifies, or whether she should get nothing at all even when she is completely unable to maintain herself, is fast becoming a 'Muslims vs. the Rest' issue.

To many Muslims, even a harmless judgement that a 70-year-old indigent woman divorced by her husband after forty-five years of marriage and five children should get a little allowance is proof that the Hindus want to destroy their identity, to swallow them up. To the Hindus, even an academic defence of the Shariat is proof that Muslims are being pandered to, that in its weakness the country has allowed them 'special privileges'. It is proof positive to them that the Muslims owe primary loyalty to Islam rather than to the country. It is proof conclusive that behind the defence of Shariat is the design to retain polygamy, and behind *that* is a conspiracy to outstrip the Hindus by producing more children....

This road leads to bitterness, recrimination, riots and murder.

The Need to Get Down to Specifics

The cure is to get down to specifics. The question is not whether my 'primary loyalty' is to Islam or to India – as far as I can make out, not just the 'primary' but the 'overriding' loyalty of the Hindu and the Muslim alike is to himself – but what provision of Muslim personal law is just and excellent and should therefore be made applicable to all, and what provision is inequitable and retrograde and to which therefore no one should be subjected.

The Hindu must confine himself to these specifics. He will discover that there are provisions in the Shariat that *should* be made applicable to all. Thus, for instance, he will find that in Muslim marriages it is mandatory to secure the consent of the bride. If she has been married as a minor and the marriage has not been consummated, she has the right to repudiate the marriage on reaching puberty. Similarly, the provision that a person can dispose of only a third of his property in his will, that the remaining two-thirds automatically devolves to heirs in fixed proportions, forces a Muslim to leave a fixed proportion even to a scoundrel who may have tormented him, but it also prevents him from being unjust to anyone out of pique.

The Hindu will also discover that many provisions of Hindu personal law are inequitable and should be replaced. For instance, it is almost impossible for a wife whose husband has taken a second wife to bring him to book for bigamy. Similarly, when a couple is getting divorced, there is a *presumption* that the husband will be better able to look after the adult children and should therefore have the custody of the children as their 'natural guardian'. The presumption is unwarranted, it places the wife at the greatest

disadvantage; the fear of losing the children forces many a wife to
continue to suffer.

The Muslim too will do well to focus on specifics. The more
he makes this also into a Hindu-Muslim issue, the more he will
instigate a backlash. Nor can one hope to shut off inquiry and
debate by asserting divinely ordained immunity. For one thing, the
scriptures of others also claim to have originated from God or
to be reporting what He said. The Bible is full of 'God spakes'.
The Institutes of Manu claim no less: 'He [the Imperishable One]
having composed these Institutes [of the sacred law], Himself
taught them, according to the rule, to me alone in the beginning...,'
(*The Laws of Manu,* 1.58) '...Wise Manu sprung from the Self-
existent, composed these Institutes [of the sacred law],' (*Ibid,* 1.
102) 'The Lord Prajapati, created these Institutes [of the sacred
law] by His austerities alone....' (*Ibid.,* 11.244). May the Christians, the Hindus and others not then claim similar exemption
from inquiry, discussion, reform? Moreover, the confidence that
our scripture is divine, that the Prophet is the Perfect Man whom
Allah sent down to mankind as the great exemplar, should make
us not reluctant but eager to engage in free and rational discourse
about the doctrine, the Prophet and everything that flows from
them. The more free and rational and abundant the discussion
is, the more swiftly will their excellence be established.

Each of us should also see that the best way to guarantee
our interests – of each of us as individuals and of all of us together
– is not by clutching on to this fig-leaf of separateness or that, but
of working together to strengthen the institutions of a modern,
secular State. Every badge of separateness spurs others to assert
separateness too – notice the demand that was put forward
recently that the Sikhs too should be allowed to have their own
personal law, notice also the hardening of the sentiments of
Hindus *qua* Hindus. It is precisely for this reason that when our
Constitution was framed it was clearly recognized that the
different communities were being allowed to retain their personal
laws purely as a temporary expedient, and that – as Article 44
says – the endeavour of the State will be 'to secure for the citizens
a uniform civil code, throughout the territory of India.' Steps
were taken to reform Hindu law, and the reforms were carried
through in the teeth of the opposition of obscurantists, who too
were insisting that personal law and religion were inseparable,

that the law, like the religion, was divinely ordained and could not therefore be altered by human hand, that amending one would endanger the other. All these specious assertions were wisely set aside. The law was updated and reformed. Hinduism did not collapse.

Why Reform Stopped

Ever since the mid-nineteenth century, Muslim law too was being reformed slowly. Whereas under Muslim law the penalty for apostasy was not just the loss of rights in property, the automatic dissolution of the marriage bond etc., but death, the Caste Disabilities Removal Act of 1850 banished all laws and usage which impaired the rights of property, inheritance or any other rights of an individual 'by reason of his or her renouncing, or having been excluded from the communion of, any religion, or being deprived of caste.' The jurisdiction of the Qazis was abolished, and where the personal law of different communities continued it was thenceforth to be administered by magistrates appointed by the State. Muslim criminal law was replaced by the Indian Penal Code of 1860 and the Criminal Procedure Code of 1898. Muslim law of evidence was replaced by the Evidence Act of 1872. This put a host of matters of personal law – the presumption of death, the legitimacy of children, etc. – within the purview of secular, modern legislation. In the same year, the Contract Act was put in force and applied equally to all – Hindus and Muslims alike. As the textbooks record, the Married Women's Property Act of 1874, the Majority Act of 1875, the Transfer of Property Act of 1882, the Guardians Wards Act of 1890, the Indian Succession Act of 1925, one by one extended the ambit of modern, secular, common principles to spheres that had been regarded as the exclusive preserve of the separate personal laws of different communities.

Moreover, even in spheres where the different personal laws continued to operate, the procedure to be followed in the courts, the nature of evidence to be taken into account, etc., came to be governed by the common Codes and Acts. Reform continued apace. Thus while, as we shall see, a tradition of the Prophet would seem to recommend that daughters be married off at the age of twelve, and while child marriages were as customary in Islamic society as in other traditional societies, the Child Marriages Restraint Act of 1929 began the process of the State laying down the minimum age for marriage. Similarly, while Muslim law gives unfettered, complete and exclusive rights to the husband to divorce his wife, and confers none on the wife whatsoever – save what the husband may in his discretion grant her – the Dissolution of Muslim Marriages Act of 1939 began the process of redressing the balance by enabling the wife to initiate the proceedings too on specified grounds. Principles of equity from English law were gradually grafted on to the Muslim law of gifts. And so on.

This process of reform and integration stopped dead with the Partition. Apart from a few stray extensions – such as the Special Marriage Act of 1954, which gives all couples the option to register their marriages under this Act and thenceforth be governed by common, modern, secular laws – the country abandoned all efforts to update or reform Muslim law, or to move towards a common code.

The reason has not been any new, suddenly discovered veneration for personal law but the trauma of Partition – the urge to 'leave bad enough alone' – that is, the reason has been expedience, not principle.

The consequences are before us. These symbols of separateness continue. What is good in the law of this or that community is not extended to all. What is iniquitous in it continues to torment members of that community. And anomalies reign: a Muslim husband remains free to cast away his wife by pronouncing a single word thrice, while a Christian couple – even if they amicably agree that their marriage is not workable – must wait for *three* judges of a *High Court* to confirm their divorce!

The Secular Approach

Three points should be obvious. First, under our Constitution, by the very nature of our State, no religious or other group has any inherent or perpetual right to insist that it will be governed by laws different from laws that apply to the generality of citizens.

Second, every tradition has much that is valuable, just as every tradition has much that is today regressive – whether it was progressive at one stage or not. The excellence of a tradition on one point is no justification for continuing an inequity on another. Similarly, the inequities of one tradition are no justification for the inequities of another. Dowry murders among Hindus do not justify the fact that Muslims can discard a wife so arbitrarily, any more than the fact that Muslim husbands have this terrible power justifies dowry murders among Hindus. We should imbibe the best from each of the traditions, just as we must reform each of them.

Third, all our traditions – Hinduism, Islam and all the others – are equally the common heritage of each one of us. Each of us therefore has the fullest right and the equal duty to examine, to debate, to urge the adoption or reform of any one and all of the traditions. And each of us must exercise this right and discharge this obligation without the slightest trace of self-consciousness for being a Muslim or a Hindu.

'You had better write a critique of Hindu personal law also,' a friend counsels me, 'otherwise you will be accused of being communal.' But that precisely is the kind of self-consciousness that we must rid ourselves of. A parallel paper can certainly be written about Hindu personal law. And the occasion for writing it will arise when the Hindus start saying that modern, secular laws should not be applied to them, that the laws of Manu and Vashishta and Apastambha should not be altered since they are divinely ordained.

Today these claims are being put forward on behalf of Muslim personal law and therefore they must be examined in reference to that law. That is the subject I will deal with, objectively, in a forthright manner, with reference to the texts and the provisions themselves. There is a lot of ground to cover and I am not going to waste space making parallel points about Hindu law just to 'prove' my secular credentials, just to 'prove' that I am approaching the matter as an Indian and not as a Hindu.

Propositions

It must have struck the newspaper reader that in all the commotion that has been raised against the Shah Bano verdict, no Muslim leader or organization has argued that the verdict is unjust, that casting off a 70-year-old indigent woman without any maintenance after 45 years of marriage and five children is right and just.

The assertion, instead, is that discarding her in this way is in accord with Allah's word and the Prophet's practice, that, therefore, asking a Muslim to pay anything – be it Rs 25 or Rs 500 – as alimony is compelling him to violate his religion.

Five propositions are being urged to create this impression:

❏ Every bit of Muslim personal law is derived from the Quran and the *sunna*, i.e. the practice of the Prophet;

❏ Being divinely ordained, it cannot be altered by a merely human agency like a court or a legislature;

❏ Muslim law – deriving as it does from the Quran and the practice of the Prophet – is perfect, in that it is excellent, i.e. it is the ideal basis for an ideal society; and that it is complete, i.e. it anticipates all eventualities, all circumstances of time and place, and provides just answers for all of them;

❏ It is a seamless garment – if one thread of it is pulled out, all of it will come apart;

❏ In Islam there is no partition between personal law, law in general, and life; Islam provides an integrated code for all aspects of life; therefore, to ask a Muslim to do something contrary to Muslim law is in fact to compel him to violate his religion as a whole.

In contrast to these propositions, I shall argue that

❏ What we know as Muslim law today owes more to clerics than to the Quran or the traditions of the Prophet;

❏ From the earliest times – that is , from the days of the revelation itself – it has been supplemented, and changed;

❏ It bears – and manifestly so – the stamp of the time, place, and circumstances in which it originated;

❏ Muslims, like the rest of humanity, have grown beyond the beliefs, practices, institutions of that time in every aspect of life from cosmology to medicine to law; growing beyond what was said and done at that time has not injured Islam;

❏ If there is no difficulty in acknowledging that what was said and done about a host of these matters is indeed dated, why is it sacrilegious to recognize the same thing in the case of marriage or   divorce   or alimony or inheritance?

❑ On the other hand, if we insist that every word of what was said
then is excellent and eternal, if we insist that every command
of, say, the Quran must be   followed, if we insist that
everything it lays down is one   seamless garment, we end up
with another set of problems: are we then to reintroduce and
live by what it   says,   for   instance,   on apostasy, on *Jihad*?

❑ Therefore, the only way to consider the question is to examine
the specific provisions of the law;

❑ These may have been progressive in the context of seventh
century Arabia, but by the standards of equity and justice
mankind has reached today − in part, no doubt as a result of
the example   and   efforts   of giants like the Prophet − the
provisions are regressive;

❑ And this result is not fortuitous, for the specific provisions
are rooted in a conception − of women, for instance − which
bears the stamp of seventh century Arabia.

In short, the fundamentalists are   right: in asking the husband
of the 70-year-old Shah Bano to pay her a maintenance allowance,
the Supreme Court   has gone contrary to Muslim personal law.
But that is a reason not for reversing the verdict;   it is a reason
for re-examining Muslim personal law   in the light of modern,
secular principles.

Basis

Formally, Muslim personal law is said to be derived from four
sources: the Quran; the *sunna*, that is, the practice of the Prophet;
ijma, that is, consensus (of the community? of jurists? of divines?
of those possessed of piety, of devotion to Islam, etc.? − there are
differences on all this); and *qiyas*, that is, reasoning by analogy.

Everyone knows about the Quran, of course. The original of the
Book is believed to exist in heaven. It was revealed by Allah to His
apostle, Mohammed, through the angel Gabriel, from time to time.
It was put together in its present form after the death of
the Prophet during the reign of the third Khalifa, Usman.

The practice and   words of the Prophet form the second source of the law. These are described in the *hadis*, i.e., 'the traditions'. The first compilations began to be put together about 125 years after the Prophet's death. Several compilations were made. Six of these are regarded as canonical. Of the six, two – the compilations of Bukhari and Muslim – are the most revered. The two of them lived in the third century after the Prophet. (I will have occasion to refer to the two compilations often. All references to them are to the following editions: *Sahih al-Bukhari*, Volumes 1 to 9, Islamic University, Medina Al-Munawwara, Kazi Publications, Lahore, 1979, *Sahih Muslim*, Volumes 1 to 4, Kitab Bhavan, Delhi, 1978.)

These records of the practice and words of the Prophet are revered almost as much as the Quran, for, Allah said, 'I have sent you two things, and you will not go astray as long as you hold them fast. The one is the Book of God, and the other the *sunna* of the Prophet.' While there are some traditions which say that a rule from the *sunna* cannot override a verse of the Quran, there are others that affirm that a verse from the Quran cannot be used to abrogate a rule derived from the *sunna*. Modern texts put the two at par. Thus, for instance, our most widely used text says, 'As a source of law, *hadis* is as binding as the principles of the Koran,' 'In the word of God is included, of course, the Koran but the divinely inspired *sunna* of the Prophet ranks equal' (Mulla's *Principles of Mohamedan Law* by M. Hidayatullah, 17th edition, 1972, Tripathi, Bombay, pp. xii-xiii). The importance of this will become evident soon enough.

Ijma played a very important part in the formative stages of the law. The acceptance of one particular version of the Quran rather than the others as the one and only authentic version, the institution of Caliphate, the growth of different schools of law – there were nineteen at one stage – and the gradual ascendance of four among them, the recognition of the authority of Shariat courts and the subsequent modifications in their jurisdiction – all these, and of course a whole host of particular points in law, arose as a result of consensus, at first among the followers of Islam as a whole and then among narrower and narrower circles.

Ambiguities in the original texts, the fact that they covered only a few of the many eventualities that arise in life, change and the new requirements that expansion entailed are what made this practice necessary. Legitimacy followed. The practice was said to derive from the fact that Allah had endowed Muslims with the necessary ability to innovate and adapt. Had Allah not said, 'You are the best of peoples ever raised up for mankind'? (*Quran*, 3.310) Similarly, three hundred years after he died, the Prophet was also recorded to have said, for instance, 'My followers will never agree upon an error.' It followed that if through *Ijma* they now agreed on a point, their decision necessarily had to be right.

Innovations and substitutions through *Ijma* were made easier by recognising that, while the texts were of course inviolate, there was the right of *ijtihad*, that is to interpret them, to use one's reason, to deduce logically.

'It is incumbent on you to follow the most numerous body,' the Prophet was recalled as saying and implicit in this, it was said, was the permission to the majority to form an opinion. 'Whatever Muslims hold to be good,'he was recalled as saying, 'is good before God.'(The word 'whatever' was to be strictly circumscribed later on, but for the time being this too was taken to contain the permission for members of the community to decide on their own by consultation among themselves.)

Strictly speaking, as the Quran was said to be not just excellent but complete in all aspects – i.e., as it was said to provide not just the basis for the ideal society, but also to anticipate and provide the answer for every possible situation – Allah Himself having said, 'Today I have perfected your religion for you, and have *completed* My blessing upon you, and I have approved Islam for your religion,' (*Quran*, 5.4-5) – in view of all this, *ijma, ijtihad*, etc. should not really have been necessary.

But they proceeded apace. And, as is obvious, while retrospective sanction for them may have been couched in the words of Allah or the Prophet, the consensus was being arrived at, the interpretations and constructions were being made, not by the Divine Lawgiver or the Prophet but by ordinary mortals like any of us.

As the decades passed, two things happened. No basis had been laid down for ascertaining the consensus. The verses of the Quran and the traditions of the Prophet that were being cited had referred to the entire community of believers. As Islam spread, as different States were formed, each proclaiming adherence to it, as they began or continued their wars against one another, it became more difficult to ascertain the consensus of the community of believers.

Second, the freedom implicit in *ijma* and *ijtihad* led to a welter of opinions on every point, to endless disputations, to dangerous free-thinking.

Reaction took two forms. *Ijma* was narrowed down to mean the consensus, not of the community, but of the jurists and the Qazis, and, later still, of the jurists and, for different groups, the Qazis of different areas – of Medina for some, of Damascus for others, and so on. Traditions were now cited to show that the Prophet's practice had not been to consult all and sundry but only the few who were qualified to give an opinion – his select companions. Indeed, it was recalled that he had warned, 'Allah will not deprive you of knowledge after He has given it to you, but it will be taken away through the death of the religious learned men who, when consulted, will give verdicts according to their opinions whereby they will mislead others and go astray' (*Bukhari*, 92.410, 411). Next, the right to interpretation too was progressively restricted to 'those qualified to exercise it' – the *mujtahids*, the few 'who strive'. Soon, in fact just about 300 years after the Prophet's time – that is, almost a thousand years ago – 'the doors of *ijtihad*'were officially and formally 'closed' on the grounds that all points had been already clarified and that, in any case, piety had fallen to such a state that there were no men left who were qualified to exercise the right to interpret. Sure enough, there were traditions which supported this closure, traditions which recalled that the Prophet himself never gave a decision on his opinion or on *qiyas* but that he confined himself strictly to following the word of Allah (as Allah, it was recalled, had enjoined all to do – e.g. *Quran* 4.105), traditions which recorded that when the Allah was silent on a matter, the Prophet too kept silent (e.g., *Bukhari*, 92.412-13).

Ijma of the community came thus to mean whatever had come to prevail, whatever had come to be accepted one way or another, as evident from the actual practice of the believers. And *ijma* of the learned came to mean the *fatwas* and opinions of the learned, later still of the Qazis of the particular area. *Ijtihad* was replaced by *taqlid*, the practice of abiding – abiding literally and one hundred per cent – by the rulings of the learned who had lived earlier and the Qazis.

The learned and the Qazis, in turn, came to depend on kings and courtiers. Some of them continued to be men of learning and piety. Most of them ended up as the clergy of every other religion: preoccupied with externals, factionalists, using religion and law to further their personal and sectarian interests, apologists bending the law to legitimise what the king and courtiers were doing in any case. And so on. Several of them had to be punished for embezzling funds, for amassing wealth etc. In his outstanding work, *The Indian Muslims*, (George Allen and Unwin, London, 1967), Professor Mujeeb recounts in detail the progressive inter-dependence of the Qazis, the princes and the courtiers, as well as the consequences for what we today know to be the Shariat.

A single illustration will have to suffice. The admonitions of the Quran against dissolute behaviour in general and wine in particular are well known. Notice now how the clerics state the law in *Fatawa-i-Qadi Khan*: 'It is written in the book of *nikah* [marriage] that a person both of whose parents are Muslims is *Kufw* [eligible for marriage].' But, as Professor Mujeeb reminds us, the jurist introduces variations:

If a person is *openly* immoral (for instance, he drinks wine openly and staggers and stumbles while passing through streets), he will not be considered eligible for a virtuous young woman. But he will be eligible if he conceals this fact and does not let it become evident.... If an openly immoral person is treated with respect by the people, for instance, because he is a courtier, then he will be considered eligible, but if he is a common sort of man, he will not be.

Naturally, the clerics used the law and the power to lay it down, not just to legitimise the conduct and performance of their patrons and their class, but also to wage their own little faction fights, and to indulge their own notions. Professor Mujeeb recounts how two famous jurists – Qadi Shihabuddin Daulatabadi and Shaikh Abdul Fath Jaunpuri – 'engaged in a bitter contro-versy,' how they 'abused and cursed each other,' on the question of whether the saliva of a cat was clean or unclean (Mujeeb, *op. cit.*, pp. 76-7). He recalls how another cleric caused great con-sternation by declaring that it was a deadly sin to let a midwife cut the umbilical cord of a new-born child, that this was Hindu custom which should not be imitated, and that a Muslim father should perform the operation himself (*Ibid.*, p. 396). Scores of other examples can be given.

Now, for the question that we are considering, two points
are important. First, all the decisions connected with this process
– the introduction of *ijma*, the opening of the doors of *ijtihad*,
the narrowing of *ijma* to a few, then to the few of one region or
another, its final extinction, the closing of the doors of *ijtihad* –
each of these decisions was made by ordinary human mortals,
neither by Allah nor by the Prophet. Second, what we know as
Muslim law today is the amalgam of the dicta, the *fatwas*, the
inclinations of these very ordinary, very human beings.

It is made out that each and every bit of what we know to be
Muslim personal law is from the Quran, that therefore amending
any part of it will amount to mutilating the Quran. Contrast this
with the facts of history and evolution sketched above. And
contrast them too with the actual practice that our courts follow
while administering the law. Citing judgements, a recent text
summarizes the position:

> In India the traditional law of the Muslims is to be accepted
> as it is found in the book of authority. The courts or
> the lawyers do not have to locate the principles of law
> in the Quran or the *sunna*. Nor have they to look or arrange
> for *ijma* [consensus of the jurists] on any particular issue. As
> regards other sources mentioned above [*qiyas*, etc.] the courts
> neither have to employ them nor to ask any contemporary
> jurist to do so in a given case.
>
> Thus, each source of law recognised under the classical theory
> is now, in India, rather dormant. The courts cannot exercise
> the power of *ijtihad*; nor do they recognise the authority of
> any *mujtahid* of our age. Under the Indian law the courts
> have to act as *muqallids* [conformists] in respect of the
> Sunnis (who agree that the doors of *ijtihad* are closed) as well
> as the Shias (who, in theory, believe in the continuing
> possibility of *ijtihad*).
>
> The courts in India have firmly accepted the principles [of]
> *taqlid* by laying down and acting upon the rules stated
> below: (i) In administering Muslim law no court should
> attempt to put its own construction on any Quranic text.(ii)
> No court should examine the conformity of any traditionally
> settled legal principle with the relevant text of the Quran. (iii)
> No reported *hadis* should be taken by the courts literally so

as to deduce from it a new rule of law. (iv) The lawyers of the modern age cannot be allowed to introduce new rules of law by claiming that they logically follow from the texts of the Quran or the *sunna*. (v) No court should in any way circumvent or deviate from the law as settled by the jurists of the past even if it does not sound 'modern', 'just', or 'logical'. (Tahir Mahmood, *The Muslim Law of India*, Law Book Company, Lucknow, 1980, pp. 13-14. Mahmood cites the relevant cases for each rule. See also *Mulla's Principles of Mohamedan Law, op. cit.*, Sections 34-6.)

Two conclusions are manifest. First, as far as our courts are concerned, Muslim personal law is *completely* frozen. *There is not the slightest possibility of reform from within the corpus.* And, second, it has been frozen in a mould not set by the original texts – the Quran and the accounts of the practices of the Prophet – but fabricated by ordinary mortals like us, mortals whose rulings, *fatwas* and the like bear only too clearly the impress of their particular concerns, their time and circumstances.

And yet the impression is put out that to amend any bit of the law will be to mutilate the Quran itself.

The question for us is: what do we find when we go back to first principles – to the Quran, that is, and the traditions of the Prophet?

The Quran

The Quran has about 6000 verses. About 70 of these – on one count, about 80 – deal with personal law. Twenty-five deal with divorce, 10 with marriage, 5 with fornication and adultery, 10 and 3 with inheritance and legacies respectively, 6 with orphans and minors, 7 with maintenance of divorced wives and widows, and 3 with maintenance in general.

It is thus a small corpus – specially because many of the verses repeat or reiterate what has been said elsewhere. From the beginning, therefore, there has been the most extensive elaboration of, the most extensive grafting onto, the most extensive discoveries and inventions about these few verses. For instance, as noted above, around 10 or so verses are all that there is on the law of inheritance in the Quran. Yet this branch

of the law has been developed into a most extensive and
intricate maze extending, quite literally, to the farthest reaches of
the imagination. While in the Quran Allah confines Himself to
spelling out the shares that are to devolve on near-relatives – like
parents, sons, daughters, wives etc. – our jurists (as Goldziher, one
of the greatest scholars of Islam, notes) have written treatises
setting out the share in the estate that may be claimed by a male
ascendant at the fifth degree of removal from the deceased
if the latter dies childless. 'Since in popular belief the
metamorphosis of man into beast is within the range of natural occurrences,' Goldziher continues with appropriate examples,

> the jurists inquire in all seriousness into the legal status of
> enchanted persons and their responsibilities under the law.
> Since, on the other hand, demons frequently assume human
> shape, the jurists assess the consequences of such
> transformation for religious law; serious arguments and
> counter-arguments are urged, for example, whether such
> beings can be numbered among the participants necessary for
> the Friday service. Another problematic case that divine law
> must clarify: how is one to deal with progeny from a marriage
> between a human being and a demon in human form (a
> further eventuality admitted in popular belief)? What are the
> consequences in family law of such marriages? Indeed, the
> problem of *munakahat-al-jinn* (marriages with *jinn*) is
> treated in such circles with the same seriousness as any
> important point of the religious law (Ignaz Goldziher,
> *Introduction to Islamic Theology and Law*, Princeton, 1981,
> pp. 63-4; the original in German was printed in 1910).

Apart from the lengths to which the law had to be and was
in fact developed, it was apparent from the beginning that some
of the injunctions of Allah in the Quran just could not be
fulfilled in practice. Conventional solutions – that is, solutions
put together by ordinary human beings confronted with
insoluble conundrums, with impractical requirements – were
devised around these provisions of the law.

Two brief examples – one from the law of inheritance and one
from that of marriage – will have to suffice.

Verses 4.12-15 and 4.175 of the Quran specify the shares that fall to heirs upon the death of a man. The verses distinguish between the case when a man dies leaving no children and when he is survived by children. In the latter case, there are further distinctions depending on whether there are sons or not, and, in either case, on whether the number of daughters is one, or more than two (what is to be done when there are two daughters is not quite clear).

Consider the case when a man is survived by children, among others. The relevant commands are as follows:

> God charges you concerning your children. To the male the like of the portion of two females; and if they be women ['daughters' in this context] above two, then for them two-thirds of what he leaves, but if she be one then to her a half, and to his parents to each one of the two, the sixth of what he leaves...;
> But if you have children, then for them [the wives] of what you leave an eighth, after any bequest you may bequeath, or any debt.

Now whether there is one daughter or more the share of the wives, mother and father remains at 1/8, 1/6 and 1/6 respectively. If there is one daughter, then she receives 1/2 of the estate. The share of each son must be double that of this daughter. Thus, if there is one son his share will be double of a half, that is, one; if there are two sons each must get double of a half, that is, each must get one. And so on. The consequence is that the total shares add to about *two* with one son, to *three* if there are two sons, etc. But there is, after all, a total of only *one* to distribute!

When there are two daughters, it isn't clear what should be done because the verses only specify 'if there be women *above* two' and 'if she be one'. When there are three or more, the same problem starts arising after a while.

Clearly, the injunctions just cannot be adhered to by mere mortals. The jurists therefore do the obvious thing: they scale down all the shares proportionately to ensure that, even though the precise figures given in the Quran are violated, the total to be distributed adds up to one. Now, this is an eminently sensible solution, but it is a *conventional* one thought up by mere mortals, in clear violation of the command of God.

As a second example, consider the question of adultery. The

Quran is very firmly set against it. After rumours had touched Aisha herself, God revealed that henceforth there must be four witnesses 'to the fact' (4.19; the incident forms the starting point of *Sura* 24 in the Quran; Aisha's account of it and of how the consequential Revelation then followed is recounted at length in the traditions, for instance *Muslim* 35.6673.) Once the witnesses testified against the women, Allah said, 'then detain them in their houses till death takes them or God appoints for them a way' (*Quran*, 4.15). At another place (24.2) it prescribes that she be flogged with a hundred lashes. As is well known, the punishment that the law-books prescribe is not immuring (i.e., walling in till the woman suffocates to death) as divinely decreed but stoning to death, or a hundred lashes.

The way this replacement of the command of God by a practice that had prevailed in the area but had fallen into disuse is justified is typical. First, of course, there is the practice of the Prophet himself. The traditions record instances in which when persons themselves came and told him that they had committed adultery, he had them stoned to death. There is next the tradition attributed to Aisha that a *Sura* of the Quran that now has 73 verses originally had 200 and one of those was the verse on stoning. Umar also confirmed that there had been a verse to this effect(*Bukhari*, 82.816).

As can be imagined, the latter traditions of Aisha and Umar have raised more problems than they have solved. In the Quran some verses abrogate others. Did some or any of those 127 abrogate or throw new light on some or any of the ones that remain?

The point is that on several matters, conventional solutions have been found to modify or get around the specific commands of the Quran from the time of the Prophet himself. In fact, 'finding a way around' a provision of the Quran by a legal trick (*hiyal*) became a discipline in itself. Abu Hanifa, one of the greatest jurists of Islam, and the founder the school of law which the overwhelming population of Muslims in India follow, was specially renowned for his skill in putting together the necessary inventions (Goldziher, *op.cit.*, pp. 57-65). Tricks were found to get around the Quran's prohibition of drinking, its injunctions about what kind of meat alone may be eaten, etc. (*Ibid*, pp. 57-63). A typical example from Schacht, one of the most thorough scholars of Islamic Law, will suffice:

For instance the Quran prohibits interest, and this religious prohibition was strong enough to make popular opinion unwilling to transgress it openly and directly, while at the same time there was an imperative demand for the giving and taking of interest in commercial life. In order to satisfy this need, and at the same time to observe the letter of the religious prohibition, a number of devices were developed. One consisted of giving real property as a security for the debt and allowing the creditor to use it, so that its use represented the interest; this transaction forms a close parallel to the sale with the right of redemption. Another, very popular, device consisted of a double sale (*bay' atan fi bay's*) of which there are many variants. For instance, the (prospective) debtor sells to the (prospective) creditor a slave for cash, and immediately buys the slave back from him for a greater amount payable at a future date; this amounts to a loan with the slave as security, and the difference between the two prices represents the interest; the transaction is called *mukhatara* or, more commonly, *'ina'*. Euphemistically, it is also called *mu'amala*, 'transaction' and the money-lender 'trader', because traders also acted as money-lenders. This custom prevailed in Medina as early as in the time of Malik. There were hundreds of these devices, extending over all fields of the law of contracts and obligations, many of them highly technical, but all with a scrupulous regard for the letter of the law.... (Joseph Schacht, *An Introduction to Islamic Law*, Oxford, 1964, p. 79).

The provisions of the Quran on law can be discussed at great length. For the present two points are all we need to note. First, in contrast to the impression that is sought to be conveyed, the impression that Muslim personal law is one seamless garment every bit of which is derived from the Quran, in fact only a very small part of the Quran deals with it, and the verses that deal with it cover only a small proportion of the subjects that today constitute Muslim personal law.

Second, several of the provisions on these matters have been added to and substituted by conventional devices from the very beginning.

The Sunna

The second ostensible source of the law – namely, the practice of the Prophet – presents even greater problems. In the case of the Quran we have, at least since the days of Usman, a text which is reliable. While there are several collections of narratives about what the Prophet said and did, there are the gravest doubts about their accuracy.

The Prophet had an overpowering and a magnetic influence on his people. They used to go to him for decisions and advice on all sorts of matters – the cosmos, beliefs, mode of prayer, sacrifice, what to eat and how, sex, dress, manners, property, law and a hundred other things. His spontaneous remarks on these matters were for them law.

After he died, specially because of the circumstances in which he died (on his deathbed he had asked for material to write something down, in all probability to indicate who should be the Khalifa; this was denied – on the apprehension, say the Sunni historians, that he might abrogate something vital of the Quran in his delirium; to prevent him from recording his decision that his son-in-law Ali should be the Khalifa, say the Shia historians), strife and contention began among the closest companions as well as among their followers. At the same time, people further and further away from the heartland began to embrace Islam.

In all corners, whenever an issue arose the believers wanted to know what the Prophet had said or done about it, what his opinion or ruling had been. This was due both to the veneration in which he was held and to the fact that each contender, each disputant felt that the only way to justify his position was to trace it to the practice of the Prophet himself.

Such intense demand brought forth a ready supply. The *hadis,* the accounts or traditions of the Prophet, multiplied by the hundreds of thousands. Dynasties – the Ummayads and following them the Abbasids who displaced them – had traditions manufactured to establish their right to rule and their virtues. Traditions turned up in which the Prophet was seen to have prophesied that a ruler with the name X or Y from place A or B would ascend to leadership and bring prosperity to the people. Traditions turned up to prove that the Prophet had certified the superiority of this place or that, of Syria in some, Basra in others, of Fas in the Maghrib, of Shershil in Algeria, of Qamuniya. Nor were these certificates confined to rulers and places. The great jurist Abu Hanifa – the founder of the Hanafite school of law that most Indian Muslims follow – was born about 70 years after the Prophet died. But to establish his pre-eminence his followers had no difficulty in discovering a tradition in which the Prophet had said, 'In my community will rise a man called Abu Hanifa who will be the torch of the community.'

Alarmed by the torrent, the faithful then produced traditions in which the Prophet was shown to have forecast that after him many fabricators would circulate false accounts of what he had said or done and put words in his mouth to legitimise themselves and their ways, and to have warned that such fabricators would roast in hell. But these were followed by traditions in which, while he was seen to have prophesied the production of traditions all right, his attitude to the productions was represented as being more indulgent. In a typical tradition, for instance, he says, 'After my departure, a number of sayings attributed to me will increase in the same way as sayings have been ascribed to previous prophets. What therefore is told to you as a saying of mine you will have to compare with the Book of God, and what is in accordance with it is by me, whether I have in fact said it myself or not.'

But what was 'in accordance with the Book of God' is precisely what the contenders differed about. The result was that the fabrication continued. In fact, the manufacturing of *hadis*, so long as one was doing so to enhance piety or adherence, itself came to be looked upon as a pious act. As a result of this 'pious fraud,' as Goldziher correctly termed it, the stock of accounts about the Prophet's *sunna* went on multiplying. No wonder, the specialist on the *hadis*, Asim Al Nabil surveying the scene about a century and a half after the Prophet, exlcaimed, 'I have come to the conclusion that a pious man is never so ready to lie as in matters of *hadis*.'

Affairs reached an appalling state. Thus the compiler of the most revered collection – Bukhari – recorded that he had been led to sift the true *hadis* from the chaos by a dream in which he saw himself driving flies away from the Prophet's corpse.

He and the other compilers used the most elementary tests to winnow the material. Each tradition, for instance, is based on an *isnad* – a preface saying 'A heard from B who heard from C...that when K was with the Prophet, he heard him tell Y that....' But if it turned out that when C was alive B was already dead, the tradition was rejected as unreliable. Even though the tests were elementary in the extreme, and even though they were confined almost exclusively to an assessment of the *isnad*, the results of these diligent and pious compilers testify to what they found.

Thus Bukhari laboured 16 years, interrogating a thousand sheikhs living in far-away places, and complied six hundred thousand traditions. Ultimately he included only, 7397 (on another account 7295) in his *Sahih*. And, as Guillaume points out, if the repetitions are eliminated, the number of distinct *hadis* is only 2762. That is, of every two hundred that Bukhari examined, he found *one hundred and ninety nine* to be unreliable.

The experience of the other compilers was similar. Abu Daud examined five hundred thousand. Of these, even on those elementary tests, he was able to retain only 4800. And in regard to even this selection he states that he was including not just the authentic *hadis*, but also 'those which seem to be authentic and those which are nearly so.'

'Where such a preponderance of material is judged to be false,' records Guillaume, 'nothing but the successful application of modern canons of evidence can restore faith in the credibility of the remainder....' The problem doesn't of course end with the fact that such an overwhelming proportion of the *hadis* had to be rejected. The ones that were retained and which now ostensibly form the basis of Muslim law are themselves riddled with the severest difficulties.

For instance, much depended on whether a transmitter was regarded as truthful or not. Of the 40,000 odd 'companions' by and through whom the traditions had been transmitted, Bukhari found only about 2000 to be reliable. The Shias, of course, reject all traditions that do not originate with Ali and the Prophet's family. But even among the Sunnis, assessments about the degree to which transmitters can be relied upon continue to differ to the widest possible extent. Thus, for instance among the most prolific of transmitters is Abu Huraira, a constant companion of the Prophet for three years or so. A significant proportion of the traditions that figure in each of the great compilations – about a sixth in Bukhari's case – originate from him. Accounts about him range all the way from a stout defence, to his being hit with a whip by Umar, the second Khalifa and eminent companion of the Prophet, for transmitting fabrications, from explanations of how he probably heard and saw more of the Prophet than the others to his being threatened by Umar with banishment unless he stopped transmitting his concoctions.

Not only have such disagreements about the reliability of the individual transmitters continued, there have been equally vast disagreements about what should be done about the traditions transmitted by the person *after* evidence about the person's reliability or unreliability has been gathered. Thus, for instance, Bukhari and Muslim proceeded on the assumption that only those *hadis* should be incorporated in the corpus which had been transmitted on the authority of persons who were universally esteemed to be trustworthy. (As the facts about Abu Huraira indicate, Bukhari and Muslim themselves cannot be taken to have applied this rule with any strictness.) Abu Daud and Ibn Hanbal, on the other hand, proceeded on the opposite rule – that only those traditions should be rejected which had been transmitted by persons who were universally deemed to be unreliable.

The final problem is the predictable one. The traditions are contradictory. Some traditions say that the traditions themselves should not be written down, while others imply that they should be – and Abu Daud reports one to the former effect and one to the latter, one after the other. Some imply that the traditions merely amplify and cannot override a verse of the Quran, others that a verse of the Quran cannot abrogate a tradition. The compiler Tirmidhi is particularly diligent in listing contradictory *hadis*.

An entire discipline therefore had to be constructed to set out the principles by which flagrantly contradictory *hadis* may by 'reconciled.' The great Shafi's *Risala* devotes chapters to it.

Is it any surprise, then, to learn that even a man like Ibn Qutayba, one of the most zealous advocates of the school that insists on deriving every point possible of law from the traditions, concedes a greater role to *ijma*, to ascertaining the consensus of the community, than to looking up the relevant *hadis*, on the ground that 'the truth was more likely to be contained in the *ijma* than in tradition. The *hadis* is subject to many vicissitudes, due to the negligence of those handing it down, confused explanations, the abrogations which may have occurred, the unreliability of informants, the existence of two contradictory *hadis*....The *ijma* of the community is free from such vicissitudes.... This is the reason why people hand down *hadis* going back to the Prophet but follow in practice other ways.' That from a most zealous advocate, not of *ijma*, but of *hadis*! And we have already seen what happened to *ijma* as a basis of the law.

Now, all this and much, much more about the *hadis* has been established meticulously by a host of scholars. It can be easily looked up in widely available and well-known works of Goldziher (e.g. *Muslim Studies*,Volume II, Allen and Unwin, London, 1971, Original 1890), A.Guillaume (e.g., *The Traditions of Islam*, Oxford, 1924, reprint Khayats, Beirut, 1966), Joseph Schacht (e.g., *The Origins of Muhammadan Jurisprudence*, Oxford, 1948), G.H.A. Juynboll (e.g., *The Authenticity of the Tradition Literature*, Leiden, E.J. Brill, 1969) or even in Hughes' *Dictionary of Islam* and *The Encyclopaedia of Islam.*

We look up none of it. Instead, as our most widely used textbook does, we just keep chanting in blissful ignorance, 'As a source of law *hadis* is as binding as the principles of the Quran....'

Conventional, Not Divinely Ordained

Abu Ḥanifa, who founded the Hanafite school of law, placed little reliance on the traditions. His disciple, Abu Yusuf, whose appointment by Harun Al Rashid as the Chief Qazi over Malik ensured the eventual predominance of the Hanafite school, placed as much reliance on them as on other sources of the law. Inclinations and decisions differed. The point is that like everything else connected with the traditions – their collection, the criteria by which they would be accepted or rejected, the rules by which the contradictory ones would be reconciled etc. – the decision about the extent to which they would form the basis of law was a conventional one, a decision made by ordinary mortals. It was not Allah's command, nor that of the Prophet.

What was true of the traditions was equally true of the other bases of the law. Abu Hanifa would emphasise reasoning, logical deduction, analogy, consensus of the learned. Ibn Hanbal would insist that the Quran and the traditions alone must form the basis.

Even after the role of a particular source of law was recognised, the widest possible differences arose and persisted about every aspect of it. Consider the third source – *ijma*.

Can it settle questions on all matters of faith and law or only on the latter? Can it settle all questions in relation to either or only questions on which there is no clear verdict in the Quran and the *hadis*? Is the consensus to be of the community or only of the learned? Must the agreement be unanimous or will the opinion of the majority do? Is it to be the opinion of the community or the jurists of one region or of the entire world of Islam? Does the consensus become effective as soon as it is arrived at or only after all those whose opinion has been sought die without changing their opinion? Must all who are consulted express their consent actively or can we presume that their silence is consent? Who are to be excluded from the process – infidels only or heretics also? Only those heretics who proclaim and propagate their views or all? All who violate the Shariat or only those who flagrantly violate it?

Is the *ijma* of the companions alone binding? Who are to be reckoned as the companions – only the ten that the Prophet specifically certified would go to heaven, all who lived and fought along with him, or all the 30,000 who lived in Medina at that time? If the companions themselves disagreed on a matter, can law be established by the consensus of a community or the jurists? Would that not amount to certifying the heresy that some of the Prophet's companions were misled?

In arriving at a consensus, is a generation limited to choosing one of the positions from among those that have already been adopted by previous generations or can it strike out completely on its own?

Any standard, even reasonably comprehensive work on the subject (e.g., M.A. Khadeer, *Ijma and Legislation in Islam*, Shivaji Press, Secunderabad, 1974) will establish two points on every single question of this kind: the answers ranged from the most emphatic 'Yes' to the most emphatic 'Never'; second, the answers were arrived at conventionally by ordinary men, they were not ordained by Allah or the Prophet. And yet they determined the very basis of the law.

As a result of differences on such questions, nineteen

schools of law grew up. Eventually, four survived. The decision
to adhere to one school rather than another too was a conventional one – influenced as it was by the time and place in
which one grew up. There was no divinely ordained basis
for adhering to one school rather than another. Regions, even
individuals, differed as to their preferences and many changed
from one school to another. Goldziher recalls the case of a 12th
century theologian who earned the appellation 'Hanfash' because
he belonged successively to three of the schools.

Even within a school, convention rather than divine
ordinance rules in practice to this day. Consider what is to be
done when the three principal authorities within the Hanafite
school differ. Here is how our textbook summarizes the practice
in India: where there is a difference of opinion between Abu
Hanifa, the founder, and his two principal disciples – Abu Yusuf
and Imam Muhammad – the opinion of the disciples is to be
preferred; where the two disciples disagree, the opinion of Abu
Yusuf is to be preferred; where the two disciples differ from Abu
Hanifa and also among themselves, the opinion of Abu Yusuf is
to be preferred (cf. *Mulla's Principles of Mohamedan Law, op. cit.,*
p. 27). Now, these are just conventional rules of thumb – and yet
today they constitute the very foundation of Muslim personal
law. There is nothing divinely ordained about them. In fact, the
most fundamental rule of our courts – that they will look not so
much at the original text of the Quran and the *hadis* but at what
the textbooks say – is itself nothing but a rule of convention. It
has no basis in the Quran or the *sunna*, to say nothing of course
of its having any basis in our Constitution or our laws, and
yet it determines the entire way in which Muslim Law is
administered today. But should our courts or legislatures so much
as talk of re-examining this rule, the cry is sure to go up that they
are interfering in the Shariat, all of which is divinely ordained, etc.

But we are getting ahead of the argument. We should return
to the Quran and the *hadis.*

The Stamp of Time and Place

The argument thus far confronts us with a cruel problem. If
we acknowledge the fact that the *hadis* are unreliable, we are left
with nothing but 70 odd verses on which to build the entire edifice

of personal law. And these verses, we have already seen, are not an adequate foundation for it.

Let us now look at the matter from the opposite point of view. Let us totally disregard all the evidence about the unreliability of the *hadis* and, instead, proceed in the belief that everything narrated in the canonical collections is completely trustworthy. What happens then?

One is struck first by the fact that as with several specific injunctions of the Quran, Islamic society has disregarded or gone beyond the *sunna* of the Prophet. Several examples can be given. One, this one from the law of evidence, will have to suffice.

The Prophet judged matters exclusively by oral testimony. Often, as reported in several traditions, he settled a matter solely on the basis of one witness swearing to a fact on oath. Another method was for the contending parties to accuse and curse each other. Thus, for instance, recall the rule specified in the Quran that there must be four witnesses 'to the fact' of adultery to substantiate the charge (4.19). But when a husband accuses his wife of adultery, and there are no witnesses, all he has to do is to swear to the charge four times and, on the fifth time, ask that the curse of Allah be upon him if he be lying. The wife, if she wants to contest the charge, must similarly deny it four times on oath and, the fifth time, call down the curse of Allah upon herself if her husband has spoken the truth (*Quran*, 24.6,7). (The denial saves her from the charge of adultery, but the marriage stands automatically dissolved, and the wife loses all her rights. But to that we will revert later.) The Prophet on occasion thought mutual cursing to be a fit method for settling not just legal but theological matters too. Thus when differences arose between him and the Christians of Najrah about the divinity of Jesus, he suggested that they curse each other and the view of him whose curses worked would prevail (cf., *The Life of Muhammad*, translation of Ibn Ishaq's *Sirat Rasul Allah* by A. Guillaume, OUP, Karachi, 1978, pp. 270-7).

Now, this is the *sunna* on what kind of evidence to entertain -- oral testimony, often that of only one witness, mutual imprecation, no cross-examination, no written documents, etc. In fact, over the centuries in the Islamic world as much as elsewhere, written documents have come to take precedence over oral testimony. They are examined as elsewhere for veracity, consistency, etc., just as cross-examination of witnesses has been introduced (on all this see, Joseph Schacht, *An Introduction to Islamic Law, op. cit*, for instance, Chapter 11, 'Theory and Practice').

That is the first thing that strikes one if one proceeds on the assumption that the *hadis* are totally and completely reliable. They may be a faithful record of the Prophet's *sunna,* but the Islamic world has grown beyond them in practice.

Next, one is struck by the fact that much of what is said and prescribed in the traditions is so obviously dated, it so manifestly bears the stamp of the time and place in which the Prophet and his companions moved, it so obviously reproduces beliefs of that time, it so embarrassingly reflects the fact that the information available then was limited, that one can't quite affirm that one will live by and only by the prescription of the *hadis.*

Scholars have shown how the institutions that the Prophet prescribed, how the norms he laid down were derived from the compulsions of a medieval, part-settled, part-nomadic, desert tribal society. The point can be illustrated with even greater ease by listing examples from other spheres of knowledge and life, examples that are so obviously dated that no extensive argument or documentation is required to establish that they reflect, not eternal verities, but the information, the beliefs, in many cases the superstitions and folklore then current.

Allah, we are told, created the heavens without any visible pillars and put mountains on the earth, as paperweights it would seem, 'lest it shake with you' (*Quran*, 31.10). The Prophet certifies that at sunset the sun goes and prostrates itself underneath the Throne of Allah and, next morning, it takes Allah's permission to rise again. The permission is granted ordinarily, says the Prophet, but a time will come when 'it will be about to prostrate itself but its prostration will not be accepted, and it will seek permission to go on its course, but it will not be permitted, but it will be ordered to return whence it has come and so it will rise in the West,' and this, he certifies, is what is meant by the statement of Allah that the sun will run its course for the term that has been fixed for it by Allah's decree (*Bukhari*, 54.421). On the authority of the companions, the traditions certify that the sun and the moon move in a circle, 'They move like the hand-mill,' and that Allah has created the stars for three purposes – to decorate the sky, to guide travellers and as missiles to stone the devils with (*Ibid.*, 54.3 & 4).

Notions about day-to-day occurrences are equally quaint. The Prophet says,

> When you hear the crowing of cocks, ask for Allah's Blessings for [their crowing indicates that] they have seen an Angel. And when you hear the braying of donkeys, seek refuge with Allah from Satan for [their braying indicates that] they have seen Satan.
>
> (*Bukhari*, 54.522)

The Prophet certifies that the rats are Israelites who had got lost. And his proof is straightforward. The Israelites were forbidden to eat the meat or drink the milk of camels. They were, however, allowed to eat the meat and drink the milk of sheep. The Prophet says that the Israelites who had got lost,

> Were cursed and changed into rats, for if you put the milk of a she-camel in front of a rat, it will not drink it, but if the milk of a sheep is put in front of it, it will drink it (*Bukhari*, 54.524).

These could have been only a few of the Israelites, though. The generality must have become apes and swine. The Quran twice reports how, for their transgressions and contumacy, Allah brought down the curse upon them, 'Be ye apes, despised and rejected' (*Quran*, 2.65, 7.166). At another place it reports that He changed them into 'apes and swine' (*Quran*, 5.65).

Bukhari etc. have entire 'Books' on the Prophet's verdict about what this dream means or that, the general theme being that good dreams are from Allah and bad ones from Satan (for instance, *Bukhari*, 87.113-15). To ward off the effect of the latter, one must seek refuge in Allah from Satan and spit to the left (once in some accounts, thrice without saliva in others, e.g. *Bukhari*, 87.115, 124,133). There is a corresponding differentiation between sneezing, which is said to be from Allah, and yawning, which is said to be from Satan (e.g., *Bukhari*, 72.242, 245).

The injunctions about medicine too bear the stamp of what was thought and believed then. Sickness is an expiation for sins (e.g., *Bukhari* , 70.544). It is also the sign of Allah's favour, for He shall remove it (*Ibid*, 70.547-51,571). Diarrhoea, the Prophet says, should be cured with honey (*Bukhari*, 69.588, 614; *Muslim*, 5492), pleurisy with sea or Indian costus and olive oil (e.g., *Muslim*, 5487-8) sniffed as an incense. The Indian qust cures seven diseases from throat trouble to tonsilitis (e.g., *Bukhari*, 71.596, 613,616). Black cumin or Nigella seeds are said to be a cure for all diseases except death (*Bukhari*, 71.591; *Muslim*, 5489-90). The dust of Medina mixed with the saliva of pious Muslims cures disease, ailment or 'any injury'(e.g., *Muslim*, 5444). Fever, we are told repeatedly, is 'due to the vehemence of the heat of Hell,' and so the cure is to 'cool it with water' (*Bukhari*, 71.619-22; *Muslim*, 5476-85).

Although he advises that a person in an area struck by plague should not leave it and persons elsewhere should not go to it, and that one should not mix healthy cattle with unhealthy ones, the Prophet states categorically that there is neither infection nor contagion (e.g., *Bukhari*, 71.615, 665, 667; *Muslim*, 5507-16). Much is said about the effects of the evil eye and how they are to be neutralised. Spells and chants are prescribed as cures for the evil eye, of course, but also for skin eruption, scorpion stings, bleeding (e.g., *Bukhari*, 71.632-48; *Muslim*, 5428-57).

What should one do if a house-fly falls into something one is drinking? 'Dip all of it' in the drink, the Prophet enjoins, 'and then throw it away, for in one of its wings is a disease and in the other there is healing,' that is, the antidote to the poison and cure for the disease (*Bukhari*, 54.537,71.673).

Examples of this kind can be multiplied many times over. (And of course they are not exclusive to these texts or to Islam.) For our purpose two points are relevant. First, the knowledge they convey is clearly dated -- they reflect the beliefs of and the information available in the Middle East 1400 years ago. Although these are said to be the words and opinions of the Prophet, no one would assert that they are eternal truths.

The second point is more crucial: there is nothing in the Quran or the *hadis* to say that the dicta on these matters are 'less eternal' than, say, the dicta on polygamy, or divorce, or alimony. Why is it that while we seem quite at ease in acknowledging that the dicta on these matters may be dated, we revolt at the

suggestion that   the prescriptions on marriage, divorce etc. may
also reflect no more   than the conditions, notions, requirements of
eighth century Arabia?

And if authority must be sought, there is, as always, the well-
known tradition set out in the standard compilations, like *Muslim*
and *Mishkat*.   When the Prophet was in Medina, he saw the
people fertilising date trees in a particular way. He asked them why
they were doing so.'It is an ancient custom,' they said. He advised
that   the yields may be   higher if they did not do so. They
followed his   advice. The trees   bore little fruit. When they
complained to him, he said, 'I am   no more than man; when I
order you anything   regarding   religion, receive it, and when
I order you about the affairs of this world, then I am nothing
more than man.'

Now, if growing date-trees is an 'affair of this world', why
is alimony not? Or marriage? Or divorce? Especially in Islam,
where marriage is not a sacrament at all, but a contract?

I mention the *hadis* merely to make the point that there
is no way of distinguishing between the traditions as well as the
verses of the Quran on the basis of *the subject* they deal with.
If they are sacrosanct and binding on one subject, they must be
deemed to be equally sacrosanct and binding on all. But reform
isn't just a matter of citing a convenient *hadis*. For each *hadis*
the reformers can cite, the fundamentalist can cite five. And there
are different versions to contend with. In the date-tree *hadis* for
instance, the phrase 'when I order you on the affairs of this world'
is replaced in one version by 'when I order you on the basis of
my opinion.'So, the theologian will argue, while on date-trees we
can proceed independently of the Prophet's opinion – there being
no command of Allah in the Quran on the subject – we cannot
do so in the case of marriage etc. We can't get around the problem
by quotation mongering. But we are anticipating the argument.

A Seamless Garment

We notice that if we acknowledge the traditions to be unreliable,
then we are left with little on which to base the claim that Muslim
law is divinely ordained. On the other hand, if we insist that,
like the Quran, the texts are trustworthy, so much of what they
say is so manifestly dated that one cannot but agree that all of

it has to be re-examined in the light of the knowledge that has become available since.

If, however, just as in our piety we decided to set aside everything that modern scholarship has revealed about their reliability, we now shut our eyes to all knowledge that shows the traditions to be dated, and we continue to maintain instead that the Quran and the *hadis* are eternally excellent and are a seamless garment, not one thread of which can be pulled out or replaced, we end up with an even graver problem.

For we must then declare how far back we want to go in restoring the law of Allah and the Prophet. The law on evidence, on punishments, on apostasy, on *Jihad*? If God's words on polygamy are to be construed as a permission-in-perpetuity, what about His words on slavery, on concubines?

A few examples will show how untenable is the position that we land ourselves in if we insist that the law and the injunctions are eternal, excellent for all time, and of a piece.

The scale of punishments is medieval. Allah enjoins, 'So to the thief, whether male or female, cut ye off their hands in recompense for their doings. This is a penalty by way of warning from Allah Himself, and Allah is Mighty, Wise,' unless the thief repents and turns to Allah, in which case Allah will 'turn to' him in compassion (*Quran*, 5.41-2). The Prophet makes the command specific: 'The hand of a thief should be cut off for stealing a quarter of a dinar,' 'Allah curses a thief who steals an egg, for which his hand is to be cut off, or steals a rope, for which his hand is to be cut off' (*Bukhari*, 81. 781-91). As for sincere repentance, the traditions seem to imply that the punishment having been carried out in this world, that part is up to Allah in the next, for the Prophet says, 'And whoever commits any of the above crimes and receives his legal punishment in this world, that will be his expiation and purification. But if Allah screens his sin, it will be up to Allah who will either punish or forgive him according to His wish'(*Ibid.*, 793).

We have already noted that a woman against whom four witnesses testify that she has committed adultery must on Allah's command be walled in till she dies, 'or God appoints for her a way' (*Quran*, 4.15), or along with the man be flogged with a hundred stripes (*Quran*, 24.2). 'Let not compassion move you in their case,' Allah stresses, 'and let a party of the believers witness their punishment' (*Ibid*). By the Prophet's example both must be stoned to death (e.g., *Bukhari*, 82. 803-10, 814-16). Even at that time, there were objections that the Quran did not ordain stoning, but Umar (and Aisha, as we have seen earlier) testified that there *had* been a verse to that effect which was not now in the Quran (e.g., *Bukhari*, 82.816). The Prophet ordered persons to be stoned to death even when there were no witnesses and the persons were confessing on their own (*Ibid.*, 805-6, 810, 815). The stonings were on occasion carried out in the tiled courtyard right in front of the Prophet's own mosque, and in the place where the Id prayers used to be held (*Ibid.*, 809,810).

Thus, the injunctions of Allah are clear, as is the *sunna* of the Prophet. Should the punishment be revived and should it be meted out on the type of evidence that was found to be acceptable then?

Similarly, today we have freedom of religion. This includes the right not just to practise my religion but to practise the religion of my choice. But by All's command, and by the Prophet's example, he who changes his religion from Islam must be put to death. Allah's commands are emphatic. Talking of disbelievers, he says that no Muslim should take them either as friends or helpers until they embrace Islam,

> Then, if they turn their backs, take them, and slay them
> wherever you find them.   (*Quran*, 4.91)

The Prophet is equally emphatic. 'Whoever changes his Islamic religion', he says, 'kill him' (*Bukhari*, 84.57).

And the mark, not of so grave a thing as apostasy but of a mere deviation which merited such punishment, could be quite innocuous. Here, for instance, is the *hadis*: 'Disagreement and division will arise among my people', the Prophet forecasts. 'Some will speak well but do evil; they will recite the Quran but it will go no farther than their throats; they *will* swerve from their religion as an arrow goes through the animal shot at and will not return till an arrow comes back to the place where it was strung. They are the worst of men and animals. Blessed are they who kill them and are killed by them! They summon people to God's Book, but they have no part with us. He who fights them, is nearer to God than they!' God's Messenger was asked by what mark such persons could be identified; he said it was a clean-shaven face. (Mishkat al-Masabih, Muhammad Ashraf; Lahore, Volume 1, pp. 753-4; on the first part, see also, e.g. Bukhari, 84.64, in which the Prophet exhorts, 'So wherever you find them, kill them, for whoever kills them shall have reward on the day of resurrection.') Hence, strictly speaking, every Muslim who shaves his beard must be taken to be an apostate, and must be executed.

His actual practice in this was guided by Allah's injunction that the punishment for those who fight against Allah and his Messenger, those who go about creating disorder and do not repent before they are vanquished, is that

They shall be slaughtered or crucified, or their hands and feet shall alternately be struck off, or they shall be banished from the land.

(Quran, 5.37-8)

Recall the incident cited earlier. Some persons from the tribe of Ukl came to the Prophet and embraced Islam. The climate of Medina did not suit them. The Prophet ordered them to go to the herd of milch-camel and drink the milk and urine as medicine. After recovering from their illness, they reverted from Islam, killed the shepherd and ran off with the camels. The Prophet had them caught. He then ordered their hands and legs to be cut off, their eyes to be branded with heated pieces of iron. He ordered that the cut hands and legs should not be cauterised so that they bleed to death. 'And when they asked for water to drink,' records the hadis, 'they were not given water' (Bukhari, 82.794-7; Muslim, 4130-7).

Thus, once again the injunctions of Allah are unambiguous and emphatic. So are the injunctions of the Prophet and his sunna. Should these replace the freedom of religion that our Constitution guarantees to every Indian? The answer cannot but be 'Yes' if we maintain that Islamic law is one seamless whole, and altering any part of it is desecration of the religion.

So much for what should constitute a crime and what scale of punishment it should invite. How and by whom should the punishment be carried out? For instance, today enforcing criminal law is the function of the State. But the Quran and the sunna of the Prophet enshrine retaliation as a principle. We have already seen how in the Quran Allah declares,

O believers, prescribed for you is
retaliation, touching the slain;
freeman for freeman, slave for slave,
female for female. But if aught is pardoned
a man by his brother, let the pursuing
be honourable, and let the payment be
with kindliness. That is a lightening
granted you by your Lord, and a mercy;
and for him who commits aggression
after that – for him there awaits
a painful chastisement.
In retaliation there is life for you,
men possessed of minds; happily you
will be God – fearing.   (*Quran,* 2.173-5)

And, therefore, says the Quran,

The holy month for the holy month;
holy things demand retaliation.
Whoso commits aggression against you,
do you commit aggression against him
like as he has committed against you;
and fear you God, and know that God is
with the Godfearing.   (*Quran,*2.190)

Allah reiterates what He says He has already sent down in the
Torah – the command of equal retribution:

And therein We prescribed for them:
'A life for a life, an eye for an eye,
a nose for a nose, an ear for an ear,
a tooth for a tooth, and for wounds
retaliation'; but whosoever forgoes it
as a freewill offering, that shall be for his
an expiation. Whoso judges not
according to what God has sent down –
they are the evildoers.   (*Quran,* 5.49)

He repeatedly faults the Jews for not adhering to His injunctions
in this as in other matters.

Accordingly, the Prophet was scrupulous in enforcing 'an eye for an eye' etc., and in upholding the right of the family of the victim to either carry out the punishment in retaliation or, as allowed by Allah (*Quran*, 2.178, 5.49), transmute it into blood-money. The incidents are set out in the *hadis*, although in one the Prophet is seen as himself killing between two stones a person named by a dying victim as being the assaulter (e.g., *Bukhari*, 83.15-24).

Notice that, in all probability, the Quran and the Prophet were merely continuing the practice of seventh or eighth century Arabia. It can even be said that in a way they were humanizing it. We learn in the traditions, for instance, that among the Israelites, blood-money was not permitted, and the only code was 'an eye for an eye'. The Quran and the Prophet are credited in the *hadis* with introducing the option (e.g., *Bukhari*, 83.20). But society has evolved. Must we today revert to retaliation as the operational principle, to 'an eye for an eye' as the working scale? The answer cannot but be 'Yes' if we insist that the injunctions of the Quran and the practice of the Prophet are one seamless whole.

Consider next, not just a crime, or an operational principle, or punishment in a specific case, but an entire social institution. Slavery was common in Arabia at that time. The Quran and the Prophet recommended that Muslims treat their slaves well, that they refrain from forcing their female slaves into prostitution. They made freeing individual slaves a virtuous act, an act that could be the expiation for a few transgressions. The Quran even envisaged the possibility of a Muslim freeing his slave and after she had accepted the faith, etc. marrying her.

But both the Quran and the Prophet assumed that slavery as an institution would continue. For instance, the Quran, in laying down that a Muslim may have up to four wives at a time, often refers in addition to slave or female concubines that a man may keep – concubines on whose number, of course, no restriction is placed (*Quran*, 4.3,28,29,23.3-6).

It isn't just that slavery is assumed to continue and that nothing is said against the institution as such. The *sunna* of the Prophet, the second and co-equal source of Muslim law, for instance, lays down that the slave must serve his master diligently. 'When a slave acts sincerely towards his master and worships God well,' the Prophet says, 'he has a double reward.' 'How excellent it is,' he says, 'for a slave to be taken in death by God when worshipping his lord well and obeying his master! How excellent it is for him.' The master, he says, may beat the slave, though he should avoid hitting his face. A slave who runs away, he says, is an infidel. From all this follows naturally the suspension of the general law of equal retribution. Thus, for instance, a Muslim is to be killed if he unlawfully kills a Muslim, but not if he kills a slave (cf., for instance, *Muslim* 3. 4097-101; *Mishkat, op. cit* 2, pp. 714-5, 813; Hughes' *Dictionary, op. cit,* p. 599).

Are we then to reintroduce or permit the continuance of this social institution? If the law is to remain as it is laid down by the Quran and the Prophet's practice, we must indeed.

Jihad

As a final example − of the scores and scores that can be given − consider not just a specific transgression, a specific punishment, a specific rule of operation, or even a specific institution. Consider what the Quran and the *sunna* of the Prophet enjoin as a major, overriding duty, a duty that affects the relations of Muslims with all others in the society or State in which they happen to live − the duty of *Jihad,* of engaging in Holy War, so as to convert the universe into *Dar-ul-Islam,* the Land of Islam.

At the turn of the century, when the Muslim intelligentsia was very keen to erase from the British mind the memory of 1857, when it wanted to replace the image of Muslims as 'rebels' by the image of Muslims as the most loyal subjects, Sir Syed Ahmed Khan Bahadur, C.S.I. and his associates were at pains to underplay this mandatory duty (as a representative of this genre see Moulavi Cheragh Ali, *A Critical Exposition of the Popular 'Jihad', showing that the wars of Mohammed were defensive; and that aggressive war, or compulsory conversion is not allowed in the Koran,* Thacker, Spink & Co., Calcutta, 1885). It is clear in retrospect that such works were mere apologetics, called for by time and circumstance.

On few things does the Quran lay down the law as forcefully and unambiguously, on few things does it repeat its command as often as on the duty to engage in *Jihad,* or the great merits that accrue to the believer from doing so.

When the nascent movement was in difficulties, for instance, in Mecca and in the initial years in Medina, Allah recommended an indulgent tolerance. 'Say', He commanded,

> O unbelievers,
> I serve not what you serve,
> and you are not serving what I serve,
> nor am I serving what you have served,
> neither are you serving what I serve.
> To you your religion, and to me my religion! (*Quran,* 109.1-5)

Or, as in 2.256, 'Let there be no compulsion in religion.'

Once the Prophet's hegemony was established in Medina, however, Allah's commands become minatory. The Quran as a whole bears the stamp of these days. It divides the world into believers and non-believers; it states again and again that the non-believers are incorrigible as God has deliberately led them astray; that, even after doing so, 'If God had willed He would have avenged Himself upon them,' but that He has left the task to the believers, so that 'He may try some of you by means of others' (*Quran,* 47.5-7); that therefore it is the duty of the believer to 'slay them wherever he find them,' to make ' a wide slaughter among them,' to vanquish them till Islam reigns all over, that in doing so the believer is only hastening the chastisement that the unbelievers have themselves invited upon themselves; that by doing so he assures himself a place in Paradise.

As you read the following representative verses from the Quran, notice two things. Notice how emphatic, unambiguous are Allah's commands. Notice also that they are far more frequently repeated than the commands on, say, alimony. If we insist that the injunction on alimony -- and it is one that can be derived only by implication – cannot be altered, must we conclude that in this age and place, as much as in every other, every believer will be living by the injuctions on *Jihad* too?

The commands to engage in *Jihad* are indeed the leitmotiv of the Quran. Do not be the aggressor, says Allah, for Allah does not like aggression (though on this see below), but fight the unbelievers,

And kill them wherever ye shall
find them and eject them from
whatever place they have ejected
you; for civil discord is worse
than carnage.... fight therefore
against them until there be no
more civil discord, and the only
worship be that of God; but if
they desist [i.e. if they give in]let there be
no hostility, save against the wicked. (2.186-9; see also 8.40)

'O believers,' Allah commands,

fight the unbelievers, who are near to you,
and let them find in you a harshness;
and know that God is with the God-fearing.   (9.125)

'Now, if the hypocrites do not give over,' He says,

and those in whose hearts there is sickness,
and they that make commotion in the city,
we shall assuredly urge thee against them
and then they will be thy neighbours there only a little;
cursed they shall be, and wheresoever
they are come upon they shall be seized and slaughtered all —
God's wont with those who passed away
before; and thou shalt find no changing the wont of God.
                                                            (33.60-4)

'O Prophet.' Allah commands,

struggle with the unbelievers and
hypocrites, and be thou harsh with them;
their refuge is Gehenna — an evil
homecoming.   (9.74)

Do not be like the Israelites, Allah admonishes the faithful, who
did not fight even after God had granted their wish of having a king
who would lead them in battle (2.244-9). Instead, remember,

Prescribed for you is fighting, though it be hateful to you;
Yet it may happen that you will hate a thing
which is better for you; and it may happen that you
will have a thing which is worse for you;
God knows and you know not.   (2.212)

Fighting in Allah's way is the bargain that you have made with
Allah, the believer is told, the bargain that will guarantee you a
place in Paradise; therefore rejoice in fulfilling your part of
it, for, remember, Allah will certainly fulfil His part:

God has bought from the believers their selves,
and their possessions against the gift of Paradise;
they fight in the way of God; they kill, and are
killed; that is a promise binding upon God
in the Torah, and the Gospel, and the Koran;
and who fulfils his covenant better than God?
So rejoice in the bargain you have made with Him;
that is the mighty triumph.   (9.113)

For this reason exhortation follows exhortation, command
follows command – sell the present life for the life to come; fight
in the way of God, against Satan's way, against the way of the
idols; in doing so a mighty wage awaits you whether you slay or
are slain; obey sincerely for God knows your secret thoughts (for
a typical exhortation of this kind, see, *Quran* 4.70-87).

The   duty to vanquish the non-believers, to annihilate their
way,   is urgent,   imperative, indeed inescapable, says Allah,
because   the   non-believers   are completely and   irrevocably
incorrigible. There just is no alternative to fighting and subduing
them. This assessment of those who do not agree with its message
is special to the Quran, and we should see how emphatic and
inescapable is the duty that follows from the assessment. Asks
Allah,

What, do you desire to guide him
whom God has led astray?
Whom God has led astray, thou wilt not find for him a way.
                                                        (4.90)

The design of the unbelievers, He says, is that 'you should disbelieve as they disbelieve, and then you would be equal' (4.91; similarly, see 4.142). Therefore, 'O Messenger', Allah exhorts,

> let them not grieve thee
> that vie with one another in unbelief,
> such men as say with their mouths, 'we believe,'
> but their hearts believe not...
> Whomsoever God desires to try,
> thou canst not avail him anything with God.
> Those are they whose heart God desired not
> to purify; for them is degradation
> in this world; and in the world to come,
> awaits them a mighty chastisement....   (5.45)

'God guides not the people of the unbelievers,' the Quran says. In fact, 'What has been sent down to thee from thy Lord will surely increase many of them in their insolence and unbelief.' 'So grieve not,' it says again, 'for the people of the unbelievers' (5.70-5). The Quran repeatedly recalls how Allah had sent clear guidance to the Israelites and how they perverted it. This too is Allah's design, it says:

> Had God willed, they would not
> have done so; so leave them to
> their forging.   (4.135-9)

'Surely the worst of beasts in God's sight,' it says,

> are those that are deaf and dumb and do not understand.
> If God had known of any good in them
> He would have made them hear; and if
> He had made them hear, they would have turned away,
> swerving aside.   (7.20-5)

The idolators, of course, say that God is the one who must have willed them to be idolators. Why then should they be punished for it? The question, a very pertinent one, is stamped out — 'Even so the people before them cried lies till they tasted Our might' — and the believers are exhorted to repeat, 'To God belongs the argument conclusive, for had He willed, He would have guided you all' (cf. 6.149-51; and also 14.35-45).

Therefore, the unbelievers have been made that way be Allah Himself. You *cannot* make them learn. They are Allah's enemies and yours (8.42). They have been made that way so that your devotion to Allah may be tested by what you do to them (47.5-7). A terrible chastisement awaits them in the hereafter, but the unbelievers themselves hasten it and invite it upon themselves right here through your hands:

> What, have they not journeyed in the land
> so that they have hearts to understand with
> or ears to hear with? It is not the eyes
> that are blind, but blind are the hearts within the breasts
> And they demand thee to hasten the chastisement....
>
> (22.45-6)

As Allah has ordained the chastisement, as the unbelievers themselves hasten it upon themselves, your duty is clear. Ask them to embrace Islam. If they do not, then 'make a great slaughter among them,' 'slay them wherever you come on them.' Tie up the remaining securely, and then either kill them or set them free for ransom. Such are the blood-curdling duties that the Quran enjoins. 'If they withdraw from you,' it says,

> and do not fight you, and offer you
> peace, then God assigns not any way to you against them....
> If they withdraw not from you, and
> offer you peace, and restrain their hands,
> take them and slay them wherever you come on them;
> against them We have given you a clear authority.   (4.93)

(For similar commands see *Sura* 8; for instance, 8.70-6.)

Indeed, Allah, as we have seen, is specific. 'This is the recompense,' the Quran says, for 'those who fight against God and His Messenger, and hasten about the earth to do corruption there,' and who do not repent 'before you have power over them':

> They shall be slaughtered, or crucified,

or their hands or feet shall alternately
be struck off, or they shall be banished
from the land....   (5.37-8)

'When you encounter the infidels,' enjoins Allah,

strike off their heads till ye have made
a great slaughter among them, and of the
rest make fast the fetters.
And afterwards let there either be free dismissals or
ransomings,
till the war hath laid down its burdens. Thus do....   (47.4-5)

Free dismissals or ransomings, thus are allowed, but *after* 'a great
slaughter' has been made among them. 'It is not for any Prophet,'
Allah reiterates, 'to have prisoners until he makes a wide slaughter
in the land.' The reason is plain: 'You desire the chance goods of
the present world' 'in the form of ransom, Allah admonishes, 'and
God desires for you the world to come; and God is All-mighty, All-
wise' (8.68).

Thus, the fount of Muslim law most emphatically prescribes
Jihad as a major duty. Bukhari, Muslim and the other compilers
devote entire 'Books' to recording how the Messenger of Allah
followed these commands. As far as Muslim law is concerned,
therefore, the injunction is twice reinforced.

'*Jihad* in the way of Allah! *Jihad* in the way of Allah,' we hear
the Prophet proclaim, is what 'elevates the position of a man in
Paradise to a grade one hundred [higher]and the elevation between
one grade and the other is equal to the height of the heaven
from the earth' (*Muslim*, 4645). '... I love to fight in the way
of Allah,' he declares, 'and be killed, to fight and again be killed,
and to fight again and be killed.' He declares that if only he had
the means, or his fellow-believers themselves had the means, he
would equip all of them for *Jihad* (*Muslim*, 4678-83, *Bukhari*,
52.54). 'Who is the best of men?' The Prophet is asked. 'A man
who fights in the way of Allah spending his wealth and staking
his life,' he affirms. (*Muslim*, 4652-7; *Bukhari*, 52.45). Every
injury to an unbeliever tots up a meritorious deed for the faithful,
the traditions recall Allah saying (*Bukhari*, 52.15,16). 'A man
came to Allah's Apostle,' the *hadis* records, 'and said, "Instruct
me to such a deed as equals *Jihad* [in reward]." He replied, "I

do not find such a deed"....' (*Bukhari*, 52.44).

The *hadis*, the second and co-equal source of Muslim law, are in raptures about the rewards that accrue from *Jihad* – booty in this world (this apparently had not been legal at that time, the Prophet made it so) and Paradise in the next. Fighting even once in *Jihad* brings rewards greater than all this world and all that is in it (*Muslim*, 4639-44; *Bukhari*, 52.50-2). No one who dies and receives some good from Allah in the hereafter would ever want to return to this world, the Prophet says, even if he were offered the whole world and all that is in it as an inducement, except for the one who has been martyred in *Jihad*. So great will be the honour that he will receive from Allah that he would desire to return to this world and be killed ten times in the cause (*Muslim*, 4636-8; *Bukhari*, 52.53).

As the duty is an overriding one, all means are permissible. 'War is stratagem,' the Prophet says, 'War is deceit' (*Muslim*, 4311-12, 4436; *Bukhari*, 52.267-9). Thus, one may lie, one may kill the enemy while he is asleep, one may kill him by tricking him (e.g., *Bukhari*, 52.264-5, 270-1, 248-55).

The believers are told to desist from the wanton cruelty that might create aversion to Islam, that might provoke unnecessary hostility, that might destroy what could be useful. But all these things are to be viewed from a utilitarian standpoint. Thus, one should avoid slaughtering women and children, unless it happens in the exigencies of the assault (e.g., during a night raid). When a group surrenders agreeing to have its fate decided by a companion of the Prophet, the latter sends for him and asks him to decree the fate of the captives. 'I decide that the fighting men be killed and that the offspring be taken into captivity,'he declares. 'You have given regarding them,'the Prophet compliments him, 'the decision of a King,' 'God's decision' (e.g., *Mishkat, op. cit.*, 2, pp. 840-1).

There are accounts and accounts of spoils, of quarrels over them, of women being taken and used. Thus the great Imam Malik, in discussing the permissibility or otherwise of *azl, coitus interruptus*, records the *hadis:*

> Ibn Muhairiz reported: I went to the mosque and found Abu Said Khudri sitting there. I asked him about *azl*. He said: We went with the Apostle of Allah (may peace be upon Him) to the Battle of Bani Mustaliq and there we seized some women

of the enemy as captives. We were moved to passion and felt
it difficult to abstain. At the same time, we desired to sell those
women and obtain money; we therefore, intended to do *azl*.
We then thought that as the Apostle of Allah (may peace be
upon Him) was present, it would be undesirable to do so
without referring the matter to him. We asked him and He said:
'There is no harm, for whatever life the Lord intends to bring
into the world, will come into being until the day of
Resurrection' (Imam Malik, *Muwatta*, Muhammad Ashraf,
Lahore, 1980, pp. 268-9).

These then are the injunctions of the Quran, this the *sunna*
of the Prophet in regard to *Jihad*. Is it any wonder that the
secondary law books state the law as unequivocally?

The *Fatawa-i-Alamgiri* – the great compendium of extracts
from the works of the Hanafi school of law compiled on the orders
of Aurangzeb – lays down that *Jihad* is the noblest of
professions. The compendium most frequently relied upon in
India is of course the *Hedaya* of Sheikh Burhann'd-din Ali (d. AD
1198). Translated by Charles Hamilton in 1791 by orders of Warren
Hastings, it has since been the foundation of what we know as
Muslim law in India today.

It restates Allah's injunction to 'slay the infidels,' and recalls
the Prophet's words, 'War is permanently established till the Day
of Judgement.'

It sets aside all pretence about *Jihad* being defensive. 'The
destruction of the sword is incurred by the infidels,' it lays down,
'although they be not the first aggressors, as appears from the
various passages in the sacred writings, which are generally
received to this effect.'

One should normally invite the infidels to embrace Islam
before attacking them, 'but yet if he [the Musalman] do attack
them before thus inviting them, and slay them, and take their
property, neither fine, expiation nor atonement are due, because
that which protects [namely, Islam], does not exist in them, nor
are they under protection by place [namely, the Musalman terri-
tory], and the mere prohibition of the act is not sufficient to sanction
the exaction either of fine, or of atonement for property; in the
same manner as the slaying of the women or infant children
of infidels is forbidden; but if, notwithstanding, a person were

to slay such, he is not liable to a fine.'

If they do not surrender to Islam, if they do not pay the capitation tax, invoking Allah,

> the Musalmans must then, with God's assistance, attack the infidels with all manner of war-like engines (as the Prophet did by the people of Tayeef), and must also set fire to their habitations (in the same manner as the Prophet fired Baweera), and must inundate them with water, and tear up their plantations, and tread down their grain; because by these means they will become weakened, and their resolution will fail, and their force be broken; these means are therefore all sanctioned by the Law

Women, children and the disabled should not be slain, it says, 'But yet if any of these persons be killed in war, or if a woman be a queen or a chief, in this case it is allowable to slay them, they being qualified [i.e., being in a position] to molest the servants of God. So also, if such persons as the above should attempt to fight, they may be slain, for the purpose of removing evil, and because fighting renders slaying allowable.'

Peace may be made when advisable, it says, or broken when necessary, giving the infidels due notice, unless they act perfidiously, in which case they may be attacked without warning.

All movable property must be confiscated. As for the rest, it says, affairs should be so arranged that 'the inhabitants are merely the cultivators of the soil on behalf of the Musalmans, as performing all the labour, in the various modes of tillage, on their account, without their [i.e, the Musalmans] being subjected to any of the trouble or expense attending it.'

As for the prisoners, it lays down, 'The Imam, with respect to captives, has it in his choice to slay them, because the Prophet put captives to death – and also because slaying them terminates wickedness – or, if he choose, he may make them slaves, because by enslaving them the evil of them is remedied, at the same time that Musalmans reap an advantage; or, if he please, he may release them so as to make them free men or Zimmies....' The idolators of Arabia or apostates are not to be released. In any case, they should not be allowed to return to their country, 'as this would be strengthening the infidels against the Musalman.'

He who converts to Islam should not be killed. He should not however be sent to his country. He can retain his liberty, the property that is 'in his hands' and his infant children. But his lands, his wife, her foetus, his adult children etc. all become public property, says the law book.

This then is the law – as enjoined by the Quran, as proclaimed by the Prophet's *sunna*, as set out in the law books.

Must we revert to it? We must, if Muslim law is the seamless garment that we are being told it is.

Inequitable

Thus, if we acknowledge the results of modern scholarship, we are left with little on which to base Muslim personal law. If we continue to maintain that, evidence or no evidence, the traditions, etc. are authentic, we notice that much of what they and the other texts say is obviously dated. If we disregard this evidence also and insist that every word in the Quran and the traditions is eternally true and therefore eternally binding, we have to decide whether we should reintroduce the provisions regarding criminal law, the law of evidence, institutions like slavery, and the whole stance towards non-Muslims, culminating as it does in the mandatory, ineluctable duty of *Jihad*.

Each of these positions, we have seen, leads to untenable results. None of them is able to provide the blanket cover that is today being claimed on behalf of Muslim law. We thus have no alternative but to examine each provision of personal law by itself. If it is excellent, we must urge that it be applied to all. If it is medieval, there is no ground on which we can justify the subjection of any one to it.

Now, the provisions of personal law that are most in the public mind today – those on polygamy, divorce, and alimony – discriminate against women clearly and heavily.

Polygamy is sanctioned by the Quran and sanctified by the example of the Prophet – who had nine wives, on one count twenty – and that of his companions. Two verses from the Quran are pertinent:

If you fear that you will not act justly towards the orphans, marry such women as seem good to you, two,

or three, or four; but if you fear that you will not be
equitable, then only one, or what your right hand owns; so it
is likelier you will not be partial.

(4.3)

and

You will not be able to be equitable between your wives, be
you ever so eager; yet do not be altogether partial, so that you
leave her as it were suspended.

(4.128)

Notice, first, that the Quran allows four wives; second, that
it allows four wives *at a time* – one can keep acquiring more,
provided one keeps divorcing the requisite number from the
existing stock. Third, in addition to the four wives, the Quran
allows concubines, the ones that 'your right hand owns'. There
is no restriction as to the number of these that one may keep.

In spite of these facts, the Quran marks an advance over the
situation which is said to have prevailed then in Arabia. From an
unlimited number, it limits the number of wives to four. Apologists
and reformers have gone further and have maintained that in fact
the Quran prescribes monogamy. According to them, in verse 4.3
it makes the permission to marry up to four wives *conditional* –
the condition being that the husband should have no fear that he
will not be equitable to them, and that in verse 4.128 it has said
that howsoever eager he may be to do so, this is a condition that
he is not likely to be able to fulfil.

It is a well-intentioned argument, but a disingenuous one.

Verse 4.3 does not lay down a condition. It sets out an
enabling clause. A word about the context of the verse will clarify
the matter.

The preceding verses show, and the tradition states (*Bukhari*,
62.35) that the anxiety here is about an orphan girl who is in
a man's custody and whom he decides to marry for her wealth.
Allah says that rather than doing so you should marry two, three
or four women, that, if you fear you will not be equitable towards
them, marry one and use the concubines. This way you will be
kept from being unjust to the orphan. The number of wives and
concubines that you may need to ward off this injustice is a
secondary concern of the verse.

Moreover, the satisfaction about the possibility of being equitable that is required is the *subjective* satisfaction of the husband – 'but if *you* fear...' says the Quran.

The second verse in question (4.128) puts no embargo on having four wives. In fact, it *assumes* that there are more wives than one and says that while, try howsoever hard you will, you will not be able to be completely equitable to each of the wives, take care not to be so partial as to neglect one completely.

Third, the injunction about being equitable, it is said, does not mean that one has to have identical *feelings* towards each of the wives. That is recognised as being impossible. What is required here is that one must be equitable towards the wives in the matter of providing lodgings, maintenance, in visiting them, etc. This construction draws force from the traditions. The Prophet was exempted by Allah from many of the restrictions and requirements that were decreed for the followers, and so the requirement about being equitable did not strictly apply to him. But if anyone *could* have been equitable, in view of his excellence it was the Prophet. Now, in the well-known tradition, he makes the important distinction that settles the matter. 'O God,' he says, 'I make an equal partition amongst my wives *as to what is in my power*; do not, therefore, bring me to account for *that which is not in my power, namely, the affections.*' Several traditions indicate how among his nine wives Aisha was the closest to him and how this occasioned some misgivings among the other wives. Surely, if even the Prophet could not be expected to be equitable in regard to the affections, what is required of mere mortals is merely that they be equitable in regard to maintenance, lodging, etc. And this requirement is no effective bar to polygamy.

Furthermore, in the traditions the Prophet is extolled for the number of wives he had, and others are exhorted, 'Marry, for the best person of his [i.e., Muslim] nation [i.e., Muhammad] of all other Muslims, has the largest number of wives'(*Bukhari*, 62.5-7; also A.J. Wensinck, *A Handbook of Early Muhammadan Tradition*, Leiden, E.J. Brill, 1927, p.143). Even if we do not go by the Prophet's example in this matter because of the special exemptions Allah ordained for him, and because of the exceptional excellence which enabled him to be more equitable among wives than others can be, there is the example of his companions. Many of them had many wives, and they certainly cannot be accused of either going against or misunderstanding the Quran or the Prophet on the matter.

One must therefore conclude regretfully that the modern apologists and reformists are wrong, and that in holding four wives at a time to be legal the law books like the *Hedaya* are correct.

The question of divorce is much simpler. The husband has absolute, unfettered and exclusive power to cast his wife aside. There are many ways in which a marriage can be ended – by mutual cursing, by mutual consent. These are all set out in the law books. What concerns us here is that the husband has the right to throw out his wife by pronouncing '*talaq*' thrice, that he need assign no reason whatsoever for doing so, that, while conciliation, etc. may be attempted, if he sticks to his resolve, the wife has no recourse at all, there is no authority or court to which she can appeal. The husband can decree the divorce even in the wife's absence, indeed he may do so even through a representative.

The wife, of course, has no corresponding power. She may, under certain circumstances, request a divorce, but whether she will secure it or not depends on the sweet-will of the husband. The only circumstance in which she can end the marriage is when the husband has delegated to her the power to divorce herself. But even in this case her ability is hemmed in by the requirement that she must prove that the power was in fact delegated to her.

Second, the moment she is divorced, the wife loses all rights. All she gets is her dower. The husband is to pay her a maintenance allowance for only three menstrual periods, or three months. If she is pregnant then the period is up to the delivery of the child or three months, whichever is earlier.

The question here is not whether the wife's blood relatives – her sons, brother, father, etc. – can maintain her or not, a point that is being made currently in relation to Shah Bano. The point is that there is no obligation whatsoever on the husband to furnish her with anything after that short *iddat* of three months. This is important in particular because this is so in spite of the absolute, exclusive, unfettered power that the husband has to discard his wife, and because the obligation is to cease *irrespective of whether the divorced woman can or cannot find a way to maintain herself.*

In the traditions the Prophet warns that nothing is more hateful to God than divorce, that no one should make a sport of it, etc. But these are recommendations. They do not dilute the husband's power in the matter one whit.

The View of Women

Now, these provisions are not fortuitous. They cannot be got around by tricks, by quoting three or four words from the Quran or citing one or two sayings of the Prophet. They are rooted in the view that the Quran and the *hadis* have of women.

'Your wives are your field,' says the Quran, 'Go in therefore to your field when or how you will, but do first some act for your soul's good...'(2.223).

In explaining the verse the traditions narrate: 'Jews used to say: "If one has sexual intercourse with his wife from the back, then she will deliver a squint-eyed child." So this verse was revealed....' *(Bukhari,* 60.51). The act for the good of one's soul that is to be done is not specified in the Quran. One possibility is suggested by the traditions. The Prophet says, 'If anyone of you on having sexual relations with his wife said [and he must say it before starting],*"Bismillah, Allahumma Jannibni-Sh-Shaitan wa Jannib-ish-Shaitan ma razagtana"* [i.e., 'In the name of Allah! Protect me from Satan and protect what you bestow upon us (i.e., an offspring) from Satan'], and if it is destined that they should have a child then Satan will never be able to harm that offspring' *(Bukhari,* 4.143 and 62.94). The probability that this is the sort of counsel which is intended by the verse about the act one must do before 'going into one's field' is reinforced by another tradition. The prophet Solomon, son of the prophet David, we are told, said: 'Tonight I will go round [i.e., have sexual relations with] one hundred women [my wives] everyone of whom will deliver a male child who will fight in Allah's Cause.' On that an angel said to him: 'Say: "If Allah will," But Solomon did not say it and forgot to say it. Then he had sexual relations with them but none of them delivered any child except one who delivered a half person. The Prophet said, 'If Solomon had said: "If Allah will", Allah would have fulfilled his [afore stated] desire and that saying would have made him more hopeful' *(Bukhari,* 62.169).

In the *Sura*, 'Women,' the Quran says, 'Do not covet that whereby God in bounty, has preferred one of you above another,' and declares,

Men are the managers of the affairs of women for that God has preferred in bounty one of them over another, and for that they [i.e., the men] have expended of their property [in the dower, in maintenance, etc.].
Righteous women are therefore obedient, guarding the secret of God's guarding. And those you fear may be rebellious admonish; banish them to their couches, and beat them. If they then obey you look not for any way against them; God is All-high, All-great.

(4.34)

The woman is therefore clearly the inferior one. Believers are advised to be kind to their wives, not to keep or take back the dower at the time of casting them away, etc. but the general position is unambiguous. The woman is to obey. The man, if necessary, may admonish her, banish her, beat her.

Specific provisions follow from this general view. A woman, if divorced, must wait for three menstrual periods. During this probationary interval (decreed so as to avoid subsequent disputes about paternity) the husband may resort to her if he changes his mind: 'Women have such honourable rights as obligations,' the Quran adds, 'but their men have a degree above them' (2.228). Similarly, in the matter of inheritance, daughters are to get one half of the share of sons (4.12,175).

Several traditions also ask the husbands to be considerate to their wives. But the general view of women is, if anything, worse. Women are looked upon as things to be enjoyed: 'The whole world is to be enjoyed,' the Prophet says, 'but the best thing in the world is a good woman' (*Mishkat*, 1, p. 658). They are also temptresses that one has to beware: 'Whenever a man is alone with a woman,' the Prophet says, 'the devil makes a third.' 'Do not visit women whose husbands are away from home,' he says, 'for the devil circulates in you like your blood' (*Mishkat*, 1, p. 663). And wives are seen as objects into whom one should expend one's passion when thus tempted by other women: 'A woman advances in the form of a devil and retires in the form of a devil,' the Prophet says. 'When one of you is charmed by a woman and she affects your heart he should go to his wife and have intercourse with her, for that will repel what he is feeling.' The point is reiterated in another tradition in which the Prophet, after a personal incident, says, 'If any man sees a woman who charms him, he should go to his wife, for she has the same kind of thing as the other woman' (*Mishkat*, 1, p. 662).

Men are exhorted to look after their wives. But these are also looked upon in the conventional medieval way, as pots to vent one's passions in: 'Young men' counsels the Prophet,

> those of you who can support a wife should marry, for it keeps you from looking at strange women and preserves you from immorality; but those who cannot should devote themselves to fasting, for it is a means of suppressing sexual desire (*Mishkat*, 1, p. 658).

And as vehicles of procreation:

> Marry women who are loving and very prolific, for I shall out-number the peoples by you (*Mishkat*, 1, p. 659).

The Quranic concept of women being a man's tilth, his field that he may go into when or how he will, finds many echoes in the traditions, sometimes literally. The question is put, 'O Abu Said, I have some slave-girls who are better than my wives, but I do not desire that they should all become pregnant. Shall I do *azl* (*coitus interruptus*) with them?' And the companion answers, 'They are your fields of cultivation, if you wish to irrigate them do so, or if you desire otherwise, keep them dry' (*Muwatta, op.cit.*, 1221).

If the wife resists her husband's overtures, the Prophet says, she commits sin, and is cursed: 'If a man invites his wife to sleep with him and she refuses to come to him,' says the Prophet, 'then the angels send their curses on her till morning' (*Bukhari*, 62.121-2). and 'He who is in heaven is displeased with her till her husband is pleased with her' (*Mishkat*, 1, p. 689). The duty of the wife thus is clear: 'When a man calls his wife to satisfy his desire she must go to him even if she is occupied at the oven' (*Mishkat*, 1, p. 691). When a young man explains that his wife 'keeps on fasting and I am a young man who cannot contain himself,' the Prophet specifies, 'A woman may fast only with her husband's permission' (*Ibid.*, pp. 693-4).

The good wife is one 'who obeys him if he commands her, pleases him if he looks at her, is true to him if he abjures her to do something, and is sincere to him regarding her person and his property if he is absent' (*Mishkat*, 1, pp. 660,694). Husbands are counselled to treat their wives well, in part because doing so is virtuous and in part for a utilitarian reason: 'The woman is like a rib; if you try to straighten her, she will break; so if you want to get benefit from her, do so while she still has some crookedness' (*Bukhari*, 62.113, 114). Therefore, while, as the Prophet says, 'A man will not be asked about why he beat his wife,' (*Mishkat*, 1, p. 693), if she has to be beaten, she should be beaten lightly, that is, not as one would beat a slave-girl: 'Give her a command,' the Prophet counsels a man who comes to ask his advice on what he should do about the foul tongue of his wife, 'and if there is any good in her she will accept it; but do not beat your wife as you would beat your young slave-girl' (*Mishkat*, 1, p. 692; see also *Bukhari*, 62.132).

The proper relationship between husband and wife is thus put by the Prophet: 'Worship your Lord and honour your brother. If I were to order anyone to prostrate himself before another, I would order a woman to prostrate herself before her husband; and if he were to order her to convey stones from a yellow mountain to a black one, or from a black mountain to a white one, it would be incumbent on her to do so.'

This is so, he says, 'because of the special right over them [i.e., over the wives] given to the husband by God' (*Mishkat*, 1, pp. 691, 693, 694).

'After me,' says the Prophet, 'I have not left any affliction more harmful to men than women' (*Bukhari*, 62.33; *Muslim*, 6603-5 similar). After he has viewed heaven and hell, the Prophet reports that women are the ones who constitute the majority in hell (*Bukhari*, 2.28, 62.124-6, 76.456, 553; *Muslim*, 6596-6601). The reason seems to be not that they lack piety but that they are ungrateful to their husbands. The tradition has the Prophet saying, 'Then I saw the [Hell] Fire, and I have never before seen such a horrible sight as that, and I saw that the majority of its dwellers were women.' The people asked: 'O Allah's Apostle! What is the reason for that?' He replied, 'Because of their ungratefulness.' He was asked, 'Do they disbelieve in Allah [are they ungrateful to Allah]?' He replied, 'They are not thankful to their husbands and are ungrateful for the favours done to them . Even if you do good to one of them all your life, when she sees some harshness from you [sic] [at another place the words are 'and then she sees something in you [not to her liking,] she will say, " I have never seen any good from you"' (Bukhari, 62.125; 2.28).

It is no wonder therefore that women are to count for half of men in inheritance, that the evidence of two women is to equal the evidence of one man – 'This,' says the Prophet in relation to the latter, 'is because of the deficiency of a woman's mind' (Bukhari, 48.826). And it is even less of a wonder that the Prophet should affirm, 'Never shall succeed such a nation as makes a women their ruler' (Bukhari, 88.219).

The laws that are so heavily weighted in favour of men flow naturally and inexorably from this basic view of women. And that is why there is no way round them.

Reforms in Muslim Countries

The manifest inequity of these laws and their obsolescence have led one Muslim country after another to reform them wholesale. Many have tried to dress the reforms up by asserting that they are derived from or are based on the Shariat itself. Some have invoked 'the principle of necessity' and instituted reforms on this basis. Some have based these on Takhsis-al-qada, the right of a ruler to specify what will and what will not be within the jurisdiction of the courts.

Another even more openly eclectic method has been talfiq, i.e. 'patching up' by combining the opinions of different schools and jurists.

Others have been more inventive and have enlarged the latitude of choosing one school of Islamic law or another out of recognition. They have decided to choose not just this school or that, but to choose school 'X' on point 'A', school 'Y' on point 'B' and so on. Not just that. Differences of opinion within a school have been pressed into service. The countries have decided that even after choosing one school on a particular point, they are not bound by the settled or dominant view of that school on that point, but will choose from among all of the views that have been expressed on that point by any of the adherents of that school. This realistic expedient too has been elevated to the level of principle and given a fine sounding name –*takhayyur*.

Now, one can raise anything to the point of principle and sanctify it by giving it an Arabic or a Persian name. And, I suppose, if a fig-leaf helps, it is good. But these are transparent subterfuges. The main points to remember are: because of the press of reality, almost all Muslim countries have reformed personal law, as also every other aspect of Islamic law; and that in doing so they have derived the new formulations from widely disparate sources – the Napoleonic code, the codes of Britain, Italy, even Japan.

The changes are set out exhaustively in the standard texts (for instance, Norman Anderson, *Law Reform in the Muslim World*, University of London, The Athlone Press, London, 1976; Tanzil-Ur-Rahman, *A Code of Muslim Personal Law*, Vol.1, Hamdard Centre, Karachi, 1978). Even a few examples will show both that the new laws have gone beyond the Quran, the *sunna*, etc. and also that the laws applicable in these countries now, even on matters such as polygamy, divorce etc. are far more equitable than the ones in India.

The Ottoman Commercial Code of 1850 which was adopted throughout the Ottoman Empire and Egypt and features of which were incorporated in Saudi Arabia too, was, as Anderson puts it, 'squarely based on French law and owes virtually nothing to the Shariat.' Outside the Ottoman Empire, French law has been the basis of commercial codes in former French colonies, and British law in former British colonies.

The same thing is true of criminal law – both on substance and procedure, starting with the Ottoman Penal code of 1858. The new codes in each instance have been based on French and Italian laws on the subject and on the (British) Indian Penal Code of 1860.

Nor is the position any different in relation to the civil codes. The Egyptian Code of 1948, which in turn formed the basis of the codes of Syria, Libya, Iraq, etc., was based on Napoleon's Code. It incorporated features from German, Italian and Japanese laws also. It retained just a few provisions of the Shariat. The Persian Civil Code of 1939 too incorporated much from the French.

Even on the specific matters that are under discussion today in India – marriage, divorce, etc. – these countries have gone way ahead of our laws.

On marriage, two illustrations will suffice. As is well-known child marriages were customary in Islam, as in other traditions such as Hinduism. The Prophet himself married the indomitable Aisha when she was six, the marriage being consummated when she was nine. The Prophet was in his fifties; they remained happily married till the Prophet's death, nine years later. The traditions also have him saying that it is written in the Torah, 'If any one does not give his daughter in marriage when she reaches twelve and she commits sin, the guilt of that rests on him' (*Mishkat,* 1, p. 667). But today in all parts of the Islamic world child marriages are outlawed.

Polygamy too has been restricted in country after country. It has been completely prohibited in Tunisia by Article 18 of the Law of Personal Status, 1956. In 1964 Tunisia decreed that not only would a second marriage make the husband and the new wife liable to criminal punishment, the marriage itself would be invalid. Similarly, Article 223 of the Constitution of the Ismaili Khojas of East Africa says, 'Polygamy is strictly prohibited.' Under the Constitution, a marriage can be solemnized only if neither has a living spouse.

Other countries have taken steps in two directions. First, they have laid down conditions that must be fulfilled before the husband can take another wife, and, second, they have decreed that institutions or persons other than the husband – the courts, the Qazis, etc. – must satisfy themselves that the conditions laid down are indeed met in the particular case.

In Pakistan, the Muslim Family Law Ordinance of 1961 provides that no husband, during the subsistence of an existing marriage, can contract another one without the previous permission in writing of a government-appointed 'Arbitration Council'. Under it the husband is obliged to state in writing his reasons for wanting to marry again, and also to specify whether the permission of the existing wife has been obtained. The Council then asks him and his existing wife to nominate representatives. Next, it ascertains whether another marriage is 'necessary and just.' Even if the Council sanctions another marriage, the wife can apply to the Collector for a revision and, says the law, 'His decision shall be final and shall not be called in question in any court.'

Under the Moroccan Code of 1958, the Qazi is first to investigate whether there is any fear that, as a result of the new marriage, the existing wife will be treated unequally. The wife can specifically ask him to investigate any particular injury that she is liable to suffer as a consequence.

Under the 1959 law of Iraq permission for a second marriage is to be refused unless the court is satisfied that the husband has the financial capacity to maintain more than one wife and that, in addition, the second marriage will yield some 'lawful benefit'. Moreover, if there is the apprehension that the wives will not be treated equally, the permission is to be refused, in this case by the Qazi.

Under the 1968 law in Singapore, another marriage can be contracted only after the permission of the Chief Qazi, and this permission is seldom given.

Under the Family Protection Law that the Shah enacted in Iran in 1975, a husband had no right to take on a second wife unless the existing wife either consented to the marriage or a series of very specific conditions were fulfilled: i.e., unless it was established that the wife was unable or unwilling to cohabit, or that she had become insane, or that she was suffering from an incurable disease, was addicted to drugs, drinking, gambling, etc. or that she had deserted him, or that she was sterile, or had been convicted of a crime entailing punishment for five years or more. Moreover, if such permission was granted on these grounds, the existing wife could at once petition the court to have her marriage dissolved.

Even in little South Yemen, under a 1974 law, a second marriage is not permitted without the written permission of the appropriate district court, and the court is not allowed to give its permission unless there is a medical certificate showing that the wife is barren (and also unless it is shown that the husband did not know of this at the time of marriage), or a medical certificate showing that the wife suffers from an infectious, chronic and incurable disease.

Under the Turkish Code, no person can marry again unless he proves that the previous marriage has been dissolved by the death of the other party, or by divorce or a decree of nullity.

There have been corresponding advances in the law of divorce. First, steps have been taken towards putting the wife at par with the husband in initiating and ensuring divorce. Second, the courts and others have been brought into the process. Third, in some countries, although the number is fewer, the husband's power to act arbitrarily has been hemmed in.

The Tunisian law puts the wife completely on a par with the husband in this matter. Under Article 31(3) a wife may insist on a judicial divorce for any reason or none, provided she is prepared to pay such compensation to the husband as the court specifies.

Under the Pakistan Ordinance, a wife can sue for divorce where her husband has taken another wife in contravention of the provisions of the Ordinance. The case law has gone further and established that on the petition of the wife, the courts can decide on a divorce where *they* find – i.e., *the judges and not the husband* – that the temperaments of the two are irreconcilable or that the marriage has broken down.

In the Middle East, the Ottoman Law of Family Rights began this process as far back as 1917. Under it, if the original marriage contract provided that the husband shall not take another wife and he did so, the original marriage stood dissolved. Second, the wife could ask for a divorce if the husband deserted her or was afflicted by a dangerous disease.

Subsequent reforms in Egypt, Sudan, Jordan, Syria, Tunisia, Morocco, Iraq, Iran took the matter further. They enlarged the list of 'defects' on grounds of which the wife could initiate a divorce – these ranged from addiction of various kinds to commission of an offence repugnant to family honour or the prestige of the wife – and they added new grounds, for instance, the failure to maintain the wife in the condition that was appropriate or to which she was accustomed. As noted earlier, the Indian Dissolution of Muslim Marriages Act of 1939 also marked a major step forward in this respect.

In country after country the law now provides that no divorce is to be effective or to be recognised until the courts have passed a decree to that effect. Under the Tunisian law of 1956, no divorce that is pronounced outside a court of law has any legal validity whatsoever. In Pakistan, the husband must give notice to the wife as well as the local Chairman. The latter is to appoint an Arbitration Council, and this Council is to first attempt a reconciliation.

A few countries – Iran under the Shah was a leader in this – have gone further and restricted the power of the husband to ask for divorce. Under the Iranian law, for instance, a husband could divorce a wife only upon obtaining 'a certificate of impossibility of reconciliation' from a court, and this certificate could be given only if he could prove his case on specified grounds.

Even on alimony, there has been a little progress. The Constitution of the Ismaili Khojas of East Africa provides in Article 273 that 'if, upon dissolution of a marriage, the Council is of the opinion that the husband was responsible for the breaking up of the marriage, it may award to the wife such monetary compensation as it may deem just and reasonable in addition to the *Mahr*.' The Tunisian law provides that where the husband (or the wife) is the one who insists on a divorce, the Court shall decree the compensation that he (or she) shall pay. The Moroccan law requires the husband to pay the wife a parting, conciliatory gift 'in proportion to his means and her circumstances.'

Conclusion

There is therefore no shortage of precedents. Nor is it difficult to find 'grounds' for such changes in this or that passage from the Quran or in the traditions of the Prophet. 'I desire only to set things right,' says the Quran, 'so far as I am able,' (11.90) and one can argue that what is to be respected and practised in regard to proclamations such as this is the commitment and aspiration to continually 'set things right'. There is the tradition referred to earlier about the date-trees in which the Prophet affirms that while on religious matters he is the better judge, on temporal matters his followers are. There is the tradition too, in which he says, 'Islam was born alone, and will become alone again, as at its beginning. Happy the solitary men. Those are they who will come to reform that which will be debased after me.' One can argue, as Iqbal did in his famous lectures on *The Reconstruction of Religious Thought in Islam*, that 'the doors of *ijtihad*' were 'closed' for purely historical reasons and that, a thousand years having gone by, it is time for them to reopened.

More than any of these, one can draw inspiration from *the tendency* inherent in the Quran and the Prophet's injunctions.

They did not abolish slavery, true; but, it can be argued that they tried to humanise it. They did not abolish polygamy, true; but they prescribed a maximum where there had been none. Their view of women bears the stamp of the time, true; but they took a step forward by enjoining that the women should be treated well. They did not place women on a par with men in regard to property, true; but they incorporated in their institutes the right of a woman to have property of her own. Instead of getting stuck at the letter of the Quran and the *hadis*, therefore, we can focus on the tendency inherent in them, and thus press forward with reforms.

As has been suggested above, one can, if one tries hard enough, find in the rich and varied stock of the religion such justifications for adjusting old formulations to new realites. And if such citations help, they should be put together.

But we should be forewarned: in any such contest of quotation-mongering, the fundamentalists are bound to win. As suggested above, the laws, in fact, derive from the world-view of seventh century Arabia, and a few stray quotations cannot dislodge their claim to be what was enjoined.

The straightforward way is the only one which will be effective. This way is as follows:

❏ Each provision of each of our codes – and not just the Muslim one – must be re-examined in the light of modern secular principles;

❏ A new draft Code based on what is best in them as well as in codes in force elsewhere in the world should be drawn up;

❏ The task of preparing this Code must be entrusted, not to the clerics and priests and theologians of, any religion but to modern, secular jurists;

❏ Once prepared, the Code should first be enacted as an option so that all Indians can choose whether they want to be governed by this Code or by the one specific to their religion;

❏ As a final step, of course, this modern, secular, common Code should replace the existing parochial ones.

There are two preconditions for reform along these lines. The

first is a great campaign of education. On all such matters, almost
invariably, we leave the debate to the least informed and the most
reactionary elements in our society. We must ourselves get
back to first principles. We must ourselves read the primary texts.
We must ourselves prepare catalogues of the reforms that have
been enacted in other countries and circulate them throughout the
length and breadth of our country. We must ourselves affirm that
this is not a 'Hindu v. Muslim' question, but a question of
human rights, in particular, of ensuring justice to some of the
weakest in our country — namely women. And throughout this
campaign, the opinions that must be sought are not so much of
the Hindu priests or the Muslim *ulema* but of the ones who are
most handicapped by the laws.

Second, each section of our people must shed two notions.
The first is that its security lies in fortifying its separateness. Our
security and prosperity lies in our working together to strengthen
the mores and institutions of a modern, secular State. The second
notion is the one that sees the essence of religion in such externals
as rituals on the one hand, and in whether or not alimony is to
be paid on the other. Discarding such externals will get us all the
more swiftly and surely to the essence of our religions.

And as our priests and politicians whip up our fears and
passions, all of us must remember that what is cutting the ground
from under our old laws or institutions, what is 'endangering' them
is not the 'other' religion but that great solvent — time — and its
accompaniment — change.

— October 1985

X

The Muslim Women's Bill

The General Secretary of the Indian Union Muslim League, G.M. Banatwala, introduced his Bill to undo the Supreme Court's judgment on the Shah Bano case on 15 March, 1985. It was due to come up for discussion in the Parliament. In August, Arif Mohammad Khan, then Minister of State in the Ministry of Home Affairs, was at a reception for the Assam student leaders (the Accord had just been signed). He met the Prime Minister, Rajiv Gandhi and mentioned that he would like to speak on Banatwala's Bill. 'No, you might as well stay out of it,' Rajiv said. 'After all, you will just be saying what the others are saying.'

'That is just the point,' Arif told him, 'I don't want to say what the others are saying. I am convinced that asking a husband to help look after an indigent woman whom he has divorced is in accord with the spirit of the Shariat.'

The Prime Minister was suddenly interested. But after a few general remarks, he walked off to talk to the other guests.

He returned to Arif. He now approved the idea of Arif speaking on the Bill. He encouraged him to consult others also, scholars as well as other leaders of Muslim opinion.

Arif met Mr Justice V. Khalid, who had earlier decided an important case on a related question. Referring to the decision of the Kerala High Court, that a divorce given 'under compulsion or in jest or in anger' would be 'perfectly valid', the Judge had said in a subsequent case, 'My judicial conscience is disturbed at this monstrosity. The question is whether the conscience of the leaders of public opinion is also disturbed.' The Judge told Arif that he was absolutely right, but he counselled the Minister against opposing Banatwala's Bill. Rightly or wrongly, he said, the whole community had come to feel that the Supreme Court had interfered in its personal law.

Arif met Tahir Mahmood, a Muslim professor of law, who had

authored a standard textbook on Muslim personal law. Arif had learnt that an entire chapter containing the plea for a common civil code had been removed from the new edition. The professor too asked Arif not to oppose the Bill. The reason the professor gave had nothing to do with this Bill but with what he thought of the conduct of the Supreme Court on some other case involving Hindu Law.

'But I ask you a simple question,' Arif said. 'If a well-to-do husband throws out his wife, and the wife has no way at all to keep body and soul together other than to go about begging or selling her body, if her relatives cannot maintain her, if the Muslim community, being poor, cannot provide for her, and if we then ask the husband to give her at least some maintenance, will we be contravening the Shariat? Will we be going against the spirit of Islam or acting in accordance with it?'

The professor agreed that asking the husband to do so would be in accordance with the spirit of Islam, and that there would be no contravention of the Shariat. Conversations of this kind confirmed Arif in his resolve to speak up on the issue.

It was decided that Arif would speak on behalf of the Government on Banatwala's Bill. This was quite in order. Every private member's Bill is 'addressed to' a particular ministry. The ministry then responds on behalf of the Government. Banatwala's Bill had been addressed to the Ministry of Home Affairs. Arif was then the Minister of State in this Ministry.

The Home and Law ministries had already prepared notes on the subject. Both had pointed out that personal law did not come into the question at all. Section 125 of the Cr. P.C., they said, was just meant to control vagrancy. The State had the right as well as the duty under the Constitution to control vagrancy. The religious argument, which was the premise of Banatwala's Bill, should therefore be rejected at the threshold.

In his speech on 23 August, however, Arif took a different tack. He established the liberal position on the basis of Quranic texts, and the *sunna* of the Prophet, that is, in terms of the Shariat itself.

He was loudly cheered by Congress MPs as well as by the Opposition. Najma Heptullah, the Deputy Chairman of the Rajya Sabha, was among those who wrote to him. '*Allah kare zare zuban aur ziyada*' (may God add lustre to your golden words), she wrote.

The official of the Home Ministry who had prepared the brief complimented him too. 'Our line would not have worked,' he told Arif. 'Yours was the effective way.'

The Session ended. The Council of Ministers was meeting. Rajiv Gandhi expressed satisfaction at the way the Session had gone. He pointed to tasks ahead.

'The hero of the Session has been Arif', said Mrs. Ram Dulari Sinha, who too was then Minister of State in the Ministry of Home Affairs.

The Prime Minister agreed and told them that he had already sent Arif a letter congratulating him on his speech. He had, indeed – on 25 August. He had not just congratulated Arif on his personal performance, he had said how happy he was to note the widespread appreciation that the speech had evoked in the country.

At a meeting of the Cabinet Committee on Political Affairs a few weeks later, the Prime Minister again praised the stand Arif had taken. Arif was an asset to the party, he said. One could find many liberals in the community, he said, but seldom did one come across a man of such courage. This warm praise was reported to Arif by a member of the Committee.

A few days later, talking to three journalists, V.P. Singh, the Finance Minister, used identical words to commend Arif. One of the journalists told Arif what Singh had said.

Things began to sour, however, as the campaign for the 1985 Assam elections got under way. 'Arif has alienated the Muslims,' it was said. 'We must do something to win them back.'

Z.R. Ansari, another Minister of State, now spoke up in Parliament, denouncing not just the judgment of the Supreme Court but the Court itself. He characterised the judges as *teli-tambolis* (common oil-pressers) who had set themselves up as scholars and interpreters of law. At the Supreme Court, Justice V.D. Tulzapurkar raised the matter more than once in the morning get-togethers of the judges and urged the Chief Justice to write to the Prime Minister protesting against the tirade. The Chief Justice eventually did so. The Prime Minister wrote back saying that he had counselled Ansari.

Arif felt let down. After all, he had spoken on behalf of the Government, after talking to the Prime Minister, after being briefed by officials of the Law Ministry as well as of his own Home

Ministry. He had incurred the opprobrium of many Muslims. Urdu papers and leaders of the Muslim League had been denigrating him, saying that he was opposing Banatwala's Bill 'to strengthen his hold on the ministerial chair'.

His misgivings were soon allayed. To his surprise, he was told that the Prime Minister, who was visiting Oman, had personally substituted Arif's name for that of another Minister to accompany him on the visit. Arif was given to understand that this had been done to counter the impression that the Prime Minister had decided to dissociate himself from Arif's stand on the Shah Bano case.

The trip confirmed Arif's hopes. In fact, it was suggested to him that the Ansari business was meant strictly for consumption in Assam. Arif chose to believe this rather than what Rajiv Gandhi had himself said at Ansari's subsequent conference − that the Government was considering changes in the law that would take Muslims out of the purview of Section 125.

Early in February 1986 Arif was told that the Government was in fact thinking of introducing a Bill to this effect. He met among others A.K. Sen, the Union Law Minister. Sen told him that the Government had 'come to an understanding with the religious leaders'. These leaders, Arif was astonished to learn, had now been accepted by the Government as spokesmen of the Muslim community. They included leaders of the Muslim League, the Muslim Majlis, the Muslim Personal Law Board, the Majlis Ijtihad ul Muslameen − each of them a rank communal organisation.

He was told that the Bill would have the parents and other relatives of the divorced woman maintain her, and, if they could not, the Bill would have the *wakf* boards do so.

Arif pointed to the gross injustice of the Bill, how the law would now relegate Muslim women to a position abjectly inferior to that of other women in the country. He also pointed out that the clause about the *wakf* boards was quixotic. He had personal knowledge of the financial position of the *wakf* boards from his work in Uttar Pradesh. On the eve of festivals they have to run around asking for handouts from the State Government even to pay a little advance to their employees, he told Sen. In any case, where does the Quran say, what part of the Shariat says, that blood relatives must maintain a divorced woman or that *wakf* boards should do so? In fact the assets and proceeds of *a wakf* can be used only for the purposes for which it has been created, he said.

Sen agreed on every point, but kept saying that the religious leaders thought this could be done.

Arif was now convinced that if the Government persisted in introducing the Bill, he would have to resign. Over the next two weeks he met few people, and he began to stay away from his office bit by bit.

A.K. Sen finally introduced the Bill on 25 February. The Bill hurt Arif but Sen's remarks while introducing it hurt even more. The Law Minister said that it had been the consistent policy of the Government that in matters pertaining to a community, priority should be given to the views of the leaders of that community.

An MP interjected, had the Government not seen the statement that 125 eminent Muslims had signed? They included the seniormost diplomats, a sitting member of the Planning Commission, a vice-chancellor, senior officials of the Government itself, and they had pointed out that the Bill would set the community back.

They are just 'dancers and actors', shouted Ibrahim Suleiman Sait, the President of the Muslim League. No one in the Government contradicted him.

Arif was horrified. It was the 'sole spokesman' business *a la* Jinnah all over again. He wrote out a two-line letter of resignation and twice proceeded to meet Rajiv Gandhi the Prime Minister. Both times he returned to his seat.

The introduction of the Bill was over around 4.30 p.m. On his way out he told V. George, personal secretary to the Prime Minister, that he would be sending a letter for the PM and that George should hand it over as soon as he received it.

'But aren't you coming for the 6 o'clock meeting?,' George asked him. (The Council of Ministers was to meet, and Arif was to have attended it.) 'No, I may not be able to attend it,' Arif told him, 'but please see to it that the PM gets the letter before the meeting starts.'

Arif went home, sent his letter, and left his house for another place. The letter was duly handed over to Rajiv Gandhi. There were phone calls to Arif's house but the callers were told that he wasn't home.

The next morning he was called to see Arun Singh, an aide

close to the Prime Minister, and Minister of State for Defence. Singh had Arif's resignation letter with him when the two met in the outer lobby of the Parliament. They spent over an hour together. Arun was, as always, polite, soft-spoken and understanding. He told Arif that he – Arif, that is – had gone up in his esteem, that what he was doing was indeed the thing a man of principle would do . No man of honour could have done less. But, he said, it would have the unfortunate consequence that from now on no one would dare to even differ. Everyone would cite what happened to Arif. For this reason, Arun said, he should withdraw the resignation. Arif explained his difficulty in the matter. He had spoken at length on the question. He had incurred the opprobrium of many in his community for doing so. He felt that the Government was dealing with rank communalists and fundamentalists. This was against everything the Congress had stood for. The injustice that would be inflicted on Muslim women...we were going back to the pre-Partition days.

Arun Singh agreed with everything. He told Arif that he understood his difficulty in the matter. He might himself have resigned in such a situation, he said. He agreed on the fundamentalists too. Whatever reasons were given in favour of the Bill, he said, the fundamentalists were bound to claim it as their victory.

Arif's resignation would embarrass the Prime Minister personally, Arun explained. In any case, Arif had done what his conscience required him to do. And what if the Prime Minister now turned down his request to be relieved of office, Arun asked.

He would have to stay, Arif said. But he would be of no use to the Government or the party. He would just shuttle between his home and his office. He could never go to his constituency or elsewhere. You say the fundamentalists are the leaders, he said. But the people voted for the Prime Minister, they voted for you, for all of us, not for the fundamentalists.

Arif was next called to meet Arun Nehru, a cousin of Rajiv Gandhi, and at that time the Minister of State for Internal Security. They met thrice, each time in the same outer lobby in the full view of many MPs. The conversation followed the pattern of the earlier one. Nehru too agreed with every point Arif put forward, and lamented that such a situation had arisen. But now they were under a 'compulsion'. The 'compulsion' was not spelled out. But

Arif gathered that the agitation and the hysteria that had been whipped up had had their intended effect.

Like Arun Singh, Arun Nehru too appreciated Arif's difficulty. He too said that he also might have resigned in a similar situation. But what if, Arif having sent in his resignation, the PM did not accept it?

Finally, Arif met Rajiv Gandhi at 9.15 that evening. They were together for half an hour. The Prime Minister was courteous, even sympathetic. Arif went over the points one by one. Rajiv seemed to appreciate each of them. He too put the blame on the unfortunate situation that had arisen. He did not defend the Bill much.

His final question was to ask Arif what should be done so that people would not say that he, Rajiv Gandhi, had dumped him. Arif thanked him for the sentiment but explained that the Prime Minister was in the best position to judge what should be done in the circumstances.

I have not known Arif. Our paths have crossed only once before. He was once kind enough to read an article of mine in 1980 and file a privilege motion against me. This time around, he was kind enough to agree to come over to my house and discuss the events narrated above.

It is clear that he has taken a stand on a principle. He is concerned that the Government has lent respectability to rank communalists, that it has accepted the fatal assertions, first, that Muslims alone can speak for Muslims, and, second, that among Muslims the fundamentalists alone can speak for Muslims. This, he has told Rajiv Gandhi and his aides, and he affirms today to his colleagues in the Congress, takes us back to the pre-Partition days. Then too, he recalls, this is precisely what the Muslim League used to say, this is precisely what the Congress fought against.

He is convinced that the Bill is bad on merits, that it goes against the tenets of Islam, that it will compound the grave injustice from which Muslim women already suffer. He has done a great deal of work on the question. As we talked on the law in my study, two volumes of the nine of *Sahih al-Bukhari* (the most highly revered collection of the traditions of the Prophet) happened to be lying among the pile on the table.

'Here, look at this,' he said. 'This is Volume 7, isn't it? Look at pages 199 and 200.' He opened them and began reading out the chapter entitled, 'The gift given by a husband to a divorced lady for whom *Mahr* has been fixed, by virtue of the statement of Allah.' He came to the verse,

There is no blame on you if you divorce women while yet you have not touched them nor appointed unto them their dower (*Mahr*). But bestow upon them (a suitable gift)... Truly Allah is all-seeing of what you do.   (*Quran*, 2.236-7)

'And Allah also said,' he continued reading from Bukhari,

And for divorced, maintenance (should be provided) on a reasonable (scale). This is a duty on the pious. Thus Allah makes clear His signs to you in order that you may understand.
(*Quran*, 2.241-2)

Nine Muslim countries, he said, already have laws that require the husband to provide maintenance to the wife he divorces. A Pakistani Alim, he has been told, has written in a Lahore newspaper that the assertion of some Muslims in India, that in decreeing maintenance the Indian Supreme Court has thwarted the Shariat, is derogatory to Islam. To buttress his case, he quoted the paragons of fundamentalism itself – from Maulana Maudoodi to Mustafa as Sibaee to Abu Zohra.

Many Ministers are articulate, even I have met a few of them. But this is the first time that I have met a Minister who can pick up the right volume of a canonical text and at once turn to the right page.

It is rare to have a Minister stand up for a principle these days. Therefore, even if this was all there was to the matter, it would still be a significant event. But there is much more to it.

First, the cost of having as our Prime Minister a person who does not have an adequate background on public issues is becoming clearer by the week. The most charitable interpretation that one can put on this episode is that Rajiv Gandhi just did not know what he was about, that faced with a few demonstrations the Government funked, that, in a panic, it thought that the only way to buy peace was to strike a deal with the obscurantists. Because of his lack of background the Prime Minister does not seem to be able to appreciate the point of principle involved in an issue or the wider implications of a step.

But the episode reveals something even more disturbing. The Government remains what it was to begin with—a Prime Minister, a cousin, and one school-friend. Today one Minister after another says in private how he regrets the Bill, but he says nothing in public. (The Bill was not considered by the Council of Ministers at all before it was introduced in the Lok Sabha. It was put to the Council after it had been introduced by A.K. Sen on 25 February, and then it was, of course, presented as a *fait accompli*.) In this case even the Prime Minister and his two closest associates do not seem to enter a defence of the measure in private. It is as if the Government is sleep-walking. They speak of 'the unfortunate situation that has arisen', of 'compulsions'. 'It was a political decision,' the Prime Minister at last told the Congress Parliamentary Party on 28 February.

There is, of course, a lack of background, and of preparation on public issues. But there is also an obstinacy. 'The moving finger having writ, moves on,' we are being told, 'Not all thy piety nor wit...'

There is moreover no question of elementary loyalty. A colleague is encouraged to take a stand. The stand, in some myopic vision, later seems inconvenient. He is dumped. And there is the incipient chicanery: 'Leaders of the community have been consulted.' In fact all that has been done is that a deal has been made with the obscurantists. 'A comprehensive background paper will be circulated setting out provisions of the law as they prevail in Islamic countries.' No paper is circulated. 'There was some delay on this matter on our part,' says the Prime Minister. That is not what I hear. My information is that the material was collected, and it was ready. It was collected in part by our embassies in Muslim countries, I am told. But it showed that one Muslim country after another had in fact modernised its family laws. That is why the promised paper was not circulated. And it stands to reason. A Prime Minister who is so particular about sticking to 'time-bound programmes' is not likely to have so lightly forgotten his pledge to Parliament to circulate the background paper. The provision about *wakf* boards is touted when in fact Arun Nehru, A.K. Sen, Arjun Singh, among others, know that these boards are in no position to help indigent, castaway women. Once again the Government is dressing its funk in principle, this time in the primacy it says it has always accorded to the views of the leaders of the community.

The signal will not be lost on anyone. Certainly not in Punjab. Having expressed so much solicitude for the personal law of the Muslims, how will this Government deny the demand for a separate 'Sikh personal law' that the Akalis had put forward and which is duly listed in the official White Paper on the Punjab agitation? And surely if our Parliament is to codify personal laws of different religious communities, it must be guided by the clerics of each community. But it is the Parliament of what the Constitution describes as a Sovereign Socialist Democratic Republic, it is a Parliament that is by the same Constitution enjoined, as much as each of the citizens who elect it, to 'endeavour to secure for the citizens a uniform civil code throughout the territory of India', 'to renounce practices derogatory to the dignity of women', and 'to develop the scientific temper, humanism and the spirit of inquiry and reform.'

* * *

The Ministries' View

Banatwala's contention was in effect that Sections 125 and 127 of the Criminal Procedure Code must be amended to ensure that a divorced Muslim woman should have no right whatsoever to claim even the most niggardly maintenance after the period of *iddat*, which is around three months.

Section 125 (which corresponds to Section 488 of the old Cr. P.C. of 1898) is a very mild provision. Under it a magistrate may ask a husband to provide up to a maximum of Rs 500 a month for the maintenance of his wife, provided two conditions are fulfilled: the magistrate must satisfy himself, first, that the husband has 'sufficient means', and, second that the wife is 'unable to maintain herself'.

It had been contended that Section 488 of the old Cr.P.C. on which Section 125 of the new Cr.P.C. is based did not apply to Muslim husbands. The matter was settled by Justice Krishna Iyer, then a Judge of the Kerala High Court, in 1970. He held:

The Indian Constitution directs that the State should endeavour to have a uniform civil code applicable to the entire Indian community, and, indeed, when motivated by a high public policy, Section 488 had made such a law. It would be improper for an Indian court to exclude any section of the community born and bred upon Indian soil from the benefit of that law.

The subsequent history is recounted compactly in a standard book on Muslim personal law (Tahir Mahmood, *Muslim Personal Law*, 1983). The original edition of the book had a chapter with many progressive things to say about moving towards a common civil code; in the new edition the author noted: 'On a deeper study of the subject I realised that time had not yet come for me to formulate a final opinion on certain points covered by the book,' and therefore dropped the entire chapter from the book! Dr. Mahmood records what happened:

In 1973 when a comprehensive Bill for the revision of the Criminal Procedure Code was moved in Parliament, section 488(3) was sought to be re-enacted with a modification to the effect that the courts could make an order for maintenance in favour of a divorced wife also. The proposed modification was vehemently opposed by various sections of orthodox Muslims on the ground that under Islamic law a husband is bound to maintain a divorced wife only during the period of *iddat* (nearly three months) and not thereafter. Numerous articles appeared in the Urdu press opposing the proposed amendment of section 488(3). *The opponents of the new measure took advantage of the political situation prevailing at that time in the country. They succeeded in capitalizing on it and, at the instance of the ruling party, Parliament chose to budge.* As a rare instance in the legislative history of India discussion on the draft of the (new) Criminal Procedure Code was reopened in Parliament at a very unusual stage. The provision as finally enacted laid down that though the courts could grant maintenance to a divorced wife, at the time of so doing they should give due consideration to whether she had already realised from her husband in full her post-divorce entitlement under the personal law of the parties. This was obviously meant to protect Muslim personal law on the point as traditionally interpreted. The way in which the amendment as originally proposed was modified, seemingly satisfied the orthodox Muslims.

The concession was apparently a severe blow to Muslim women, and it certainly put them in a position far inferior to that of other women in India.

In a series of subsequent judgments, however, the courts held that the compromise did not snuff out the rights of indigent Muslim women who had been cast off by their husbands.

In 1979 the Allahabad High Court held that Section 127(3), which was the concession that the fundamentalists had been able to extract from a beleaguered Government, in fact 'grants *additional rights* to a divorced Muslim woman for receiving maintenance beyond the period of *iddat* till such time as she has not married after her divorce. This additional benefit does not conflict with the rights which already accrue to her under Muslim law.'

In 1980 the Supreme Court pinpointed the matter further. It held that Section 125 would not apply only 'on proof of payment of a sum stipulated by customary or personal law *whose quantum is more or less sufficient to do duty for maintenance allowance.*'

Now, Muslim personal law requires only that the *Mahr* be paid. It was argued on the part of Muslim husbands that, as they had paid the *Mahr*, Section 127(3)(b) extinguished such obligation as may fall upon them under Section 125.

The courts held that this was not so. The *Mahr*, they specified, is an amount that the husband agrees to pay at the time of marriage out of regard for the bride. It has to do with the conjugal life that follows upon marriage. It has nothing to do with divorce and the obligations that must follow upon it. *Mahr* is not arrived at with any reference to what the wife would require for maintenance should she be divorced. As the Supreme Court said, 'The quintessence of *Mahr*, whether it is prompt or deferred, is clearly not a contemplated quantification of a sum of money in lieu of maintenance upon divorce.'

As Muslim personal law does not require the husband to pay anything to maintain the wife he discards, the courts said, and as the proviso of Section 127(3)(b) comes into operation *only if the wife has under personal law been paid something for maintenance*, there is nothing in Muslim personal law which will exempt the husband from the obligation which is cast upon him by Section 125.

The Shah Bano judgment was but a reaffirmation of such expositions of the law.

This was the background to Banatwala's Bill, 'addressed to' the Ministry of Home Affairs.

In its search for the relevant material, the Ministry consulted among others the Law Ministry. In his note dated 25 May 1985, the Legal Advisor to the Law Ministry categorically stated that the Supreme Court had correctly interpreted the law, and opined that 'provisions of maintenance for a divorced wife do not conflict with the Mohammadan personal law.' He cited what Parliament had been told on behalf of the Government 12 years earlier and concluded: 'A careful reading of the judgment would show that the honourable court has simply interpreted the relevant provision of the Cr. P.C. without any interference with the Muslim personal law as such.'

The Law Secretary was, if anything, even more emphatic. 'The Muslim personal law is of a civil nature whereas Section 125 is a provision contained in the Criminal Procedure Code,' he said and added that 'The Bill to amend Sections 125 and 127 of Cr.P.C. should be opposed.'

The Law Secretary's note on the file is worth reading in full:

I have perused the judgment of the Supreme Court rendered in *Mohd. Ahmed Khan Vs Shah Bano Begum & Ors.* with due care and attention. While performing its constitutional duty of interpreting section 125, particularly clause (b) of the explanation to sub-section (1) of the said section, the court has held that a Muslim wife who has been divorced and had not re-married is entitled to maintenance under section 125 and that this provision does not conflict with Muslim personal law. In support of this conclusion, reliance has been placed by the court not only on authoritative commentaries but also on *Aiyats* No. 241 and 242 from the Holy Quran. According to the court, these *Aiyats* leave no doubt that the Quran imposes an obligation on a Muslim husband to make provision for or to provide maintenance to the divorced wife. The court has also construed the expression *'Mahr'* to mean a sum payable to the wife out of respect to her. Another point decided by the court is regarding the true scope of sub-section (3) (b) of section 127 vis-a-vis the right to claim maintenance by a divorced woman under section 125. The decision of the court cannot be regarded as an encroachment on the Muslim personal law. The Muslim personal law is of a civil nature, whereas, section 125 is a provision contained in the Criminal Procedure Code.

In view of the foregoing, the Bill to amend sections 125 and 127 of Cr.P.C. should be opposed.

In view of the importance and sensitive character of the matter, ministers may also kindly see.

The note was signed by the Secretary, B.S. Sekhon, on 31 May 1985. The opinion was then endorsed by H.R. Bhardwaj, Minister of State for Law on 1 June and by A.K. Sen, the Cabinet Minister, on 2 June.

On the basis of this unanimous opinion of the Law Ministry as well as other material, the Ministry of Home Affairs prepared a comprehensive note. This note, dated 24 July 1985, shows that the judgment of the Supreme Court was only the latest occasion for the fundamentalists to raise a hue and cry. Banatwala had introduced similar Bills in the Lok Sabha in April 1979 and March 1980. The Ministry also recalled that the Committee on the Status of Women had opposed any amendments being made to the Cr.P.C. which would further worsen the position of Muslim women. The Ministry recorded that

The provisions of sections 125 and 127 are a sort of social legislation meant to prevent vagrancy. It does not seem necessary to amend the provisions of section 125 or 127 (3) (b) to nullify the interpretation given by the Supreme Court in the judgment. Further, according to the provision of the section, maintenance allowance will be payable only in cases where the husband is possessed of sufficient means. It should, therefore, not cause any serious burden on the husband of the divorced wife.

In view of all this, the Ministry said, the Bill should *not* be accepted 'either in its present form or in any modified form'.

So emphatic was its view that it said that even if an effort
was made to keep the Bill alive by sending it to a Select
or Joint Committee or by having it circulated to elicit public
opinion, that too should be rejected.

Once again, both because of the unambiguous nature of
the views expressed and the background information it contains,
the relevant portions of the note are worth reading in full:

Section 125 of the new Cr.P.C. relates to the grant of maintenance to wives, etc., and corresponds to section 288 of
the repealed Code of Criminal Procedure, 1898. Under the
old section 488, if a person having sufficient means
neglected or refused to maintain his wife, a magistrate could
order the payment of maintenance to her in summary
proceedings. This right was available only to the wife and so
a person could deprive a woman of her maintenance by
divorcing her, even if proceedings had already been
instituted under section 488. The provision thus had serious
limitations in so far as poor divorced women were
concerned, particularly of the Muslim community in which a
divorce can be brought about suddenly.

The Joint Committee of Parliament on the Code of Criminal
Procedure Bill, 1970, considered the provision of section 488,
and the hardship which it caused to the Muslim women. The
Joint Committee decided that the benefit of the provision
should be extended to a woman who has been divorced by
her husband so long as she had not remarried after divorce.
Accordingly, the definition of 'wife' was added in the bill. As
reported by the Joint Committee (clause 125), 'wife' was
defined as including a woman who has been divorced or has
obtained a divorce from her husband and has not remarried.
The provision was passed by the Rajya Sabha and the Lok
Sabha. But immediately after the adoption of all the clauses
of the bill in the Lok Sabha, the Government requested for re-
consideration. In order to allay the fears of the Muslim
community that the bill interfered with their personal law,
an amendment was moved to clause 127 of the bill. It
enabled the magistrate to cancel the order for
maintenance if the woman had received the whole
or any sum agreed to be paid to her on divorce. The

observations made   by   the   then MHA [Minister for Home
Affairs] and Shri Jyotirmoy Bosu during the debate in the Lok
Sabha on 1 December 1973, on the amendment to substitute
sub-section (3) of   section   127   by another sub-section are
given below:

Shri Ram Niwas Mirdha: 'I will tell you the purpose of this
amendment.

'As I said, under customary or personal law of Muslim communities, certain sums are due to divorced women. Once they
are paid, the   magistrate's order giving maintenance could
be cancelled. Now, whether the maintenance should be reasonable or unreasonable, is not the point. The hon. member
has not disputed this. He has said that it should be reasonable
and it should be given in that light. I am not in the position of
accepting the hon. member's own view and commentary on the
Holy Quran.'

Shri Jyotirmoy Bosu: 'I quoted the translation as done by
Allama Yusuf Ali which   reads: "For   divorced   women
maintenance should be provided on a reasonable scale." This
is the duty of the righteous, right-thinking person. This is very
clear, absolutely clear and crystal clear. The Holy Quran
clearly lays   down   that   a   right-thinking person will give
adequate money to the divorced lady to live and survive.'

Shri Ram Niwas Mirdha: 'If that holds good, this provision
may   not come into operation. This provision was considered
sufficient to take care of the special   arrangements between
the parties   and under the personal law of Muslims and was
incorporated   in   sub-section   (3) of section 127.'

Thus the provision in the new code is that under section 125
Cr.P.C. if any person having sufficient means neglects or
refuses to   maintain his wife, unable to maintain herself, a
magistrate of the first class may, upon proof of refusal, order
such person to pay maintenance to his wife at such monthly
rate not exceeding Rs 500 in the whole, as such magistrate
thinks fit. 'Wife' under this section, has been defined as
including a woman who has been divorced by or has obtained
a divorce from her husband and has not remarried...

The Supreme Court in *Bai Tahira Vs Ali Hussain* (AIR 1979
SC 362) has held that no person can claim under section 127
(3) (b) absolution   from   his   obligation under section 125

towards a divorced woman, except on proof of payment of sum
stipulated by customary or personal law whose quantum is
more or less sufficient to do duty for maintenance allowance
and is not illusory. Justice Krishna Iyer delivering his
judgment observed: 'The payment of illusory amounts by
way of customary or personal law requirement will be
considered in the reduction of maintenance rate but cannot
annihilate that rate unless it is a reasonable substitute. The
legal sanctity of the payment is certified by the fulfilment of
the social obligation not by a ritual exercise rooted in
custom.'
It is to this interpretation that Shri Banatwala, M.P., has
taken objection. He has, therefore, suggested that a new sub-
section should be inserted to section 125 Cr.P.C. to the effect
that no woman who has been divorced by, or has obtained a
divorce from, her husband shall be entitled to receive an
allowance, if she has received, or if she has been offered and
she has refused, the whole of the sum which under the
customary or personal law applicable to her was payable
on such divorce and that the quantum of the amount payable
shall not be questioned in any court on any ground. He has
also suggested that clause (b) of sub-section (3) of section 127
should be deleted.
The Ministry of Law, Justice and Company Affairs, who were
consulted, expressed the view that the judgment of the
Supreme Court in *Bai Tahira vs Ali Hussain* (AIR 1979 SC
362) had not intruded into the personal and customary law
applicable to the parties...
The Supreme Court has delivered judgment on 23.4.1985 in
Criminal Appeal No. 130/81 (*Mohd. Ali Khan Vs. Shah Bano
Begum and others*) wherein the courts have interpreted the
provisions of sections 125 and 127 of the Cr.P.C. and reconsid-
ered its earlier judgments in *Bai Tahira* and *Fazlunbi's* cases
(copy at Annexure-II). The important observations made by
the court are summarised below: (i) section 125 of the Cr.P.C.
is truly secular in character and the religion professed by
a spouse or by the spouses has no place in the scheme of the
provisions; (ii) the liability imposed by section 125 to maintain
close relations, who are indigent is founded upon the
individual's obligation to the society to prevent vagrancy and

destitution; (iii) there is no conflict between the provisions of section 125 and those of the Muslim personal law on the question of Muslim husband's obligation to provide maintenance for a divorced wife, who is unable to maintain herself; (iv) 'Mahr' referred to in section 127 (3) (b) is not a sum payable on divorce. 'Mahr' or 'Dower' is a sum of money or other property which the wife is entitled to receive from the husband in consideration of the marriage. If Mahr is an amount which the wife is entitled to receive from the husband in consideration of the marriage, that is the very opposite of the amount being payable in consideration of divorce. The Mahr, according to some, is an obligation imposed upon the husband as a mark of respect for the wife. The provision contained in section 127 (3) (b) is based on the misconception that dower is an amount payable 'on divorce'; (v) Mahr not being payable on divorce, does not fall within the meaning of section 127 (3) (b) of the Cr.P.C.

The provisions of sections 125 and 127 are a sort of social legislation meant to prevent vagrancy. It does not seem necessary to amend the provisions of section 125 or 127 (3) (b) to nullify the interpretation given by the Supreme Court in the judgment.

Further, according to the provision of the section, maintenance allowance will be payable only in cases where the husband is possessed of sufficient means. It should, therefore, not cause any serious burden on the husband of the divorced wife.

In view of the position explained above, it is proposed that the bill may not be accepted either in its present form or in any modified form. The bill may, therefore, be opposed. Any motion and/or amendment which may be moved for the circulation of the bill to elicit public opinion or its reference to select or joint committee may also be opposed.

Here then was the unambiguous and emphatic view of the relevant Ministries. And this was the position that was stated by Arif Mohammad Khan, Minister of State for Home Affairs, on behalf of the Government in his speech in Parliament on 23 August 1985.

As we know, the Government thereafter funked and struck

a deal with the fundamentalists. Clearly, the Bill must be defeated.

The first step is for Arif Mohammad Khan to testify to the facts. He is still reticent out of a false sense of 'loyalty to the party', false   because true loyalty to the party must consist in making sure that the principles on which it was built prevail, and out of a personal regard for Rajiv Gandhi, which regard should in fact lead Arif to try and restrain the Prime Minister on this matter so that even greater blunders are avoided.

Second, the Opposition owes a duty to the country. To start with, it must have the Government explain why the background paper which had been promised was not circulated, and, assuming that the only cause was, as the Prime Minister put it, 'a little delay on our part', to insist that it be circulated before the Bill is debated. It should also ask the Government to lay before the Parliament the full texts of the opinions prepared by the Home Ministry and the Law Ministry and other relevant documents.

Finally, Congress MPs should stand up. A great deal is at stake. They must demand that they be allowed to vote according to their conscience and then defeat the Bill. Should a whip be issued, they should defy it and defeat the Bill. By doing so, they will be serving the country and incidentally also absolving themselves of Rajiv Gandhi's charge, made in Bombay last December, that the party consists of men and women without character.

* * *

A Cynical Fraud

What the courts have held unambiguously about the provisions of Sections 125 and 127 (3) (b), the Supreme Court reaffirmed in the Shah Bano case. It isn't just that the Law and Home Ministries--the Ministries that were concerned with the matter--said in their confidential files that the Supreme Court's decision in the Shah Bano case had been correct. The comic fact is that the principal note in the papers that the Government has at last circulated among MPs to justify the new Bill says that the Supreme Court has correctly decided the case!

Here is what it says was the intention behind the new Section:

The new provision [i.e. Section 127 (3) (b)] was drafted with great care. There was no reference to the word '*Mahr*' (or Dowry) in the provision and this was done deliberately because '*Mahr*' was a sum agreed to at the time of marriage in consideration of conjugal life and had nothing whatever to do with the subject matter of the legislation, namely maintenance, after divorce (which in fact is the opposite of conjugal life).

The draft was intended to provide that if the parties had agreed or their customary or Personal Law so provided, that a specific sum of money should be paid as and by way of maintenance after divorce and if the whole of such sum had been paid, the Magistrate who awarded the maintenance could alter or cancel his order. It is clear that unless there was a specific provision for maintenance after divorce, section 127 (3) (b) will not come into operation.

Further, this note which has been circulated to justify a Bill that aims at overturning the Shah Bano judgment, concludes by saying:

From the foregoing it will be clear that the interpretation of the Supreme Court in the Shah Bano case does *not* militate against the intention either of the Government or of the Parliament at the time when the provision was enacted or at any earlier stage. It may be noted in this connection that *no new interpretation was adopted in Shah Bano's case.* The matter came up before courts in a number of cases after 1974, and the Supreme Court has, in the 2 cases decided in 1979 and 1980, adopted only this interpretation of the provision. No serious objection was taken by any one when these cases were decided.

That is the comic part. The quixotic part is the provision about the *wakf* boards. The Bill says that in case the parents, brothers, etc. of the cast-off wife cannot maintain her, these boards will. What is a *wakf*? What are these boards? What is their condition? Can they discharge an open-ended responsibility of this kind?

A Muslim creates a *wakf* when he endows his property *in*

perpetuum and irrevocably for a charitable purpose. There is an important caveat, however. The endowment having been created, and the owner having in a sense irrevocably extinguished his rights over the assets, the benefits from the property may not immediately pass on to the beneficiaries, for instance the poor for whom the endowment has been created. The endower may, for instance, consecrate the property but reserve the profits for himself, or provide out of it for the current as well as future subsistence, not just of himself, but also of his relatives and descendants. The Prophet is reported to have declared that 'a man providing subsistence for himself, his children and his people and for the maintenance of his and their position, is giving charity in the way of God.' It is also reported that the Prophet 'used to participate in [*lit.* eat out of] the produce of the lands dedicated by him....' Therefore, it has been held to be lawful for a believer to create a *wakf* but to simultaneously lay down that the manager – *the mutawalli* – he appoints, 'will pass the produce to me while I live, then after me to my child and my child's child and their *nasl* forever, while there are any,' and that *only after that* would the proceeds go to the poor. (On all this see the authoritative exposition of Syed Ameer Ali, *Mahommedan Law*, Volume 1, Thacker, Spink & Co, 1912; specially chapters X and XI; the foregoing quotations are from pp. 281-2.)

We do not quite know how many *wakfs* there are in India at present. For twenty years they have been estimated to number around a lakh. Their properties have been variously estimated to be worth anywhere between Rs150 crores and Rs700 crores. Similarly, their income has been estimated to be anywhere from five to a potential 25 crores a year.

While *wakfs* are the creation of pious Muslims, *wakf* boards, one for each state, are creations of our legislatures. They have been constituted under Central and State *Wakf* Acts. There are separate boards for important shrines, most notably the *dargah* at Ajmer. There are also local *wakf* committees. Members of all these are partly nominated and partly elected.

The boards have been set up to ensure that the *wakfs* are managed properly. The *wakfs* in turn are supposed to contribute five to six per cent of their net income to the boards.

At the apex – although it is only an advisory body – is the

Central *Wakf* Council. It is meant to advise the Central Government on policy, and also to undertake a few welfare schemes directly. The *wakf* boards are supposed to contribute one per cent of the net income of the *wakfs* in their jurisdiction to the Council for its expenses and schemes. In 1984-5 it received about Rs 6 lakhs on this account, and Rs 50 lakhs as a grant from the Central Government. (The boards receive their subsidy from the respective states.)

In the last twenty years every single study which has examined the *wakfs* has concluded, to use one of the milder expressions that the evidence calls forth, that they are in a terrible, perhaps an irretrievable mess. In the view of one and all, the person who has done the most to reduce them to their sorry state is the one who was supposed to have managed the properties on behalf of God, the *mutawalli* himself.

The *Wakf* Inquiry Committee which submitted its final report in 1976 correctly called him 'the king-pin of *wakf* administration'. It noted that 'with the lowering of the general standards of morality and integrity in all sections of society, the increasing tempo of materialism, and dilution of spiritual values, the number of black sheep among the *mutawallis* have naturally grown enormously during the past few decades.' It recalled how sky-rocketing land prices and the like had 'put a premium on temptation.' 'During all our tours of the states,' it said, 'all sections of Muslim community have represented to us hundreds of instances of illegal alienation and transfer of *wakf* properties by the *mutawallis* and with their connivance an equally large number of unauthorized occupation by squatters....' It talked of thousands of instances in which they had wilfully concealed the *wakfs* and not registered them. It talked of their having 'flagrantly ignored' the requirements of law, of their 'playing so much havoc with the *wakfs* and of making a lot of money out of it'.

While every *mutawalli* was supposed to submit the budget of the *wakf* to the *wakf* board of the state, the Committee recorded that 'the percentage of compliance in this regard is not even point nought one per cent.' It noted that while the law ostensibly contained many safeguards against selling, leasing, mortgaging the land, etc. of the *wakfs*, the *mutawallis* had been circumventing these 'easily and successfully'. So extensive and ingenious were their violations , for instance on the matter of leasing out the lands surreptitiously, that the Committee said, 'No statutory provision, howsoever perfectly worded, can meet all the contingencies and the contrivances that are being adopted and will continue to be adopted by the *mutawalli* to circumvent the law.'

The situation – not just in relation to *mutawallis* but the boards too – is just as bad today as it was ten years ago when the Committee examined it. The remarks of one Muslim MP after another during the discussions in the Rajya Sabha and the Lok Sabha on 23 July and 27 August 1984, when amendments to the Central *Wakf* Act were being discussed, testify to this.

Ghulam Rasool Kar said, 'I feel that *wakf* properties have come into the hands of persons who, by exploiting religion, want to influence and overawe the Government.' They were such clever persons, he said, that they were inflaming Muslim sentiments to further their personal interests, to fortify their hold on the chair. He spoke of a *dargah* in Kashmir whose income of Rs one to one and a half crores was being used, he said, 'for political exploitation'. The persons controlling *wakf* properties, he said, looked upon them and were using them as their personal property, as their *jagirs*.

Maulana Asarulla Haq testified that 'thousands of lakhs' were being received at the *dargahs*. 'But we know well,' he said, 'that from this lakhs are embezzled, people pocket them.'

In the Lok Sabha, Syed Masudal Hossain was incensed enough to exclaim, 'Yes, some *mutawallis* should go to hell. For some *mutawallis wakf* properties have become a personal business. Allah does not come and gobble the land that is given in the name of Allah. The *mutawallis* gobble it up.'

In brief, while many pious Muslims have created *wakfs* for charity, the *wakfs* have become instead a poorly managed real estate business, a business in the hands of unscrupulous agents who have used the cloak that they are discharging a religious function to violate the law, Islamic as much as secular.

The *wakf* boards have been constituted to ensure that the *wakfs* are well and faithfully administered. Instead, the Union Minister for *Wakf* Boards said in Bhopal on 30 April 1983, they have become 'dens of corruption'. He cited the instance of a *wakf* property worth Rs seven crores which had been leased for 99 years on terms that would yield an income of only Rs 2.5 lakhs over the entire period.

In the 1984 debates, Maulana Asarulla Haq cited as typical an instance from his personal knowledge: a flood washed away a graveyard; the Government gave a valuable piece of land to make up the loss; instead of using it as a graveyard, the *wakf* committee carved it into plots and earned a lot of money by selling these; in addition lakhs were made, he said, by using 'lement' instead of cement for constructing the houses.

Assad Madni charged that 'persons are being appointed to *wakf* boards because of their contacts. There is no category, there are no criteria for selecting them. Those who auction off and have auctioned off crores worth of property are sitting in the *wakf* boards.' 'They are appointed to the boards,' he said, and then, 'through the *wakf boards*, help is taken for elections and politics. This is the state of affairs.' The nominations had ruined the boards, he said, and the boards had ruined property worth hundreds of crores which had not been destroyed even by the Partition.

Rafiq Alam said that persons who were appointed to the boards had nothing to do with *wakfs*. Their sole concern was to further their personal ends and to see how they can swallow the property.

Abdul Rashid Qabli complained of the manner in which politics marred the boards and he dilated upon the consequences.

In all this the MPs were once again confirming the sorry state that the *Wakf* Inquiry Committee had documented. It had said:

> The *wakf* boards have admitted in their replies to our queries, that they have not been able to perform even a few of the most important duties and responsibilities entrusted to them under the Central *Wakf* Act, such as inspection of major *wakfs*, framing of proper schemes, carrying out the audit of at least five per cent of the *wakfs* under their jurisdiction, with the result that almost all the statutory provisions of the Act have remained a dead letter all these years.

For instance, on the matter of inspecting accounts, it had noted that the boards had not been able to inspect the accounts of even one per cent of the *wakfs* in their charge. As noted earlier, in only 'point nought one per cent' of the cases had the *mutawallis* submitted budgets, and even these the boards had not examined. It noted that while there were 'tall orders' in the law, in fact 'in the absence of a proper machinery of control and supervision, coupled with the paucity of staff and its brazen inefficiency, and in the context of several thousands of *wakf* institutions in regard to which these orders have to be complied with, it is no wonder that these sections (on accounts, etc.) have been observed almost in their total breach.'

On an average a board received Rs 2 to 2.5 lakhs, it had noted, almost all of which was spent on the Travel Allowance and Dearness Allowance of the members.

The Committee recounted the most distressing facts even about boards such as those of Tamil Nadu and Andhra which it called 'the better of the worse'. Its narrative of 'the problem boards' like Punjab and Delhi was of course even more dismal.

The *wakfs* as well as the boards are embroiled in disputes of several kinds. As the Committee noted, 'There is no gain saying the fact that litigation has virtually become a festering wound which is eating into the very vitals of *wakfs*.' Often the disputes go beyond mere litigation. In 1975 the dispute between the Delhi *wakf* board and the Imam of Jama Masjid resulted in an enormous riot that left ten dead and a hundred injured.

'As far as the future is concerned,' the *Wakf* Inquiry Committee pointed out, 'we cannot envisage that large sized *wakfs* will be created.' The Committee held that 'the steady and continuing deterioration in the economic conditions of the Muslim community' would ensure this dismal prognosis. One can think of several other reasons also, the organized loot of *wakfs* being one.

And as for the existing *wakfs*, they have remained unamenable to reform. In fact, whenever the Government has intervened (for instance, when it has had to supersede patently corrupt, fractious and mismanaged boards), whenever it has tried to acquire the powers to supervise the boards effectively (for instance, when in 1984 it urged additional powers for the commissioners), it has been accused of interfering in the religious affairs of Muslims, of trying to 'nationalise' a religious institution 'through the back-door'.

Nor can any non-Muslim be blamed for the plight of the *wakfs*. While piloting the Bill on 23 July 1984, the Law Minister told the Rajya Sabha at some length and with some emphasis, 'But you have to admit, though I do not want to say it, our brothers, our

Muslim brothers, our *mutawallis*, our board members are the ones who have done all this.' 'The anger you have,' he told the Muslim members, 'the anger you have in your heart is very little against me, it is largely against your associates.' 'You pointed to what happened in Punjab, Haryana,' he said, 'Who were the members? Your Muslim brothers and mine.'

This is the bitter truth. But unfortunately no reform movement has arisen among Muslims to set the *wakfs* right. Muslim 'leaders', i.e. Muslim MPs, office bearers of the Muslim League, heads of Muslim religious and theological organizations, have instead been asking for three things: first, that larger subsidies be given to the *wakf* boards; second, that the *wakfs* be granted various kinds of exemptions – from income tax, from land ceiling laws, from the Rent Control Act, from the limitation that cases against persons who have occupied one's land be filed within a specified period; third, even as some have accused the Government of trying to nationalise the boards by the back-door, others have been urging that the Government to do more to improve the management of the boards and the *wakfs* and to do so directly. For instance, they have urged that the Government directly strengthen the boards' capacities to audit accounts, that the district administrators be instructed that getting *wakf* properties vacated is their personal responsibility, etc.

The minor point in all this is that many of those who are now shouting that the Supreme Court has interfered in Muslim personal law, have themselves been clamouring that the Government should intervene directly, that, to use the expression that Ghulam Rasool Kar used, not once but four times in the Rajya Sabha, it should do so with 'iron hands', with 'firm hands', that it should use harshness –*sakhti*–to rectify this very integral part of the same Muslim personal law. The main point in the context of the present Bill however is that nothing has as yet been done to improve the functioning of the *wakfs* or the boards. In these circumstances to say, as the Bill does, that if the parents, etc. cannot provide for the cast-off wife, the *wakf* boards will, and to tout this provision as if it is a remedy that will really be available to an indigent, cast-off woman is as cynical a fraud upon our people as can be imagined.

The reasons for the fraud are plain. As putting the responsibility of looking after the cast-off wife on the parents, etc. was

patently inadequate, the Government wanted to pretend that it
was also providing a reserve, 'institutional' solution. The fundamentalists were as keen on the pretence. From their point of
view the main thing was that the Government had recognised
their right to lay down the law. But there is a somewhat more
down to earth reason too. The *wakf* boards have no money.
The Parliament having put this new responsibility on them,
the Government must increase the subsidies to the boards. Leaders
in control of the *wakf* boards are reported to have already
asked the Government to give the boards Rs 50 crores a
year on this account!

Should this Bill be passed, Government funds will end up
fortifying the hold of what official committees, Government as
well as Muslim MPs, etc. have themselves testified are the
venal, corrupt and retrograde elements in our society, and the
game will not stop there. After all, how can it be that our secular
State will provide its funds to look after divorced *Muslim*
women alone? Why not divorced Sikh, Christian, Parsi, or, for
that matter, divorced Hindu women also?

* * *

Arguments of the Managers

Managers of the Congress-I have begun a concerted campaign to
inveigle MPs and others into supporting the Muslim Women's
Bill. Plain falsehoods are being purveyed as facts. Arguments
that are specious in the extreme are being peddled as the genuine
stuff.

Each of these must be examined because it bears on the
issue, and because it gives us a glimpse into the nature of our
rulers. Do they know what they are talking about? Are they so
naive as to think that such grave matters can be handled by clever
drafting? How far will they go to find alibis for a mistake? Is
there a pattern here? A mistake is made in Kashmir. Two years
must pass, an entire part of the country must be brought to the brink
of concluding that it cannot get justice in the country, the situation
must go completely out of hand before the mistake is rectified. A
question is mishandled in Gujarat. Two or three hundred must die,
the apparatus of governance must be brought to a point where
every part of it is fighting another, and all parts of it are fighting

the people, before the obvious thing is done.

The assertions, then, by turn, and the facts about each of them.

'But at the time of framing our Constitution we gave an undertaking that personal laws will not be interfered with.'

Quite the contrary. The decision of the Constituent Assembly was that personal laws of different communities *will* continue to be reformed and that we *will* move towards a single civil code common to all our citizens. This decision is embodied in Article 44 of the Constitution.

Since then the duty to remove injustices, etc. from archaic personal laws has become all the greater. Article 51A now specifies our Fundamental Duties. Among these, as we have noted earlier are the following:

❑ to renounce practices derogatory to the dignity of women;
❑ to develop the scientific temper, humanism and the spirit of inquiry and reform.

The former binds us to doing away with polygamy, doing away with the absolute, arbitrary power to discard wives, etc., features that are parts of the Shariat and which are derogatory to the dignity of women, indeed which reduce the wife to living in terror of the husband's whim. The latter binds us to countering, and not pandering to religious obscurantists.

'But the Constitution guarantees freedom of religion and therefore we cannot interfere with personal law.'

Articles 25 and 26 are the ones that guarantee freedom of religion for each of us. They specifically state that the freedom to practise a religion is subject to public order, morality and health. In addition, Article 25 specifies *inter alia* that nothing in the Article shall prevent the State from making any law regulating or restricting any secular activity, and from providing for social welfare and reform.

Therefore, even in the context of the Articles that deal specifically with the Right to Freedom of Religion, the authority of the State to reform personal laws is threefold:

❑ If a personal law is injurious to public order, morality or health, the State has the clear authority to alter it, even if it is an essential part of religion;

❑ The State has overriding authority to pass laws for ensuring social welfare and reform;

❑ It has overriding authority to regulate any secular activity associated with religious practice; as is often emphasised, in Islam, marriage is a contract and not a sacrament.

'But we have never interfered with Muslim personal law.'

Quite the contrary. For more than a century now laws have been enacted that have modified, circumscribed and completely replaced provisions of the Shariat.

As is well known, and has been noted above, the Shariat is an integral code. Provisions regarding what we now call 'criminal law' or the 'law of evidence' are as germane to it as the provisions regarding 'personal law'. Muslim criminal law was abolished by the Indian Penal Code of 1860 and the Criminal Procedure Code of 1898, Muslim law of evidence by the Indian Evidence Act of 1872. And so on.

On the civil side too, one enactment after another has altered, circumscribed and abrogated Muslim personal law. Two examples from the laws relating to matrimonial affairs that should suffice have already been cited. Child marriage was as common among Muslims as it was among Hindus. The Child Marriages Restraint Act of 1929 made such marriages illegal for Muslims as much as for others. Similarly, under Islamic law the husband has absolute, arbitrary power to cast his wife out. The wife has no corresponding power to free herself from even the cruelest of husbands. The Dissolution of Muslim Marriages Act of 1939 took a giant step towards redressing this imbalance by specifying a number of circumstances in which a Muslim wife could initiate divorce proceedings.

The reform has continued throughout. Just a year and a half ago our Parliament for the fourth time amended the Central *Wakf* Act of 1954.

'But with this new Bill the Parliament is legislating Muslim per-

sonal law. This itself is a great advance.'

The right of our Parliament to legislate personal law is well established. No new law needs to be passed just to demonstrate it again.

This is how the most recent textbook on Mohammedan law puts the matter:

> The courts in India have to apply Muslim law *subject to the provisions of all those general legislative enactments,* relating to or affecting one or another of the matters in the area of family law and succession, etc....
> Numerous legislative enactments and provisions, however, deal in India exclusively with the institutions of Muslim law. While some of them modify substantive provisions of Muslim law, the rest are of a regulatory nature. *The courts have to apply the classical Muslim law subject to and in accordance with all this legislation.* In no case can a court hold any legislative provision to be *ultra vires* the classical Muslim law, notwithstanding the contrary opinion of the theologians. *Legislation, thus, constitutes the supreme source of Muslim law in India.*

The author is the same Tahir Mahmood I have mentioned before, a Muslim academic, and the very man who, the Government says, drew up drafts of the new Bill! We do not need a bad law to once again affirm the right and authority that are already so well established.

'But the Supreme Court was wrong to go about interpreting the Quran. Personal law can only be interpreted by religious authorities.'

First, the Supreme Court did not arrive at the Shah Bano judgment by interpreting the Quran. It did so on the basis of Sections 125 and 127(3)(b) of the Criminal Procedure Code. All that the Court said was that it was fortified in the decision by the incidental fact that the decision conformed to the Shariat. As we know by now, the Law and Home Ministries, and also the briefing note that has been circulated to the MPs by the

Government itself, have emphatically stated that this is all that the Court did.

Second, the verses from the Quran were introduced into the proceedings not by the Court *suo moto*, but by the counsel for the Muslim Personal Law Board, which was intervening against Shah Bano. The Court at once asked him whether the translation was authentic. Yes, he said emphatically, it is, adding that, after all, he was citing it himself. On examining the verses and hearing the further citations by the counsel for Shah Bano, the Court found that the verses led to a conclusion which was the exact opposite of what the Muslim Personal Law Board had sought to urge by bringing the Quran into the argument!

Third, for over a century personal law has been applied and interpreted not by clerics and theologians but by our normal, secular Courts. The jurisdiction of the Qazis and Pandits was abolished over a century ago, the very office of the Pandit or Qazi as assistant-to-the-magistrate was abolished.

That is why cases travelled from magistrates to High Courts, and thence to the Privy Council. And that is why they travel to the Supreme Court today. In all these cases, passages from the Quran, the *hadis*, from Islamic jurists have been routinely cited to arrive at or to fortify decisions. Often they were cited precisely to lay down what their real meaning was. Much of what we know today as Muslim personal law is the creation of British magistrates, judges, the Privy Council, etc. For that reason till 1947 it was often referred to as '*Anglo*-Mohammedan Law'.

'*But why did the Court mix up the question of whether or not a Muslim husband has to pay maintenance with whether or not we should have a common civil code?*'

That is just amazing. May the Supreme Court, which is there to see that things are done according to the Constitution, not even press the hope – and *that is all that the Court did in this case* – that we will act in accordance with an Article of the Constitution? By this manufactured, retrospective hyper-sensitivity, Government spokesmen are just trying to fabricate alibis for their failure to stand up to the fundamentalists. (Incidentally, as Danial Latifi, the senior counsel who appeared for Shah Bano, points out in *The Radical Humanist,* he did not introduce the so was the counsel for Shah Bano's husband. He is the one who told the Court that they, i.e. the husband's side, were for a common civil code applicable to all Indians!)

'But the Bill does not absolve the husband. Section 3(1)(a) has been deliberately drafted to say, a divorced woman shall be entitled to a reasonable and fair provision and maintenance to be made and paid to her within the iddat period by her former husband. It does not say 'for the iddat period', but 'within the iddat period.' We hope the Courts will hold that , because of these words, the husband must pay for maintenance beyond the iddat also and do so within it.'

The assertion is plain silly. A man divorces a woman when she is, say, twenty-five-years old. Will the Section require that he or the Court consult the acturial tables, estimate the number of years she is liable to live, calculate the amount she will need to maintain herself in the standard of living to which she is now accustomed, multiply these, and that the husband cough up the entire amount within three months? And what happens if she remarries? Is she then to repay the remaining amount? With interest, surely?

But more than this, there is the scheme of the Bill. This is crystal clear and does not permit the construction that is being put on the word being 'within' rather than 'for'. The Bill clearly divides that post-divorce period into two sub-periods – the three months of *iddat* and the period beyond that. To the former Section 3(1)(a) applies, and the responsibility for maintenance is put on the husband. To the latter Section 4(1) applies and the responsibility is put on everyone except the husband. This is clearly stated in the respective sections and I just cannot understand how a patently misleading construction is being put out to the MPs.

'Instead of limiting the responsibility for maintaining the divorced woman to just one husband, the Bill broad-bases it: it makes a number of relatives responsible for maintaining her.'

The assertion fails both on grounds of principle and practicality.

The point of principle is as follows: a Muslim husband has

absolute, arbitrary and exclusive power to cast his wife aside with or without assigning any reason. Should he not have some corresponding obligation towards her? The Courts have said, 'Yes'. The Bill says, 'No, nothing beyond three months, nothing whatsoever, whatever the respective circumstances of the husband and the wife he discards.' This is unjust in the extreme.

The impracticality is also patent. A case with just one respondent – the husband – takes a decade. We can imagine what will happen when there are three or four respondents, as there often will be under the Bill.

'But the Bill says that the magistrate will issue his order within one month of the woman filing her application. This is a great advance.'

An outright lie, if ever there was one. First, the clause, (3.3), in which this one month limit is specified applies only to the maintenance to be provided during the three-month *iddat* period. Nothing is specified about the time within which the magistrate is to issue his order for the post-*iddat* period.

Second, implicit in the Bill itself is the acknowledgement that while the one-month limit is laid down, it is seldom going to be met even for maintenance in the three months of *iddat*! Notice how Section (3) concludes: 'Provided that if the Magistrate finds it impracticable to dispose of the application within the said period, he may for reasons to be recorded by him, dispose of the said application *after the period.*'

It is disingenuous in the circumstances to tout the one-month limit as a great boon that the Bill provides to women.

'But no other country has provided for maintenance. This Bill at least does that.'

This too is untrue.

❑ The Tunisian law provides that where the husband (or wife) is the one who insists on a divorce, the court shall decree the compensation that he (or she) shall pay;

❑ The Moroccan law requires the husband to pay the wife a parting amount 'in proportion to his means and her circumstances;'

❏ In Egypt too the woman upon divorce is now entitled to the
   Mahr, as well as an amount to cover maintenance for two
   years;
❏ Article 273 of the Constitution of the Ismaili Khojas of East
   Africa provides that, 'If, upon dissolution of a marriage, the
   Council is of the opinion that the husband was responsible
   for the breaking up of the marriage, it may award to the wife
   such monetary compensation as it may deem just and reasonable in addition to the *Mahr*.'

There are other instances also. Why must Muslim women in
India not be entitled to what Muslim women elsewhere already
have by right? Why must women in India who happen to be
Muslim not be entitled to what women who are not Muslim are
entitled to?

Even more important than these specific provisions is the fact
that all these countries – from Tunisia to Indonesia – have
legislated comprehensive reforms in the marriage-divorce laws
and that what has been done on maintenance is a *part of that
package*. The proposed Bill comes as an isolated measure with
no prospect of the comprehensive reform of marriage-divorce
laws. And it is retrograde in itself.

In contrast to what has been done in all these countries this
Bill heaps yet another hardship on women. As it is, to our shame
and misfortune, the birth of a daughter is regarded among millions
as a curse. Now it will be regarded as doubly so: the parents will
say, 'Not only have we to bring her up for fifteen years only to have
her go elsewhere, she may be thrown back at us any time.'

*'But that is just the point. This Bill will encourage parents to have
the marriage of their daughter registered under the Special
Marriages Act so that she will be at once liberated from the thrall
of the religious personal laws.'*

I am mystified to hear this argument. It would betoken a
greater cunning than I think the Government would like us to
believe it possesses. In any case, one cannot simultaneously claim
that the Bill is full of boons for the wife, and also claim that it
inflicts such prospective hardships on her and the parents that they
will be induced to register the marriage under secular laws. And
this quite apart from the fact that, should they insist on doing so,

they are liable to have even greater difficulties in locating a husband for their daughter.

'But there is a limit to what a Government headed by a Hindu Prime Minister can do in reforming Muslim law.'

This is nothing but an argument of convenience. The Prime Minister is not a practising Hindu. He does not perceive himself as one. The country does not perceive him as one. We are Indians and should act as such.

Moreover, no one is asking the Prime Minister to rush about revolutionising Muslim law. The point about the Bill is that it arrests, it turns back the reform that was taking place on its own, gradually, step by step.

'But the Prime Minister's prestige is at stake.'

This is being presented as the final, conclusive argument to Congressmen.

A person – even a Prime Minister – gains in 'prestige' by acknowledging an error, by rectifying it. Second, those who are so concerned about the Prime Minister's prestige had better assess what it will be six months or a year after the Bill is enacted and its consequences – in particular, its consequence in legitimising Hindu fundamentalists – take shape.

Most important, no one's prestige – not even that of the country's Prime Minister – can be a reason for doing an unjust thing, for doing the country wrong.

None of the assertions survives even elementary scrutiny. A mistake has been made. That is unfortunate. But these things happen. Much the worse thing to do is to persist in a mistake. The ill-effects are compounded. And in this case the consequences will certainly be very grave. Inevitably, step by fateful step we will be certifying the 'separate nations' theory.

It is indeed a moment of truth.

* * *

This chapter is based on articles written in February and March 1986. The last section was based on arguments that the

Prime   Minister   had been furnished with and which he himself
pressed upon several persons including me. The Bill was of course
passed, but the   passage   was   unique.   The Congress   felt it
necessary to issue a three-line whip ordering each Congress MP
to vote for the Bill. Accordingly, all, including those who spoke
against it in the debate, including Arif Mohammed Khan himself,
voted for it.

Books, Bans and Fatwas

XI

Fomenting Reaction

Ram Swarup, now in his seventies, is a scholar of the first rank. In the 1950s when our intellectuals were singing paens to Marxism, and to Mao in particular, he wrote critiques of communism and of the actual — that is, dismal — performance of communist governments. He showed that the 'sacrifices' which the people were being compelled to make had nothing to do with building a new society in which at some future date they would be the heirs to milk and honey. On the contrary, the 'sacrifices' were nothing but the results of terrorism, pure and simple — of State terrorism, to use the expression our progressives use for all governments save the governments which have used it most brutally and most extensively. And that this terror was being deployed for one reason alone: to ensure total dominance, and that in perpetuity, for the narrowest of oligarchies. He showed that the claims to efficiency and productivity, to equitable distribution and to high morale which were being made by these governments, and even more so by their apologists and propagandists in countries such as India, were wholly unsustainable, that in fact they were fabrications.

Today, any one reading those critiques would characterise them as prophetic. But thirty years ago so noxious was the intellectual climate in India that all he got was abuse, and ostracism.

His work on Hinduism and on Islam and Christianity has been equally scholarly. And what is more pertinent to the point I want to urge, it has been equally prophetic. No one has ever refuted him on facts, but many have sought to smear him and his writing. They have thereby transmuted the work from mere scholarship into warning.

A ban

I mention all this because of one of those announcements – this one by the Delhi Administration – which we do not notice but which in the end stoke reaction. Newspapers carried a little paragraph a fortnight ago that his book *Hadis ke madhyam se Islam ka adhyayan* had been banned, and all its copies had been forfeited, on the gound that it 'deliberately and maliciously' outrages 'the religious feelings of the Muslims by insulting their religion and their religious beliefs.'

The forfeiture is exactly the sort of thing which has landed us where we are: where intellectual inquiry is shut out; where our traditions are not examined, and reassessed; and where as a consequence there is no dialogue. It is exactly the sort of thing too which foments reaction.

Facts

What has been banned now is the Hindi translation of the book.

The original in English, *Understanding Islam through Hadis*, was published in the US in 1983. The '*Hadis*' are '*traditions*', that is accounts of the life of the Prophet. There are six canonical collections of these traditions – those of Imam Bukhari and Imam Muslim are the most revered.

These devout and scrupulous divines went to great lengths to collect and verify accounts of what the Prophet had said and done. The volumes – nine of Bukhari, four of Muslim – cover the entire gamut of life. Along with what was revealed in the Quran, these compilations have been fundamental guides through the ages for all Muslims: the Prophet having been the ideal personage, his conduct has been the ideal to follow and emulate; and these compilations have been taken as the most authentic accounts of that conduct.

Ram Swarup's book is based wholly on what is set out in Imam Muslim's compilation. The scheme itself of the book follows that compilation. Paragraph after paragraph ends with noting the number of the *Hadis* from *Sahih Muslim* of which it is a summary. Imam Muslim's account of an incident or an expression is put in context where necessary by material derived from other sources.

But these too are wholly the orthodox sources revered by

Muslims the world over: the *Sirat Rasul Allah* by Ibn Ishaq (the first authoritative biography of the Prophet), the *Tarikhi-i-Tabri*, the works of Waqidi etc.

Not one incident, not one remark or rule on the matter at hand is derived from anything other than these revered and orthodox sources.

Now, as I noted, the original was printed in 1983 in the US.

The Indian publisher procured the plates etc. from the USA and reprinted it in India in 1984.

The book went into a second reprint soon.

In 1987 the text was translated into Hindi. The translation was sent to the binder in December 1987.

A Muslim gentleman, who said he lived next to the binder and therefore got to know of the book, sent a protest to the Delhi Administration.

The publisher, binder etc. were arrested, and then released on bail.

The book was referred by the Delhi Administration to the Screening Committee. The Committee examined the book, found it to be wholly and entirely based on orthodox and revered sources; it noted too that no action had been taken on the English version of the book which had been in circulation by then for five years, and, as no consequences had followed upon its circulation, decided that no prosecution was warranted.

The police were so informed, and formal orders to this effect were issued by the Delhi Administration on 5 September 1988.

Even so, in deference to pressure from the same lobbies on the police, and therefore a request from the police the case was, as the file notes, 'kept pending for further assessment of the situation by the police.'

On 4 January 1990, the Deputy Secretary, Home (General) of the Delhi Administration wrote to the police a second time. '... I am directed to say', said the Deputy Secretary, 'that the case was re-examined by this Administration and after considering all the aspects and legal points, the action/decision conveyed to you vide this Administration's letter of even number dated 5th September, 1988 (by which the police had been told that no action should be taken against the Hindi translation of the book) may be treated as final.'

But the publisher, printer, binder were still out only on bail, and the case was coming up periodically in the court.

Eventually on 28 September 1990 the magistrate passed his final order. He noted that he had given the complainant – the gentleman whose missive had led to the arrest of the publisher etc. – several opportunities to make good his complaint. That in spite of these, the complainant had not done so. That under the relevant Section of the Penal Code the case could be taken cognisance of only if prior permission had been given for prosecution by the relevant government. That the government had, not once but twice, reviewed the book and had concluded that no action was warranted.

He therefore discharged the matter.

That was as late as 28 September 1990: seven years after the original book was published; two years after the Screening Committee had cleared it.

But, lo and behold, just two months later, on 27 November 1990, the Delhi Administration declares that contrary to what it has itself twice decreed the book is not only objectionable, it is deliberately and maliciously so.

The Law

The relevant sections of the Penal Code state and a host judgments by the Supreme court affirm that:

❑ The impugned publication must be read as a whole, that expressions, metaphors, sentences, paragraphs must not be torn out to establish the charges;

❑ That taken as a whole, the test must be what the ordinary man with ordinary common sense, prudence and understanding will deduce from the publication, not the constructions that some abnormal or hypersensitive man may put on it;

❑ That the publication must constitute 'an aggravated form of insult to religion', and the author must have 'deliberately and maliciously' set out to outrage the religious feelings of others.

The rationale for such principles (the law and judgments are summarised in 'Is reform incitement?', elsewhere in this volume) is obvious: were we to depart from them all reform would be punishable as all reform is bound to offend those who are habituated to and benefit from age-old prejudices and practices.

Nor can the law and order bogey be invoked to stifle free speech. The Supreme Court has held that under Article 19 (2) free speech can be restricted for 'public order' – and that it has said connotes not a mere breach of the peace, not a mere 'law and order problem', but 'the prevention of disorder of a grave nature'. Moreover, the danger of this widespread disorder must not be remote, conjectural or far-fetched, it must be recognisable and specific. And it must be shown to arise directly from what is said, written, or exhibited.

True, there may be threats by 'X' and 'Y' groups that they will take to the streets unless the publication is banned. But, the Supreme Court has held, and that too just last year, it is the function of the State to safeguard the liberties our Constitution guarantees against such threats and consequences. 'Freedom of expression which is legitimate and constitutionally protected', it declared last year, 'cannot be held to ransom by an intolerant group of people'. To curtail it in the face of threats of demonstrations and processions or threats of violence 'would amount', the Court said, 'to the negation of the rule of law and surrender to blackmail and intimidation.'

And in Practice

That is the law. And in practice?

❑ Some busy-body shoots off a letter;
❑ A nervous and illiterate administration stomps on the scholar and his work;
❑ If there is a ruckus or the apprehension of it from the other side also, it bans some other publication too, as the Delhi Administration has done in the current case, declaring that *that* one is liable to injure the feelings of the other group;
❑ The fundamentalists use the ban to prove to their ignorant followers that the religion is indeed under attack, and that but for them it would go under.

The sequence has but one end. It stokes reaction.

'Secularists' are unnerved by the reaction Advani's *rath* has evoked among Hindus. But it is not the *rath* which evoked it. The 'victories' in having Shah Bano reversed, in having Rushdie banned, – 'victories' which were loudly applauded by the 'secularists'; the success in convincing political parties – with maps and lists – that Muslims as Muslims would decide their fate in hundreds of constituencies; to say nothing of the 'victories' of the violence in Punjab and Kashmir – the reaction is the cumulative result of these distortions in our polity.

If these had not been there, the temple would never have become an issue. And if they persist, the temple will just be prelude.

– 8 November 1990

XII

Is Reform Incitement?

Each time the fundamentalists and self-styled leaders of religious communities are unable to answer a critique, they pounce on the author and the publication with the charge that the latter have offended their 'religious feelings.'

Complaints are filed with the police and other authorities demanding that action be taken, that the author etc. be arrested for inciting hatred between communities, for offending religious sentiments and all. The authorities in turn register cases, ask for explanations and issue summons. Often, it seems to me, they do so just to get the fundamentalists and 'leaders' off their back by making a show that some action *is* being taken; at least sometimes, it seems, they do so because of a less than complete knowledge of what the law on the matter is.

The problem is compounded, I am afraid, by many of our standard law books. They present an unjustifiably discouraging view of the law and judgments on the matter. In some instances it is only too evident that the authors have gone merely by the headnotes of the judgments, by one or two paragraphs in them and thereby conveyed impressions about the judgments which are greatly at variance with the contents of the judgments. These books present, for instance, the Bombay High Court's judgment in the well known case *G.V. Godse vs. Union of India* and the Supreme Court's judgment in *Babu Rao Patel vs. State (Delhi Administration)* as if under these even truthful accounts are liable for action under Section 153A. In fact, as we shall see, such constructions are derived from reading but a sentence or two, not even a passage or two from the judgments.

The principle is clear. The law is liberal enough. And so it is vital that the press should not give in to these feints of the fundamentalists.

The Principle

Every attempt at reform is liable to dislocate those who are steeped in existing mores; it is certain to dislocate the 'leaders' and *mathaadhishes* − to dislocate, that is, the principal benefiaries of the existing practices − even more. Ordinary believers are generally innocent of the fact that all too often the very thing they revere is the shackle which is holding them back. The *mathaadhishes*, on the other hand, are resourceful and cunning. They immediately sense that the reform will cut away the ground from under their feet. They are therefore compelled to, as well as able to, misrepresent matters to a point where the ordinary believers can be made to feel that the author has written something which does grave injury to or constitutes mockery of some pillar of their faith.

We can therefore readily imagine what the consequences will be if we were to proceed on the principle that nothing which causes offence to the religious feelings of any group − in practice, this means to the religious feelings of any group as proclaimed by the *mathaadhishes* of that group − must be published.

❑ The way the shrines of a religion are managed is regarded as an internal affair of that religion's community. Many of the shrines are misused. Talking about this misuse − e.g., of the Golden Temple − causes offence − e.g., to many in Punjab. Should the press, therefore, stop talking about the misuse?

❑ Should we not talk about the barbarity of Sati on the ground that to do so causes offence to many in Rajasthan?

❑ Just as there are persons doing saintly work, there are some fakes among godmen. Many believe in the latter and do so intensely. Rationalists raise questions about the fakes. This offends the devotees. Should the press not report the questions raised by the rationalists on the ground that they cause offence to some?

❑ Today a holy stone, a holy book are venerated as idols. Practices like prayers at the graves of saints, the wearing of amulets, all smack of the very idolatry which the Prophet and the Sikh Gurus condemned so severely. Should we not, even when the occasion demands, talk about such practices on the ground that doing so may cause offence?

❏ The campaign to open up temples to untouchables causes offence to many orthodox Hindus. Should the press then not report the campaign, to say nothing of espousing the cause of temple entry, a cause so dear to Mahatma Gandhi?

❏ The extortions of the Syedna are well-known as are the terrible tragedies that excommunication by him inflicts on thousands of Bohras, as is the terror to which he subjects this entire community. At grave cost and risk to their lives Bohras like Asghar Ali Engineer are campaigning for reforms. Their campaign and their writings certainly cause offence to the Syedna and his henchmen. Should the press therefore stop carrying their writings and reports about their campaign?

The answer is obvious. And the answer that holds for practices also holds for priests, for places of worship, for texts. And it holds equally for the practices, priests, places of worship, texts of *all* religions.

The Law

The law on the matter is just as clear.

Three provisions of the Indian Penal Code are relevant – Sections 153A, 295A and 298.

Section 153A reads as follow:

(i) Whoever –

    (a) by words, either spoken or written or by signs or by visible representations or otherwise, promotes or attempts to promote, on grounds of religion, race, place of birth, residence, language, caste or community or any other ground whatsoever, disharmony, feelings of enmity or hatred or ill-will between different religious, racial, language or regional groups or castes or communities, or

    (b) commits any act which is prejudicial to the maintenance or harmony between different religious, racial, language or regional groups or castes or communities, and which disturbs or is likely to disturb the public tranquillity...

shall be punished with imprisonment which may extend to three years, or with fine or with both...

Section 295A reads as follows:

> Whoever, with deliberate and malicious intention of outraging the the religious feelings of any class of citizens of India, by words, either spoken or written, or by signs or by visible representations or otherwise, insults the religion or the religious beliefs of that class, shall be punished with imprisonment of either description for a term which may extend to three years, or with fine, or with both.

And Section 298 reads as follows:

> Whoever, with the deliberate intention of wounding the religious feelings of any person, utters any word or makes any sound in the hearing of that person or makes any gesture in the sight of that person or places any object in the sight of that person, shall be punished with imprisonment of either description for a term which may extend to one year, or with fine, or with both.

I shall first summarise the position regarding Sections 295A and 298.

Two sets of operative words in these Sections are vital. As is obvious, Section 298 can be invoked only against words that have been *uttered*, or *sounds that have been made* within the hearing of a person, or *gestures* that have been made or *objects that have been placed* within the sight of the complainant. The courts have reiterated what is obvious from the wording of the Section, namely that an article written and published is none of these and therefore is not actionable under this Section (e.g., *Shalibhadra Shah vs. Swami Krishna Bharati, 1981, Criminal Law Journal*, Gujarat, p. 113).

As many complainants seek to arraign the press under this Section, the complaints are liable to be dismissed at the threshold on this ground alone.

Intention

The more important point is that the fact that something said or done injures the religious feelings of some group is not sufficient to make it actionable under either of the Sections. Section 298 requires that the person should have spoken the word etc. '*with the deliberate intention of wounding the religious feelings* of any person.'

Section 295A provides an even more stringent test: to be actionable under it the words, signs, representations must have been put out '*with deliberate and malicious intention of wounding the religious feelings* of any class of citizens of India.' The intention must be established to be 'deliberate' as well as 'malicious.' And the aim must be not only, as in Section 298, to 'wound' but to 'outrage' the religious feelings of a person or group.

The courts have reiterated the requirements in several cases.

The matter was stated clearly and emphatically in one of the first case in independent India on the question. In this case the courts held in the context of Section 298 that:

The essence of the offence under S. 298 consists in the '*deliberate intention*' *of wounding the religious* feelings of other persons. *A mere knowledge of the likelihood that the religious feelings of other persons may be wounded would not suffice nor a mere intention to wound such feelings would suffice unless that intention was deliberate* (*Criminal Law Journal*, 1952, Orissa, p. 149).

Similarly in the case of Section 295A it has been held that:

Further, as pointed out by the Supreme Court in the case of *Ramji Lal Modi vs. State of U.P.* (AIR 1957 SC 620) (Supra) S. 295A does not penalise any and every act of insult to or attempt to insult the religion or the religious beliefs of a class of citizens, which are not perpetrated with the deliberate and malicious intention of outraging the religious feelings of that class. Insults to religion offered unwittingly or carelessly or without any deliberate or malicious intention of outraging the religious feelings of that class do not come within the scope of the Section. *It only punishes the aggravated form of insult to religion when it is perpetrated with the deliberate and malicious intention of outraging the religious feelings of that class* (*Criminal Law Journal*, 1986, p. 182, at p. 188).

Nor is the test fortuitous. It is precisely because almost every attempt at reform is bound to offend someone – even many of those who are under the yoke of the evil sought to be reformed – that the law-makers have laid down that to be actionable the intention has to be, not reform or scholarly research for instance, but to outrage the religious feelings of others, and 'deliberately' and 'maliciously' to do so.

Additional Criteria

In deciding cases under these Sections the courts have laid down three additional principles which are important safeguards for the press.

First, they have held that in assessing whether the words offend the religious feelings of another, the test to be applied is the reaction of an ordinary person and not that of a hypersensitive one. In a well-known case the Court put the principle succinctly:

> The mere fact that the author could have used synonyms for certain words and he could have expressed the matter in milder terms is immaterial. The test that has to be applied in such case is not that of an abnormal or hypersensitive man but that of an ordinary man of ordinary common sense and prudence (*Criminal Law Journal,* 1971, p. 1026, at p. 1031).

There is scarcely a person writing in the mainstream press in the country who writes with the deliberate and malicious intention of outraging the religious feelings of others. It is also a fact that the complaints for which pressmen are arraigned before the police, the courts or the Press Council seldom originate with 'ordinary men of ordinary common sense and prudence'. Most often they are put up by self-styled leaders who are always on the lookout for 'issues' by stoking which they can further their claims to being the protectors and guardians of their followers. It is a good rule therefore for pressmen to delve into the antecedents of the complainants and also to ferret out the propaganda which has accompanied the complaint. The well-orchestrated and patently false propaganda – 'X has demanded that the Quran be banned in India' – is most often sufficient by itself to establish whose intentions are deliberate and malicious.

Second, the courts have held that the intention of the author or publisher is to be assessed primarily from the publication itself, not from what may be alleged about him in general. And, third, that the item which has been complained of must be seen as a whole; intention and offence must not be gleaned from isolated sentences. While quashing the ban on a book which was proclaimed by one of the Judges to contain references to the Prophet which were 'provocative, derogatory and denigratory' in which the Prophet was 'brought to light before us as cunning, sexy and greedy,' the Supreme Court held as follows:

> That the intention prescribed by the relevant section of the Penal Code is to be gathered primarily from the language, contents and import of the offending publication.... That the onus lies on the applicant to dislodge and result the *prima facie* opinion of the Government that the offending publication is punishable under one or other of the relevant sections of the Indian Penal Code; and furthermore it is well settled that the offending publication is to be viewed as a whole and the intent of the author has to be gathered from a broader perspective and not merely from a few solitary lines or quotations (*Criminal Law Journal*, 1985, at pp. 806 and 809).

In brief, the courts have held that for a publication to fall afoul of Sections 295A and 298:

(a) the intention of the author to hurt the religious feelings of other must by *deliberate* and *malicious*;

(b) that the test to be applied for this purpose is *the reaction of the ordinary man with ordinary common sense and prudence* and not the reaction of some abnormal or hypersensitive person;

(c) that the intention must be gleaned primarily from the language and contents and import of the publication itself;

(d) that the deliberate and malicious intention to outrage the religious feeling of others must permeate the article as a whole.

No pressman would want protection greater than the one these tests accord.

Section 153A

Until 1961 the IPC used to have an 'Explanation' after Section 153A. This read:

> It does not amount to an offence within the meaning of this section to point out, without malicious intention and with honest view to their removal, matters which are producing or have a tendency to produce, feelings of enmity or hatred between different classes of Her Majesty's subjects.

Thus, on a number of occasions the courts had held that intention was of the very essence of the crime under this Section. The 'Explanation' was deleted in 1961. It was felt accordingly that a publication would henceforth be liable for prosecution even if the author or publisher did not intend to cause enmity, hatred or ill-will between communities. The matter repays scrutiny.

With the 'Explanation' deleted, on the face of it Section 153A is much more restrictive than Sections 295A and 298. It does not require deliberate or malicious intention to bring an author or publication within its ambit. It speaks not of feelings being outraged but of 'disharmony, feelings of enmity or hatred' or ill-will being created or an attempt being made to create them. And the result it puts as the test is the breach or the attempted or likely breach of 'public tranquillity'. The Section has become an even bigger bug-bear for pressmen because some of the key judgments have been presented by the law books and lawyers as saying that even if the publication contains no more than a truthful account of the facts of history or a religion it is liable to be open for prosecution if it affects or is even likely to affect 'public tranquillity'.

In fact, the courts have continued to look not just at the effect or likely effect of the publication but also at its purpose. They have noted, for instance, that one who does not either 'promote or attempt to promote' class hatred is not, even under the bare words of the Section alone, liable to prosecution. As the Allahabad High Court without reference to the pre-1961 'Explanation' put it in *Wajih Uddin vs. State:*

... that section only makes an act punishable if it promotes or attempts to promote feelings of enmity or hatred between different classes of the citizens of India. The language of the section is exact. There is neither any ambiguity nor vagueness about it. What has been made punishable has been stated in unambiguous, precise and clear words. *The provision cannot be used to punish any one except those who either attempt to promote or promote class hatred or class enmity.* The language used in the section is not of an all pervading nature and does not suffer from being all embracing with the result that because of language no one who does not either promote or attempt to promote class hatred or enmity can be convicted.... (*AIR Allahabad* 335 (V 50 C 93) at 336).

Godse's Case

The criteria which have been set out in different judgments are summarised most conveniently by the Bombay High Court in the well known case, *G.V. Godse vs. Union of India*:

While inquiring whether such a charge can be sustained on the data disclosed in the order of forfeiture, namely the offending passages read in the context of the book as a whole, it is important to remember that: (1) Under Section 153A it is not necessary to prove that as a result of the objectionable matter, enmity or hatred was in fact caused between the different classes. (2) Intention to promote enmity or hatred, apart from what appears from the writing itself, is not a necessary ingredient of the offence. It is enough to show that the language of the writing is of a nature calculated to promote feelings of enmity or hatred for a person must be presumed to intend the natural consequences of his act. (3) The matter charged as being within the mischief of Section 153A must be read as a whole. One cannot rely on stray, isolated passages for proving the charge nor indeed can one take a sentence here and a sentence there and connect them by a meticulous process of inferential reasoning. (4) For judging what are the natural or probable consequences of the writing, it is permissible to take into consideration the class of readers for whom the book is primarily meant as also the state of feelings between the different classes or communities at the relevant time. (5) If the writing is calculated to promote feelings of enmity or hatred, it is no defence to a charge under Section 153A that the writing contains a truthful account of past events or is otherwise supported by good authority. If a writer is disloyal to history, it might be easier to prove that history was distorted in order to achieve a particular end as, e.g., to promote feelings of enmity or hatred between different classes or communities. But adherence to the strict path of history is not by itself a complete defence to a charge under Section 153A. In fact, greater the truth, greater the impact of the writing on the minds of its readers, if the writing is otherwise calculated to produce mischief (1971 *Criminal Law Journal*, 324 at p. 340).

At first reading this enunciation seems to be all that is needed to shackle the press from printing anything about which some group might be made to work itself into a fury and thereby endanger public tranquillity. For the summary seems to imply that even if the author may not have intended to disturb tranquillity, even if tranquillity may not actually be disturbed, even if the account given in the articles is a truthful one, in fact specially if it is truthful one, the publication is open to conviction under this Section.

In fact, the apprehensions are set at naught by the judgment itself. The case arose because the Delhi Administration passed an order against a book by Gopal Vinayak Godse, the brother of the assassin of Mahatma Gandhi, ordering its forfeiture. Readers who have proceeded merely by the foregoing statement would be surprised to learn that in fact the Bombay High Court held in favour of Godse's brother and, not only held the forfeiture to have been wholly unjustified, but also decreed that the Administration pay the costs of litigation to Godse.

While it had said in the summary enunciation that things said in the publication may be true and yet fall foul of Section 153A, the Court went to great pains to examine the passages in Godse's book which the Administration had asserted were objectionable. In instance after instance we find the Court examining the veracity of the passage and concluding that other accounts, for instance those of Pyarelal, of Maulana Azad etc., showed that the author had sufficient grounds for saying what he had said; and this is one of the main reasons on account of which it strikes down the order of forfeiture. These passages include Godse's assertion to the effect that Pakistan had been given cash balances at Mahatma Gandhi's instance, that men and women had been moved by Nathu Ram Godse's deed, that they had offered great and spontaneous support to him and his relatives after the assassination, that Sardar Patel had opposed Gandhiji on the payment of cash balances and so on.

Again and again the Court points out that the book must be read as a whole and that its purpose must always be kept in mind. Again and again it holds that the book in question deals with the policies which led to the Partition of India and that it does not deal with any current communal issue. It holds that to ascertain the purpose for which the book is written, apart from the contents of the book itself, things that are said in the preface etc. should be examined.

In fact, the Court holds that even if in a particular case the facts turn out to be at variance with the assertions in the book, one cannot deduce automatically that the intention of the author is to create enmity and hatred among the communities. As the Court puts it:

> ... Pyarelal's book bears out the petitioner in a large measure and in any event no charge can be be made against him that in regard to the events surrounding the fact history has been distorted by him. It is also necessary to remember that if the claim of an author that he is an historian is not fully borne out, one cannot infer from that alone that the author had an oblique intention in straying from the strict path of history. Much less can one infer that such an oblique intention was of the nature mentioned in Section 153A of the Indian Penal Code (1971 *Criminal Law Journal, op.cit.*, pp. 345-6).

It repeatedly dismisses the pleas of the prosecution regarding several passages by affirming that sentences and passages cannot be torn out of context to make a fanciful charge stick. As the Court puts it:

... a passage here or a passage there, a sentence here or a sentence there, a word similarly, may if strained and torn out of context supply inflammatory matter to a willing mind. But such a process is impermissible . We must read the book as a whole, we must not ignore the context of a passage and we must try and see what, reasonably, would be the reaction of the common reader. If the offending passages are considered in this light, the book shall have to be cleared of the charge levelled against it. [The reader will find additional examples to the same effect on pages 344, 347, 348 and 351 of the judgment.]

It holds the same about similes and metaphors. Acknowledging that the language of the author is powerful, that the scheme of the book is purposeful, it strikes down the apprehension of the Administration on the ground that the latter is picking up passages, metaphors, sentences out of context. As the Court puts it.

A metaphor may mean volumes in one context but you cannot tear it from its context so that you can speak volumes about it (*Ibid,*   p.   343).

Equally important, it holds that the book, the passages must be assessed in the light of what a common reader can reasonably be expected to do upon reading the passages. Obtuse and strange constructions are not to be the guide in these matters. In dismissing an interpretation of the Advocate General, for instance, we have the Court saying:

We, however, think that the inference which the learned Advocate General wants us to draw is rather far-fetched.... In our opinion, such an inference would require a dissection far too meticulous to be within the reasonable bounds of a common reader.... (*Ibid,* p. 347).

In regard to another passage, we find it saying:

...we think that far more is being read in such passages than is intended by the author or than can be reasonably inferred by the readers. The context in which these extracts are reproduced in the eighth chapter has to be borne in mind and the context is that the author wants to establish that Savarkar was implicated in the trial wholly out of ulterior motives.... (*Ibid.*, pp. 347-8).

We have it saying yet again:

... we have read and re-read these passages but we are unable to share the view that they are objectionable on the ground stated in the order of forfeiture. The inferences which are sought to be drawn from the passages seem to us far-fetched. That, in our opinion, is not how the common reader will react to the passages. For example, if one turns to the passage at page 221....

Similarly, while a bald reading of criterion four listed in the paragraph quoted above – namely, that in judging the natural or probable consequences of the writing, one should consider the class of readers for whom the publication is primarily meant – may seem to give the authorities a handle, the Court itself uses the criterion to infer that the book is unlikely to have the consequences which the Government is apprehending. While noting that Godse's language is powerful, that he has written the book with a definite purpose, the Court holds that the language is so Sanskritised that the ordinary reader will not be able to find the incendiary material in it which the Government is claiming marks the whole book. To quote the Court:

...we have a fair acquaintance with the Marathi language but we must frankly confess that many a passage had to be read with more than ordinary care in order to appreciate why it is said to be of an objectionable nature. A common reader has, we suppose, neither the leisure nor the learning to digest the wealth of words which the book contains. He shall have to delve deep into the book to resurrect some stray incendiary material.... (*Ibid.*, p. 343).

The theme of the book was that Gandhiji had been assassinated for his policy of appeasing the Muslims, which in turn had led to the Partition of India. This was a fundamental charge. The assassination thereby was not just explained, it was in a sense 'extolled'. But, says the Court, that is no ground for forfeiting the book under Section 153A:

> ...there is no doubt that Gandhiji's murder has been extolled and one cannot possibly appreciate it. But the question before us is not whether the book is bad for that reason. Our task is to see whether the glorification of Nathuram or the justification of his dastardly act can be said to be reasonably connected with the problem of Hindu-Muslim amity.... (*Ibid.*, pp. 349-50).

The Government took objection to the parts of the book in which Nathuram Godse and Apte, upon becoming convinced that they would be executed, stated as their last wish that their ashes be cast into the Indus. This the Government said was liable to cause offence to Muslims and thereby endanger public tranquillity. The Court rules the apprehension out with the following words:

> The author says that after it was clear that the sentence of death was to be executed, Nathuram and Apte were asked to express their final desire. They said that their one desire was that their ashes should be immersed in the Indus. The account of the conversation between the author and Apte in regard to this matter shows the reasons why such a desire was expressed. The Indus which had become red by bloodshed was once a part of India. We are unable to appreciate that the observation made by the author in the context of this attitude can promote feelings of enmity and hatred between Hindus and Muslims in India. The chapter contains, if anything, an exhortation that what once belonged to India, and had become a part of Pakistan, should be won back by India. The Muslims who are citizens of India are not likely to feel aggrieved by any such exhortation, because such a problem arising out of attempted resurrection of lost territory is political, not communal.. (*Ibid.*, p. 349).

The Court holds that the book might as a whole find an echo

in many hearts for its language is powerful and its scheme purposeful, that the author has given strong expression to his views, that the author has dealt with many bitter facts, but that neither the passages nor the book can be held to fall within the mischief of Section 153A because its purpose is to examine the facts leading to the Partition of India and to the assassination of Mahatma Gandhi and not to create enmity between the communities.

History

This very principle has been followed again in the well known case, *M/s Varsha Publication Pvt. Ltd. vs State of Maharashtra*, in which the Court observed as follows:

> We have already observed that the very purpose of writing the article is a sort of historical research and it is based on a number of reference books and other material. It is true that sometimes in a given case even a truthful account may come within the mischief of S. 153A. But this will be too broad a proposition. Different considerations will prevail when we are to consider a scholarly article on history and religion based upon research with the help of a number of reference books. It will be very difficult for the State to contend that a narration of history would promote violence, enmity or hatred. *If such a convention is accepted, a day will come when that part of history which is unpalatable to a particular religion will have to be kept in cold storage on the pretext that the publication of such history would constitute an offence punishable under S. 153A of the IPC.* We do not think that the scope of S. 153A can be enlarged to such an extent with a view to thwart history. For obvious reasons, history and historical events cannot be allowed to be looked as a secret on a specious plea that if the history is made known to a person who is interested to know the history, there is likelihood of someone else being hurt. *Similarly, an article containing a historical research cannot be allowed to be thwarted on such a plea that the publication of such a material would be hit by S. 153A. Otherwise, the position will be very precarious. A nation will have to forget its own history and in due course the nation will have no history at all.* This result

cannot be said to have been intended by the Legislature when S. 153A of the IPC and S. 95 of the Cr. P.C. were enacted. *If anybody intends to extinguish the history (by prohibiting its publication) of the nation on the pretext of taking action under the above Section his act will have to be treated as a malafide one (Criminal Law Journal, 1983, at p. 1454).*

Rational Criticism

The point that rational criticism in restrained language cannot be deemed to be an offence was reiterated recently by the Allahabad High Court in the well known *Azizul Haq Kausar Naqvi* case. The full bench of the Allahabad High Court put the offence sought to be checked by Section 153A at par with what has come to be known in British law as 'blasphemous libel.' It recalled how Starkie on Libel had enunciated this offence:

A wilful intention to pervert, insult, and mislead others by means of licentious and contumacious abuse applied to sacred subjects, or by wilful misrepresentations or artful sophistry calculated to mislead the ignorant and unwary, is the criterion and test of guilt. A malicious and mischievous intention, or, what is equivalent to such an intention in law as well as morals, a state of apathy and indifference to the interest of society, is the broad boundary between right and wrong.

Citing British judgments ranging over a hundred years, the Court concluded,

It is thus firmly established both in India and in England, that criminality for the offence of blasphemous libel or criminality under Section 153 A of the Indian Penal Code, does not attach to the things said or done but to the manner in which it is said or done. If the words spoken or written are couched in temperate, dignified, and mild language, and do not have the tendency to insult the feelings or the deepest religious convictions of any section of the people, penal consequences do not follow.... (*AIR 1980 Allahabad,* Full Bench 149 at 159, 160).

Harsh Words

In the earlier and well known case of *State of Bihar vs.Ghulam Sarwar* the Patna High Court had quoted several earlier judgments to emphasise that the intention of the author etc. is the essence of the offence under Section 153A, that courts cannot accede to doctrines of 'constructive intention,' that malice must not be imputed without definite and solid reason. It also emphasised that the publication must be read as a whole and assessed with reference to the circumstances in which it was put out. It quoted the earlier judgment in Debi Soren's case to the effect that the offending matter must be considered,

> as a whole and in a fair, free and liberal spirit, not dwelling too much upon isolated passages or upon a strong expression used here and there; in other words an attempt should be made to gather the general effect of the speeches as a whole [*AIR 1965, Patna*, 393 (V 52, C 112) at pp. 395-396].

The full bench of the Allahabad High Court took the matter further in *Lalai Singh Vs. State of U.P.* It reiterated that in judging a book one must bear in mind its underlying purpose. It held that as the underlying purpose of the publication in question was reform, as it was to remove the evil of untouchability, the book was perfectly justified in the criticism which it had heaped upon Hinduism and the upper castes. 'Rational criticism of religious tenets couched in the restrained language,' said the Court , 'cannot amount to an offence either under Section 153A or under Section 195A of the Penal Code'[1971 *Criminal Law Journal* 1773 (V 77 C 505) at p. 1775].

It emphasised that the passages and the publication must be judged in accordance with the normal susceptibilities of a reasonable person. 'Even on a cursory perusal,' the Court said in this context, 'many of these passages clearly fall within the category of legitimate criticism and are such that no reasonable person of normal susceptibility could possibly object to....' (*Ibid.*, p. 1775). 'But these passages too,' said the Court, citing some strong expressions of the kind to which we shall revert in a moment, 'if read in the setting in which they occur, with particular reference to the subject of untouchability, will be found to be innocuous and unlikely to give offence to any reasonable person' (*Ibid.*, p. 1775).

Given these criteria, it held that though the book had characterised the Hindu religion as 'blemished'; though it had asserted that 'Hindus lack sympathy, equality and independence'; though it had maintained that 'in Hinduism there is no room for feelings of humanity and that in Hinduism progress for the individual is impossible'; though in its view 'untouchability is the base of Hinduism,' Brahminism is 'our enemy from birth' and deserves to be 'annihilated', high-caste Hindus are 'arrogant, selfish, hypocritical and false,' and 'exploit others, inflict mental suffering on them and treat them with contempt'; though the book regarded the preaching of Vedanta as 'mockery of humanity'; though it held that in view of its actual practice towards untouchables the religion was just 'idle chatter'; though in the author's view the word Hindu was made up of '*hin*' for '*hinsa*' and '*du*' for '*dushyati*' ; though the author had maintained that the Vedas were composed by hundreds of people who were 'undeveloped and uncultured,' 'fools or madmen'; though it characterised the Gita, which many revere, as 'a song of shepherds,' as a 'political book,' as 'an irreligious book'; though the book maintained that Lord Ram could not be respected because of his murdering a sage, Shambuk; though it characterised Lord Hanuman as unchaste – the book was perfectly in order.

The Court based its vindication of each of these passages on the ground that the passages were but part of an argument, the argument being that untouchability must be removed. As the book's purpose therefore was to continue the reform which even such a great person as Mahatma Gandhi had striven for, the passages, were though strong, innocuous and could not be objected to. Moreover, said the Court, the strictures, for instance about Lord Ram and Hanuman are justified by what is said in, for instance, Valmiki's *Ramayana* itself. 'The original text of the Valamiki's *Ramayana*,' said the Court,

...has been shown to us and we find that it describes both the killing of Shambuk by Ram and the presentation of the 16 maidens to Hanuman by Bharat. That being the case, it is difficult to see how the repetition of these stories can be said to be an insult to the Hindu religion or to promote disharmony and hatred. In the eyes of orthodox Hindus the Valmiki Ramayana has the status of a holy book or scripture; and nothing that is mentioned therein can possibly be taken offence to or construed as an insult to Hinduism, however much it may be at variance with modern ideas of morality and ethics...(*Ibid*, p. 1776).

Hence, said the Court, the order of the Government for forfeiture of the book was wholly unjustified, and could not be sustained. It therefore set aside the order and awarded costs to the petitioner. It also ordered that all the forfeited copies of the book be returned to the petitioner forthwith.

Before the orthodox – in this case the orthodox Hindu – concludes that in sanctioning such strong expressions the Court went too far, he must remember that the principles laid down apply equally to the discussion of *all* religions and *all* texts. It follows from judgments like *Lalai Singh* that when the object is reform, when the facts and affirmations in a publication can be borne out by reference to authorities, in particular to authorities held in reverence by the protagonists of the religion itself, the publication cannot be taken to offend the adherents of that religion. The publication must be judged in the context and purpose for which it has been written – namely, reform and rational inquiry.

Controversies are Endless

This view finds further corroboration in another recent case though it involves a film rather than a publication *per se*. Farzana Bi approached the Court to stop the further exhibition of the film *Nikah*. One of her grounds was that the film misrepresented Muslim Personal Law when it implied that a husband who had divorced his wife could marry her again provided she had in the meantime been married by another man, the second marriage had been consummated and the second husband had divorced her. The Court held, first, that the proposition was supported by authorities, and it relied on a recent book on Muslim Personal Law for this purpose. Second, it held that merely because something is at variance with what a person or group of persons holds Islam to teach, the offending proposition is not actionable under Section 153A. 'So far as matters of religion are concerned,' the Court said, 'there is often controversy even in the highest religious quarters. Such controversies are endless and cannot be resolved by courts of law' (1983 *All Law Journal*, Lucknow Bench 1133, at p. 1134). The judgment is worth quoting at length for it reaffirms salutary principles:

...the petitioner is, of course, entitled to her own views in regard to the true interpretation of Quran Sharif on the subject. No one is preventing her from holding or expressing those views. She is free to rebut the view expressed in the film by any public rejoinder. However, the Constitution guarantees freedom of expression to persons holding different views. In the famous words of Justice Holmes '... If there is any principle of the Constitution that more imperatively calls for attachment than any other it is the principle of free thought – not free thought for those who agree with us but freedom for the thought we hate' (*United States vs. Schwimmer*, 1929, 279 US 644, 654, 655).

Likewise, another famous American Judge Brandeis observed as follows in the well-known case of (*Miss*) *Whitney v. California* (1926) 274 US 356, vide *The World of Law* edited by Epraim, London (1960 Edition) at pages 593-598:

'Fear of serious injury cannot alone justify suppression of free speech and association. Men fear witches and burned women. It is the function of speech to free men from the bondage of irrational fears. To justify suppression of freedom of speech there must be reasonable ground to fear that serious evil will result if freedom of speech is practised. There must be reasonable ground to believe that the danger apprehended is imminent. There must be reasonable ground to believe that the evil to be prevented is a serious one.'

The learned Judge quoted the following inspiring words of Thomas Jefferson in support of this reasoning:

'We have nothing to fear from the demoralising reasons

of some, if others are left free to demonstrate their errors and especially when the law stands ready to punish the first criminal act produced by the false reasoning; these are safer corrections than the conscience of the judge ....'(*Ibid.*, at pp. 1134-5).

Thus, on examination it is clear that our courts have consistently held to these liberal principles. The standard law books often cite *Babu Rao Patel vs. State (Delhi Administration)*, (1980 *Criminal Law Journal*, 529) in which the Supreme Court upheld the order of the Delhi Administration against a publication. But it is clear upon reading this brief judgment that the Court did not in any way depart from the criteria which courts had earlier laid down again and again. It merely pointed to passage after passage which showed that the articles in question were 'not even a thinly veiled political thesis,' that they were obviously smears hurled at an entire community, smears which could certainly be held to be liable to foment enmity and ill-will between communities.

Vires

The liberal construction of Section 153A is fortified by another, all-important consideration. Section 153A can only be read in the context of Article 19 (1) (a) of the Constitution which guarantees freedom of speech and Article 19(2) which allows the State to impose reasonable restrictions on free speech for specified purposes. The purpose that lies closest to the present context is 'in the interest of public order.' In fact, whenever the constitutionality of Section 153A has been challenged, the courts have held that it is *intra vires* precisely because Article 19(2) allows the State to impose restrictions in the interests of public order. (See, for instance, *Wajih Uddin vs. State*, *op. cit.*, paras 3 and 4, and *Gopal Vinayak Godse, op. cit.*, para 61, in which Section 153A is held to be *intra vires* precisely on this ground. For vindication of Section 295A on the same ground see *Ramji Lal Modi vs. State of UP*, 1957 SCR 860.)

The test, therefore, has to be not the mere inference that a publication is liable to cause ill-will, hatred or enmity in some persons. The test has to be that the ill-will, hatred and enmity that the publication is liable to cause will be such as to threaten public order. Now, the courts have repeatedly held that public order cannot be deemed to be jeopardised merely because it is liable to cause some breach of peace, or because a law and order problem is liable to arise. As the Supreme Court put it in the well-known case *Ram Manohar vs. State of Bihar*, the public order which is sought to be safeguarded entails 'the prevention of disorder of a grave nature'. The expression does not cover disorders of lesser gravity and ones which are of local significance alone. It said:

> ...disorder is no doubt prevented by the maintenance of law and order also but disorder is a broad spectrum which includes at one end small disturbances and at the other the most serious and cataclysmic happenings. Does the expression 'public order' take in every kind of disorders or only some of them? The answer to this serves to distinguish 'public order' from 'law and order' because the latter undoubtedly takes in all of them. Public order, if disturbed, must lead to public disorder. Every breach of the peace does not lead to public disorder. When two drunkards quarrel and fight there is disorder but not public disorder. They can be dealt with under the powers to maintain law and order but cannot be detained on the ground that they were disturbing public order. Suppose that the two fighters were of rival communities and one of them tried to raise communal passions. The problem is still one of law and order but it raises the apprehension of public disorder. Other examples can be imagined. The contravention of law always affects order but before it can be said to affect public order, it must affect the community or the public at large.... [*AIR 1966,* SC, 740 (V 53 C 140) at 745 and 758.]

The Court has reaffirmed this distinction often, maintaining that

> It has been held in a series of decisions of this Court that the concept of law and order is not identical with the concept of public order. Public order is an aggravated form of disturbance of public peace. It affects the general current of public life (*Bhupal Chandra Ghose vs. Arif Ali*, A 1974 SCC 255; see also *Madhu Limaye vs. S.D.M. Monghyr, AIR 1971* SC 2486).

This being the case, unless someone deliberately sets out to create hatred, enmity or ill-will between communities in such a manner that ordinary readers with ordinary common sense, with ordinary susceptibilities, with ordinary prudence, are liable to be enraged to such an extent that public order affecting the community at large is liable to breakdown, the publication will be protected by our courts. No writer, editor or publisher would want freedom wider than that.

The Law and Order Bogey

The foregoing principles have been reaffirmed with great emphasis by the Supreme Court in its recent judgment, *S. Rangarajan vs. P. Jagjivan Ram & Ors* (SC, 30 March, 1989). In this case efforts were made to prevent the exhibition of a film in which the reservation policy of the Government was criticised. Even though censorship and pre-censorship of films have come to be accepted on the presumption that films have a much greater impact on the audience than does the written word; even though the statutes dealing with films, such as the Cinematograph Act, specifically provide for censorship and pre-censorship; and even though in accordance with these notions the Supreme Court held in the present case that 'as regards films, censorship by prior restraint is not only desirable but also necessary'; in spite of all this the Court removed all restraints on the exhibition of the film and upheld the principles which we have been discussing. It recalled with approval the observation in *Naraindas v. State of Madhya Pradesh* [1974 (3) SCR 624] in which the Court had held:

It is our firm belief, nay, a conviction which constitutes one of the basic values of a free society to which we are wedded under our Constitution that there must be freedom not only for the thought that we cherish, but also for the thought that we hate. As pointed out by Mr. Justice Holmes in *Abramson v. United States* (250 U.S. 616): 'The ultimate good desired is better reached by free trade in ideas – the best test of truth is the power of the thought to get itself accepted in the competition of the market.' There must be freedom of thought and the mind must be ready to receive new ideas, to critically analyse and examine them and to accept those which are found to stand the test of scrutiny and to reject the rest.

It also recalled with approval what had been said in *Sakal v. Union of India* [1952 (3) SCR 842 at 866]:

This Court must be ever vigilant in guarding perhaps the most precious of all the freedoms guaranteed by our Constitution. The reason for this is obvious. The freedom of speech and expression of opinion is of paramount importance under a democratic Constitution which envisages change in the composition of legislatures and governments and must by preserved.

Going further it observed:

Alexander Meiklejohn perhaps the foremost American philosopher of freedom of expression in his wise little study neatly explains: 'When men govern themselves, it is they – and no one else – who must pass judgment upon unwisdom and unfairness and danger. And that means that unwise ideas must have a hearing as well as wise ones, unfair as well as fair, dangerous as well as safe, un-American as well as American.... If then, on any occasion in the United States it is allowable, in that situation, to say that the Constitution is a good document, it is equally allowable, in that situation, to say that the Constitution is a bad document. If a public building may be used in which to say, in time of war, that the war is justified, then the same building may be used in which to say that it is not justified. If it be publicly argued that conscription for armed service is moral and necessary, it may likewise be publicly argued that it is immoral and unnecessary. If it may be said that American political institutions are superior to those of England or Russia or Germany, it may with equal freedom, be said that those of England or Russia or Germany are superior to ours. These conflicting views may be expressed, must be expressed, not because they are valid, but because they are relevant.... To be afraid of ideas, any ideas, is to be unfit for self government' [*Political Freedom* (1960) at 27].

He argued, if we may say so correctly, that guarantees of freedom of speech and of the press are measures adopted by the people as the ultimate rulers in order to retain control over the Government, the people's legislative and executive agents.

The Court then went on to recall,

Brandies, J, in *Whitney v. California* [274 US 375-8 (1927) propounded probably the most attractive free speech theory:

'...that the greatest menace to freedom are inert people; that public discussion is a political duty...: It is hazardous to discourage thought, hope and imagination; that the path of safety lies in the opportunity to discuss freely supposed grievances and proposed remedies, and that the fitting remedy for evil counsels is good ones.'

What Archibald Cox said in his article though on the First Amendment is equally relevant here:

'Some propositions seem true or false beyond rational debate. Some false and harmful political and religious doctrines gain wide public acceptance. Adolf Hitler's brutal theory of a "master race" is sufficient example. We tolerate such foolish and sometimes dangerous appeals not because they may prove true but because freedom of speech is indivisible. The liberty cannot be denied to some ideas and saved for others. The reason is plain enough; no man, no committee, and surely no government, has the infinite wisdom and disinterestedness to accurately and unselfishly separate what is true from what is debatable, and both from what is false. To license one to impose his truth upon dissenters is to give the same license to all others who have, but fear to lose, power. The judgment that the risks of suppression are greater than the harm done by bad ideas rests upon faith in the ultimate good sense and decency of free people' (*Society*, Vol. 24, p. 8, No. 1, November/December 1986).

After citing all these observations with approval the Supreme

Court advanced the law by clarifying two points. First it held that the danger which is alleged to be liable to follow the dissemination of an idea must not be remote, conjectural or far-fetched, it must be proximate and it must have a direct nexus with what is being said or exhibited. This is how the Court put the matter:

> ...there does indeed have to be compromise between the interests of freedom of expression and social interests. But we cannot simply balance the two interests as if they are of equal weight. Our commitment to freedom of expression demands that it cannot be suppressed unless the situations created by allowing the freedom are pressing and the community interest is endangered. The anticipated danger should not be remote, conjectural or far-fetched. It should have proximate and direct nexus with the expression. The expression of thought should be intrinsically dangerous to the public interests. In other words, the expression should be inseparably locked up with the action contemplated like the equivalent of a 'spark in a powder keg.'

Finally, while the Tamil Nadu Government and others had been pleading that the exhibition of the film would create very serious law and order problems in the state, while they had been citing the threats held out by several groups and their warnings that they would proceed to damage theatres screening the film, the Court observed:

> We are amused yet troubled by the stand taken by the state Government with regard to the film which has received the National Award. We want to put the anguished question, what good is the protection of freedom of expression if the state does not take care to protect it? It the film is unobjectionable and cannot constitutionally be restricted under Article 19(2), freedom of expression cannot be suppressed on account of threat of demonstrations and processions or threats of violence. That would tantamount to negation of the rule of law and a surrender to blackmail and intimidation. It is the duty of the State to protect the freedom of expression since it is a liberty guaranteed against the State. The State cannot plead the inability to handle the hostile audience problem. It is its

obligatory duty to prevent it and protect the freedom of expression.

The Court concluded its judgment with words which apply in particular to the sort of circumstances which we are considering. It said:

> Freedom of expression which is legitimate and constitutionally protected, cannot be held to ransom by an intolerant group of people. The fundamental freedom under Article 19(1)(a) can be reasonably restricted only for the purposes mentioned in Article 19(2) and the restriction must be justified on the anvil of necessity and not the quicksand of convenience or expediency. Open criticism of Government policies and operations is not a ground for restricting expression. We must practice tolerance to the views of others. Intolerance is as much dangerous to democracy as to the person himself.

Fundamental Duties

An even stronger safeguard is provided by Article 51A of the Constitution which enjoins Fundamental Duties on the press as it does on all citizens. The Article binds us *inter alia* to respect the ideals and institutions of our Constitution, to cherish and follow the noble ideals that inspired our freedom struggle, to promote harmony and the spirit of common brotherhood amongst our people, to renounce practices derogatory to women, to value and preserve the rich heritage of our composite culture, to develop the scientific temper, humanism and the spirit of inquiry and reform, to strive towards excellence in all spheres of individual and collective activity so that the nation consistently rises to higher levels of endeavour and achievement.

A mere glance at the list shows that articles about which the fundamentalists and propagandists have raised such hue and cry — articles on the Shah Bano matter, on the banning of Rushdie's book — were written in pursuance of precisely these mandatory duties.

In a recent ruling the Press Council itself has recognised the import of Article 51A for the press. On the April 9, 1987, an editorial   was published in the *Indian Express*   commending a judgment of the   Supreme Court in which it had furthered the cause of Muslim women. It included a   sentence   in which I had said that Muslim Personal Law   allows   a husband   to have up to four wives at a time and an unspecified   number of concubines and mistresses.

A   reader took   offence, and complained to the   Press Council. The Council   accepted   the fact that the Quran, the *hadis*, the   books on Muslim Personal   Law,   as   well   as   the   words   of   several other authorities   supported   what   had   been said   in the   sentence. More important, the   Press Council accepted the contention   that, truth   and fundamental   rights apart, the paper was bound by Article 51A to   take up   such   causes   and write about them (cf: *RV Patel against   Indian Express*, Press Council, 1988).

Conclusion

Thus   the   law is liberal. The rulings have been liberal. It is   not against   these that the writer must steel himself. It is   against   the pusillanimity of the State which allows harassment and   prosecution of reformers to   buy   peace for the moment, against the verbal terrorism of the   fundamentalists, against the fear of being abused and labelled   by the pseudo-liberals who dress up their cowardice as 'secularism',   the abuse   that   is   of the very persons who have done so   much   to   stoke communalism in India by pandering to it.

– August 1989

XIII

But What about the Verses Themselves?

There was a time when the greatest care, the most thorough examination, the gravest deliberation would precede the banning of a book.

Two weeks ago, a handful, whose boast it is to this day that they have not read Rushdie's novel, demanded that it be banned. The Government complied.

And Rajiv Gandhi's boast is no less: he too has not read the book. And he is firm: the ban will not be lifted.

And now comes the ban on importing a film. No one claims to have seen it. And in this case the Government has acted without much of a demand for a ban!

The book was banned, Rajiv says, 'because it was felt that it might hurt the feelings of certain groups of people' – that premonition having been arrived at, naturally, without reading the book.

The film is to be kept out presumably because it too may hurt the feelings of certain other groups of people, as it suggests that Jesus succumbed to a temptation.

The book on which that film is based was written over thirty years ago. It has been available in our bookshops all these decades, and is available today.

But it Enhances

And what is its offence? To suggest that Jesus might have fallen to temptation? But that can only enhance our debt to Jesus. I still remember as a boy listening to Panditji. By looking upon these great figures as having been perfect, as having been divine from the very moment they were born, he used to say, we miss their greatness. We miss the significance of their endeavour, of the great, sublimely human effort by which they raised themselves above the ordinary material of which we are all made. We miss the splendour of how, in spite of the frailties and temptations to which we are all subject, they brought back the divine ambrosia for mankind. The case of the great books is no different, he said. 'Many Hindus look upon the Vedas as revealed scripture,' he wrote. 'This seems to me to be peculiarly unfortunate, for thus we miss their real significance – the unfolding of the human mind in the earliest stages of thought...'

Consider the argument the other way. You ban a film or a book which suggests that Jesus fell for a solitary temptation. That lapse does not diminish his divinity or the greatness of his message in the slightest. You ban the book nonetheless. What then will you do about the book that knocks down the very divinity of Jesus, that strikes at several of the most important events on which the Christian faith rests – the belief, for instance, that Jesus was not the son of man, of Joseph, but of God; the belief that he was crucified so terribly, the belief that he thereafter rose and ascended to heaven?

What will you do to the book which says not once but repeatedly that Jesus was NOT the Son of God? Which declares the very notion of the Trinity – the conception so central to Christian theology and belief – to be blasphemous? Which says that it was not Jesus who was crucified, but another man who looked like him? And, of course, as he was not crucified, subsequent events such as the Resurrection never occurred.

May it not be 'felt' about such a book that 'it will hurt the feelings of certain groups of people'? In fact, is it not certain to not just offend, but to strike at the very foundations of the belief of every devout Christian? Will you then ban it also?

The Book

Before we consider doing anything so foolish, you better know that the book is the Quran itself. It states repeatedly that Jesus was not the Son of God.

'O ye people of the Book,' Allah says, 'overstep not bounds in your religion: and of God speak only truth. The Messiah, Jesus, son of Mary, is only an apostle of God, and His Word which

He conveyed into Mary, and a Spirit proceeding from Himself....'
(4.169).

'Infidels now are they,' Allah declares, 'who say "Verily God
is the Mesiah Ibn Maryam [son of Mary]," SAY: And who could
aught obtain from God, if He chose to destroy the Messiah Ibn
Maryam, and his mother, and all who are on the earth together?'
(5.19).

'Infidels now are they,' Allah proclaims again, 'who say "God
is the Messiah, son of Mary...."' (5.76).

'The Messiah, son of Mary,' Allah says conclusively, 'is
but an apostle; other apostles have flourished before him; and his
mother was a just person [i..e, as one, of the most authoritative
translators explains, she did not give herself out to be a goddess];
they both ate food [i.e., as the translator explains, they were both
human beings, subject to the usual wants and liabilities of ordinary
persons]' 'Behold!,' Allah tells the faithful, 'how we make clear to
them the signs! Then behold how they [the unbelieving Christians,
that is] turn aside' (5.79).

Thus, 'O people of the Book! Outstep not the bounds of truth
in your religion....' (5.81)

'The Jews say, "Ezra (Ozair) is a Son of God,"' Allah
recounts, 'And the Christians say, "The Messiah is a Son of God"
Such the sayings in their mouth!,' He scoffs. 'They resemble the
sayings of the infidels of old! God do battle with them! How are
they misguided.'

'They take their teachers, and their monks and the Messiah,
son of Mary, for Lords beside God, though bidden to worship one
God only,' He says. 'Fain would they put out God's light with
their mouths....' (9.30-2).

And there is a reason why their belief is sinful: 'It beseemth
not God to beget a Son,' Allah says (19.36).

'Jesus is no more than a servant whom We favoured,' Allah
says, 'and proposed as an instance of divine power to the children
of Israel....' (43.57).

The function of Jesus is not, as in the Bible, to deliver
the conclusive message of God. He is pictured as just a latter
day John. That is, his function is merely to forecast the future
coming of Prophet Mohammed.

Blasphemy

Now, as Jesus is but the son of Mary, as he is just an apostle like so many others, the notion of the Trinity – a notion that puts Jesus and the Holy Ghost at par with God – is nothing but blasphemy.

'Believe therefore in God and his apostles,' says Allah, 'and say not "Three" [There is a Trinity] – Forbear – it will be better for you...' (4.169).

'They surely are Infidels, who say, "God is the third of three,"' Allah proclaims. 'For there is no God but one God; and if they refrain not from what they say,' He warns, 'grievous chastisement shall light on such of them as are Infidels' (5.77).

'These!', Allah warns, 'they are veritable infidels! And for the infidels have We prepared a shameful punishment.'

'And those who believe in God and his apostles, and make no difference between them – these! We will bestow on them their reward at last....' (4.150,151).

The Crucufixion

So, Jesus as the Son of God is out, the Trinity is out, and so is the crucifixion.

'Yet,' says Allah, 'they [the Jews] slew him not and they crucified him not, but they had only his likeness...' (4.155-156).

Nor are these affirmations in the Quran accidental. They are central to the mission of the Prophet. For the doctrine in brief is that Allah has sent many an apostle, among them Moses and Jesus, but that the followers of these falsified their scriptures, and that is one reason why He has had to send the Prophet, the final one, the Seal of Prophets, to bring them back to the true path.

'Among the Jews,' Allah tells us, 'are those who displace the words of their scriptures, and say... perplexing with their tongues, and wounding the Faith by their revilings....' (4.48).

'O people of the Scriptures!,' Allah announces, 'Now is our Apostle come to you to clear up to you much that ye concealed of those Scriptures, and to pass over many things....' (5.18).

Does all this not strike at the very root of the faith of a Christian? Is it not liable to hurt his feelings? But is a ban the remedy? Or is it understanding and the effort to make those who may be offended understand?

The Law and the Book

Our law says (and do spare a minute to read it):

(1) Whoever

(a) by words, either spoken or written, or by signs or by visible representations or otherwise, promotes or attempts to promote, on grounds of religion, race, place of birth, residence, language, caste or community or any other ground whatsoever, disharmony or feelings of enmity, hatred or ill-will between different religious, racial, language or regional groups or castes, or communities, or

(b) commits any act which is prejudicial to the maintenance of harmony between different religious, racial, language or regional groups or castes or communities, and which disturbs or is likely to disturb the public tranquillity...shall be punished with imprisonment which may extend to three years, or with fine, or with both.

(2) Whoever commits an offence specified in sub-section (1) in any place of worship or in any assembly engaged in the performance of religious worship or religious ceremonies, shall be punished with imprisonment which may extend to five years and shall also be liable to fine.

We ban a novel, a film on the ground that 'it was felt that the book might hurt the feelings of certain groups of people,' without reading it or seeing it.

What then of the book which commands us,

When the Lord your God brings you into the land which you go to possess ... and when the Lord your God delivers them over to you, you shall conquer them and utterly destroy them. You shall make no covenant with them nor show mercy to them....But thus shall you deal with them: You shall destroy their altars, and break down their sacred pillars, and cut down their wooden images, and burn their carved images with fire...?

What of the book that ordains that if 'certain base fellows' in a city preach that we serve gods other than the ones specified in this book,

> You shall put the inhabitants of that city to the sword, destroying it utterly, all who are in it and its cattle with the edge of the sword. You shall gather all its spoil into the midst of its open square, and burn the city and all its spoil with fire, as a whole burnt offering to the Lord your God; it shall be a heap forever, it shall not be built again...?

What of the book which says that when the inhabitants do not agree to the terms of peace you specify, which naturally include complete surrender and conversion, and instead fight you, you must upon taking the place,

> put all its males to the sword, but the women and the little ones, the cattle and everything else in the city, all its spoil, you shall take as booty for yourselves, and you shall enjoy the spoils of your enemies, which the Lord your God has given you as your inheritance, you shall save alive nothing that breathes, but you shall utterly destroy them...?

What of the book that does not just lay down this as the law in general, but goes on to hold as the example to follow that of the Prophet who, upon being told by his followers that they had indeed killed every male in the city sparing only the women and the children, flew into a rage and ordered them to return and, kill every male among the little ones, and 'kill every woman who has known man by lying with him. But all the young girls who have not known man by lying with him, keep them alive for yourselves....'?

And which then informs us triumphantly that thirty-two thousand little girls were thereby kept for debauchery and use?

The book?

The Bible: Deuteronomy, 7.1-6, 13.12-16, 20.10-18; and Numbers, 31, 1-54.

This, according to the Bible, is what you must do if the persons you encounter do not agree to worship the God it specifies, and Him alone. Now, the Quran says that unless the people worship the Allah IT specifies, and none but Him — He, of course, being different from the God of the Bible – you must

> Strike off their heads till you have made a great slaughter
> among them, and of the rest make fast the fetters....(47.4-5)

The exhortation is indeed the leitmotiv of the Quran. 'And
kill them wherever ye shall find them,' Allah enjoins, 'and eject
them from whatever place they have ejected you; for civil discord
is worse than carnage; fight therefore against them until there be
no more civil discord, and the only worship be that of God...'
– that is, till universal peacc reigns as everyone has been
converted to Islam (2.186-9; see also 8.40).

'O believers,' Allah enjoins, 'fight the unbelievers, who are
near to you, and let them find in you a harshness....' (9.125; see
also 9.74).

This, indeed, is the bargain Allah has struck with you, the
Quran says – that you will kill or be killed in trying to exterminate
the infidels and Allah will in return give you your place in
Paradise (9.113).

We are told again and again that we just cannot guide them
to the right path, Allah Himself having sent them astray after
having concluded that they have no merit in them (4.90; 5.54;
4.135-9; 7.20-5, etc.). And so the only recompense for 'those
who fight against God and His Messenger, and hasten about the
earth to do corruption there,' and who do not repent 'before you
have power over them,' is:

> They shall be slaughtered or crucified, or their hands or feet
> shall alternately be struck off, or they shall be banished
> from the land....(5.37-8)

You may sell them for ransom, but only after you have wreaked
'a great slaughter' among them. 'It is not for any Prophet,' Allah
says, reiterating what He has enjoined in 47.4-5 cited above,
'until he makes a wide slaughter in the land.' And there is a
reason for it. 'You desire the chance goods of the present world,'
in the form of ransom which you will obtain by selling and
releasing them, Allah tells us, 'and God desires for you the world
to come' – which you will obtain by the wide slaughter (8.68).

Nor do you have any choice in the matter. For it is laid down:

It is not for any believer, man or woman, when God and His Messenger have decreed a matter, to have the choice in the affair. Whosoever disobeys God and His Messenger has gone astray into manifest error (33.36).

Conclusion about Banning

Compare the extent to which such mandatory requirements may 'hurt the feelings of certain groups of people' – and not just the feelings – with what some film or some fictional novel might do. And what I have cited are just a few of the provisions on *Jihad*. And the Quran and the Bible are just two of the texts that enjoin it. *Sahih Bukhari, Sahih Muslim*, the revered accounts of what the Prophet said and did, do so in vivid, often gory detail. As do the law books from *Fatwa-e-Alamgiri* to the *Hedaya*. And *Jihad* is just one of the topics in the texts that 'might hurt the feelings of certain groups of people'.

The point is not that because a novel or a film has been banned, such texts too should be banned. On the contrary. The point is that as we have learnt to live with and to outgrow such mandatory texts, we should not allow hustlers to bulldoze us into banning mere novels and films.

Next, if a novel or a film is to be banned because it 'might hurt the feelings of certain groups of people', must every liberating book not be banned too – from Thomas Paine's *Age of Reason* to Bertrand Russell's *Religion and Science*, from the works of theologians like Kung and Schillebeeckx to those of rationalists who today work to make us see through our god-men? These most certainly offend 'certain groups of people' – many of them, like the books of Kung and Schillebeeckx, two of contemporary Europe's leading theologians, have been officially censured by the Catholic Church, for instance. Are we to ban Swami Dayanand's *Satyartha Prakash* because someone (without reading it) says that it insults the great Sikh Gurus? And in return excise portions out of the Guru Granth Sahib because the worshippers of Kali say that these abuse them?

And is that the way to the twenty-first century or to the sixteenth?

It isn't just that there are hundreds and hundreds of such books. It is that they have been among the great liberators. By the very act of lifting mankind out of religiosity, they have enabled it to get closer to perceiving the truly spiritual.

'But you don't see the point. These provisions and books are about doctrine, about practice. Rushdie's book is about the person of the Prophet. The film is about the person of Christ.'

Since the seventeenth century, book after book has dealt with the person of Jesus. Christology has become a distinct discipline under which each incident, each account of each incident has been examined. And ever so often proclaimed to be wanting.

And as for the Prophet's person, so greatly have the times changed and with them the mores that, on the rule applied to Rushdie's book, you'd have to start by prohibiting the reproduction of the accounts of the Prophet's life and deeds – those of Imam Bukhari and Imam Muslim, accounts that are revered by the devout almost as much as the Quran itself. I can state this from personal experience – on the testimony, that is, of the wrath that the Urdu press and the leaders of the current campaign against Rushdie's book heaped on me for merely reproducing a few, relatively innocuous passages from these accounts during the controversy over the Muslim Women's [Further Enfeeblement] Bill.

'But you still don't get the point. These are old books. We have all got used to them. A new novel, a new film – that is different. That is a new thing. People will notice it and be enflamed to act by it.'

Quite the contrary. No one would have been enflamed by a mere novel, a mere film, few would have even heard of them but for the fact that the Government, capitulating to fundamentalists, has banned them. Now everyone will hear about them.

As for effectiveness, it isn't the newness or the antiquity which determines that, it is the regard in which people hold the text. Who can say that the Quran does not mould the character of the devout Muslim or the Bible that of the devout Christian? That a mere novel, a mere film will have a greater influence on their behaviour than these sacred texts?

About Politics

The regression that this episode marks on the principle of

free inquiry, of national discourse is, of course, great. The precedent has now been set to ban a book without reading it, to ban a work of art without seeing it. That is bad enough.

The regressive effects for politics will be infinitely worse. For the second time in two years the Government has anointed the Shahabuddins as the new Jinnahs. For the second time it has conceded that those of one religion alone can speak on matters that are said to affect them, and that among Muslims the Shahabuddins are the sole spokesmen of the community. The consequences will be worse than were those of the encouragement which Mrs Gandhi and Sanjay gave to Bhindranwale.

'But you don't understand. There is a difference. Yes, the passages you quote, the whole doctrine can offend the Christians, the Hindus. But the fact is that it does not. That is the difference. That is why the Government has to be extra careful about books like Rushdie's. That is why it has to heed the Shahabuddins on the Muslim Women's Bill.'

That from the key rationaliser – more accurately, from the only rationaliser left now – in Rajiv's entourage. And what signal does such a premise send to other communities, to the Hindus for instance?

That they too should work themselves into a fury.

Are we surprised then that the Shiv Sena is spreading like fire, like the fire, that is, which will consume the country? That the Vishwa Hindu Parishad is finding so much support for its stern line on the Ram Janma Bhoomi matter?

The cure for the apprehension that a novel or a film 'might hurt the feelings of certain groups of people' is not to pander to the new Jinnahs who use the ignorance, the religiosity of our people to enflame them and thereby fortify their own leadership. It is to reason with the people, to educate them, to make them understand.

– 19 October 1988

XIV

'But you are Quoting Out of Context'

*If you have power, **Jihad** is incumbent upon you. If you have no power, it is unlawful.*

Sir Syed Ahmed Khan

'When a dog goes mad, we kill it with poison. When a man goes mad, we send him to a lunatic asylum. We must decide what should be done in the case of Arun Shourie....'

'Arun Shourie has launched a campaign to ban the Quran in India....'

'He is anti-Islam....'

'He has no right to discuss the Quran and Islam....'

'Apologise within twenty-four hours or else....'

A well-orgainsed campaign of calumny, of misrepresenting an article I had written ('But what about the verses themselves?', *Indian Express*, 19 October 1988), a campaign to enflame the laity, a campaign to frighten a writer into silence.

That it was a campaign, and that it was orchestrated is evident. Scores upon scores of 'letters to the editor' making the same points, in the same words, the same sequence. Identical articles. Telegrams upon telegrams – bearing the same message in the same words, 'Publish Maulana X's article immediately or else....' Printed post cards bearing different signatures. Posters. A march or two to the offices of the *Indian Express*. Two similar complaints – one to the police in Hyderabad (demanding among other things that I be arrested under the National Security Act), another to a magistrate in Srinagar.

Now, abuse should not be answered. Threats need not be. The question that remains is: what exactly do the persons complain of? Three things, as far as I can make out:

❑ That I have quoted edicts of the Quran – e.g., on the duty to
   engage in *Jihad* – 'out of context';
❑ That I have quoted some isolated verses from the Quran about
   Jesus and the Christians so as to disrupt the hitherto cordial
   relations between Christians and Muslims; and
❑ That, true or not, I had no right to draw attention to the verses
   as doing so was liable to offend others, in this case the Muslims.

So, it is to these that I shall attend.

'Out of Context'

For the second time in two years – the first occasion was the
Shah Bano controversy – these propagandists have shown how rash
and how bereft of forethought they are.

In this case, as in that, unable to deny the precise edicts from
the Quran that were quoted, they have invoked the argument,
'But the passage is being quoted out of context.' 'The verses
were written 1400 years ago, in the context of a medieval desert
society,' they say. 'Circumstances are very different today. What
relevance can quoting them have in this day and age?'

A Genuine Problem

Now, it is the strangest possible thing to hear this argument
from those who claim to speak on behalf of the orthodox position
on a scripture such as the Quran. But it is best to begin with a
genuine problem: a special feature of the Quran itself which
can lead followers – or at the least enable them – to confine its
edicts and rules to this 'context' or that. It isn't just that the
Quran was revealed in bits and pieces. A very large proportion
of the revelations were all too clearly meant to help the believers
vault over specific predicaments. Although the verses are as
generally worded as they can be, in the eyes of the devout these
revelations are so strongly tied up with the context in which they
were called forth that they can only too easily put the followers
in the habit of – and give them the excuse for – reading the
revelations in general so as to confine each to a very narrow

context. A few examples will show how easily the unwary apologist can fall for this temptation or alibi.

When the Prophet was in Mecca, beleaguered and harassed, Allah counselled toleration, moderation. 'Say,' He told the Prophet, 'O unbelievers.... To you your religion and to me my religion' (*Quran* CIX), 'No compulsion is there in religion,' He proclaimed (2.256).

But as the Prophet's power grew in Medina, Allah exhorted the Prophet and his followers to *Jihad,* to ceaseless struggle till Islam was established over all humanity.

When the Prophet first reached Medina and needed the help of the Jewish tribes which controlled the city and its environs, the Prophet was inspired to woo them, to choose Jerusalem as the *Qibla,* as the direction in which the faithful were to bow in prayer, to adopt as the day of fasting the tenth day of the Jewish month of Tishri, *Yom Kippur,* the Day of Atonement, to adopt the Jewish practice of praying at midnight also. Allah also announced that the faithful could eat Jewish food and marry Jewish women.

But as the Prophet's position stabilised and as the Jews continued to resist accepting the Prophet's hegemony and doctrine, as they continued to resist believing his assertion that they had distorted the scriptures which God had given them, Allah, immediately after the victory at Badr, revealed that henceforth the *Qibla* should be the *Kaba* in Mecca and not Jerusalem, that the fast, the *Ramzan,* should be in the month in which the battle of Badr had taken place, that the Jews could not be trusted. And so the great massacre of the Jewish clan Banu Qaynuga followed.

When the Prophet was contending with the Jews, Allah told him that they were his implacable enemies, and that the Christians were the ones who were nearest to him and his friends. And this He said was because of the priests and monks among them:

> Thou wilt surely find the most hostile of men to the believers are the Jews and the idolators; and thou wilt surely find the nearest of them in love to the believers are those who say, 'We are Christians', that because some of them are priests and monks, and they wax not proud... (*Quran,* 5.85)

But when the Christians too proved to be intractable, when they too failed to accept the Prophet's hegemony and his doctrine any more than the Jews, Allah exhorted the Prophet never to take the Christians any more than the Jews as friends:

> O believers, take not Jews and Christians as friends; they are friends to each other. Who so of you makes them his friends is one of them. God guides not the people of the evildoers.... (*Quran*, 5.56)

And, this implacability, this intractability Allah now said arises in large part because of those very monks and priests who had been commended earlier. Christians are now said to have taken their monks as Lords apart from God in exactly the way the Jews have taken their *Rabbi* (*Quran*, 9.30-3). The monks who had been extolled for their humility are now seen along with the *Rabbis* to 'consume the goods of the people in vanity', and to bar the people from Allah's way. They are seen by Allah to 'treasure up gold and silver' instead of spending it in His way. Instead of being the reason for befriending the Chrisitians, the monks join the *Rabbis* in being ones to whom the Prophet is enjoined to convey 'good tidings of a painful chastisement' (*Quran* 9.34).

And this intractability of the Christians as much as of the Jews is not going to end, says Allah. He says that He has Himself sown enmity and hatred in their hearts, an enmity which will last to the Day of Resurrection:

> And those who say 'We are Christians' we took compact; and they have forgotten a portion of that they were reminded of. So we have stirred up among them enmity and hatred, till the Day of Resurrection; and God shall surely tell them of the things they wrought (*Quran*, 5.17).

Just as He has in the hearts of the Jews:

> And what has been sent down to thee from thy Lord will surely increase many of them in insolence and unbelief; and We have cast between them enmity and hatred, till the Day of Resurrection. As often as they light a fire for war, God will extinguish it. They hasten about the earth, to do corruption

there; and God loves not the workers of corruption (*Quran*, 5.69).

The relationship with the Christians thus culminated, as one of the most thorough Christian commentators on the Quran notes, in the way in which the relationship with the Jews had ended – i.e., in hostility and war and bloodshed. (For instructive surveys of the changing revelations in regard to Jews and Christians, see Richard Bell, *The Origin of Islam in its Christian Environment*, Macmillan, London, 1927, pages 151-60; Alfred Guillaume, *Islam*, Penguin, London, 1979, and Maxime Rodinson, *Mohammed*, Penguin, London, 1971, *et passim*). Let us pass to notice other examples briefly.

Allah forbids fighting in the Holy Month. But a raid on the Meccan caravan on the express instructions of the Prophet leads to blood being shed. There is much booty. But as the fighting has occurred in the Holy Month, there is in addition much unease; there are protests also. Allah reveals that while fighting in the Holy Month is a serious matter, the crimes of the Meccans were greater, and so the fighting was justified:

> They will question thee concerning the Holy Month, and fighting in it. Say: Fighting in it is a heinous thing, but to bar from God's way, and disbelief in Him, and the Holy Mosque, and to expel its people from it – that is more heinous in God's sight; and persecution is more heinous than slaying.... (*Quran*, 2.213)

When the Prophet returns to Mecca, Allah feels conciliation and prudence are called for. The revelation thus comes:

> Have you considered al-Lat and al-Uzza and Manat, the third, the other? (*Quran*, 53.19-20)

these three being goddesses whose idols alongwith those of hundreds of others were being worshipped in the *Kaba*.

And it is followed by the certification: 'These are the cranes exalted, whose intercession is to be hoped for.'

Now, this is certain balm for the Meccans. Upon hearing this they feel that the Prophet has at last partially come around to their view – accepting their goddesses as ones who could effectively intercede with God on behalf of the worshippers. They are assuaged. The Prophet's return is eased.

But that having come to pass, the Prophet is made to see that the latter sentence certifying to the efficacy of the worship of the goddesses has been inveigled into his mind by Satan, that it is not from Allah (hence the expression, 'The Satanic verses'). And so he returns to implacable hostility towards idolators and idols. (For a compact account of the episode see, for instance, William Montgomery Watt, *Muhammad at Mecca*, Oxford University Press, pp. 101-9; also his *Islamic Revelation in the Modern World*, Edinburgh, 1969, p.19.)

The examples can be multiplied many times over. Allah was particularly sensitive to the needs of the Messenger, and so revelation after revelation came down to deal satisfactorily with the Prophet's needs. These permitted what was needed with regard to the Prophet's needs as the founder of a new State, they also dealt satisfactorily with the Prophet's personal inclinations and needs – with the allegations against his favourite wife, the irrepressible Ayesha, with whether he could marry his adopted son's wife, with his departing from a vow of abstaining from his wives for a month, with whether he could alter the turns of the women etc. The revelations saw the Prophet out of many a situation, so much so that on one typical occasion concerning her and the other wives Ayesha remarked to him, 'I feel that your Lord hastens in fulfilling your wishes and desires' (*Sahih Bukhari*, Book 60, Chapter 240, *Hadis* 311-2). But it is not necessary to multiply the examples. They can be gleaned from the Quran and the collections of *hadis*.

The Consequence

This feature of the Quran, namely that the revelations seemed to take account of the circumstances of the community and the Prophet, is perhaps understandable, for it is entirely possible that Allah, having chosen Muhammad as the one through whom He would send His message to mankind, was concerned to protect His Messenger and his fledgling band of followers. But understandable in the context of the initial years or not, the variability of the revelations to match circumstances must be taken to have ended with the end of the Prophethood of Muhammad. This should be obvious. By not bearing it in mind, commentators and scholars have led themselves into a grave consequence. In their careless hands the feature of revelations varying with the Prophet's circumstances has become the occasion, if not the excuse, for them to read their own compulsions and preferences into the Quran. This tendency in turn has done great injury to the claim of the faithful regarding the integrity and universality of the Quran and its message. An example or two will make the consequence obvious.

For instance, each time sanguinary verses on *Jihad* are recalled these days, so-called scholars start asserting that they are being quoted 'out of context'. History gives the clue.

The *Hedaya*, the great compendium of Sheikh Burhann'd din Ali (d. AD 1198), the one that has been the basic text in determining Muslim law in India, binds the faithful to follow Allah's injunction and 'slay the infidels'. It reminds us of the Prophet's admonition, 'War is permanently established till the Day Of Judgment'. *Jihad* is not to be defensive, it says. 'The destruction of the sword is incurred by the infidels,' it proclaims, 'although they be not the first aggressors, as appears from the various passages in the sacred writings, which are generally received to this effect....'

Aurangzeb, reigning when Muslim power was at its zenith in India, had Muslim law codified in the famous *Fatwa-e-Alamgiri*. It lays down that *Jihad* is the noblest of professions, and in doing so it goes faithfully by the edicts of the Quran and the numerous *hadis* on the matter. Its mandatory provisions are if at all possible even more sanguinary than those of the *Hedaya*.

This is what the Quran, the *hadis* and other authoritative books are proclaimed to say when Muslim power is in ascendant, when it is at its zenith.

Aurangzeb dies. The Mughal empire begins to fall apart. The great revivalist Shah Waliullah arises. How does he interpret the edicts of the Quran on *Jihad*?

Here is how the Pakistani authority on the Shah puts the matter:

Besides, what Shah Sahib feels so sorry about and for which he so bitterly laments, is the apathy and negligence on the part of Muslims towards *Jihad* which in fact is continuous and permanent. So long the spirit of *Jihad* was alive among them,

they were made successful and victorious wherever they
went, but no sooner it disappeared from them, than they were
subjected and held in contempt everywhere. The verse of the
Holy Quran, 'And fight on with them until there is no more
tumult or oppression, and there prevail justice and faith in God
altogether and everywhere, but if they cease, verily God does
see all that they do,' clearly points out to the necessity of the
continuation of *Jihad* till the emergence of Islam as a dominant
force....

Maulana Ubedullah Sindhi, while shedding light upon the
verse, 'It is He Who sent His Apostle with guidance,' explains
as under:

This verse publicly invited people towards an
international revolution, and its primary object is to make
all people agree on one point. In history we see that a certain
community professes a certain religion, and then subsequently
that religion becomes the sacred part of its national life. In
the like manner, there came into existence a separate religion
for every community. But the Quran presents to the world one
religion for all, and its sole aim is to make that religion prevail
upon all other religions. There are, however, only two ways
for achieving this prevalence. One way is to make it dominate
other religions through preaching and exhortation; but had
this way been possible, there would not have been any
necessity for taking up arms and waging wars, and all the
people would have accepted this religion of their own accord;
but the words at the end of the verse, 'Even though the
polytheists like it not,' do signify that it would be to the
dislike of the polytheists to see Islam dominating. The verse
clearly points out the fact that their dislike would certainly
come in the way of Islam. The other way is the creation of
a most powerful centre which could make Islam prevail
through the use of force. It is being given out these days that
domination should be achieved through peaceful methods,
in other words, there is no need to fight and bring about a
revolution; but it must be remembered that the nature of man
is such, that it is not always possible to put up with it
peacefully, and sometimes one is compelled to the use of force.

During the reign of the Orthodox Caliphs (*Khulafa-i-rashidin*), Islam most probably spread through the sword and the use of force and not through the force of argument or by reconciliation (G.N. Jalbani, *Teachings of Shah Waliullah of Delhi*, Ashraf, Lahore, 1967, pp, 122-4).

In his famous, 'Address to the Muslim Kings' Shah Waliullah cites the very verse – 'and fight against them till no insurrection is left....' (Quran, 2.193) – for citing which critics accuse me of 'quoting out of context'. Here is the Shah's counsel to Kings on the subject:

> I say to the kings that the Will of the Almighty God has decreed that you should draw your swords and do not put them back in their sheaths until a Muslim is not made distinct from a *mushrik* [polytheist], and the unruly leaders of infidelity and impudence (*kufr wa fisq*) are not relegated to the ranks of subjugation. Make sure that nothing is left in their hands that can incite them to rebellion again. 'And fight against them until no insurrection is left.....' The governors of the provinces should be expert in warfare. Such officials should be allowed to keep troops comprising twelve thousand men infused with love for *Jihad*, and possessing undauntless [*sic*] courage against the insurgents and rebels. When this is done the Will of God will require you to pay your attention to the welfare of your subjects. You should enforce such a system of government that allows nothing to go against the tenets of *shariat*. This, and this only, will ensure a peaceful and happy life for the people....

And here is his 'Address to the soldiers':

> I say to the military men that God has created you so that you should wage *Jihad*: exalt His name, promulgate the truth, and eradicate infidelity from its roots. But you have forgotten the purpose for which you were created. Now the horses you rear and the arms you collect are meant only for adding to your riches. Your hearts are devoid of the missionary zeal for *Jihad*. You are addicted to wine and hemp; you get your beards clean shaven, and let your mous-

taches grow. You oppress human beings by robbing them of
their commodities without making any payment. By God, you
have got to go to Him one day! Then He will let you
know what you have been doing in the world (A.D. Muztar,
Shah Waliullah, A Saint-Scholar of Muslim India, National
Commission of Historical and Cultural Research, Islamabad,
1979, pp. 80-2).

Such is the meaning which is deduced from the injunctions of
the Quran immediately after the period of Aurangzeb.

1857 happens. The Mughal empire is finished. Sir Syed Ahmed
Khan is the dominant Muslim intellectual. His sole anxiety is to
convince the British that of all their subjects the Muslims are the
most loyal. Not only have the Muslims not taken to *Jihad*, he writes
repeatedly, as the British Government is allowing them freedom
to practice their religion, Muslims just *cannot* embark on *Jihad*,
they are barred from doing so by the provisions of the Quran
itself. Even if the British were to deprive them of this freedom,
all that Muslims can do, says Sir Syed, is to emigrate to another
country. He goes so far as to say that the Muslims would be
wrong, that they *were* wrong to take offence at being asked
to bite cartridges greased with swine lard, food offered by
Christians being lawful to Muslims by the injunctions of Allah and
the Prophet. Indeed, there can be no *Jihad*, he proclaims,
as Christians have been designated by Allah to be the ones whom
the Muslims will find the closest of friends. (He repeated the
assertions incessantly, as can be gleaned from any representative
collection of his work; for instance, *Writings and Speeches of
Sir Syed Ahmed Khan*, Shah Mohammad (ed.), Nachiketa,
Bombay 1972; some representative passages are cited in the
essay, 'The Gloss-over School,' above).

Notice what is happening: Sir Syed simply omits revelations
of the Medina period, and keeps repeating one or two passages
again and again. He just omits the subsequent revelations
forbidding friendship with Christians, and just goes on citing
one verse – the one in which, as we shall see in a moment, Allah
extols Christians at the expense of Jews and idolators.

By the time Maulana Azad comes to write his well known
Tarjuman al-Quran the need is for ecumenicism. This need of
the times is reflected in the constructions he puts on the very same
verses.

In direct contrast to the *Hedaya*, the *Fatwa-e-Alamgiri,* the exhortations of Shah Waliullah and centuries of expositions by other scholars, the Maulana says that *Jihad* can be waged only for defensive purposes, only to *safeguard* religious liberty, never to propagate the faith. The latter, he says, is to be done through persuasion alone (*Tarjuman al-Quran*, Syed Abdul Latif Trust, Hyderabad, Vol. 2, pp. 121-6).

The Maulana focuses on *Jihad* in its literal sense – i.e., 'to strive in the way of God' – and this way, he says, is love, peace, universalism.

We can see by now what is changing from commentator to commentator, from Shah Waliullah to Sir Syed to Maulana Azad, to say nothing of 'scholars' of our own time. Indeed, the expression 'to strive in the way of God' itself provides an excellent illustration of the point.

As Goldziher showed long ago, the Kharijites and other insurrectionists relied on exhortations such as verse 9.112,

God has bought from the believers their selves and their possessions against the gift of Paradise; they fight in the way of God; they kill and are killed....

– i.e., on the very verse for citing which I am accused today of 'quoting out of context' – to ride to deliberate martyrdom fighting 'godless' rulers.

Later, when the clerics had developed closer relations with the rulers, it was held that *Jihad* waged out of opposition to authority does not ensure martyrdom.

And the notion 'to strive in the way of God' was extended to cover the undertaking of a voyage that entailed sea-sickness, the collection of taxes for the ruler, the pursuit and propagation of religious learning, the discharging of obligations to one's parents, the giving of alms in charity, constructing a public well. These and many similar activities were all taken to be 'striving in the way of God', and doing any of them was put at par in the merit it ensured with dying in *Jihad* in the strict sense. (See, for instance, Ignaz Goldziher, *Muslim Studies,* 1890, Vol. 2, Allen and Unwin, London, 1971, pp. 350-6.)

What then is the doctrine on *Jihad* left to us by such a process, such an approach – of 'looking at the verses in their context'?

It is put pithily by Sir Syed. The Doctrine, he said, is that *'If you have power, Jihad is incumbent upon you; if you have no power, it is unlawful'* (Cf, Bashir Ahmed Dar, *Religious Thought of Sayyid Ahmed Khan*, Institute of Islamic Culture, Lahore 1971, p. 79. Dar commends this interpretation as being 'realistic').

Nor does what has been authoritatively held about *Darul Harb* provide any way out. Quite the contrary. *Jihad* is mandatory for the faithful in *Darul Harb*, that is, in the Land of War. The question therefore is: 'Is India *Darul Harb*, the Land of War, or *Darul Islam*, the Land of Peace?' The Ulema of Deoband, the most authoritative seminary of Islamic theology and law in India, has answered the question decisively. In the *Fatawi Dar-ul Ulum* (*Dar-ul Ulum, Deoband*, compiled by Maulana Mufti Mohammed Sahib, *et al.*, Volume XII, pp. 268-69) the divines recall how the Fatwa declaring Hindustan to be *Darul Harb* was issued first by Hazrat Shah Abdul Aziz Muhaddas Dehlavi and how it has been reiterated periodically since then. They then hold as follows:

In August 1947 the country became independent but the cruelties perpetrated on Musalmans, and the kind of murders and bloodshed that followed independence have no parallel in history. For this very reason the Sheikh-ul Islam, Maulana Madani, even after Independence, called this country, on account of its state of affairs, *Darul Harb*. And some others termed it *Darul Aman*, a variant of *Darul Harb*. In any case, though the country is now free, Musalmans and Islam have no share [in the fruit] of Independence. The life and property, dignity and honour, of a Muslim are not secure so far. And in the eyes of the government these have no value. Some special Musalmans have of course benefited from Independence but they are in a minority and this has happened in the earlier government too. The *millat-i-Islamia* continues to be unhappy. In future perhaps God would provide a solution.

This, then is the decisive, the authoritative statement of 'the context'. Where does it leave the apologists of the tradition, the ones who would explain away the passages on *Jihad* in the Quran by asserting that they were written long ago for a medieval, Arabian context?

And *Jihad* is but one example. Consider another.

Invoking the injunctions of Allah and the Prophet that the entire community of believers is one indivisible body, that it is the duty of all believers to rush to the aid of each, Shah Waliullah invites Ahmad Shah Abdali to invade India. The Battle of Panipat follows. And the disastrous consequences. Concerned that the doctrines of the Wahabis are causing suspicion among the British, Sir Syed sanitises them. He declares that far from Muslims of India having affinity with or commitment to Muslims elsewhere, Islam requires no Muslim ruler – not even the Caliph – to come to the succour of Muslims under some other ruler, nor does it require Muslims under one set of rulers – especially Muslims under such benevolent rulers as the British – to aid or obey a Muslim ruling over some other country. The Caliph, he says, is no more than a *Sultan* ruling over his own country – that Muslims in India are not to heed him (Cf., Shah Mohammad, *op. cit.*, pp. 253-261).

Just a few decades later when an already decayed Caliphate is abolished, Muslim leaders go back to the older interpretation and insist that by striking at that *functus officio*, the Caliph, the British and others are striking at Islam. Maulana Mohammad Ali, going by the injunctions that Shah Waliullah had based himself on, proclaims that should the King of Afghanistan invade India every Muslim would be bound by his religion to aid that King against the British Government of India.

Jesus

The attitude to Jesus, in particular to what the Quran proclaims about Jesus, exemplifies the same phenomenon. Today our 'scholars' and propagandists proclaim that Islam has always held Jesus in the highest regard. Some even seem to imply that the Quran, and Islam in general, hold almost the same views about Jesus as do the Christians.

Some of the verses have already been referred to. The Quran says again and again that Jesus was *not* the Son of God, that he was *not* crucified, that those who put others at par with God by believing in notions such as the Trinity smear God.

The matter is put beyond doubt by the traditions. Thus we have the Prophet reporting that Allah had told him that those who maintain He had a son abuse Him. This is how the matter is put:

> Narrated Ibn Abbas: 'The Prophet said, 'Allah said, "The son of Adam tells a lie against Me though he has no right to do so, and he abuses Me though he has right to do so. As for his telling a lie against Me, it is that he claims that I cannot recreate him as I created him before; and as for his abusing Me, it is his statement that I have offspring. No! Glorified be Me! I am far from taking a wife or offspring"' (*Sahih al-Bukhari*, Book 60, Chapter 10, *hadis*-9).

The Prophet also maintained that Jesus would return, that he would marry and have children, that he would rule and dispense justice according to the *Shariat*, that he would break crosses and kill swine, that he would lead Muslims in prayer to Allah, that he would remain for 45 years, after which he would die and be buried along with the Prophet in the latter's grave (cf, *Mishkat al-Masabih*, Book 26, Chapter 6).

The virgin birth of Christ, the miracles attributed to him, his crucifixion etc. have all been contested most vigorously by Muslim scholars from the very beginning. Polemics between Muslim and Christian scholars and clergy on matters such as these have been vicious. On the Muslim side works of Al-Jahiz, Ibn Hazm, Ghazzali himself, Ahmed Ibn Zayn, Al-Abidin, Rehmat Ali, down to Sir Syed, and on the Christian side those of Father Xavier during the reign of Jehangir, Pfandar, Sir William Muir, Tisdall and other polemicists, all testify to the fierce battles which have raged on these matters.

Controversies arose during the life of the Prophet himself. He was convinced that Jesus had been ordered by Allah to forecast his, i.e. Muhammad's, coming. He was also convinced that Jesus had in accordance with this command actually forecast his coming [the verse in question actually has Jesus forecast the coming of one 'Ahmed':

> And when Jesus Son of Mary said, 'Children of Israel, I am indeed the Messenger of God to you, confirming the Torah that is before me, and giving good tidings of a Messenger who shall come after Me, whose name shall be Ahmed' (*Quran*, 61.6)

but Muslims have assumed, as the Prophet himself did, that 'Ahmed' in the verse refers to the Prophet, i.e. to Muhammad. Christian scholars naturally have not missed the opportunity of pin-pointing this incongruity].

As this forecast is not mentioned in the Bible, the Prophet – as well as all Muslim scholars following him – have maintained that both the Old and New Testaments have been corrupted by the Jews and Christians. They have, of course, maintained that the scriptures have been corrupted by the Jews and Christians in other respects also.

Almost all Muslim scholars have held steadfastly to what the Quran teaches about Jesus. As on the matter of *Jihad* a few have waivered from time to time and from concept to concept. For instance, Sir Syed in his *Essays on the Life of Mohammad* characterises the Trinity as 'the worst of corruptions,' he characterises the authority which the Catholics have given to the Pope as being 'so ignominious a yoke', he maintains that it is Islam which has liberated Christians from this yoke by inspiring Luther. (See, for instance, his 'Essay on the question whether Islam has been beneficial or injurious to human society in general and to the Mosaic and Christian dispensations,' in *Essays on the Life of Mohammad*, 1870, reprint, Idarah-I-Adabiyat-I, Delhi, 1981, pp. 38 – 40.) In his famous *The Mohammedan Commentary on the Holy Bible* (1862-1865) he accepts the Christian doctrines of the virgin birth of Christ, of crucifixion, of resurrection, but in his equally famous *Tafsir-al-Quran* he denounces each of these dogmas. (For a compact account see, Bashir Ahmed Dar, *Religious Thought of Syed Ahmed Khan, op.cit.*, pp. 94 – 106.)

By the time Maulana Azad came to write his famous *Tarjuman al-Quran*, it was possible to adhere to the Quran in a more straightforward manner. In fact, in a sense nationalist Muslims and nationalist Hindus were fighting together against foreign rulers who happened to be Christians. The Maulana himself was sincerely devoted to the cause of Hindu-Muslim unity, and he was a spirited and vigourous fighter against foreign rule.

We thus have the Maulana telling us that Jesus was not divine on the ground that to attribute divinity to him would contradict the unity of God, that to entertain the notion that Jesus is the Son of God is 'clear infidelity to God'. He says that it is their

'excessive zeal in religious matters' which has led the Christians
to raise Jesus to the status of God and thereby to arrive at notions
such as the Trinity. In proclaiming Jesus to be the Son of God,
the Maulana says, Christians have taken 'undue advantage' of
Jesus speaking of God as 'Father'. In accordance with the Quran
the Maulana says that the doctrine of Christ being the Son of
God is 'a clear invention of his followers.' In talking of what he
calls the 'serious error' of the Christians in putting Jesus and Mary
at par with God, the Maulana says that notions such as this and
the Trinity are things which the Christians have 'coined for
themselves'. He attributes the notion of the crucifixion of Jesus to
the 'delusion' of those who sought to kill him. (See, for instance
Abul Kalam Azad, *The Tarjuman al-Quran*, Syed Abdul Latif
Trust, Hyderabad, Vol. 2, pp. 157, 269, 273, 288, 328, 309-10; Vol.
3, pp. 391, 399-405.)

Christian scholars on the other side have through the
centuries cast the strongest aspersions on the Prophet for what
he said about the contents of their Bible, in particular on his
reports that Allah had told him about Christians and Jews
corrupting their scriptures and departing from the message that
He had sent them. They have dubbed the Prophet's objections
to Jesus having been 'begotten' as 'silly'. They have attributed
his opposition to the notion of the Trinity to the fact that he
mistook them to imply that the Trinity referred to the Father,
Mother and Son and that as this 'sexualised' the concept it became
anathema to him. They have referred to his reconstruction of the
principal sacrament of the Christians as 'stupid'.

They have attributed the fact that in recounting many of
the events mentioned in the Old Testament and in the Gospels, the
accounts in the Quran differ from the accounts in the Jewish and
Christian scriptures to the fact that the Prophet had no direct access
to the scriptures, that he, went by fragments of information which
he picked up about these stories from minor, often heretical sects
which wandered about Arabia in those days. They have gone
further and maintained that even these stories he could not
recount fully as he had but a short memory and that therefore
his retelling of them was often not of what he had heard as
of what he thought he had heard from these persons who
themselves had no comprehensive knowledge of the contents of
the scriptures. Many of course have gone much, much further and

questioned the fact of revelation itself – attributing the successive revelations to psychological and other 'maladies' which they say afflicted the Prophet. (As two relatively tame examples, see Duncan Black Macdonald, *Aspects of Islam*, Macmillan, London, 1911, pp. 247-48, and Richard Bell, *The Origin of Islam in its Christian Environment,* Macmillan, 1926, pp. 100-61.)

Muslim scholars have poured much scorn on the contradictions in the accounts of events given in the Old and New Testaments. They have asserted that the Christians deliberately removed many books from the Bible which bore out what was contained in the Quran about many events. (See, for instance, Sir Syed's *The Mohammedan Commentary on the Holy Bible*, Ghazepore, 1862, and Allygurh, 1865.) Jewish and Christian scholars in their turn have argued at great length and in scrupulous detail that what the Quran presents as revelations of Allah are just restatements, and in their reckoning restatements of garbled versions of what is stated in the self-same Old and New Testaments. (As representatives of the genre see Abraham Katsh, *Judaism in Islam*, New York University Press, 1954; W. St. Clair Tisdall, *The Sources of Islam,* T. & J. Clark, Edinburgh, 1901; Richard Bell, *The Origin of Islam in its Christian Environment*, *op. cit.*, and his *Introduction to the Quran,* Edinburgh University Press, 1953, pp. 139-172.) Scholars have emphasised that this all-too-obvious concordance had led to unease even in the time of the Prophet. Some accused the two important transmitters of traditions – Kab al-Ahbar and Wahb b. Munnabih – of smuggling Jewish legends into the Prophet's consciousness and narratives. This charge of *Israliyat* became a matter of vigorous contestation. (See, for instance, A. Guillaume, *The Traditions of Islam, An introduction to the study of Hadith literature,* Khayats, Beirut, 1966; and G.H.A. Juynboll, *The Authenticity of the Tradition Literature*, E.J. Brill, Leiden, 1969.)

While Muslim scholars have questioned some of the miracles attributed to Jesus in the New Testament – for instance, that of the clay birds – Jewish and Christian scholars have shown how, from the position in the Quran where the Prophet is seen consistently to refuse to perform miracles for establishing his authenticity, saying that the Quran itself is the miracle that he has brought, over the centuries miracle after miracle similar to the ones reported in the case of Jesus came to be attributed to

Muhammad. (See, for instance, Ignaz Goldziher, 'Hadith and New Testament,' in *Muslim Studies*, 1890, Allen and Unwin 1971, Vol. 2, pp. 346-62.)

Such is the history of the fierce polemics. But now the mere recalling of a few verses about Jesus from the Quran itself leads the propagandists to charge that I am trying to divide Muslims and Christians, that I am trying to disrupt what has hitherto been a close and cordial sharing of dogma, to disrupt what has been a shared and common reverence for all prophets – Jesus as much as Muhammad.

What is Really Happening

We can see well from these examples what context it is that is changing: not the context of the revelation, but the context of the commentator. As the latter context changes, chiefly as the Muslim elite has power or does not have it *vis-a-vis* others, one set of verses is picked up and projected as being the essence of the Quran. To do so is not to interpret the Quran, much less to live it. It is to select from it what is convenient.

Surely, this is hardly the way to proceed in relation to a book that one reveres. It is to reduce a Holy Book to a manual for legitimising our convenience of the moment.

And it is undesirable for another reason: such sleights of mind, such procedures of reading 'context' into the plain teachings of the Book leave followers and their readers without an anchor. They legitimise opportunism and hypocrisy. They yoke a Holy Book to the task of doing so.

Context-mongering thus is to be shunned at all costs.

The Greater Problem

The point is fortified by two further considerations. As can be gleaned from the six canonical collections of the *hadis*, information about the precise context in which each revelation occurred is fragmentary, it is often contradictory. And, as can also be seen from the *hadis*, the Prophet as well as his companions themselves used to cite individual verses, and fragments of individual verses, in several *different* contexts.

But more important than all these is another consideration. It is a basic one. Indeed, it is fatal to the context-mongers.

And that consideration is this: the Quran is said not just to be true in some undefined, general sort of way. Every word in it is said to be true and eternally so, to be true in all circumstances, in all contexts. The faithful cannot but adhere to this position in the strictest sense. In fact, it is this belief, and everything that follows from it, which makes a person a believer. Thus, for instance, consider the position of the Quran *vis-a-vis* that of the Prophet; the Quran is venerated not because it was given to humanity by the Prophet: the Prophet is venerated because it was through him that Allah chose to bequeath the Quran to humanity.

The Sunnis cannot have even the little room for manoeuvre which some Shiites have tried to retain. As is well known, these Shiite sects have maintained that the Quran is the *created word of Allah*. As it is the created word of Allah, they have held, it can be reinterpreted, some would hold even revised, added to, subtracted from *by some other entity* – for instance, another Prophet *–who has also been created by Allah.*

This view has been denounced as heresy by the orthodox – maintaining as they do with Abu Hanifa, that '... he who says that the word of God is created is an infidel.' They have declared instead that the Quran is the *uncreated word of Allah*, that it has existed unchanged from and will continue to exist unchanged to eternity. This view has of course led to complications of the kind that have plagued the Advaitins who have tried to impute the same status to the Vedas – the complication, namely that if the Quran has existed co-equally with Allah, the undifferentiated unity of the latter before He created the universe etc. is ruptured. But for the moment, all that concerns us is the fact that, being the uncreated word of Allah, the Quran is context-proof, every word of it is true in all circumstances, in all contexts.

That is the position. That position is the hallmark of their faith. And our propagandists are so rash that to overcome a momentary difficulty they violate the fundamental tenet of the faith, they confine the Quran to the pen of specific contexts.

An example or two will perhaps bring home to them how great an injury they inflict by their argument.

Assume for a moment that some old book on geography or cosmology says that the earth is flat, stretched like a carpet in a Bedouin's tent, that the sky is a roof or tent over it, that it does not fall upon us because it is held up by God, that mountains have been placed on the flat earth as heavy rocks on a carpet so that it may not shake like us when the storms blow. Assume that some old geography book says all this. We can set it aside without any qualm today. We can say that the author had written all this before Magellan sailed around the world in his ships and proved it round, we can proceed on the assumption that things stated in that text need not now be taken seriously as the book was written in the Pre-Magellanian context.

But if the Quran says so (and it does; cf: *Quran*, 2.20, 13.3, 21.33, 22.64, 31. 8-9, 78.6, 91.6) we must take the assertions to be facts, facts that are true not just in 'the pre-Magellanian context', but true for ever. No believer can dismiss the affirmations as even sympathetic Christian authorities on Islam like William Montgomery Watt are apt to do, i.e. as being just the remnants 'of the simple picture of the world presumably held by the pre-Islamic Arabs of the desert' (W.M. Watt, *Islamic Revelation in the Modern World*, Edinburgh, 1969, p. 38). For it is not some pre-Islamic Arab who is speaking in the Quran. It is Allah Himself.

What holds for some thousand-year-old book on geography holds equally for a book that is revered by some other religion, say, the Bible. The orthodox Muslim can without any qualm find fault with its account of creation — God creating the universe in six days and then resting on the Sabbath as He felt tired etc. He can dismiss the account as being pre-scientific, as having been rendered obsolete by what we now know of the way in which and the time over which the earth took its present shape, about the way man evolved. He can dismiss it as being an account which we ought to discard in the post-Copernicus, post-Darwin context.

But when Allah tells us in the Quran that He created the heavens and the earth in six days (9.3, 11.9), that He created the heavens, the earth and in addition everything between them in six days (25.60, 32.3, 50.37, 57.5), that He created the earth in two days, its sustenance in four days, and demarcated the heavens into seven in two days (41.7-12), when the Prophet supplements this with the data that just as there are seven heavens there are seven earths, one beneath the other with a distance between each equal to 500 years' journey (*Mishkat al-Masabih*, Book 26, Chapter 1, Part 3), the believer must take all this to be true, to have been true always, and to be true for evermore.

The believer can, as Muslim scholars have done for centuries, scoff with Thomas Paine at the fact that the Bible describes creation twice and the two accounts differ, and on that ground alone he can dismiss both the accounts. But when he notices the apparent discrepancy between the various statements of the Quran on the matter (for instance, among those quoted above), or between what Allah says in the Quran and what is attributed to the Prophet ('Allah created the earth on Saturday, created the mountains in it on Sunday, created the trees on Monday, created what is objectionable on Tuesday, created light on Wednesday, set forth the animals in the earth on Thursday, and created Adam in the late afternoon on Friday....', *Mishkat al - Masabih*, Book 26, Chapter 17, Part 3) the believer must not dismiss either of the contradictory accounts. He must contemplate the matter, till he comes to see the contradiction as being only a paradox.

The believer can dismiss with impunity the usual fables about *jinns* and angels and spirits, but he cannot but take every verse in the Quran about them to be true and wholly and eternally so. (And Allah talks repeatedly in the Quran about *jinns* and angels and spirits, about the good ones among them and the evil.) How can he set these aside on the ground that they date from 'a medieval-context', or from a context in which people had little knowledge of nature and its phenomena and were therefore apt to attribute some of these to *jinns* and spirits? For in the verses it is not some medieval scholar but Allah who is testifying to their reality, to their nature. To hold anything else would be to reduce the Quran to the level of any other book containing stories of *jinns* and spirits, of devils and angels.

Assume that some conventional book or law — the Indian Evidence Act, say, or the Criminal Procedure Code, or one of our laws governing marriage or divorce — lays down that the charge of adultery will be taken to be established only if four testify that they have themselves — i.e., with their own eyes — witnessed the act of adultery. We can scoff at it, and demand that the requirement be changed — it being almost impossible to expect that adulterous couples will be so obliging as to copulate to the gaze of four eye-witnesses. But when the Quran lays this down as the test (as it does in 4.19), then that is the test which must hold forever.

And it is no argument to say that the requirement is relevant only for the context in which it was revealed – namely, the allegation against the Prophet's favourite wife, Aisha, herself, when she was found missing from the caravan and turned up later riding a camel with a passerby (cf: *Quran*, Sura 24; *Sahih Muslim*, 35.6673).

Is the verse (59.76) 'whatever the Messenger has given you, take; what he has refused you, refuse,' to be confined merely to the distribution of booty after a particular victory, that is to the event which sparked the revelation, or is to be taken as it has been by the faithful through the centuries to refer to the entire corpus of revelations received through the Messenger of Allah, Muhammad? Are the verses (74.11-25) to warn us against the acquisitive greed in each of us or are they to be taken to refer to the acquisitive nature of one unbeliever alone – Wahid b. Mugriah?

If rules and the edicts of the Quran are to be confined in this way to merely the occasions on which they were revealed, hardly any of them would be left. That much follows from the pattern of the Quran itself. The Book was not revealed to the Prophet in one go. Nor was it revealed in any systematic order. It was revealed bit by bit, verse by verse, sometimes part-of-a-verse by part-of-a-verse over several years. Each verse was revealed in response to a particular situation, a particular crisis, a particular problem. To now confine the edict or rule or notion enshrined in the verse to the specific context in which the latter was revealed is to completely destroy the universality of the Quran, to destroy the very feature, that is, which is said by the faithful to mark the Quran out as the Book of Books.

Nor can one sever parts of the Quran one from the other – one cannot say, for instance, that the parts dealing with geography, and cosmology, and *jinns* and spirits are superseded by subsequent knowledge and therefore need not be taken seriously but the ones dealing with divorce and alimony are eternal. No part is any less, and no part any more the revelation of Allah than any other part.

In fact, the very ones who are now saying that the verses on Jesus and *Jihad* are dated, that these pertained only to the contexts in which they were revealed, are the very ones who just a few months ago, in the context of the Shah Bano controversy, were saying that the provisions of the Quran are eternal and just cannot be disregarded or altered or confined to any particular context (e.g., that of medieval Arabia) without destroying Islam itself.

In brief, the only position that the believer can possibly take in regard to each and every verse of the Quran is the one taken by Shah Waliullah, the founder of Muslim revivalism in the subcontinent, and other teachers – namely, that the universality of the provisions of the Quran must not be shackled to the context or occasion of the particular revelation, that the provisions must be taken as absolute, applicable in all conditions and situations, limited only by their sense and by what is provided in other verses. (See, for instance, G.N. Jalbani, *The Teachings of Shah Waliullah of Delhi*, Ashraf, Lahore, 1967, pp. 17-19; and A.D. Muztar, *Shah Waliullah, A Saint-Scholar of Muslim India*, National Commission of Historical Research Islamabad, 1977, pp. 94-95.)

The alternative course will leave the propagandists providing not interpretations of the Quran, but *selections* of it. That course will knock the bottom out of their claim to be believers, to say nothing of their claim to be the spokesmen of the faith.

Is the convenience of the moment so compelling that they should desert their claims altogether?

November 1988

New Troubles

XV

The Troubles at Jamia

The Point We Evade

' "....I think the ban should be lifted," says Mushir-ul-Hasan, Pro-Vice Chancellor of Jamia Millia Islamia,' reported SUNDAY. 'I think', Hasan told the correspondent, 'every person has a right to be heard and to be read.' He added that, as happens in all cases of this sort, banning Rushdie's book had given it greater notoriety and in addition given our country the image of being 'intolerant and undemocratic'. As such the ban in his view, the report said, 'qualifies as an indefensible move'.

Students of Jamia Millia Islamia paralysed the university. Liberals got up and acted − that is, they wrote a letter to the editor saying Hasan had a right to speak his mind. Hasan buckled, issuing three statements 'clarifying' his position: he expressed 'sincere and profound regret over my remarks' and maintained that he had never wished to demand that the ban on Rushdie's book be lifted.

The liberals were at a loss for words.

Now, none of us may sit in judgment on a man beleaguered. Anyone of us may react in the same way. Rushdie himself had felt compelled to announce his re-conversion to being a Believer and to express regrets for the hurt the book had caused. The point at issue thus is not Hasan's courage but the pressure which the students have felt entitled to exert on him and how, even while castigating it as undemocratic, the liberals have flinched from talking about the set of beliefs which lead the protagonists to the conviction that they are entitled to bend another man, that they are entitled to silence him.

Two phases

Each time a controversy like this arises, and the facts are pointed out, we are told that actually Islam preaches tolerance and peace. Allah, we are reminded, told the Prophet, 'Let there be no compulsion in religion: Truth stands out clear from error...' (Quran, 2.256); that He told him to 'Invite (all) to the Way of Thy Lord with wisdom and beautiful preaching, and persuade them in ways that are best and most gracious...' (Quran, 16.125); that He admonished Muslims, 'And if ye catch them out, (in a controversy), catch them out no worse than they catch you out' and that the best course is to show 'forbearance' (16.126). 'O, unbelievers,' Allah urges Mohammed to tell them, '.... to you your religion, and to me my religion' (109.5).

But the fact is that these conciliatory verses pertain to the earlier period when the Prophet was trying to persuade the various clans in Mecca, including those who made their living off the various idols in the Kaba. Once he had to leave for Medina, and specially after he began welding the Arabs into a State, Allah commanded him to be harsh in the extreme. Reviewing the drastic change, and recalling the new commands to fight the unbelievers so that they either submitted or were put to death, the famous Iranian scholar Ali Dashti says in his Twenty Three Years : A study in the Prophethood of Mohammed, 'Mohammed's announcement of this edict ... indicates that with Islam in power, polite and rational discussion with dissentials was no longer deemed necessary. The language of future discourse with them was to be the language of the sword.' 'Mohammed is the Messenger of Allah,' Allah proclaimed, 'and those who are with him are hard against the unbelievers, merciful one to another...' (48.29). Allah repeatedly warned the faithful that many will say one thing in their presence and another when 'they are alone with their evil'. They shall spare nothing to ruin you, Allah warned the faithful, they yearn for you to suffer; 'Hatred has already shown itself of their mouths, and what their breasts conceal is yet greater,' He warned. 'They but wish that ye should reject Faith as they do, and be on the same footing (as them),' He warned. Do not take them as friends, He admonished, be harsh in dealing with them (for instance, Quran, 2.14-16, 3.118-120, 4.89, 4.140, 5.60.)

'They swear by God that they said nothing (evil),' Allah

pointed out in a vital verse that the agitators will find apposite, 'but indeed they uttered blasphemy. And they did it after accepting Islam; and they meditated a plot which they are unable to carry out: this revenge of theirs was (their) only return for the bounty with which God and His Apostle had enriched them! If they repent, it will be best for them. But if they turn back (to their evil ways), Allah will punish them with a grievous penalty in this life and in the hereafter. They shall have none on earth to protect them or help them' (9.74). 'O, Prophet,' Allah therefore commanded, 'strive hard against the unbelievers and the Hypocrites, and be firm against them. Their abode is Hell – an evil refuge indeed' (9.73).

How are Rushdie and Hasan – both Muslims, both whom Allah has enriched by His bounty of the one true faith – to be dealt with in terms of such commands? Where is the room in any of this for the principle liberals cherish, namely that, 'Every person has a right to be heard and be read'?

The point is this: while liberals etc. always take comfort in the revelations Allah had sent down to the Prophet when the latter was yet alone and his followers few, and try to make out that a liberal Islam can be founded on these, Islam itself has been founded on the commandments to harshness which Allah sent down once the Prophet had established himself in Medina. The entire history of Islamic rule bears testimony to this.

The Prophet's Example

In instances such as those of Rushdie the point is even sharper, there is in fact no room for relenting. And the reason for that is two-fold. Islam is founded on, it revolves around the personality of the Prophet. Any thing that casts a shadow on that personality is therefore taken to undermine Islam. There was of course, as has been pointed out, an attempt – for instance by the Asharite school, in particular by its great theologian, al-Baqillani – to maintain that the central thing was the Revelation – the Quran – the one through whom it was made being of lesser importance. But it was soon evident how such a position would leave Islam vulnerable, and so most have insisted that the Prophet's conduct, motives, personality must not be called into question in any way. This position leaves no room for Rushdie.

But there is not just the negative point – 'If such licence is allowed in regard to the Prophet, Islam itself will be endangered' – there is the positive example. The Prophet's life, what he said and did, is the ideal example which every Muslim must aspire to follow – in every particular, and to the fullest extent.

Now, the Prophet himself was very particular about what people said about him. Upon conquering Mecca for instance the Prophet proclaimed an amnesty for all except six persons who, he ordered, must be killed wherever and whenever they were found: his previous scribe who had said that he had renounced Islam upon seeing that the Prophet altered the text of the Revelations at his – i.e., the scribe's – prompting (he was saved by his proximity to Othman, though against the Prophet's inclination); two slave girls who were reported to have sung satires about him, and their master etc. Similarly, Abu Afak was killed although he was well over a hundred years of age: the Prophet himself ordered the killing of this 'rascal' as he called Afak, as the latter had tried to make light of him. The killing of a man so old led a poetess – Asma b. Marwan – to compose verses criticising the Prophet. She too was therefore killed – 'She was sleeping with her children about her,' writes Maxime Rodinson in his well known biography of the Prophet. 'The youngest, still at the breast, lay asleep in her arms. He (Umr ibn Adi, who had been spurred by the Prophet's 'will no one rid me of this daughter of Marwan?') drove his sword through her, and in the morning he went to Mohammed. "Messenger of God," he said, "I have killed her!" "You have done a service to Allah and his Messenger, Umayr", was the reply...' These and other killings are listed in every canonical biography of the Prophet, they are listed among the expeditions of early Islam. As they originated from the Prophet whose words and deeds are the ideal which every Muslim must emulate, they constitute the norm. (To get the flavour of the Prophet's attitude to those who sought to mock him the reader will do well to read one of the most revered and earliest biographies of the Prophet – Ibn Ishaq's *Sirat Rasul Allah* which is available in the translation of the great Islamicist, A. Guillaume: *The Life of Mohammed*, Oxford University Press, Karachi, 1978, in particular, pp. 307-8, 364-9, 550-1, and 675-6 for the incidents mentioned above.)

These examples were soon codified in treatises. Annemarie Schimmel, a diligent and also one of the most sympathetic scholars of Islam, summarizes in her *And Mohammed is His Messenger* the position as it came to be. She writes : 'For how could one defame or slander a person whose name is mentioned close to that of God in the second half of the profession of faith? If someone should commit this sin, he has to be asked to return to Islam; if he refuses, he has to be put to death. Other authorities went farther; the slanderer of the Prophet was declared to deserve immediate capital punishment, which could not be averted even by contrition. And indeed Islamic historians now and then report that someone was either executed legally or lynched by an enraged mob when he had been overheard slandering the Prophet. It is ironic that one of the greatest theologians in Islamic history, the medieval reformist Ibn Taimiyya, was sentenced to heavy punishment because of his alleged "lack of veneration" for the Prophet when he spoke up against certain unhealthy exaggerations in the popular cult of the Prophet in Damascus, such as the veneration of his footprint.....'

'Reports of Muhammad's own reactions to slander and insult are contradictory,' Schimmel continues. 'Many *hadith* emphasise the Prophet's mildness and generosity in such cases; others found it necessary to give a much harder picture of his reactions. An example of the latter is Ibn Taimiyya – once himself accused of lack of reverence for the Prophet! – who composed a special work with the telling title *As-sarim al-maslul alaa shatim ar-rasuul* (The Sword Drawn against the Vilifier of the Prophet), in which he states that "whoever vilifies a prophet is to be killed and whoever vilifies his Companions is to be flogged". The latter sentence is of course directed against the Shiites, who curse the first three caliphs and other Companions....'

Freedom of speech in this setting? Taking back Khomeni's *fatwa* in view of such precedents?

It is this central fact – that the only sort of freedom of speech which Islam sanctions is the freedom to laud it – which the liberals do not want to face. But unless they do so, they will in each round be reduced to doing what they were to in this instance : writing a letter to the editor one day, and falling silent the next.

The Worsening Position

The situation in India is far worse than it is in other countries. The French Marxist scholar Maxime Rodinson's biography of the Prophet, *Mohammed*, is freely available in India and abroad: its English edition is published by Penguin. Among the things he does is to trace the Revelations which appeared from time to time – specially the ones pertaining to personal law – to the personal dilemmas the Prophet was facing at that turn. On the Prophet's order, Rodinson recalls, a caravan is way-laid, blood is shed in doing so; this has happened in the holy month; there is much consternation; but Allah intervenes revealing to the Prophet that while shedding blood in the holy month was a serious matter, the offences of the Meccans had been greater. After what is said to be a conspiracy to kill him, the Prophet lays siege to the Jewish tribe Nadir; to force their surrender he begins felling their palm trees; this causes great consternation, given how vital palm trees are in the desert to one and all; Allah intervenes and reveals to the Prophet that he had a right to do what he did. A scandal erupts when the Prophet's young wife, Ayesha, rejoins a caravan riding the camel with some other man; the Prophet is most disconsolate; Allah intervenes revealing to the Prophet that Ayesha is blameless, and asks the Prophet to have the accusers produce four eyewitnesses to the alleged act, which of course they can not. After a very delicate fiasco involving the Coptic Mariya, his wife Hafsa, and him, the Prophet resolves to spend the whole month with Mariya and to have nothing to do with any of his wives for an entire month; but on the twenty-ninth day he visits Ayesha; she remonstrates with him reminding him of his oath; Allah intervenes, revealing to the Prophet that he is absolved from his oaths, that he may divorce any or all of his wives, that he may interchange their days and the rest. The Prophet has adopted Zayd ibn Haritha as his son; he marries Zayd to his cousin Zaynab bint Jahsh; by a chain of coincidences the Prophet begins wondering whether he should himself marry Zaynab; he apprehends the opprobrium which will follow his marrying his daughter-in-law; he is in much turmoil even after Zayd has told him that he will willingly give Zaynab to him; Allah intervenes, telling the Prophet to fear not men but Him, and asks him to marry Zaynab. Revelations of this kind follow revelations − from whether, contrary to earlier revelations, the Prophet may take a Jewish girl captured as booty as his wife, whether, contrary to earlier revelations, a marriage may be consummated the same day the girl is obtained..... And so on. Rodinson sets the incidents out at length and the revelations they occasioned, recalling Ayesha's jest about how ready Allah seemed to be to answer her husband's wishes, and hypothesizes that the Revelations we revere were the working out − in the way made familiar by Freud − of the Prophet's unconscious. Now, this work is available freely, the English edition having been published by the Penguin Group. Imagine the howl which would have gone up if the book had been written by an Indian.

Ali Dashti's *Twenty Three Years* to which I have referred earlier shows in graphic detail how the Prophet's attitude to one thing after another − to power, to the Jews, to those who did not fall in line, to women − changed after his position in Medina became secure. Recalling the sea-change in the Prophet's personality, he writes, '... Like Jesus, he was (in the Meccan period) full of compassion. After the move to Madina, however, he became a relentless warrior, intent on spreading his religion by the sword, and a scheming founder of a state. A Messiah was transformed into a David. A man who had lived for more than twenty years with one wife became inordinately fond of women.' Ali Dashti sets these changes out in detail − showing in the process how the accounts which have been given to explain away the Prophet's numerous marriages, for example, do not hold, and listing twenty women he formally married and several incidents connected with them. He sets out the process by which power was consolidated, writing, 'To this end every sort of expedient was considered permissible, regardless of consistency with the spiritual and moral precepts which were being taught.' 'Among the events of the period,' he writes, 'were political assassinations, raids which were manifestly unprovoked, and attacks on tribes who had not acted aggressively but were reported by spies to be restless or unsympathetic to the Moslems...' Reviewing the increasing intransigence of the rules and exactions in this period he writes, 'Thus Islam was gradually transformed from a purely spiritual mission into a militant and punitive organization whose progress depended on booty from raids and revenue from the *zakat* tax ...' He narrates how the fear of the Prophet became the thing on account of which people submitted. Now, this book is freely available abroad, the English version having been published by George Allen & Unwin. The same book, had it been written by an Indian, would have called forth demands for a ban, demands which would certainly have prevailed.

And the situation in India has been getting worse over the years. Imagine one of us – who happens to be a Hindu – writing today, 'Excepting our own almost all the other great religions in the world are inevitably connected with the life or lives of one or more of their founders. All their theories, their teachings, their doctrines, and their ethics are built round the life of a personal founder, from whom they get their sanction, their authority, and their power: and strangely enough, upon the historicity of the founder's life is built, as it were, all the fabric of such religions. If there is one blow dealt to the historicity of that life, as has been the case in modern times with the lives of almost all the so-called founders of religions – we know that half of the details of such lives is not now seriously believed in, and that the other half is seriously doubted – if this becomes the case, if that rock of historicity, as they pretend to call it, is shaken and shattered, the whole building tumbles down, broken absolutely, never to regain its lost status...' There would be a howl – 'fascism', 'cultural imperialism' – and demands that the book be kept out of schools and universities. Yet the passage is Swami Vivekananda's – and he makes the point repeatedly in almost identical words.

Imagine a scholar today referring to the 'obvious defects of the Koran,' to the 'crudities of the Koran'. Imagine a scholar casting doubts on the revelations which came to the Prophet characterizing the claim to having received them to be a 'dubious claim', and saying about such claims, 'Such experiences always result from cerebral disorder which takes place whenever the prescribed practices are carried too far. Fixed ideas, however fantastic or imaginary, may appear to take concrete form if the mind is focused on them so as to exclude the consciousness of other sensations. A scientific study of the psychology of seers reveals the fact that "inspiration" or any other "religious experience" is the result of a pathological state brought about either accidentally or purposely through prescribed practices.' Imagine the scholar going further and writing that when Muhammad himself doubted the 'psycho-pathological symptoms' and feared that he was going mad, it was his wife, 'the worldly wise' Khadija, who stepped in and 'was quick to appreciate the spiritual value of the mental aberrations of her husband. She persuaded him that his visions were not signs of insanity, but were messengers of God. Taking advantage of his psycho-pathological state of suggestibility, she could easily make him "see" an angel entering the room to deliver to him the Message of God...' Imagine a scholar writing this today – the book would be pounded on, effigies of the author burned...

Yet the sentences are from that most effusive – and one of the shallowest apologias of Islam: MN Roy's *The Historical Role of Islam*. In brief, the situation has worsened over the decades. No one today could write even this much, and it is only the good fortune that our enthusiasts do not read these older books which allows them to continue in circulation.

The point about Khomeini's *Fatwa* is that it has worked: it has intimidated into silence scholars and writers all over the world. And the agitation against Hasan will work too: it took three years for a Muslim scholar to say as much – or, as little – as he did. It will take twice that many years for another one to say half as much.

And no one has contributed to making these things work, to smothering free inquiry and speech in this vital sphere as the liberals and secularists. We supported the ban on Rushdie's book at that time, writes a leading commentator, as we knew the reactions the book would provoke.

Is that 'prudence' not the precise thing which goads the fundamentalists to work up a fury each time they want to have their way? Is that not what they are doing now?

* * *

From That to This

The Jamia is a Muslim institution; the Vice Chancellor the government has appointed is an Ahmediya; We do not recognize Ahmediyas as Muslim; the Vice Chancellor should therefore be removed – that is the logic the Janata Dal MP, Mohammed Afzal, expounds on the floor of the Rajya Sabha.

The cry is picked up by Imam Bukhari: the Vice Chancellor is an Ahmediya, he should be removed, the Imam tells the faithful who have gathered for the Friday prayers.

'He is the real enemy of Islam', Tavleen Singh quotes Abu Nafe, a leader of the Students Islamic Organization, hectoring the Jamia students about the Prime Minister. 'For two reasons: he opened diplomatic relations with Israel and he put a Qadiani as head of Jamia Millia.'

Nor is the Vice Chancellor, Bashiruddin Ahmed, the only one who has been made a target on the charge, among others of course, that he belongs to a particular sect of Islam. There has been the under-tow of insinuations in the case of the Pro-Vice Chancellor, Mushirul Hasan, himself: one of the reasons he is being targeted, it has been urged, is that he is a Shia and the Sunnis are not able to stomach a Shia occupying such a high position in a Muslim institution.

All this − to say nothing of the role in inflaming the agitation of those who have built an illegal colony on the Jamia's land they have grabbed − at the Jamia Millia Islamia. That is, at the *National* Muslim University. That name is no accident. It bears testimony to that electric circumstance in which the University was founded, it calls to mind the ideals for which it was nurtured, it testifies even more to the way its life was intertwined with our national movement for freedom.

That Electric Moment

It was indeed an electric moment. Mahatma Gandhi had launched the non-cooperation movement against the British government's obduracy over the Rowlatt laws and the Caliphate. He had called upon teachers and students to boycott colleges and schools which received government aid or were run by it. The Ali Brothers had drawn his attention to the college at Aligarh (now the Aligarh Muslim University). Some students − led by the young Zakir Hussain − had invited Gandhiji to address the students.

Gandhiji wrote to the Trustees: please forgo the government grant; if you don't, the students will be justified in boycotting the College. The Trustees were true to Sir Syed Ahmed's teaching: they were overwhelmingly pro-British. They spurned the suggestion. Gandhiji and Mohammed Ali came to address the students. The meeting was a fiasco. Zakir − who could not return to Aligarh to be in time for the meeting − and others were crestfallen.

But in the next few days more meetings were held. Zakir Hussain, M. Mujeeb, K.G. Saiyidain .... and about 200   other students announced their decision to leave the Aligarh College. Mohammed Ali led them out in a procession to an open space.

Arguments ensued as to what should be done next: we should not vacate the premises even if the police belabour us, Mohammed Ali maintained; storm the police, the firebrand poet Hazrat Mohani maintained. Eventually, as the biographer of Hakim Ajmal Khan records, it was the   sage   counsel of Hakim   Sahib which prevailed: let us set up   a   new institution.

And so Jamia came to be set up at Aligarh − as one of the four national universities,   alongwith   the   Vidyapeeths at Bihar, Kashi   and Gujarat, which were founded to provide education to students and jobs to teachers who had left colleges and schools in response to Gandhiji's call.

Instruction   began in tents which Hakim Ajmal Khan   had arranged, and was shifted eventually to a few rented rooms.

The   fever of Khilafat subsided. There was no money to run the institution. Hakim Sahib, Dr. M.A. Ansari and others thought it best to shift it to a house in Karol Bagh in Delhi. Gandhiji concurred. Eventually 100 acres were bought for it in far away Okhla for Rs. 10,000   and its first building was begun.

Its Character

From their first breath to their last the great men who nurtured it − Hakim Sahib, Dr. M.A. Ansari, the chancellors, Dr. Zakir Hussain, its Vice Chancellor for three decades, Dr. M. Mujeeb, Dr. K.G. Saiyidain and their associates − sought to create an institution in the service of the national movement for freedom, a fount of brotherhood and   inclusiveness. Each student was to be made the true servant of India by being imbued with the pristine qualities of his   religious and ethical tradition, by becoming, as Professor Mujeeb was to record later, 'cultured, modest, thoughtful and competent.'

This was the refrain from beginning to end. We have Hakim Sahib in 1921 delivering the first Convocation Address as the *Amir-i Jamia,* that is as its Chancellor − 'We have in view,' he declares, 'the ideal of creating the sense of service towards

the country together with Islam....' We see him in December 1927
on one of his last journeys : ailing and scarcely able to bear the
strain, he has travelled all the way to Bombay to wait upon the
King of Afghanistan so that he may acquaint the King with Jamia,
a university, Hakim Sahib says, 'established by the Muslims of
India with a view to promote nationalism and also to enlarge their
mental horizons.' We have Dr. M.A. Ansari, since Hakim Sahib's
passing away the *Amir-i Jamia,* now himself ailing, at the
foundation stone laying ceremony of the building at the new site
in Okhla in 1935 – 'We desire to build an institution which, while
being Islamic in its traditions, will be national in its outlook.'
From beginning to end, that was the refrain: secular learning, as
well as being steeped in our traditions, so as to serve our country.

The traditions they talked of were, to recall Professor Mujeeb's
words, 'the common culture of the region,' – 'the Hindu-Muslim
culture of the 19th and 20th centuries.' The Islam they talked of
was to be a tolerant, compassionate, wide-open Islam: 'catholicity
and inclusiveness,' as Mujeeb recounts in his fine biography of
Dr. Zakir Hussain, were the key words.

'The syllabi,' records Hakim Sahib's biographer, 'made it
compulsory for the Muslim students to learn Islamiat, so also it
was incumbent upon the Hindu students to study Hindu ethics.
Similarly, Hindi was made compulsory for those whose
mother-tongue was Urdu and *vice-versa.* The study of Arabic and
English was to start in Class IV. Sanskrit was made a compulsory
subject for the Hindu students. Similarly, craft was made a
compulsory subject from Class V onwards. Calligraphy was made
a part of the syllabi. It was expected of the Jamiaites to put on
khaddar since it was their own fabric.'

Dr. Zakir Hussain, Mujeeb notes, introduced painting, in spite
of the prohibition against visual representation, he had plays
written and staged, he introduced co-education. And at each step
Ajmal Khan, Zakir Hussain, as well as their associates were
attacked savagely by communal Muslim opinion, and by pro-
British Muslim clerics and politicians. 'It was really an irony
of circumstances,' the Hakim Sahib's biographer informs us, 'that
the Aligarh College authorities stooped to the lowest depth and
threw away all decency and decorum to the winds. The columns
of the *Aligarh Institute Gazette* were full of the vilest abuse
and all the available English and vernacular dailies were

requisitioned for the "propaganda of invection, calumny and scandal." But Hakim Saheb stood firm and behaved with unrivalled dignity and fortitude, keeping himself engaged in the building up of the infant institution.'

Dr. Zakir Hussain, specially after he chaired the committee set up to work out Gandhiji's scheme of Basic Education, came in for assaults even more virulent, but he too persevered with the same unruffled determination.

At every step Jamia was associated with the national movement for freedom. 'The Jamia, being a national institution,' we learn from the biography of Ajmal Khan, 'encouraged the constructive programme of Mahatma Gandhi. The use of *Charkha* and *Takli* became a routine with the Jamiaites as it promoted self-help, self-reliance and self-sufficiency.' The first contribution to the Mahatma's Swaraj Fund — the one he instituted in memory of the Lokmanya — was made by the faculty and students of Jamia. The University's teachers and products travelled far and wide throughout the country preaching Gandhiji's gospel. They stood emphatically against the two-nation theory which Aligarh espoused in keeping with Sir Syed's beliefs. Gandhiji's youngest son, Devdas, became a teacher at the Jamia. At his asking, Gandhiji sent Rasiklal, a grandson dear to him, to help him. Rasik, an idealist, merely 17, died being cared for by Dr. Ansari and others at Jamia.

How it was Sustained

And with what sacrifice it was sustained ! Hakim Ajmal Khan was always importuning those who came to him, those on whom he called to contribute to the University. In spite of the wide circle of his acquaintances it remained in the direst need. We have him donating to the Jamia a part of the amount which had been earmarked for his daughter's wedding , and asking the bridegroom's parents to do the same. We have Dr. Zakir Hussain and others fixing their salaries at Rs.100 ; we have them unable to pay themselves even that much; we have them deciding to receive only Rs. 50, the rest to be received as and when the University would have the requisite funds; we have them making do with money — Rs. 10 at a time — borrowed from the neighbourhood money-lender. We have Dr. Ansari going around

with 'a begging bowl' soliciting funds, Dr. Zakir Hussain
wearing his feet to blisters trudging from house to house in
Bombay beseeching people for funds.

The University is again and again at the point of being closed
down. And then Hakim Ajmal Khan dies on a visit to the Nawab
of Rampur. The future is dire indeed.

Throughout these trials, all those directing the affairs of
Jamia have been in touch with Gandhiji. When in 1927 Ajmal
Khan and others think that Iqbal is the man to have as Vice
Chancellor, it is to Gandhiji they turn. Gandhiji writes to the poet:
'The Muslim National University calls you. If you could but take
charge of it, I am sure that it will prosper under your cultured
leadership.... Your expenses on a scale suited to the new
awakening can be easily guaranteed. Please reply Allahabad,
care Pandit Nehru.' Iqbal begs off, 'for reasons of health.'

Gandhiji keeps in close touch with the Jamia. He heaps praise
on the work of Zakir Hussain and others. He writes to the
students, he visits them, he encourages them : 'Your number is
small,' he tells them, 'but the world never overflowed with good
and true men. I ask you not to worry yourselves about the
smallness of the number, but to remember that however few
you may be the freedom of the country depends on you....' When
Hakim Ajmal Khan dies, Gandhiji tells the students that he will
do everything in his power to put the Jamia on a sound financial
footing: 'let us keep his (Hakim Sahib's) memory for ever green,'
he tells them, 'by making the Jamia a living temple of unity.'
Gandhiji institutes a fund in his memory and appeals to the country
to contribute for the Jamia. A second appeal is issued jointly
by Gandhiji, Dr. Ansari, Zakir Hussain and Jamnalal Bajaj. That
the contributions are not sufficient pains him intensely. He
remonstrates with the readers of *Navjivan* : 'Let not the Jamia
Millia be crushed between two opposing forces. Since the Jamia
Millia does not nourish the present atmosphere of hatred, the
general Muslim masses appear indifferent towards it, and if the
Hindus too should be indifferent under the presumption that
Muslims alone should support it, the Jamia Millia will be
nowhere and Hakimji's memorial will meet the same fate....' Two
months later, he despairs: 'So far as the Jamia contributions are
concerned,' he writes to Dr. Ansari, 'I suspect that we shall do
nothing beyond getting collections from personal friends....' He

asks G.D. Birla to give Rs.75,000; Birla parts with Rs. 50,000; Jamnalal gives Rs.10,000. On tour in Rangoon, Gandhiji appeals to the local Gujaratis to contribute to the Jamia. He forwards to the Nawab of Bhopal what he describes as 'a pathetic letter' from Zakir Hussain about the penury to which the Jamia has been reduced and implores the Nawab to help.... He intervenes to shield Zakir Hussain and his dedicated colleagues from the imprecations of the rough Shaukat Ali and the unwieldy Committee of Control the latter has devised to impose upon the University.

Years pass. Ajmal Khan has passed away, saddened by the continuing violence among Hindus and Muslims over petty issues. Dr. Ansari has died, saddened by the same wretchedness. Gandhiji's own dreams lie asunder. It is April 1946. The killings have begun again, they are to reach a crest soon. Gandhiji has gone to an Ashram nearby. He is to return to his residence. 'But a number of students and some members of the staff from Jamia Millia came and requested him, some time to pay a visit to their institution too,' reports the *Harijan* of that week.

'"Some time must mean now," replied Gandhiji. "Having come so far I cannot go back without going to you",' the *Harijan* continues. 'The Jamia Millia group were overjoyed. They ran ahead of him to carry the happy tidings to their colleagues and returned with petromax lanterns to lead the way. The unexpected visit put the whole place in a flutter of excitement. Dr. Zakir Hussain was away at Bhawalpur. But Mujeebsaheb was there with other members of the staff. Carpets were spread on the lawn and a happy family gathering was held there under the sky...' "I have proved my claim to being a member of the family by coming without previous notice," Gandhiji begins. A student asks him what they can do for Hindu-Muslim unity. Gandhiji repeats the advice to which no one has been paying heed.

'In a corner of the Jamia grounds stood Dr. Ansari's tomb,' Pyarelal writes concluding the account of the visit. 'Before returning home Gandhiji made a pilgrimage to it. The doctor had been like a brother to Gandhiji. During his twenty-one days' self-purification fast at Poona in 1933 when Gandhiji's condition suddenly became critical, Gandhiji sent him a message at Delhi that he would love nothing better than to die in his lap.

Back came the good doctor's reply: he would not let him die either
in his or anyone else's lap! And interrupting his visit to Europe,
he hastened to the bedside of his friend to see him safely through
the fast. A platform thrown up into a series of terraces marked
the burial place. A plain marble tablet at the foot bore the doctor's
name and the dates of his birth and death. The austere simplicity
of the monument added to the poignancy of the visit....'

Our Times

From that 'catholic and inclusive' Islam to the cries of 'Ahmediyas are not Muslims,' to the cries of Shias versus Sunnis. From
students nurtured on those values – 'cultured, modest, thoughtful
and competent' – to the louts who have paralysed the University
today.

Nor is that all. The University was set up to be, and
functioned as a *National* Muslim University – as a University set
up to train Muslims for national service. Over the last two decades
fundamentalist elements have moved to capture it. The tussle over
the current Vice Chancellor and Pro-Vice Chancellor is their
final lunge at total control. That much is evident. And now see
the stupidity to which we have reduced our laws.

While Hindus as well as Muslims were associated with setting
up the University and sustaining it, while teachers and students
have been both Hindus and Muslims, the University today
is in the eyes of the law a minority institution in terms of Article
30 of the Constitution. This is so as it was set up primarily by
individuals who happened to be Muslims, and was meant to train
primarily Muslims.

By a series of judgments our courts have laid down that while
the State can intervene in the interests of making such an
institution function better as an educational institution, while it may
intervene to ensure that it serves the interests of the minority
community better, it *CANNOT* intervene to ensure that the
institution serves the national interest better. That is the law as it
stands today.

Thus, not just, 'From that Islam to this,' not just 'From those
students and teachers to these,' but from the days when a
University was set up to serve the national cause to the day in

which, by law, the national interest cannot be invoked to save it from fundamentalists....

* * *

Not just a Right, an Absolute Duty

'Whatever the original issue might have been, Mushirul Hasan has lost the confidence of a sizeable section of the students and the staff. He cannot now discharge the duties of a Pro-Vice Chancellor. For the sake of the University, so as to enable it to resume functioning, he should himself resign.'

As the fundamentalist argument – that by advocating that the ban on Rushdie's book be lifted Hasan had himself cast a slur on the Prophet – did not get them the support they needed, the fundamentalists have been urging the foregoing, pragmatic argument. And they make themselves out to be ever so reasonable: we are not saying he should be dismissed; we are only saying that he should himself, voluntarily resign. And it is all to be for the highest of purposes – it is only to enable the University which, they add with calculated magnanimity, Hasan has himself served with such distinction as a Professor, it is only to enable that University to resume functioning again. We would even go so far as to advocate, they say, that once he gives up his Pro-Vice Chancellorship, he should be allowed to continue as a Professor at the Jamia itself.

How reasonable it all sounds. And how wrong-headed it is.

An Absolute Duty

To give in to such a demand is to hand the University over to the louts who have been leading the agitation. Even if a removal or a resignation were to ensure peace for the moment, it would, by delivering the University to such elements, ensure its death. And a capitulation of this kind, wherever it occurs, becomes an encouragement, I would say an incitement to elements of this kind in Universities elsewhere to use the same methods, in fact to such elements in institutions in general to do so : work up a fury, everyone concludes, bring the place to a halt, so that the

pragmatists 'in the interests of the institution' cave in and concede
your demands.

'But no right is absolute,' the reasonable men say. 'No one
has a right to offend others. Having done that, the man must
pay the price.'

I shall come to the sense in which the right is less than
absolute in a moment. But the first point is that whether the
right is absolute or not, there is a duty which is absolute. In a
country where it has become standard practice to get one's way
by paralysing institutions, roads, whatever, by intimidating those
who disagree with one, to stand up to the bully, to NOT yield
to intimidation is an absolute duty. Unless these intimidators are
rolled back, unless some conspicuous defeats are inflicted on
them, we will be seeing the last of academic work, free speech,
in fact excellence and norms in general. And busy as we are being
buffetted from day to day, we do not realize how frequent – and
effective – these assaults have become. In the last fortnight alone
we have had not only the attacks on Bashiruddin Ahmed and
Mushirul Hasan at the Jamia. Dr. Abid Reza Bedar, the Director
of the Khuda Baksh Library – a man devoted to academic scholarship, a man who is the picture of humility and old-world
courtesy – has been terrorised in Patna, the performance of a play
in which Shabana Azmi was acting has had to be cancelled in
Calcutta. Their crimes? That the Director has had the temerity
to say that a book on the Quran makes a point worthy of notice
about the word 'kafir'. And Shabana Azmi's? That she gave an
assessment of Satyajit Ray which differed from what Congressmen in Bengal approve.

Notice that in none of these instances had the supposed
offender endangered any great purpose. Notice too that in each
instance the attack was based on a misrepresentation of what the
alleged offender had actually said. Notice too that in each
instance the fury was contrived – one look at those clamouring
for the resignations of Mushirul Hasan or Bedar, for instance, is
enough to convince one that they are not touched by piety or
devotion. Notice most of all that in each instance these persons
took the law in their own hands. A society that does not see the
duty to stand up to these fellows, to defeat their intimidation and
force them back is writing itself off as an orderly community.

'The Right is not Absolute'

And where does the point about the right to free speech not being absolute come in? Mushirul Hasan, Bedar etc. are not claiming that they have said what they have because they have an absolute – that is, unconditioned – right to say whatever they like. In Mushir's case, he merely said – in the most innocuous and restrained way possible, and that too only when asked to state his view by a correspondent – that the ban on Rushdie's book was proving counter-productive and should for that reason be lifted. In Bedar's case, he merely drew attention to the way a word – *kafir* – had been interpreted in a scholarly work. The point at issue thus is not whether the right to free speech is absolute or not, but whether we have or not the right to say the specific things which these persons said.

Moreover, the right to free speech is a limited one in a very specific sense. Article 19(1)(a) guarantees the right to free speech. Article 19(2) specifies the grounds on which restrictions may be placed on it. These grounds are the sovereignty and integrity of India, the security of the State, friendly relations with foreign States, public order, decency or morality, or to prevent contempt of court, defamation or incitement to an offence. Given the situation in India, most would grant that there are good reasons to restrict speech on these grounds. But two things are vital. This is an exhaustive list – that is, restrictions can be placed only on these grounds. And, as the Constitution states, the restrictions must be reasonable.

Clearly, only one of these grounds is relevant in the present context: that is, public order. But just as clearly, the mild remarks which Mushirul Hasan or Bedar made cannot be brought in under this ground at all. And that for several reasons.

The courts have held that to show that something is liable to create public disorder and therefore has to be restricted one has to show not merely that the particular speech or writing is liable to create a law and order problem, but that it is liable to cause a general – that is, pervasive, vast – breakdown of public order and peace. As the Supreme Court has said, 'the contravention of law always affects order but before it can be said to affect public order, it must affect the community or public at large,' it must be 'an aggravated disturbance of public peace,' affecting 'the general current of public life.' It is impossible to bring the mild remarks in question in the net of these requirements. In fact, the Supreme Court has gone further. In *S. Rangarajan vs P. Jagjivan Ram and others*, it nailed the public order bogey. It held first that the apprehended breakdown of public order as a consequence of the speech must be 'pressing', not 'remote, conjectural or far-fetched.' Furthermore, 'It should have *proximate* and *direct* nexus with the expression. The expression of thought should be *intrinsically dangerous* to the public interest. In other words, the expression should be *inseparably locked up* with the action contemplated like the equivalent of a "spark in a powder keg".'

The point in fact is even more telling in the present instance. For in each of these cases various groups for a host of motives — from acquiring control of the University to preventing eviction from lands they have usurped — have siezed upon the remarks and have deliberately worked up a fury. Judgments upon judgments have held that to be proceeded against the writer or speaker must have had the deliberate and malicious intent to, for instance, outrage the religious feelings of someone. But here the deliberate intent is all with the agitationists: they have deliberately set out to create a law and order problem so as to silence someone else.

The *Rangarajan Vs Jagjivan Ram* case arose from exactly that sort of circumstance. Agitators threatened to burn down cinema halls if these exhibited a particular film. The Tamil Nadu government took the stand that it could not guarantee protection. The Court observed : 'We want to put the anguished question, what good is the protection of freedom of expression if the State does not take care to protect it? If the film is unobjectionable and cannot constitutionally be restricted under Article 19(2), freedom of expression cannot be suppressed on account of threat of demonstrations and processions or threats of violence. That would tantamount to negation of the rule of law and a surrender to blackmail and intimidation. It is the duty of the State to protect the freedom of expression since it is a liberty guaranteed against the State. The State cannot plead its inability to handle the hostile audience problem. It is its obligatory duty to prevent it and protect the freedom of expression.... Freedom of expression

which is legitimate and constitutionally protected, cannot be held
to ransom by an intolerant group of people....'

A final consideration nails the matter completely. Even if
restrictions on speech are justified in a particular case – and in the
present instances the remarks cannot be brought under the
provisions by the remotest stretch of imagination – even then
only the State is authorised to impose those restrictions. What
the agitationists are insisting on is that, as *they* find the remarks
objectionable, *they* shall inflict penalties on those who made them
– by intimidating them, by forcing them out of their jobs. Far from
the law sanctioning such intimidation, such taking of the law in our
own hands, it prohibits it, and prescribes penalties against it.

Not just against the State

The Preamble itself of the Constitution declares that the people
of India are giving themselves the Constitution to constitute
the Republic of India and to secure for all citizens along with
Justice, Equality and Fraternity, the 'Liberty of thought, expression, belief, faith and worship.' Article 19(1)(a), among others,
translates this resolve into a specific fundamental right – that of
free speech. As a right which every citizen has against the State,
it limits the regulations and impediments which the State may
impose upon the right of the citizen – the single, solitary citizen
as much as any group of them – to speak his or her mind. But
it is a bulwark not just against the State. It is as much a bulwark
against other citizens – against any other citizen who may seek
to stifle a citizen's voice, against any group, such as a 'majority',
which may seek to stifle it, against the entire body of citizens
which may seek to prevent a single individual from speaking his
mind. When such assaults take place it is the duty of the State
and its institutions – the judges and the executive for instance
– to create the conditions which would enable that solitary
individual to stand by his beliefs and to express them freely.

That the right is a shield against the people is as vital as
the fact that it is one against the State, and the leaders of our
freedom movement were particularly conscious of its significance. Gandhiji, in particular, as he so often used to say, ever
so often was 'a minority of one.' Indeed, every reformer is in
a minority when he commences his work. Socrates, the Buddha,

Jesus, Galileo, Gandhi, Dayananda – the life of each of them, even more so the death of so many of them testifies to the fact that the reformer stands up not just against the State, he stands up against the people – their ways, their beliefs – he stands up against the age. That is the essence, the very meaning of reform, it is the essence of innovation too – to urge people to change their ways, their beliefs, their thinking. Can it be maintained that as the majority opposed each one of them, he should not have been allowed to have his say? But that is exactly what the agitationists against Mushirul Hasan have been so often saying : 'The majority of students and teachers want him to go. And this is a democracy. The view of the majority must prevail.'

Nor is it just that every reformer stands alone, it is that he challenges, he provokes, in a very basic sense he offends – that too is evident from the way so many of them have been set upon, indeed killed. And our law – for instance the relevant sections of the Indian Penal Code, that is Sections 153A, 295A and 298, and the host of judgments on them – recognizes this clearly. For something spoken or written to be construed to have been done so as to injure the religious feelings etc. of others, the person must be established to have had the deliberate and malicious intention to outrage those feelings. The work, its content, its import, the courts have held, must be judged as a whole, and it must be judged from the standpoint not of a hypersensitive man but from that of a reasonable man with common sense. The mild statements of Hasan, Bedar etc. cannot be brought under these sections even by the most determined distortion.

At various gatherings – at the Jamia and elsewhere, for instance at the discussion organized by NEWSTRACK – the students and teachers made another point. They insisted that if Hasan had a right to speak, they too had the right and so every one should listen to them. They do indeed have the right. And every one had been listening to them with utmost patience. The difficulty was that they were interpreting their right to speak to be *a right to shout so as to keep the one they did not approve of from speaking.*

Nor have they shown any knowledge of another set of rulings of the Supreme Court. It has repeatedly held in cases involving free speech that you cannot seek to achieve indirectly what you are prohibited from achieving directly. Thus, for instance, it has held that governments cannot seek to stifle a newspaper by denying it advertisements or putting exorbitant duties on news-print, thereby jeopardising its economic viability. That, they have held, would be to leave the lips unsealed while throttling the throat. The position of the agitationists and their rationalizers including among these a Central Minister, is exactly that: well, Hasan is free to say what he likes but then 'he must pay the price' for doing so. That price is to be abused and threatened, and to 'voluntarily' give up his job. Again: the agitationists are seeking to achieve by indirect means – intimidation, removal from a job – what they are debarred from achieving directly – that is, silencing a person they dislike.

What should be Done?

The right is vital for the individual of course: the freedom to think and speak is an essential component of a fulfilling life. It is at the same time, as John Stuart Mill argued so long ago, as vital for the others, for society as a whole that the individual be free to think and speak. Truth – in science, in society, in affairs of the State – has so often been at first perceived by just a few, so often by just one individual that the only way to ensure that it will be discovered is to ensure at all times that each individual will be free to pursue it and speak it. That fundamental reason is fortified by several others in contexts such as ours.

In a democracy the people must decide; to be able to decide they must have access to facts from all quarters and to views of all hues. Moreover, even more than judicial review, this right is the guarantor of other rights: when they are stifled, the fact that we have the freedom to speak about their suppression enables us to resurrect them. Nor would there be any way to make our rulers accountable, neither to ensure that our governments remain responsive if we were not free to talk about them. The right is essential to a democracy for another reason – to ensure that change is brought about by peaceful means: if the impulse to reform is bottled up, it will either shrivel and die – and the people will be the losers – or it will burst in violent explosions – and the people will be the losers again. By ensuring that dissenters and reformers can speak, we, on the one hand, alert society to changes which need to be brought about, and, on the other, enable those who oppose the way things are to vent their rage.

When a right so precious is assaulted by louts and bullies, as it has been at Jamia, what should be done? Three things at the least:

❏ We must give every opportunity to the bullies to show themselves to the people, we must put them on TV and Video screens, as nothing will finish their 'movement' as effectively as doing so will;

❏ We must stand up to the bullies and see that they do not prevail, as this alone will safeguard the future;

❏ We must use the controversy as a 'learning moment', as the occasion to reflect on and comprehend fundamentals – our laws, our values, the consequences of giving in to bullies.

– April 1992

XVI

Conjuring up 'Rushdie the Second'

We have read the book in detail, declared the *Amarat ahl-i-Hadis,* Patna, the Islamic organization with the authority to lay down the law, in its *fatwa.* It should be banned. Its author, bereft of faith, is a *murtad,* an apostate.

Now, as is well known, under Islamic law the punishment for apostasy is death.

The one who says 'X', 'Y'...'Z' – the propositions the man was said to have enunciated in his book – is a *Kafir,* declared the *Amarat-i-Sharia,* another equally weighty authority on matters of Islamic law, in its *fatwa.*

The *Adara-i-Sharia,* a third layer-down of the law, in its *fatwa* declared that the man had repudiated the Revelations of the Quran, that he had dismissed the Traditions of the Prophets, that he was openly preaching infidelity. He is therefore a *Kafir,* the *fatwa* declared. He is for that reason excommunicated from Islam, it declared. The organization urged all Muslims to accordingly terminate all relations and contacts with the man, until and unless he repents and apologises to satisfy the canons of the *Shariat.* And in a lament the import of which could not be lost on any one, in the end it asked, 'For the protection of the foundations of our religion in a secular State, what more can we do?'

For his indecent attacks on Islam the Ulema must pass a death sentence on the author, the speaker thundered. Just as the Iranian Ulema had issued a *firman* for the execution of Salman Rushdie, a *fatwa* should be issued against this man. The speaker was Fida Hussain Ansari, of the Congress. The Bihar Legislative Council, of which he is a member, was discussing the budget of the state government. When communist members interjected to say that, as the man was a citizen of India, whatever punishment was meted out to him had to be under the Indian Penal Code, Ansari shot back, 'This is our religious issue and only Islamic law can deliver proper justice.'

Meetings, demonstrations, *dharnas* followed one upon the other. Let the Ulema just give the word, speakers declaimed. Rs 1 lakh on his head, reported the papers.

What has the man done? What is the point of the campaigners? Who are the campaigners?

The Man's Sin

The Khuda Baksh Library at Patna houses one of the best collections of medieval manuscripts. It was founded in 1891. In 1969 by an Act of Parliament it was declared to be an Institution of National Importance and its management was put under the sole control of the Government of India. The Library is administered through a twelve member Board constituted by the Government. Expenses of the Library are aided from the budget of the Government. It is therefore like any other institution aided and administered by the Government – except that it is a Library, a distinguished Library, one the hallmark of which is the collection of priceless medieval manuscripts. It is not a 'minority institution'. And it is not an 'Islamic institution' any more than medieval Indian history is the property of Islam.

Abid Reza Bedar has been its Director since 1972. He has had genuine pride in the collection and has devoted himself single-mindedly to rehabilitating the Library. He has been a stern task – master and has over the years terminated the services of four or so employees for dereliction of duty. He was to have retired in 1992. The Governor, who is also *ex officio* the head of the Board, gave him a two year extension. (Incidentally, such is the state of our affairs that when it came to assigning a reason for extending Bedar's term the Governor did not or could not do so on the straight-forward ground that the man had done a fine job and the Library needed his services; he did so on the ground that the retirement age at the Jawaharlal Nehru University, where Bedar had been working before he joined the Library, that is where he had been working 20 years ago, is 60 and not 58 !)

On 24 May 1992 there was a function at the Raj Bhavan, Patna, at which the Governor released a book, *Keynote of the Holy Quran*, by S. M. Mohsin. A social scientist of some distinction, Mohsin is now 80. His book is best described as yet another pious effort to distance Islam from its entire history. Its theme is that the keynote of the Quran is love and amity and peace. One of its chapters deals with 'Violence and forcible conversion.' Far from urging or even condoning these things, says the author, the Quran urges us to shun them. In this context he argues that the *Kafir* whom admittedly the Quran exhorts us to put down is not to be taken to mean any or every one from a different faith, not even someone who does not believe. The word is to be taken to refer only to persons who are actively the enemies of Islam — in that they prevent the faithful from living by their faith and prevent its peaceful propagation. The notion that for a believer in Islam a non-Muslim is a *Kafir*, Mohsin says, 'is illusory and unfounded.' For this notion, he says, 'the unsophisticated or fanatical diehards in the Muslim community, are mainly responsible.'

The book, as I said, is a pious rendition.

In any event, at the function at which the book was released Bedar also spoke. Five-sixths of his brief speech consisted of nothing but extracts from Mohsin's book. In the end he said :

> And, towards the end, I may draw your attention to the discussion and the points particularly raised in this book. In particular I would draw your kind attention to the word, used in the Holy book, *Kafir*. This has been a controversial word; and such words, like *Kafir*, have been misused — have been exploited, I should say — by those who have made their mission to disintegrate this great nation.

> Such misunderstandings are created by misinterpretations of the word like *Kafir*; I would not go into the detail, that is in this book. This book will, I am sure, remove so many misunderstandings that are widespread not only in the non-Muslims; in Muslims, themselves.

Nothing offensive in that. Quite the contrary, the words were innocuous, in fact mere pieties.

The Campaign

By the next morning the mischief had begun. Bedar was

accused of having faulted the Quran itself. He was accused of
having asked for changes in the language of the Quran. He was
accused of launching an attempt like the one of a Hindu who had
sought through a writ in the Calcutta High Court to have the Quran
banned. Two Urdu papers — the *Qaumi Tanzeem* and the *Azimabad
Express* — led the barrage. Bedar sent statements to them
furnishing the text of what he had said, affirming that he had not
criticised the Quran in any way. In these he went even further than
Mohsin in trying to placate diehards : whereas Mohsin had
held 'the unsophisticated or fanatical diehards in the Muslim
community' to have been mainly responsible for the wrong constructions which had come to be put on the word *Kafir*, Bedar
declared that in his speech he had had the 'Hindu Mahasabha'
— he seems to have meant the BJP and VHP — in mind which,
he said, had made a special point of misrepresenting the
word during the *Rath-Yatra*. Bedar's statements were of course
not published by the two papers.

An avalanche of swear words, the entire demonology of such
papers was instead let loose upon him, the *Qaumi Tanzeem*
carrying up to twelve items a day denouncing him. *Malun* —
scoundrel; *Dareedaa Zahan* — dirty-minded; *Rushdie saani* —
Rushdie the Second; *Dushman-i-Islam* — the enemy of Islam;
Shaatir — dishonest, crafty; *Be-din* — irreligious; *Kharij-al-Islam* —
dropout from Islam; *Murtad* — apostate; *Mulhid* — heretic; *Dahariya*
— materialist; *Kafir* — infidel; *Shaitan* — Satan; *Faasiq* — reprobate;
Iblis — Satan; *Naapaak* — filthy; *Zindiq* — a hopeless infidel; *Ibn-
al-Waqt* — opportunist — such were the epithets which the papers
and those whose statements they highlighted hurled at him.

Once the tape recording of the speech had been heard by many,
once many had read the text of what the man had said, it was not
quite possible to allege that Bedar had either faulted the Quran
or advocated that its language be amended. The charge now
became that, to use the words of the editor of the *Azimabad
Express*, by asserting that a word used in the Holy Book was
'controversial' Bedar had blasphemed the religion ! He was
accused of creating the controversey to divide the Muslims. He
was accused of having converted the Khuda Baksh Library into a
centre for anti-Islam movements. He was of course accused of
being an agent of the RSS and BJP!

Next, a little book — a pamphlet, really — *Seema ki Talaash*, which he had written 22 years earlier, was exhumed.

The pamphlet does no more than argue two things: externals are not the essence of religion; we would not injure our religion in any way, but we would help promote amity and fellow-feeling, if, in choosing to adhere to or insist on one set of externals rather than another, we paid heed to the sentiments of our fellow countrymen also. Just one example from the book will do. Islam enjoins the faithful to sacrifice animals on occasion. Bedar's point was that, as several animals had been listed sacrificing which would bring merit, believers would lose little if they paid heed to the sentiments of a neighbour who regarded the cow as his mother, and chose an animal other than the cow to sacrifice. The specific example of sacrificing animals apart, the advice was almost Gandhian – the only thing exceptional about it being that, this time round, such advice had been addressed to Muslims.

In any event, no one had paid any heed to it, and the pamphlet had been forgotten. It was now exhumed. Extracts from it – the feature of the day in the *Qaumi Tanzeem*, in posters. It was made out that to appease Hindu communalists, of which of course he was an agent, Bedar had set out to have Muslims abandon their identity and submerge themselves in the sea of Hinduism.

Demands went up to dismiss him – such a person 'has no business to hold a post in a religious institution,' it was said; to 'teach him a lesson'; to inflict 'deterrent punishment' on him – 'the time has come to stone the man,' the *Qaumi Tanzeem* reported a reader as writing; to prosecute him for spreading enmity between communities; to put 'this Second Rushdie' to death – 'Islam has been harmed more by Muslims who don a progressive dress,' the paper reported a reader saying, 'than by non-Muslims; Muslims get ready to die and kill when Islam is attacked by non-Muslims; what about these Muslims ?'; to ban his book; to approach the leaders and Embassy of Iran to obtain a *fatwa* similar to the one which had been issued in the case of the original Rushdie; to come out on the streets. Muslims were exhorted to open their eyes to the international conspiracy against Islam, to see that Rushdie, Mushirul Hasan and Bedar were agents of anti-Islam forces, to boycott Bedar completely, to decide whether he did not deserve death.... The *fatwas* of the *Amarat ahl-i-Hadis,* the *Amarat-i-Sharia*, and the *Adara-i-Sharia* became the high points of the campaign.

The contrary fatwa

Bedar petitioned the *Darul Uloom* at Deoband, in some ways the most prestigious centre of Islamic law and learning. He declared his faith in Islam to the Maulanas, he sent them excerpts from *Seema ki Talaash* which testified to the sincerity of his commitment to Muslims and Islam, he sent them an account of his work as Director of the Library.

The Maulanas at Deoband issued a *fatwa*. In it they pronounced Bedar to be a faithful Muslim. They said that excerpts from his book testified to his love and passion for Islam. It is neither right nor just, they said, to issue a *fatwa* of unbelief against such a person. 'It is a horrible injustice to expel a faithful Muslim from Islam,' they declared. They accordingly exhorted Muslims to conduct themselves towards him in the spirit of Islamic brotherhood, and not heed the *fatwas* which had been issued against him. One Maulana, while endorsing the Deoband *fatwa*, added, 'It is not appropriate to hasten and show audacity in declaring a Muslim to be a *Kafir*. Whoever does so commits injustice and betrays inexperience. I, therefore, hold that the above reply of the learned Mufti is right and correct on all counts. And those issuing the *fatwa* of *kufr* have committed an error and have done so in haste.'

The Deoband *fatwa* has been obtained by deception, the *Qaumi Tanzeem* declared. It is more of a character certificate than a *fatwa*, it declared. It has been issued after seeing only those portions of the book which Bedar showed them, it declared. The Maulanas were told that the Barelvis are after Bedar, it declared, and it is a bitter truth that there has been heart-burning and tension between the Ulema of Deoband and Bareli. The man who was sent to obtain the *fatwa* bore false witness, it declared.

The campaign continued. Students' bodies, Muslim organizations from one city after another, from cities as far away as Aurangabad jumped in. And of course the politicians.

Qaumi Tanzeem, it turned out, was controlled by Tariq Anwar, the former President of the Bihar Pradesh Congress Committee. To support him, not to be left behind by him or to out-do him, Jagannath Mishra, the current President of the Bihar Pradesh Congress Committee weighed in. Under no circumstances shall any one, Muslim or non-Muslim, be permitted to interfere with

Islam or Muslim Personal Law, Mishra declared. If anyone dubs any word of the Holy Quran to be controversial then to my mind he is communal and one who is sowing animosity, he declared. I know that the Quran of the Muslims is the Book of God and anyone who describes any word in it as controversial is doing so only to curry favour with the communalists for advancing his selfish interests, he declared. Such a person, the Director, Dr. A. R. Bedar though he may be, shall not be pardoned under any circumstances. Anything which hurts the religious sentiments of Muslims is beyond the limits of tolerance of my party and myself, he declared. Therefore, my sympathy and support are completely with whatever peaceful movement the Muslims may launch on the matter, he declared.

The Janata Dal MLA, Shahid Ali Khan, demanded an immediate ban on Bedar's book and action against him for making 'derogatory remarks' about the Quran. MLAs stormed the well of the Assembly demanding that the man be suspended, that he be prosecuted, that he be arrested. The head of the Bihar Janata Dal Momin Conference declared, 'Muslims will not tolerate any change in their personal law even if they are slaughtered' and demanded action against Bedar.

Qaumi Tanzeem reported that Arjun Singh, in whose charge is the Department of Culture under which the Library is administered, had assured early action against Bedar while accepting a memorandum against him. It reported that Laloo Yadav, the Chief Minister, too had assured early action against Bedar. The Governor relapsed into silence. He is the head, *ex officio*, of the Board of the Library. He is the one who had given the 2-year extension to Bedar. He is the one who had released Mohsin's book. He was now reported as saying that the notion of *Kufr* had never endangered national unity; he was reported as chiding Bedar; he was reported to have urged Muftis and Maulanas to issue a *fatwa* on the matter; he was reported as saying that the agitation of Muslims on the matter showed that they were vigilant; he was reported as saying that he had expressed his disagreement with Bedar at the meeting itself and that Bedar should be pardoned if he apologises and undertakes not to say such things in the future... The secular Governor in secular India about an employee of a Government-controlled institution !

Of course some spoke up for Bedar too. To his credit

Shahabuddin was amongst the first to say that he had examined what Bedar had said at the release function and that there had been nothing objectionable in it. Dr. Syed Hammid, the former Vice Chancellor of the Aligarh Muslim University, was the most forthright. Writing in *Inquilab*, the Urdu paper from Bombay, he gave the soundest possible advice. It deserves the attention of every Indian:

The Muslim community is the only one in the country in which negative tendencies dominate positive and constructive tendencies. Muslims are busy distorting their own image and destroying their own institutions. Muslims need institutions and voluntary agencies more than others to overcome their backwardness. In essence, we are ourselves responsible for our present plight.

The manner in which the Director of the Khuda Baksh Library, Patna, Dr Abid Reza Bedar was subjected to misrepresentation, humiliation and threats, is a shameful blot on our community. And this was done to a man who through his single-minded dedication, hard work and strength of character, infused a new life and vitality to a forsaken library and built up the institution.

A Patna newspaper unleashed an unseemly storm against Dr Bedar because the library declined to give it the advertisement rate demanded by it and because the Director had terminated the services of certain incompetent persons who later took up jobs in the newspaper and started their vendetta against Dr Bedar. Even more disturbing is the attitude of two religious institutions of Bihar which have passed the *fatwa* of '*Kufr*' (infidelity to Islam) without any investigation, against Dr Bedar. The role of most Urdu newspapers has been highly irresponsible. Under the circumstances, how can an average Urdu newspaper reader reflect upon issues and problems soberly and coolly when the Urdu Press is serving him such sensational fare? The BJP, VHP and other anti-Muslim bodies have charged that the *Quran* enjoins the killing of *Kafirs*. It is the duty of the Ulema, in particular, to rebut this in clear terms with sound arguments and to define the Muslim attitude towards their non-Muslim countrymen to remove any misgivings in their minds, in the light of the *Quran* and the *Hadith*.

The advice was drowned in the din of the campaigners. The result was predictable. At an early stage of the affair, fourteen eminences of Bihar's Sufi *Khanquahs* had issued a statement in Bedar's favour : they had listened to the tape of his speech, they had declared, and had compared it with the written text. 'After thorough enquiry,' they said, 'we have reached the conclusion that his address did not contain any thing which defames the Holy Quran or Islam.' Several of them now retracted their support: one said that it was wrong to assume that he had on that date supported Bedar's position as he had expressed his disapproval at an earlier date; another said that he had signed in ignorance – Bedar's hirelings had in the dark of night brought something written in English, he had signed without reading it; another declared that he had signed the statement before he had read the book *Seema ki Talaash*, the book left no room for condonation, he was therefore terminating all relations with Bedar, and he was begging forgiveness for the mistake of having supported Bedar earlier....

S.M. Mohsin, the author of, the book, commending which had started the whole thing, too distanced himself from Bedar. Bedar spoke about the word *Kafir* on his own, *Qaumi Tanzeem* reported Mohsin as saying, without reading the book; Bedar seems to have looked superficially at my book and picked up only one word; he has not been clear and honest about my book; he has only poured out the poison in his own mind....

As I write *The Times of India* reports that the situation is getting uglier. Bedar, it reports, has turned down the offer to buy peace by signing a statement declaring Hindus to be *Kafirs*, saying that it is not his function to be deciding these things. Accordingly he and his family continue to be intimidated and threatened. Obscenities are hurled at them over loudspeakers. The man, his family, the priceless collection over which he presides, all are endangered. Bedar, his wife and children live through all this defenceless, resigned, with not even a policeman to interrupt, to say nothing of intercepting the would-be assaulters. One paper, *Sangam*, which had at least occasionally been setting out the facts, has announced that it shall report nothing further on the issue: one

morning, it turns out, its edition carried a report disparaging the
man, Bedar, it had been, at least obliquely, defending. The
paper declared that the report was not its own – that the plate-
maker at the press, illiterate as he is, had been bribed by outsiders
to insert the report. A campaign not just of calumny and intimidation, therefore, but of stealth and resourcefulness!

Our Laws, Our Ways

Several things stand out:

❑ Another Rushdie has been conjured up ;
❑ The campaign has been based entirely on fabrication and distortion;
❑ The fabrication and distortion have been wilful – there was
   never any room for misunderstanding: the tape of the speech
   has been available all along, and the man had read from a
   written text which too has been available all along;
❑ The fabrications and distortions have been the work primarily
   of two newspapers; the papers are reported to have a
   circulation of only 3000 copies each, and yet these papers,
   controllers of assorted organizations – some of them surely
   little more than name-plate bodies – and the politicians have
   raised enough of a din for the impression to have been created
   that Bedar has fallen afoul of the entire Muslim community;
❑ Both the papers have been censured on earlier occasions by
   the Press Council of India – in 1981, 1984 and 1989 – for
   defaming Bedar and been directed to apologise;
❑ Politicians have fueled the flames;
❑ To defend himself Bedar has had to go not to some secular
   institution of our State or society, he has had to go to a
   religious institution, and to satisfy the office bearers there of
   his religiosity;
❑ At no point did any one think it fit to ascertain the views of
   those who were being dubbed *Kafirs*, and accordingly
   towards whom what the appropriate stance would be –
   whether they ought to be annhilated or persuaded or left to
   go their way – was being settled; even those parts of the
   'secular press' which came out in favour of Bedar shied away
   from the root of the matter – the distinction which is central

to Islam between believers and non-believers, and the duties it enjoins on the former in regard to the latter; they shied away too from questioning the presumption of Maulanas and others speaking in the name of religion that they have the right to throttle a man's freedom to think and speak, a freedom our Constitution guarantees every Indian;

❑ The campaign has endangered the priceless collection in the Library; it has been nothing short of incitement to murder;

❑ Our secular governments -- that of the centre as much as of the state-- have taken no step whatsoever to protect the library or to protect the man and his family, to say nothing of prosecuting the campaigners for inciting persons to murder ;

❑ Quite the contrary: advertisements of government departments continue to this day in the papers which have led this campaign of calumny and hatred.

Long live secularism!

— 9 September 1992

Ayodhya

XVII

Hideaway Communalism

A Chase in which

❏*The English version of a major book by a renowned Muslim scholar, the fourth Rector of one of the best known centres of Islamic learning in India, listing some of the mosques, including the Babri Masjid, which were built on the sites and foundations of temples, using their stones and structures, is found to have the tell-tale passages censored out;*

❏*The book is said to have become difficult to get;*

❏*It is traced;*

❏ *And is found to have been commended just 15 years ago by the most influential living Muslim scholar of our country today, the current Rector of that centre of Islamic learning, and the Chairman of the Muslim Personal Law Board.*

Evasion, concealment have become a national habit. And they have terrible consequences. But first I must set out some background.

The Nadwatul Ulama of Lucknow is one of the principal centres of Islamic learning in India. It was founded in 1894. It ranks today next only to the Darul-Ulum at Deoband. The government publication, *Centres of Islamic Learning in India*, recalls how the founders 'aimed at producing capable scholars who could project a true image of Islam before the modern world in an effective way;' it recalls how 'towards fulfilling its avowed aim in the matter of educational reform, it [the group] decided to establish an ideal educational institution which would not only provide education in religious and temporal sciences but also offer technical training;' it recalls how the Nadwa, 'stands out today – with its college, a vast and rich library and Research and Publication departments housed in a fine building – as one of the most outstanding institutions for imparting instruction in the Islamic Sciences;' it recalls how a salient feature of this institution is its emphasis on independent research;' it recalls how 'the library of the Nadwa, housed in the Central Hall and the surrounding rooms of the main building, is, with more than 75,000 titles including about 3,000 handwritten books mostly in Arabic and also in Persian, Urdu, English etc., one of the finest libraries of the subcontinent.' That was written 10 years ago. The library now has 125,000 books.

Today the institution is headed by Maulana Abul-Hasan Ali Nadwi. Ali Mian, as he is known to one and all, is almost without doubt the most influential Muslim teacher and figure today – among the laity, in government circles, and among scholars and governments abroad.

He was among the founders of the Jamaat-e-Islami, the fundamentalist organisation; but because of differences with Maulana Madoodi, he left it soon.

Today he is the Chairman of the Muslim Personal Law Board.

He is a founder member of the Rabitah al-Alam al-Islami, the pan-Islamic body with headquarters in Mecca which decides, among other things, the amounts that different Islamic organisations the world over should receive.

He has been the Nazim, the Rector, of the Darul Ulum Nadwatul-Ulama since 1961, that is, for well over a quarter of a century. The Nadwa owes not a small part of its eminence to the scholarship, the exertions, the national and international contacts of Ali Mian.

Politicians of all hues – Rajiv Gandhi, V. P. Singh, Chandrashekhar – seek him out.

He is the author of several books, including the well known *Insaani Duniya Par Musalmanon Ke Uruj-o-Zaval Ka Asar*, ('The Impact of the rise and fall of Muslims on Mankind') and is taken as the authority on Islamic law, jurisprudence, theology, and especially history.

And he has great, in fact he has a decisive, influence on the politics of Muslims in India.

The Father and His Book

His father, Maulana Hakim Sayid Abdul Hai, was an equally well known and influential figure. When the Nadwa was founded the first Rector, Maulana Muhammad Monghyri, the scholar at whose initiative the original meeting in 1892 was called, which led to the establishment of the Nadwa, had chosen Maulana Abdul Hai as the Madadgar Nazim, the Additional Rector. Abdul Hai served in that capacity till July 1915 when he was appointed the Rector.

Because of his scholarship and his services to the institution and to Islam, he was reappointed as the Rector in 1920. He continued in that post till his death in February 1923.

He, too, wrote several books, including a famous directory, which has just been republished from Hyderabad, of thousands of Muslims who had served the cause of Islam in India, chiefly by the numbers they had converted to the faith.

During some work I came across the reference to a book of his and began to look for it.

It was a long, discursive book, I learnt, which began with descriptions of the geography, of flora and fauna, languages, peoples and of the regions of India. These were written for Arabic speaking peoples, the language of the book being Arabic.

In 1972, I learnt, the Nadwatul-Ulama had the book translated into Urdu and published the most important chapters of the book under the title *Hindustan Islami Ahad Mein* ('Hindustan under Islamic Rule'). Ali Mian, I was told, had himself written the foreword in which he had commended the book most highly. The book as published had left out descriptions of geography etc. on the premise that facts about these are well known to Indian readers.

Sudden Reluctance

A curious fact hit me in the face. Many of the persons whom one would have normally expected to be knowledgeable about such publications were suddenly reluctant to recall this book. I was told, in fact, that copies of the book had been removed, for instance from the Aligarh Muslim University Library. Some even suggested that a determined effort had been made three or four years ago to get back each and every copy of this book.

Fortunately the apprehension turned out to be exaggerated. While some of the libraries one would normally expect to have the book – the Jamia Millia Islamia in Delhi; the famous libraries in Hyderabad, those of the Dairutual Maarifal Osmania, that of the Salar Jung Museum, of the Nizam's Trust, of the Osmania University, the Kutubkhana-Saidiya – did not have it, others did. Among the latter were the Nadwa's library itself, the justly famous Khuda Baksh Library in Patna, that of the Institute of Islamic Studies in Delhi.

The fact that the book was available in all these libraries came as a great reassurance. I had felt that if reactionaries and propagandists have become so well organised that they can secure the disappearance from every library of a book they have come not to like, we are deep in trouble. Clearly they are not that resourceful.

The fact that, contrary to what I had been told, the book was available also taught me another reassuring thing: factional fights among Muslim fundamentalists are as sharp and intense as are the factional fights among fundamentalists of other hues. For the suggestion of there being something sinister in the inaccessibility of the book had come to me from responsible Muslim quarters.

'This Valuable Gift, This Historical Testament'

The book is publication number 66 of the *Majlis Tehqiquat wa Nashriat Islam*, the publication house of the Nadwatul Ulama, Lucknow.

The Arabic version was published in 1972 in Hyderabad, the Urdu version in 1973 in Lucknow. An English version was published in 1977. I will use the Urdu version as the illustration.

Maulana Abul-Hasan Ali Nadwi, that is Ali Mian, himself contributes the foreword.

It is an eloquent, almost lyrical foreword.

Islam has imbued its followers with the quest for truth, with patriotism, he writes. Their nature, their culture has made Muslims the writers of true history, he writes.

Muslims had but to reach a country, he writes, and its fortunes lit up and it awakened from the slumber of hundreds and thousands of years. That country thereby ascended from darkness to light, he writes, from oblivion and obscurity to the pinnacle of name and fame. Leaving its parochial ambit, he writes, it joined the family of man, it joined the wide and vast creation of God. And the luminescence of Islam, he writes, revealed its hidden treasures to the light of the eyes.

It did not suck away the wealth of the country, he writes, and vomit it elsewhere as Western powers did. On the contrary, it brought sophistication, culture, beneficent administration, peace, tranquillity to the country. It raised the country from the age of savagery to the age of progress, he writes, from infantilism to adulthood. It transformed its barren lands into swaying fields, he writes, its wild shrubs into fruit-laden trees of such munificence that the residents could not even have dreamt of them.

And so on.

He then recalls the vast learning and prodigious exertions of Maulana Abdul Hai, his 8-volume work on 4500 Muslims who had served the cause of Islam in India, his directory of Islamic scholars.

He recalls how after completing these books the Maulana turned to subjects which had till then remained obscure, how in these labours the Maulana was like the proverbial bee collecting honey from varied flowers. He recounts the wide range of the Maulana's scholarship. He recounts how the latter collected rare data, how a person like him accomplished single-handed what entire academies are unable these days to do.

He recounts the structure of the present book. He recalls how it lay neglected for long, how, even as the work of retranscribing a moth-eaten manuscript was going on, a complete manuscript was discovered in Azamgarh, how in 1933 the grace of Providence saved it from destruction and obscurity.

He writes that the book brings into bold relief those hallmarks of Islamic rule which have been unjustly and untruthfully dealt with by Western and Indian historians, which in fact many Muslim historians and scholars in universities and academies too have treated with neglect and lack of appreciation.

Recalling how Maulana Abdul Hai had to study thousands of pages on a subject, Ali Mian writes that only he who has himself worked on the subject can appreciate the effort that has gone into the study. You will get in a single chapter of this book, he tells the reader, the essence which you cannot obtain by reading scores of books. This is the result, he writes, of the fact that the author laboured only for the pleasure of God, for the service of learning, and the fulfilment of his own soul. Such authors expected no rewards, no applause, he tells us. Work was their entire satisfaction. That is how they were able to put in such herculean labours, to spend their entire lives on one subject.

We are immensely pleased, he concludes, to present this valuable gift and historical testament to our countrymen and hope that Allah will accept this act of service, and scholars will also receive it with respect and approbation.

The Explanation

Such being the eminence of the author, such being the greatness of the work, why is it not the cynosure of the fundamentalists' eyes?

The answer is in the chapter *Hindustan ki Masjidein*, 'The mosques of Hindustan.' Barely seventeen pages, the chapter is simply written. A few facts about some of the principal mosques are described in a few lines each.

The facts are well-known, they are elementary and setting them out in a few lines each should attract no attention. And yet, as we shall see, there is a furtiveness in regard to them. Why? Descriptions of seven mosques provide the answer.

The devout constructed so many mosques, Maulana Abdul Hai records, they lavished such huge amounts and such labours on them that they cannot all be reckoned, that every city, town, hamlet came to be adorned by a mosque. He says that he will therefore have to be content with setting out the facts about just a few of the well-known ones.

A few sentences from what he says about seven mosques will do:

Quwwat al-Islam Mosque

According to my findings the first mosque of Delhi is Qubbat al-Islam or Quwwat al-Islam which, it is said, Qutubuddin Aibak constructed in H.587 after demolishing the temple built by Prithviraj and leaving certain parts of the temple (outside the mosque proper); and when he returned from Ghazni in H.592, he started building, under orders from Shihabud-Din Ghori, a huge mosque of inimitable red stones, and certain parts of the temple were included in the mosque. After that, when Shamsud-Din Altamish became the king, he built on both sides of it, edifices of white stones, and on the side of it he started constructing that loftiest of all towers which has no equal in the world for its beauty and strength....

The Mosque at Jaunpur

This was built by Sultan Ibrahim Sharqi with chiselled stones. Originally it was a Hindu temple, after demolishing which he constructed the mosque. It is known as the Atala Masjid. The Sultan used to offer his Friday and Id prayers in it, and Qazi Shihabud-Din gave lessons in it....

The Mosque at Qanauj

This mosque stands on an elevated ground inside the Fort of Qanauj. It is well-known that it was built on the foundations of some Hindu temple [that stood] here. It is a beautiful mosque. They say that it was built by Ibrahim Sharqi in Jami (Masjid) at Etawah H.809 as is [recorded] in *Gharabat Nigar*. This mosque stands on the bank of the Jamuna at Etawah. There was a Hindu temple at this place, on the side of which this mosque was constructed. It is also patterned after the mosque at Qanauj. Probably it is one of the monuments of the Sharqi Sultans.

Babri Masjid at Ajodhya

The mosque was constructed by Babar at Ajodhya which Hindus call the birth place of Ramchandarji. There is a famous story about his wife Sita. It is said that Sita had a temple here in which she lived and cooked food for her husband. On that very site Babar constructed this mosque in H. 963....

Mosques of Alamgir (Aurangzeb)

It is said that the mosque of Benares was built by Alamgir on the site of the Bisheshwar Temple. That temple was very tall and [held as] holy among the Hindus. On this very site and with those very stones he constructed a lofty mosque, and its ancient stones were rearranged after being embedded in the walls of the mosque. It is one of the renowned mosques of Hindustan. The second mosque at Benares [is the one] which was built by Alamgir on the bank of the Ganga with chiselled stones. This also is a renowned mosque of Hindustan. It has 28 towers, each of which is 238 feet tall. This is on the bank of the Ganga and its foundations extend to the depth of the waters.

Alamgir built a mosque at Mathura. It is said that this mosque was built on the site of the Gobind Dev Temple which was strong and beautiful as well as exquisite.

'It is Said'

'But the Maulana is not testifying to the facts. He is merely reporting what was believed. He repeatedly says, "It is said that"....'

That seems to be a figure of speech with the Maulana. When describing the construction of the Quwwat al-Islam mosque by Qutubuddin Aibak, for instance, he uses the same 'It is said....'

If the facts were in doubt, would a scholar of Ali Mian's diligence and commitment not have commented on them in his full-bodied foreword? Indeed, he would have decided against republishing them as he decided not to republish much of the original book.

And if the scholars had felt that the passages could be that easily disposed of, why should any effort have been made to take a work to the excellence of which a scholar of Ali Mian's stature has testified in such a fulsome manner and do what has been done to this one? And what is that?

Each reference to each of these mosques having been constructed on the sites of temples with, as in the case of the mosque at Benaras, the stones of the very temple which was demolished for that very purpose *has been censored out of the English version of the book*! Each one of the passages on each one of thè seven mosques. No accident, that.

Indeed there is not just censorship but substitution! In the Urdu volume we are told in regard to the mosque at Qanauj, for instance, that 'this mosque stands on an elevated ground inside the fort of Qanauj. *It is well known that it was built on the foundation of some Hindu Temple [that stood] here.'* In the English volume we are told in regard to the same mosque that 'it occupied a commanding site, *believed to have been the place earlier occupied by an old and decayed fort.'*

If the passages could have been so easily explained away by referring to the 'It is said,' why would anyone have thought it necessary to remove these passages from the English version – that is, the version which was more likely to be read by persons other than the faithful? Why would anyone bowdlerise the book of a major scholar in this way?

Conclusions

But that is the minor point. The fact that temples were broken and mosques constructed in their place is well known. Nor is the fact that the materials of the temples – the stones and idols – were used in constructing the mosque news. It was thought that *this* was the way to announce hegemony. It was thought that *this* was the way to strike at the heart of the conquered – for in those days the temple was not just a place of worship; it was the hub of the community's life, of its learning, of its social life. So the lines in the book which bear on this practice are of no earth-shaking significance in themselves. Their real significance – and I dare say that they are but the smallest, most innocuous example that one can think of on the mosque-temple business – lies in the evasion and concealment they have spurred. I have it on good authority that the passages have been known for long, and well known to those who have been stoking the Babri Masjid issue.

That is the significant thing: they have known them, and their impulse has been to conceal and bury rather than to ascertain the truth.

I have little doubt that a rational solution can be found for the Babri Masjid – Ram Janmabhoomi tangle, a solution which will respect the sentiments, the essentials of the religions of all.

But no solution can be devised if the issue is going to be made the occasion for a show of strength by either side, if it is going to be converted into a symbol for establishing who shall prevail.

The fact of Maulana Abdul Hai's passages – and I do not

know whether the Urdu version. itself was not a conveniently sanitised version of the original Arabic volume – illustrates the cynical manner in which those who stoke the passions of religion to further their politics are going about the matter.

❑ Those who proceed by such cynical calculations sow havoc for all of us – for Muslims, for Hindus, for all.

❑ Those who remain silent in the face of such cynicism, such calculations help them sow the havoc.

Will we shed our evasions and concealments? Will we at last learn to speak and face the whole truth? To see how communalism of one side justifies and stokes that of the other? To see that these 'leaders' are not interested in facts, not in religion, not in a building or a site, but in power, in *their personal power*, and in that alone? That for them religion is but an instrument which is so attractive precisely because the costs of using it – the enormous, terrible costs of wielding it – fall on others, on their followers, and not on them?

Will we never call a halt to them?

– 5 February 1989

XVIII

Takeover from the Experts

For a year and half you keep issuing statements to the press, and writing ostensibly scholarly articles, and holding forth in interviews that the Babri Mosque was not, most definitely not built by demolishing, or even on the site of a temple. Documents of the other side are sent to you. You are nominated by the All India Babri Masjid Action Committee as an expert who will give his assessment of the documents. A meeting is scheduled. Before that you meet the then Director General of Archaeology who had supervised the excavations at the site. The day the meeting is to begin the newspapers carry yet another categorical statement from 'intellectuals', again asserting the line convenient to the AIBMAC. You of course are among them.

The meeting commences. On point after point, on document after document your response is that you have not studied the evidence, that therefore you require time; that you have never seen the site, that therefore you require time to visit it.

You are not a field archaeologist you say, and will therefore nominate another person, and he too will naturally require time.... The person happens to be present. You are informed that the person has not only studied the evidence, he has met and discussed the matter with the Director General of Archaeology, and also with the previous Director General, Dr. B.B. Lal, under whose supervision the excavations had been conducted in 1975-80. Others too are named whom he has met for the purpose. But that was in another capacity, you say, now he will need time....

On behalf of the Government the officer present says that the records of the excavation – maps, four types of narrative accounts, photographs – are available, that Dr. Lal has agreed so that they can be inspected the very next day. No... we will need time....

You are on to a new tack. But why has Dr. Lal not stated a definite conclusion? In fact, it turns out, that he has: a videocassette of the interview he gave to the BBC is produced. Can't see it now as there is no VCP.... Will need time....

The next day you don't even turn up for the meeting.

An expert of the AIBMAC. A Marxist. An intellectual whose name appears invariably in the statements propagandising the AIBMAC point of view.

I summarise, but the account applies more or less to the four professional 'experts' who appeared as the AIBMAC's nominees in the meeting on January 24, 1991.

The other 'experts' of the AIBMAC were just its own office-bearers. They went one better. They 'denied' the contents, indeed it seemed the very existence of books written not just by Islamic historians and authors – the photocopies of the relevant pages from which had all been supplied weeks earlier – they 'denied' knowledge of even standard works like the *Encyclopaedia Brittanica!*

That done, the next day they did not turn up either.

The Issue Specified

The one thing on which Chandra Shekhar's Government can claim to have catalysed progress is the Janmabhoomi controversy. This was done in two ways: by getting the two sides to begin talking to each other, and by pin-pointing the issue. The issue Chandra Shekhar emphasised was: Was the mosque built by demolishing a Hindu temple or structure?

And in this Chandra Shekhar was adhering to what had been stated categorically on behalf of the Muslims: 'On behalf of Muslims,' a major protagonist of the matter had, as Justice Deoki-nandan recalls, stated in his treatise on the subject, 'I... say that if it is proved that Babri Masjid has been built after demolishing Rama Janma Bhoomi Mandir on its place, then such a mosque built on such a usurped land deserves to be destroyed. No theologian or Alim can give a *Fatwa* to hold *Namaz* on it.' And this view in turn reflected classical expositions of the law. For instance the *Fatwa-e-Alamgiri,* Justice Deokinandan notes, categorically states:

It is not permissible to build a mosque on unlawfully acquired land. There may be many forms of unlawful acquisition. For instance, if some people forcibly take somebody's house (or land) and build a mosque or even a Jama Masjid on it, then *Namaz* in such a mosque will be against the Shariat.

In consultation with the two sides, therefore, Chandra Shekhar made the issue specific. Each side agreed to submit evidence on this specific issue.

The AIBMAC Evidence

I was appalled when I saw what the AIBMAC had furnished. It was just a pile of papers. You were expected to wade through them and discover the relevance they had or the inference which flowed from them.

I read them dutifully, and was soon convinced that the leaders of the All India Babri Masjid Action Committee and the intellectuals who had been guiding them had themselves not read the pile of papers.

It wasn't just that so much of it was the stuff of cranks: pages from the book of some chap to the effect that Rama was actually a Pharaoh of Egypt; an article by someone based he says on what he has learnt from one dancer in Sri Lanka, and setting out a folk story, knowledge of which he himself says is confined to a small part of a small district in that country, to the effect that Sita was Rama's sister whom he married, etc.

It was not just that so much of the rest was as tertiary as can be – articles after articles by sundry journalists which set out no evidence.

It was that the overwhelming bulk of it was just a pile of court papers – selective court judgments, a decree without the judgment underlying it, some merely the plaints, i.e. the assertions of the parties that happen at the moment to be convenient – and it was that document after document in this lot buttressed the case, not of the All India Babri Masjid Committee, but of the VHP!

They show that the mosque has not been in use since 1934.

They show that it had been in utter neglect: the relevant authority testifying at one point to the person-in-charge being an opium-addict, to his being thoroughly unfit to look after even the structure.

They show different groups or sects of Muslims fighting each other for acquiring the property, with the descendants of

Mir Baqi, the commander who built the structure, maintaining that the lands etc. which were given to them by the British were given not so that they may maintain the structure through the proceeds but so that they may maintain themselves, and that they were given these for the services – political and military – they had rendered to the British.

It was evident too that it would be difficult to sustain the claim that the structure was a *waqf*, as was being maintained now. It was not even listed in the lists of either the Shia or Sunni Waqf Boards, as the law requires all *waqf* properties to be.

While the Babri Masjid Committee has striven now to rule out of court British gazetteers – as these, after meticulous examination of written and other evidence, record unambiguously that the mosque was built after demolishing the Ramajanmabhoomi temple – the rulings and judgments filed by the AIBMAC rely on, reproduce at length and accept the gazetteers on the very point at issue. Indeed, they explicitly decree that the gazetteers are admissible as evidence!

They show the Hindus waging an unremitting struggle to regain this place held, the documents say, 'most sacred' by them; they show them continuing to worship the ground in spite of the mosque having been superimposed on it; they show them constructing structures and temples on the peripheral spots when they are debarred from the main one.

They show the current suit being filed well, well past the time limit allowed by our laws....

On reading the papers the AIBMAC had filed as 'evidence' I could only conclude therefore that either its leaders had not read the papers themselves, or that they had no case and had just tried to over-awe or confuse the Government etc. by dumping a huge miscellaneous heap.

The VHP Documents

In complete contrast the VHP documents are pertinent to the point, and have not as yet been shown to be deficient in any way.

They contain the unambiguous statements of Islamic historians, of Muslim narrators – from the grand-daughter of Aurangzeb – to the effect that the mosque was built by demolishing the Ram temple.

They contain accounts of European travellers as well as
official publications of the British period – the gazetteers of 1854,
of 1877, of 1881, of 1892, of 1905; the Settlement Report
of 1880; the Surveyor's Report of 1838; the Archaeological Survey
Reports of 1891, of 1934 – all of them reaffirming what the
Muslim historians had stated: that the mosque was built by
destroying the temple, that portions of the temple – eg., the pillars
– are in the mosque still, that the Hindus continue to rever the spot
and struggle unremittingly to reacquire it.

They contain revenue records of a hundred years and more
which list the site as 'Janmasthan' and specify it to be the
property of the *mahants*. They also show how attempts have been
made to erase things from these records and superimpose
convenient nomenclatures on them – crude and unsuccessful
attempts, for while the forgers have been able to get at the records
in some offices they have not been able to get at them in all
the offices!

Most important of all, they contain accounts of the archaeological excavations which were conducted at the site from 1975 to
1980. These are conclusive: the pillar-bases, the pillars, the door
jamb, the periods of the different layers, the alignment of the
bases and the pillars, the stone of which the pillars are
made....Everything coheres. And everything answers the issue
the Government and the two sides had specified in the affirmative,
and unambiguously so.

'Contemporary Account'

'But where in all this is the contemporary account of the temple
being destroyed?'

At first it was, 'Show us any document'. When the
gazetteers were produced, it was, "But the British wrote only to
divide and rule (why then do you keep producing judgments of
British Magistrates, pray?) Show us some non-British document,
some pre-British document.'

Now that these too are at hand, the demand is for a
contemporary account. This when it is well-known that in the
contemporary account of the period – Babar's own memoir – the
pages from the time he reaches Ayodhya, 2 April 1528, to 18
September 1528 are missing – lost, it is hypothesised by the

historians, in a storm or in the vicissitudes which Humayun's library suffered during his exile.

It is not just that this latest demand is an after-thought. It is that in the face of what exists at the site to this day – the pillars etc. – and in the face of the archaeological findings, and what has been the universal practice as well as the fundamental faith of Islamic evangelists and conquerors such accounts are not necessary.

But there is an even more conclusive consideration. Today a contemporary account is being demanded in the case of the Babri Mosque. Are those who make this demand prepared to accept this as the criterion – that if a contemporary account exists of the destruction of a temple for constructing a mosque the case is made?

This is what the entry for 2 September, 1669 for instance is in as contemporary an account as any one can ask for: 'News came to Court that in accordance with the Emperor's command his Officers had demolished the temple of Vishwanath at Banaras....'

The entry for January 1670 sets out the facts for the great temple at Mathura: 'In this month of Ramzan, the religious-minded Emperor ordered the demolition of the temple at Mathura.... In a short time by the great exertions of his officers the destruction of this strong centre of infidelity was accomplished.... A grand mosque was built on its site at a vast expenditure.... The idols, large and small, set with costly jewels which had been set up in the temple were brought to Agra and burried under the steps of the Mosque of the Begum Sahib in order to be continually trodden upon. The name of Mathura was changed to Islamabad....'

The entry for 1 January 1705 says: 'The Emperor, summoning Muhammed Khalid and Khidmat Rai, the *darogha* of hatchet-men.... ordered them to demolish the temple at Pandharpur, and to take the butchers of the camp there and slaughter cows in the temple.... It was done.'

If the fact that a contemporary account of the temple at Ayodhya is not available leaves the matter unsettled, does the fact that contemporary accounts are available for the temples at Kashi, Mathura, Pandharpur and a host of other places settle the matter?

One has only to ask the question to know that the 'experts' and 'intellectuals' will immediately ask for something else.

Historicity

'But there is no proof that Ram himself existed; nor are any of the other facts about him proven.'

The four Gospels themselves, to say nothing of the work that has been done in the last hundred years , differ on fact after fact about Jesus – from the names of his ancestors to the crucifixion and resurrection. The Quran repudiates even the most basic facts about him – it emphatically denounces the notion that he was the Son of God, it repudiates the notion of his virgin birth, it insists that he was not the one who was crucified but a look-alike, thereby putting the resurrection out of the question altogether. And which member of the AIBMAC will say that the Quran is not an authentic recounting of the facts? Does that mean that every single church rests on myth?

Nor is the historicity of the Prophet the distinguishing feature about him. Every ordinary person living today is historically verifiable, after all. The unique claim about the Prophet is that Allah chose him to transmit the Quran. But it would be absurd to ask anyone to prove the fact of Allah having chosen him. It is a matter of faith.

Indeed, the uniqueness of the Quran itself is a matter of faith. What the faithful have and read and rever is said to be the reproduction of the original which lies in heaven inscribed on tablets of gold. And it is the contents of that original which Allah transmitted through the angel Gabriel to the Prophet. Heaven, the original on tablets of gold, Allah's decision, Gabriel – do we prove these? They too are matters of faith.

And every mosque is a celebration of those separate foci of faith.

Specific mosques are even more so. The great Al-Aqsa mosque marks the print which the Prophet's foot made as he alighted from the winged-horse which had carried him on his journey to heaven. Heaven, the Journey, the winged horse, the imprint of one particular foot – in regard to which of these would we entertain a demand for 'proof'?

The Hazaratbal mosque in Kashmir enshrines what is revered as the hair of the Prophet. Would we think of proving the matter?

And yet that is what we are insisting the devotees of Ram do.

Conclusion

The Muslim laity have been badly misled, and now been badly let down by those who set themselves up as their guardians and sole-spokesmen. First they created the scare that were any reasonable solution to be accepted on this matter Islam would be endangered. Now they have failed to substantiate their rhetoric.

Now that they seem to be finding excuses to withdraw from examining the evidence, we are liable to be plunged back into the vicious politics of manipulative politicians – that is, the precise politics which has fomented the current reaction.

We can stem the relapse. As the experts have withdrawn, each of us should secure the documents submitted by the two sides and examine them in the minutest detail. Once we do so it will be that much more difficult for propagandists to thwart this singular effort to introduce reason and reasonableness into the problem.

– 27 January 1991

XIX

Ayodhya: Some Interim Lessons

In June 1975, to go no further back than that, the Allahabad High Court held Mrs. Gandhi guilty of corrupt electoral practices, and disqualified her from holding elective office for six years. Demonstrations were organized, effigies of the Judge burnt. Mrs. Gandhi filed an appeal against the order in the Supreme Court. Her counsel told the Court, 'The nation is solidly behind (her) as Prime Minister,' and warned, 'There are momentous consequences, disastrous to the country, if anything less than total suspension of the Order under appeal is made.' The Court granted only a conditional stay. The Emergency was clamped, and thousands thrown in jail. The electoral law was altered so that the misdeeds of which Mrs. Gandhi had been held guilty no longer constituted and were deemed never to have constituted corrupt electoral practices. Justice Sinha, it was said, had been an RSS sympathizer. The people, it was said, were with Mrs. Gandhi. Legal technicalities, it was said, would not be allowed to thwart the mandate the people had given Mrs. Gandhi to abolish poverty. The progressives applauded – Arjun Singh and S.B. Chavan most vigorously.

After decades and decades of litigation and several orders of the lower courts, in September 1983 the Supreme Court finally directed that two graves of Sunnis be shifted out of a Shia graveyard in Varanasi. The Sunnis in U.P. raised a storm. The state government submitted that executing the Court's direction would endanger peace and order in the state. The Supreme Court stayed its own order for ten years. No champion of the Court protested.

In 1986 the Supreme Court declared that a Muslim husband who had thrown his aged and infirm wife out after forty five years of marriage should pay her a pittance of an alimony. Passions were whipped up. The Government changed the law so as to nullify the judgment. 'The Muslims would have been up in arms otherwise,' Rajiv's apologists explained. The secularists applauded, Arjun Singh most vigorously.

In October 1990 when VP Singh lunged for Mandal and was confronted with the question what he would do if the courts held to their previous judgments and struck down the enhanced reservations, he declared that he and his colleagues would remove the 'obstruction'. The progressives applauded.

In 1991 the Supreme Court gave its order on the Cauvery dispute : the Tribunal's order is binding it said. The Government did not enforce it : 'Karnataka will be in flames,' it was explained.

On 22 July 1992, when the defiance by the VHP was the focus of everyone's ire, a BJP member of the Rajya Sabha inquired about railway land which was under illegal occupation. The Minister of State for Railways acknowledged that 17000 acres of railway land is under illegal occupation. And that in spite of court orders the Government has not recovered the land as attempts to evict those who have illegally usurped it would rupture the peace.

In between of course there have been a host of other occasions on which orders of courts have been treated in the same way, and the BJP has released a list of them – from orders of the Rajasthan High Court asking the government to clear the illegally usurped verandahs in Jaipur's historic bazaars, to those of the Calcutta High Court to demolish the unauthorized part of a new mosque – the illegal structure was instead regularized – to warrants issued in Kerala for the arrest and production of the Imam of Delhi's Jama Masjid.

Events of the last three weeks in Ayodhya show that the Hindus – or, at the least, an organization speaking in the name of Hindus – have drawn the obvious conclusion : court orders or no court orders, one can have one's way if one creates a situation which convinces the authorities that to implement the court's orders will send the people up in flames.

Now, that is the first lesson : the Rule of Law, the authority of the State is a seamless web. When rulers overturn laws to suit their personal convenience out of greed for office – as Mrs. Gandhi did in regard to the electoral law; when courts themselves kill the law out of fear of the rulers – as the Supreme Court did during the Emergency in the *habeas corpus* and other cases ; when the rulers bend the State out of fear of one section of the population -- as Rajiv did on Shah Bano, on Rushdie; when the State is weak-kneed in facing up to those who are killing its citizens, who are out to dismember it -- as it was for years in regard to the terrorists ; when this is the case, others also conclude that the State can and should be bent, that the courts and the law, like everything else, are just a convenience of the powerful. The rise of the VHP and its intransigence, of which we have had just a glimpse, are the net result of the last decade's politics of pandering.

The second lesson is even more specific, and I am sorry to say that the courts are even more directly responsible for it. Commentators have rightly said that Ayodhya, like the anxiety over reservations, is a problem which the politicians have created and now they are dumping it on the courts. But the courts have compounded the difficulties for themselves. They have not only gone along and taken these problems on themselves, having taken them on they have prevaricated. They have allowed one legal dodge after another to be used. In the event, people have been compelled to conclude that, like the rulers, the courts are not serious about attending to the matter, that if it is left to the courts it will not get anywhere for decades. The original suite against permitting the idols to be worshipped has been wasting away for over forty years. Another suite alleging -- without specifying -- that there is a Muslim graveyard to one side of the structure has been allowed to hold things up for thirty years. The appeal that the suite of the Sunni Waqf Board is time-barred has been languishing in the Supreme Court for two years. When the acquisition of the land by the U.P. Government was challenged last October/November, the impression was given that the Supreme Court and Allahabad High Court would settle the matter by December 15, 1991. We are in July 1992, and even the hearings have not concluded as yet.

That had been the pace. And see what has happened now. The VHP begins its *kar sewa* on 9 July. And in just two weeks the Government promises to have the courts settle the matter within three months. The Supreme Court itself announces that the moment the *kar sewa* is stopped a bench will be constituted to hear the acquisition matter on a day to day basis, that it will transfer all cases concerning the matter to itself.

Clearly, what our newsmen call 'hard-liners' have been vindicated: the attention which normal pleading could not have persuaded the courts and Government to pay the matter for twenty years, *dhakka* has persuaded them to pay in just two weeks. That is not a lesson to which anyone should be driven. But the courts and the rulers are the ones who have driven that lesson home.

The third lesson is for the media, specially so as this last round has shown that we have not learnt it. As the State has been successfully bent by Sikh and Muslim communalists over the last decade, double-standards, I would say in some cases duplicity have been the hallmark of the media's treatment of events and issues. L K Advani's example – the shameful neglect by the media of the lakh and a half refugees in Jammu – has nailed the emblem of the times: had they been Muslims, Advani has asked, would the press, to say nothing of civil liberties groups have spared them as little attention? The treatment of the Ayodhya controversy has been of exactly the same kind. No paper has recalled that mosques have often been destroyed and built elsewhere in Middle Eastern countries for purposes as mundane as widening highways. No paper while stressing, 'But they say there is a Muslim graveyard there,' has recalled that in Saudi Arabia not just ordinary graves but the graves and tombs of the companions of the Prophet himself have been destroyed, and by the Government. Every paper has studiously avoided mentioning that while the Babri Masjid Committee etc. have been shouting that there is a grave-yard there, the area having been turned inside out upto a depth of twelve feet not one grave has turned up. Once it became clear that documents submitted by the two sides strengthened the VHP's case, the papers studiously neglected them. When the Babri Masjid Action Committee's representatives failed to turn up for the meetings the Government had scheduled, there was scarcely a murmur: what would have been the case if the VHP representatives had stopped coming ? It is this pattern which has done as much to raise the Hindu temper to the present pitch as the rulers did by bending the State to Muslim and Sikh fundamentalists.

And yet that pattern has continued. When Hindu shrines standing on the land belonging to the VHP, and since acquired by the UP Government, were levelled, there was much hue and cry – by the press as much as by V.P. Singh and Arjun Singh. Was there any when Hindu shrines were levelled along with shops and houses as part of the plan to beautify and render safe the area around the Golden Temple just four years ago – a levelling which incidentally was upheld by the Punjab and Haryana High Court ? In the last two weeks the one construction which would put the organizers and participants in a poor light has been the order of the day : one day the call of Singhal to *kar sewaks* to rush to Ayodhya has been reported to have evoked little response; the next the numbers have been reported to be so large that the structure is endangered; one day the VHP and the *sadhus* have been said to be obstinate and unbending, the next, when it seemed they might heed the Prime Minister's appeal, they have been said to be 'back-tracking' upon realizing that the BJP has become isolated !

The most telling illustration has been provided by the silence over the new archaeological findings. At first there was much demand for these, 'Where is the evidence that there was a temple at the site before the mosque was built ?' When the findings of the excavations which had been conducted over a decade ago became public, and these left little doubt about the fact that there had indeed been a temple at the site, archaeology itself was denounced. Papers made themselves available for tarnishing one of the most respected archaeologists in the world – the former Director General of the Archaelogical Survey of India who had led those excavations. It turns out that during the course of the current diggings additional evidence surfaced – courtyards paved with *pucca* bricks in direct continuance of the existing structure, a regular layer of a brick wall 12 feet above the brick-flooring of the courtyard, a platform of stone-slabs joined by pebbles and lime, pieces of door jambs, one of the *amalakhas* etc. Now, these are discoveries of the utmost importance. They have a direct bearing on the controversy at hand, in fact on the issue which the papers tell us the Supreme Court is to consider. How many papers have given even a cursory account of these finds or published photographs of them? This when – perhaps, 'because'? – the same finds have led two former Directors of the Archaeological Survey of India, along with others, to say that they greatly reinforce the view that a temple stood at the site before the mosque was built.

The lesson is plain : should such double-standards continue, Hindu opinion will become even less amenable to the minatory admonitions of our editorialists than it has already become. As far as politicians are concerned, I would put the point even more

emphatically. There was much glee among several Congressmen
and of course among the Left and National Front leaders,
in the weeks preceding the Presidential election that they had
once again succeeded in isolating the BJP, it had been made the
untouchable once again. As these events show, when you isolate
someone, he acts on his own! The lesson should register on the
Congress in UP in particular. 'What have you done to build the
temple?,' they have been taunting the Government there for
months. Even when the current round began they taunted, 'But why
are you beginning the construction at the gate to the temple? Why
not at the *Garbha-graha* ?' When we taunt others so vociferously,
we should not be surprised that they act on our taunts!

A Quantum Change

It would be a great mistake to underestimate the extent to which
Hindu sentiment has been hardened by the State bending to
communalists and terrorists, and by the duplicitous discourse
of our elite. Everything the Hindus say speaks to the sea-change:
'If you will bend the State on Shah Bano, on reservations, we will
bend it on Ayodhya,' 'If you will insist on having your way in
regard to the *kar-sewa* at Akal Takht, we will have our *kar-sewa*
at the Ram Mandir,' 'If you will create a vote bank of 10 per
cent of the population, we will create a mega-bank of 80 per cent.'
      There are two changes which go even deeper. When the point
has been put to the BJP and the VHP that they are wrong to
proceed by evasions – 'The land is being acquired for tourism,'
'Reconstruction, not demolition', 'Renovation, not reconstruction'
they have maintained that the way things are – the way the
courts, the media, the rulers are – they will not allow them to
proceed in a straight forward manner. The maxim of Tilak
Maharaj, it will be recalled, used to be: *Shatham prati shaathyam*,
'Wickedness to the wicked.' Gandhiji used to remonstrate with him
over this, and urge instead that the true law is, *Shatham pratyapi
satyam*, 'Truth even to the wicked.' If things continue as they are,
the Hindus will revert to Shivaji's example and Tilak's maxim,
and consign Gandhiji's.
      The second change is that the Hindus are beginning to focus
on the State as Hindus. The thousand years of foreign rule apart,
the last decade holds both negative and positive examples which

goad them to do so. The 'victories' Muslim fundamentalists wrested, for instance, were secured because they were able to bend -- to frighten -- those who were occupying the offices of State : that has signalled to the Hindus that the only way for them to prevent such things from happening is to make sure that the State is in stronger hands. The last fortnight provides the positive example. There were many in the VHP as well as the BJP who felt that they should sacrifice the UP Government if necessary for the Mandir by taking on, and then persisting in a confrontation with the central Government as well as the courts. The view which ultimately prevailed was the opposite : it had been possible to do so much within just eight months towards building the temple only because the Government in UP was theirs; for building the temple itself, if for nothing else, it was necessary that the Government there continue in office. The point registered on the sadhus also, and, apart from the assurance the Prime Minister gave them, it was one of the considerations which persuaded them to shift the *kar-sewa* to another site.

That is the point. Critics who say, 'But it has nothing to do with religion,' do not realize how very right they are. The temple at Ayodhya is not a symbol today of protest against a wrong done 500 years ago. It is a symbol of protest against the politics of the last seventy years, in particular of the politics of the last decade, the politics of vote banks, the politics of pandering, it is a symbol of outrage at the discourse of double-standards and duplicity.

'But what about the existing structure? Will it go or will it be allowed to stand?'

The answer is not in some formula. Nor is it in the hands of the Government or even the VHP. Even if some formula is agreed upon by these agencies but politics and discourse remain what they are, a harsher movement will arise with destroying the structure as an article of its faith. If politics and discourse improve, compromise will be hailed as statesmanship.

The present pause can itself mark the turn -- in either direction. If subsequent events bear out the spirit in which the Prime Minister talked to the sadhus and the assurances which were held out, things will go one way. If the Government tilts once again, if the reference to the Supreme Court is not in accord with what has been agreed to, if proceedings in the Court once again are allowed to be stalled, not just the sadhus but the Hindus themselves will conclude that they have been tricked once again. And the structure will be doomed.

— 26 July 1992

XX

The Latest Argument

At first the demand-cum-assurance was, 'If you can bring any proof showing a temple had been demolished to construct the mosque, we will ourselves demolish the mosque.' A host of documents — reports of the Archaeological Survey of India going back to 1891, Gazetteers going back to 1854, Survey reports giving back to 1838 — were produced which stated unambiguously that a Ram temple had been demolished to construct the mosque.

The demand suddenly changed. 'These are all British documents,' it was now said, 'The British concocted this story to divide and rule. Show us some pre-British document.' That this assessment of the worth of British documents was an invention to get over inconvenient facts became evident soon enough: when in response to Chandrashekhar's initiative the All India Babri Masjid Action Committee submitted documents, most of these turned out to be nothing but the rulings of sundry British magistrates! Worse, they confirmed what the Vishwa Hindu Parishad had been saying : that the mosque had not been in use since 1936; that it had been built by demolishing the Ram temple; that the Hindus had, at the cost of many lives, been trying throughout to capture the spot as they held it to be the sacred birth place of Lord Ram.

In any event, non-British, specifically Muslim documents as well as pre-British documents, including the account of an Austrian Jesuit priest who had stayed in Ayodhya in 1766-71 were produced. Each of them stated the same facts.

'But each of these is only repeating what the other is saying,' it was said. 'Show us some contemporary document.' The demand for such a document was manifestly a dodge: the one document — the *Babar-Nama* — which could have settled the matter is truncated: Babar records his reaching Ayodhya (on 2 April, 1528), the pages from then to 18 September, 1528 are missing, and are surmised to have been lost in a storm in May 1529, or during Humayun's subsequent wanderings in the desert as a fugitive. The matter however   was   soon nailed.   If the absence of a contemporary account is conclusive in this case, is the fact that contemporary accounts -- the very day's Court bulletins -- recording the destruction of the temples of Mathura, Kashi, Pandharpur and scores and scores of other places and their replacement by mosques are available proof enough to propel Shahabuddin etc. to demolish *those* mosques ?

No answer was forthcoming. Instead, there were demands for more concrete proof. This was soon available in the results of the archaeological excavations which had been conducted in 1975-'80. When attention was drawn to the pillars on which the domes etc. of the mosque rest to this day, to the carvings on these, it was said that these could well have been brought from elsewhere. But that alibi too floundered. It could not account for the pillar bases which were found three to four feet below the surface just outside the boundary wall : these were in perfect alignment with the pillars inside the mosque, and it was clear that, along with them, there must have been pillars on these bases which supported the larger structure of the temple; no one would have dragged bases of pillars from a distance and buried them outside the mosque to align with pillars inside the mosque!

So, archaeology itself was denounced. And sophistry was put out. Irfan Habib led the charge. But his own howler showed his arguments to be special pleading: if one went by the dates he ascribed on the basis of 'Carbon dating' and all, Babar would have expired in 1965 instead of 1530, the reign of Akbar would commence in 2001 instead of having ended in 1605!

Since then the case of these pleaders has been made worse by the new finds: entire walls and floor levels have now come into view, twelve to fourteen feet below the surface. No one could have picked these up from a distance and planted them under the structure !

And now the Argument is

At the discussion on Ayodhya which NEWSTRACK organized on 1 August Shahabuddin produced yet another argument. I had just quoted a signed statement he had distributed to the press as late as

15 June 1989 in which he had said, 'But the Hindu chauvinists are totally confused about their own case.... Whatever the Hindu chauvinist case, the Muslim community has, without any legal obligation, offered, as a moral gesture, to demolish the Babri Masjid – if it is proved that a temple stood on the site of the Babri Masjid and it was pulled down to construct the mosque.'' As the point at issue accordingly was whether there had been a temple at the site, I said, we should focus on the archaeological evidence to settle the matter.

Shahabuddin said that he stood by the statement. His argument was that the temple JUST COULD NOT HAVE BEEN pulled down as pulling down a place of worship to construct a mosque is against the Shariat. Incredulous, the principal correspondent of NEWSTRACK, Manoj Raghuvanshi, later asked Shahabuddin whether in that case no temple had been demolished by Muslim rulers. 'It is not a historical fact,' said Shahabuddin, 'that a standing temple in peace time was demolished by any Muslim ruler.' Assertions to the contrary, he said, are all 'chauvinist propaganda'! Even with the hedging – 'standing temple', 'in peace time' – that was quite a lump to swallow. You mean even Somnath was not demolished, Raghuvanshi asked. 'Somnath was disintegrated,' said Shahabuddin, and reaffirmed his thesis that temples could not have been demolished because pulling them down to build mosques was against the Shariat.

'Disintegrated', not 'demolished'? A disingenuous give-away, I thought: the VHP would be quite satisfied with that kind of disintegration now! Even if one accepted his contention about Shariat, the inference Shahbuddin had drawn was indefensible: it was like saying that no murders take place today because murdering is prohibited by the law!

But there is a more conclusive point : is it at all the case that demolishing a place of worship to replace it with a mosque is prohibited by the Shariat?

What was Done

Every single Muslim historian of medieval India lists temples which the rulers he is writing about has destroyed and the mosques he has built instead. In his volume, *Hindu Temples, What happened to Them, The Islamic Evidence*, Sita Ram Goel reproduces some of these accounts verbatim. Doing nothing but this, without any comments at all, takes over 170 printed pages of the book.

Nor was the practice confined to India, or to temples. Here are just two paragraphs from the entry, *Masjid*, in the first *Encyclopedia of Islam, 1931-36*:

.....It is rather doubtful whether the process (of acquiring churches) was a regular one; in any case the Muslims in course of time appropriated many churches to themselves. With the mass-conversions to Islam, this was a natural result. The churches taken over by the Muslims were occasionally used as dwellings (cf. Tabari, i. 2405, 2407); at a later date it also happened that they were used as government offices, as in Egypt in 146 (Makrizi iv. 35; cf. for Kufa, Baladhuri, p. 286). The obvious thing, however, was to transform the churches taken into mosques. It is related of 'Amr b. al-Asi that he performed the salat in a church (Makrizi, iv. 6) and Zaid b. 'Ali says regarding churches and synagogues, 'Perform thy salat in them; it will not harm thee' (*Corpus juris di Zaid b. 'Ali*, ed. Griffini, No. 364). It is not clear whether the reference in these cases is to conquered sanctuaries; it is evident, in any case, that the saying is intended to remove any misgivings about the use of captured churches and synagogues as mosques. The most important example of this kind was in Damascus where al-Walid b. 'Abd al-Malik in 86 (705) took the church of St. John from the Christians and had it rebuilt; he is said to have offered the Christians another church in its stead (see the references above, B.i; and also J.A., 9 Ser., vii. 369 *sqq*.; Quatremere, *Hist. Sult._Maml.*, 11/i. 262 *sqq*. and the article DAMASCUS). He is said to have transformed into mosques ten churches in all in Damascus. It must have been particularly in the villages, with the gradual conversion of the people to Islam, that the churches were turned into mosques. In the Egyptian village there were no mosques in the earlier generations of Islam (Makrizi, iv. 28 sq., 30). But when al-Mamun was fighting the Copts, many churches were turned into mosques, (*ibid.*, p. 30). It is also recorded of mosques in Cairo that they were converted churches. According to one tradition, the Rashida mosque was an unfinished Jacobite church, which was surrounded by

Jewish and Christian graves (Makrizi, iv: 63, 64) and in the immediate vicinity al-Hakim turned a Jacobite and a Nestorian Church into mosques (*ibid.*, p. 65). When Djawhar built a palace in al-Kahira, a *dir* was taken in and transformed into a mosque (*ibid.*, p. 269); similar changes took place at later dates (*ibid.*, p. 240) and synagogues also were transformed in this way (Masjid Ibn al-Banna, *ibid.*, p. 265). The chief mosque in Palermo was previously a church (Yakut, *Mu'djam,* i. 719). After the Crusades several churches were turned into mosques in Palestine (Sauvaire, *Hist. de Jerus, it d'Ilibron*, 1876, p. 77; Quatremere, *Hist. Sult. Maml.*, I/ii., 40).

Other sanctuaries than those of the 'people of the scripture' were turned into mosques. For example a Masjid al-Shams between Hilla and Kerbela was the successor of an old temple of Shamash (see Goldziher, *Muh. Stud.,* ii. 331 sq.). Not far from Ishtakhr was a Masjid Sulaiman which was an old 'fire-temple', the pictures on the walls of which could still be seen in the time of Mas'udi and al-Makdisi (ivth century) (Mas'udi, *Murudi,* iv. 77; B.G.A., iii. 444). In Ishtakhr itself there was a djami', which was a converted fire-temple (*ibid.*, p. 436). In Masisa, the ancient Mopsuhestia, al-Mansur in 140 built a mosque on the site of an ancient temple (Baladhuri, p. 165 *sq.*) and the chief mosque in Dihli was originally a temple (Ibn Battuta, iii. 151); as to Ta'if cf. Abu Dawud, *Salat,* bab 10. Thus in Islam also the old rule holds that sacred places survive changes of religion. It was especially easy in cases where Christian sanctuaries were associated with Biblical personalities who were also recognised by Islam : e.g., the Church of St. John in Damascus and many holy places in Palestine. One example is the mosque of Job in Shekh Sad, associated with Sura xxi. 83, xxxviii. 40; here in Silvia's time (fourth century) there was a church of Job (Mas'udi, i. 91; Baedeker, Palast. u. Syrun, 1910, p. 147.)

The Shariat

But could it not be that, like the Muslim rulers in India, these Muslim rulers of the Middle East were also doing all this in violation of the Shariat ? As we know, the Shariat is based on what the Quran says and on what the Prophet did, that is on the Sunnah. The Quran is sanguinary in the extreme, there can be little doubt on the matter. The only question therefore is about what the Prophet himself did.

The evidence is incontrovertible : it leaves nothing of Shahabuddin's latest argument. The Prophet's companions as well as his biographers -- the earliest, all devout Muslims, whose accounts are among the most authoritative sources we have of the Prophet's life -- report his ordering the destruction of a mosque as it had been set up by persons he did not think well of, they report his ordering new converts to demolish a church and establish a mosque instead at the site, they report his converting what had on all accounts become a pagan temple, with idols, paintings and all, into the greatest mosque of all -- that is, the Kaba itself. There is space to recall just an incident or two.

We learn from Ibn Sa'd's *Kitab al-Tabaqat Al-Kabir*, (Pakistan Historical Society, Karachi, Publication No. 46, Volume I, pp. 373-4) and the widely used collection of *Hadis*, *Mishkat Al-Masabih*, (Book iv. 2), of a delegation of 13 to 19 members of Banu Hanifa calling on the Prophet. We learn of them being looked after generously -- with bread, meat, milk, butter, dates. They receive instruction in Islam. They swear allegiance to the Prophet. It is time to leave. Talq b. Ali, who was in the delegation, states: 'We went out as a deputation to God's messenger and swore allegiance to him and prayed along with him. We told him that we had a church in our land, and we asked him for some of the leavings of the water he used for ablution. He called for water, performed ablution, then poured it out for us into a skin vessel, and gave us the following command, "Go away, and when you come to your land break down your church, sprinkle this water on its site, and use it as a mosque." We told him that our land was distant, the heat severe, and that the water would evaporate, to which he replied, "Add some water to it, for it will only bring more good to it."'

Upon returning they did as the Prophet had commanded. Our narrator, Talq b. Ali, became the *muezzin* of the mosque and recited the *azaan*. The friar of the church, the reverential Ibn Sa'd records, 'heard it (the *azaan*) and said, "It is a word of truth and call to truth." Then he escaped and it was the end of the regime.' (*Kitab al-Tabaqat al-Kabir, op.cit.*, Volume I, pp.

373-4). Any ambiguity there ?

Nor can Shahabuddin's claim that Shariat forbids the destruction of temples etc. in peace time be sustained in view of what the Prophet himself commanded and did. His earliest biographers — Ibn Ishaq and Ibn Sa'd, for instance — record instance after instance in which idols and temples were smashed, destroyed and burnt down at his orders. The temples of al-Uzza, al-Laat, and al-Manaat — the three godesses who are subjects of the Satanic verses in the Quran — the temples around Ta'if, those of Fils and Ruda in Tayys — are all reported by them to have been destroyed on the direct orders of the Prophet. Similarly, the biographers report the Prophet's joy when converts came and reported to him that they had destroyed this temple or that, or smashed to smithereens this idol or that. These were not instances when during a battle an army over-ran a site which happened to be a temple. These were instances of persons or tribes having come over to Islam, and then, as part of their new commitment, destroying the places of worship.

Nor, it must be noted, was the Prophet less stern about some refractory party setting up even a mosque. His orders at Dhu Awan are well known. Ibn Ishaq reports that as the Prophet approached the town, the devotees approached him saying, 'We have built a mosque for the sick and needy and for nights of bad weather, and we should like you to come to us and pray for us there.' The Prophet, Ibn Ishaq records, said that 'he was on the point of travelling, and was preoccupied, or words to that effect, and that when he came back, if God willed, he would come to them and pray for them in it.' But at Dhu Awan, upon hearing about the mosque, he summoned the followers, 'and told them to go to the mosque of these evil men and destroy and burn it.' That is exactly what the followers then did. A revelation came down from Allah and sanctified the destruction (*Quran*, 9.107).

I just do not see where Shahabuddin derives his ecumenical rule from.

But the most telling example is that of the Kaba, and the Masjid al-Haram, the mosque — the most revered in Islam — around it. And it is to this that we should turn to settle the matter.

What the Kaba was

Till the very day the Prophet took it under his control after his conquest of Mecca, the Kaba and the structure around it were a place of pagan worship with idols and paintings of all sorts of gods and goddesses.

From the earliest to the most recent biographers of the Prophet, all speak of it as such. Recalling days long before the Prophet, Ibn Ishaq reports the answer of the Hudhaylis to the King when he asked them why they too would not do in regard to the Kaba -- circumambulate the temple, venerate it, shave their heads etc. -- as they were exhorting him to do: 'They replied that it was indeed the temple of their father Abraham, but the idols which the inhabitants had set up round it, and the blood which they shed there (by sacrificing animals) presented an insuperable obstacle. They are unclean polytheists, said they -- or words to that effect.' We learn of the Prophet's arguments with the controllers of the shrine about the idols. We learn of their fear that should his iconoclasm prevail they would lose the livelihood they now secured out of the pilgrims who came to worship the idols, and accordingly their fierce opposition to the Prophet. We learn of his returning to Mecca for 'the lesser pilgrimage' and going to the Kaba 'cluttered with idols though it was.' Such are the accounts in that earliest and most authoritative of his biographies. The accounts continue to this day.

'Why did so many tribes sustain the wealth and power of the Qoraysh by coming to the Kaba ?,' the Iranian scholar, Ali Dashti, asks about pre-Islamic times in his justly-acclaimed, *Twenty Three Years, A Study in the Prophetic Career of Mohammed* (George Allen and Unwin, London, 1985). 'The reason was that the Kaba housed famous idols and contained a black stone which the Arabs held sacred .... Each group of pilgrims had to shout its entreaties to its idol while circumambulating the Kaba and running from Safa to Marwa.' 'The Kaba,' he writes, recounting the setting in which Islam was established, 'was an important idol-temple, much visited by Beduin tribesmen and greatly respected as a holy place.... The livelihood of the Meccans and the prestige of the Quoryash chiefs depended on this coming and going. The Beduin came to visit the Kaba, which was an idol-temple. If the new religion required destruction of the idols, they would not come any more....' Ali Dashti refers to the Kaba repeatedly as 'the idol-temple which the tribes had revered....', as 'the famous idol-temple.'

The temple had several idols, among them 360 statues. The Quran itself mentions the three goddesses — al-Lat, al-Uzza and al-Manaat — who were worshipped there. The most prominent idol however was that of Hubal, 'who,' the first *Encyclopedia of Islam* states, 'may be called the God of Mecca and of the Kaba.' A male figure, it was made of red carnelian. The statue stood inside the Kaba, says the new edition of the *Encyclopedia*, above the sacred well which was thought to have been dug by Abraham to receive the offerings brought to the sanctuary. Though a stellar deity, its principal function was that of a 'cleromantic divinity,' it being the custom to consult the idol by divining arrows. Hubal, the number of idols — 360 — as well as the rites associated with them, have all been taken to point to an astral symbolism, and the temple has accordingly been taken to have been dedicated to the sun, the moon and the planets.

The temple continued in this condition till the very day on which the Prophet re-entered it upon capturing Mecca. That moment of triumph is recorded in great detail by the biographers. The accounts establish both sets of facts — they establish what was in the temple at that moment, and what the Prophet did to it. Notice that the moment was exactly the kind of moment which would test Shahabuddin's claim about what is and what is not allowed by the Shariat: this was not a situation of war, quite the contrary — the Meccans had surrendered without a real fight; the protagonist was the Prophet himself, so there can be no doubt about what the Shariat — based as it pre-eminently is on what he said and did — would entail; the structure had, as we have seen, been a house of worship of an altogether un-Islamic kind for ages.

How it was Transformed

Upon entering, the Prophet went round the Kaba seven times on his camel. He then climbed into the cube — the Kaba proper. Inside he found a dove made of wood, said in the *Encyclopedia* to having been possibly devoted to the Semitic Venus. 'He broke it in his hands,' records Ibn Ishaq, 'and threw it away.' He then saw paintings of Abraham, Jesus and Mary inside the structure: by one set of traditions he had all of them destroyed, by another he had all except those of Jesus and Mary destroyed. At the noon prayer that day 'he ordered,' Ibn Ishaq reports, 'that all the idols

which were round the Kaba should be collected and burned with
fire and broken up.' That was done. Soon enough idolaters were
forbidden from the shrine.

Here then was a structure which before the Prophet had been
for several generations a place of worship of an altogether
inclusive, pagan kind. The Prophet took it over -- or reclaimed it,
as the faithful would say -- and transformed it into the greatest
mosque of Islam. Where does that leave the Shahabuddin thesis-
as-proof : 'No temple could have been destroyed to build a mosque
as doing so is against the Shariat'?

Nor does the story end there. While, as the *Encyclopedia*
puts it, 'all the pagan trappings which had adhered to the Kaba
were thrust aside,' 'it is incontrovertible that an entire pre-
Islamic ritual, previously steeped in paganism, was adopted by
Islam after it had been purified and given a strictly monotheistic
orientation.' Treating the area as consecrated ground, treating
it as a refuge, the sacrificing of animals (shifted now from the Kaba
to Mina), the various elements connected with the Haj, including
among these the stoning of the Devil by throwing pebbles, the
rushing between Safa and Marwa, the halt at Arafat -- all these,
as the *Encyclopedia* and Ali Dashti etc. point out, date from the
pre-Islamic period. Some things, as Ali Dashti notes, were
just a bit transformed. The pre-Islamic Arabs approaching for
instance the goddess Manaat would call out, 'Here I am at your
service, (*labbayka*) O Manaat.' The same call was now
addressed to Allah: '*Labbayka Allahomma labbayka*,' 'Here I am
at your service, Allah, at your service.' The retention of these
-- even after transformation -- led to great disquiet. Even Umar, one
of the most devoted adherents of the Prophet, is said to have
exclaimed on approaching the Black Stone, for instance, 'I know
that thou art a stone, that neither helps nor hurts, and if the
Messenger of Allah had not kissed thee, I would not kiss thee.'
The special veneration accorded to the Stone, to the structure, to
everything which comes in contact with it -- for instance, the
rain water which falls off it through the spout, the cloth which
is used to cover it and which is cut into pieces and sold to the
pilgrims after being taken down -- have continued to be
contrasted with the strict admonitions against idolatry. The
disquiet has not settled. Here is Ali Dashti on the decisions the
Prophet handed down upon entering Kaba :

The Prophet Mohammad's decision to set out on a visit to the
Ka'ba in 6 A.H./628 is puzzling. Did he really believe the
Ka'ba to be God's abode? Or did he make this move in order
to placate followers for whom Ka'ba-visitation was an
ancestral tradition? Was his decision, which came
unexpectedly in view of the resolve of the hostile
Qorayshites to prevent Moslems from entering Mecca, and
which led to the disappointing truce of Hodaybiya, a political
stratagem designed to impress the Qoraysh chiefs with
Moslem numerical and military strength and to draw
ordinary, unfanatical Meccans to the new religion? How could
the man who had introduced the new religion and laws and had
repudiated all the beliefs and superstitions of his own people
now revive the main component of the old tradition in a new
form? Islam's zealous founder and legislator had above all
insisted on pure monotheism, telling the people that belief
in the One God is the only road to happiness and proclaiming
that 'the noblest among you in God's sight are the most pious
among you' (Sura 49, verse 13). Had he now succumbed to
national or racial feeling? Did he want to make veneration of
Ishmael's house a symbol of Arab national identity?

However that may be, the decision was so surprising and so
inconsistent with Islamic principles that many Moslems were
upset. Several believers objected to the running between Safa
and Marwa because it had been a pagan Arab rite; but its
retention was imposed by verse 153 Sura 2, 'Safa and Marwa
are among God's waymarks.' According to well authenticated
reports, 'Omar b. ol-Khattab, who was one of Mohammad's
greatest and wisest companions, said that he would never have
kissed the black stone if he had not personally seen the
Prophet kiss it. Ghazzali, whose authority in Islamic matters
deserves respect, wrote frankly that he could find no
explanation of the *hajj* ritual but obeyed because it was an
accomplished fact.

There is one verse in the Qor'an which sheds some light
on the matter and is perhaps an answer to questions about
it. This is verse 28 of Sura 9 (*ot-Tawba*): 'O believers, it is
a fact that the polytheists are unclean. Therefore they shall not
approach the Mosque of the Sanctuary (i.e. the Ka'ba) after

this year of theirs. If you fear poverty, God will enrich you from His bounty.' According to the *Tafsir ol-Jalalayn*, this meant that God would compensate the Arabs with victories and receipts of tribute. The Sura of repentance (*ot-Tawba*) is chronologically the last in the Qor'an, having been sent down in 10 A.H./631, well after the Moslem conquest of Mecca. The ban on visitation of the Ka'ba by non-Moslem tribes was likely to disquiet the people of Mecca, whose livelihood and flourishing trade depended on the coming and going of Arab tribes and groups. Although the Meccans were of the same tribe as the Prophet, most of them had only become Moslem under duress. If Mecca should lose its prosperity, there might be a risk of widespread apostasy. That risk would be averted by making pilgrimage to Mecca incumbent on Moslems.

This explanation is of course a mere hypothesis; to what extent it corresponds to the reality can never be known. In any case no rational or religious justification can be found for the retention of ancient pagan practices in the ritual of the Islamic *hajj*....

And it is said that it is Hinduism which 'swallows' other religions by incorporating their rituals and making *Avtaars* of their deities! However that may be, the Black Stone – the veneration in which it is held, the powers which are attributed to it, the benedictions which are assumed to flow from seeing, touching and kissing it; the fact that the rituals followed can so directly be traced to pre-Islamic times, and that their retention has continued to bewilder devout Muslims like Umar and Ghazzali – all these themselves put two things beyond doubt : the Kaba was a place of pagan idol worship with an elaborate set of rituals and an entire mode of life to go with it; second, the Prophet took it over and made it the holiest shrine of Islam.

'But Where is the Proof ?'

When Shahabuddin was expounding his thesis about the Shariat not allowing the destruction of a temple for constructing a mosque, I alluded to what the Kaba had been and how the Prophet himself had made it into a mosque.

Not true, said Suleiman Sait, the Muslim League M P. The Kaba was not a temple, he said. It was a mosque from times immemorial, the foundations of it having been laid by Abraham and Ishmael – the latter are prophets of the Jews but have been proclaimed by the Quran to have been the forebearers of the Prophet.

If the VHP had said something like that about the Ram Janmasthan, Shahabuddin, Suleiman Sait and of course our 'secular' polemicists, would have asked, 'But what is the proof that Abraham and Ishmael built the Kaba?' Well, what *IS* the proof?

'The Arabs possess no historical or semi-historical records of the origin of the Kaba,' says the *Encyclopedia*, 'and we as little.' For the entire period of the Prophet's stay in Mecca after he began receiving the revelations – thirteen years – and for the first year and a half after he went to Medina, the faithful were required to bow in prayer, not towards the Kaba, but towards Jerusalem. Then came the revelation to change the *Qibla* to Kaba. From the point of view of dogma, the *Encyclopedia* notes, 'this volte-face was justified by an appeal to the "religion of Abraham" which was specially invented for the occasion (Sura ii, 129, iii, 89 etc.)....'

The 'proof' of Abraham and Ishmael laying the foundations of the Kaba therefore is just the fact that it is so stated in the Quran (*Quran*, 2.121). Now, whether an affirmation just because it is in the Quran is to be regarded as proof is entirely a matter of faith. To insist that we must accept it as such would be to urge that exact kind of proof which the Babri Masjid protagonists have been rejecting so emphatically in the case of Ram's birth-place.

The only other circumstance bearing on the affirmation in the Quran is the *Makaam Abraham*, a sort of mark on a stone which lies near the Kaba. The faithful believe that once, after the building had risen to some height, Abraham stood on that stone, and the mark on it is his footprint. The Muslims look upon the footprint with the same reverence with which Hindus would view similar marks believed to be of their *Avtaars*. But that mark in the stone does not settle the matter – for it is as difficult to prove that the mark in that stone is indeed the impress which Abraham's foot made on it as it is to prove the original affirmation in the Quran that Abraham built the Kaba. One has thus to fall back on the continuity of the tradition over such a long period, we have to fall back for proof on the fact that Muslims have long believed that Abraham built the Kaba. But that is no different from the Hindus having long believed the spot now occupied by the Babri Masjid to have been the place at which Lord Ram was born.

And the proof of all this?

Why is the Kaba vital ? After all, a point to which I shall revert in a moment, had the Prophet not said that every spot on earth is sacred, that Allah has made the entire earth a *masjid*? There are two views regarding the importance of Kaba. One is that the Kaba is the navel of the earth. It is believed to have existed before the earth was created by Allah -- on one account 40 years earlier, on one 2000 years earlier. Allah created heaven, we are told, and then the earth by stretching out the substance of the earth around this navel. Creation completed, the Kaba, we learn, now is the highest point of the earth, and its position corresponds exactly to that of the Pole Star, which, we also learn, is the highest point in the heavens. As heaven is above the earth and as Kaba is the highest point on earth, it is the place by being in which one is nearest heaven.

The other view is that it is not just the centre of the earth, but of the universe. The universe, in this account, consists of seven heavens -- one above the other -- and seven earths -- one below the other. All the fourteen levels are perfectly aligned -- the highest point in each lies perfectly in line with the highest of other levels. Now, the highest point of the seventh heaven is the Throne of Allah, the highest point on earth-- and exactly in the centre of the universe -- is the Kaba. The Kaba we see in Mecca, we are further instructed, is an exact replica of the original structure which is in heaven and which is made of gold. (The Quran too, as is well known, is an exact reproduction of the text of two tablets -- also of gold -- which are lying in heaven.)

But why was it necessary to create this replica on earth? The accounts differ. As we have seen, on one account it is Abraham who laid its foundations and with Ishmael built it on the prompting of Gabriel, the angel who, as we know, was later to transmit the revelations from Allah to the Prophet. On the other account, the structure was built by Adam.

Originally Adam was so tall that he could hear the heavenly songs around Allah's Throne directly. But after his fall he shrunk so much that the upper realms were out of his reach. Upon his importuning God sent him the tent around which and through which he could attain to the beatitudes, and this later was made into the Kaba. In answer to his pleas that Mecca had no one, that the shrine had no worshippers Allah promised that it would become the centre of pilgrimage, and that promise Allah fulfilled. The original structure was later washed away in the Great Flood. The angels spirited away and kept safe the Black Stone. That is how Abraham came to rebuild the structure later on, and Gabriel brought the Black Stone back to him. We learn that the Stone itself — now in three large and several small pieces held together by a silver band as it split in the course of a fire — was originally white : it became black upon contact with the sinfulness of the pagan period. (On all this see, for instance, the *Encyclopedia of Islam's* entry, *Ka'ba*.)

Such are the reasons on account of which the Kaba and the Black Stone are of such extraordinary holiness.

Now, which of these elements of the legends can be 'proved' in the way proof of Ram's birthplace is sought ? Yet it is precisely because of them that the Kaba is so sacred.

After the *Masjid al-Haram* in which the Kaba lies, the mosque held most sacred by the faithful is the *Al Aqsa* mosque in Jerusalem. And why so? The rock around which it is built has a mark. It is believed to be the imprint the Prophet's foot made as he alighted from the winged horse after his night's journey to this point in Jerusalem and thence to heaven : in heaven, as is well known, he met Moses and Jesus etc. Which elements of this can we prove? Heaven? The winged horse? The night's journey? That the mark is the imprint of a human foot ? That the foot of which it is an imprint was that of the Prophet? (Incidentally the mosque is built on the site where according to the other set of beliefs stood the church built by Justinian.) The *Masjid al-Khaif* in Mina is also built around a stone which the devout hold sacred : they put their heads on it. Why ? Because the stone has a mark which, it is said, was made by the Prophet placing his head on it. The *Masjid al-Baghla* in Medina enshrined the footprints of the Prophet's mule in stone. The Mosque of Ibn Tulun in Egypt was built where Musa, that is Moses, talked with the Lord .... And so on. In each instance, ask, 'What proof can I provide for the proposition on which this structure is built?'

The Prophet's Distinction

Today we are being told that a mosque can never be dismantled or shifted. It is not just that the inviolability which is being attached to the structure of a mosque is a later – much later – accretion into Islam: the first mosque in Basra, the place being an encampment then, was built of reeds so that, as the *Encyclopedia* notes, it could be taken down with the camp. It is not just that even the most revered mosques – the Kaba itself, the Prophet's mosque in Medina – have been dismantled more than once so as to replace them with more imposing structures. It is not just that to this day in the Middle East mosques are broken and then another structure bearing that name built elsewhere for purposes as mundane as widening highways. It is that doing so would seem to accord with the Prophet's view of the matter.

'I have been given five things,' the Prophet said, 'which were not given to any amongst the Prophets before me.' Among these he said was the fact that 'The earth has been made for me (and for my followers) a place for praying and a thing to perform Tayammum. Therefore my followers can pray wherever the time of a prayer is due.' (The other four things were: 'Allah made me victorious by awe (by His frightening my enemies) for a distance of one month's journey'; 'Booty has been made *halal* (lawful) for me (and was not made so for anyone else)'; 'Every Prophet used to be sent to his nation exclusively but I have been sent to all mankind'; and, 'I have been given the right of intercession (on the Day of Resurrection)' *Sahih Al-Bukhari*, the Book of Salat, tradition 429; also *Sahih Muslim,* the Book of Salat, traditions 1056-1067; there are interesting variations in the precise words: in some traditions the words 'the earth (which) has been made clean and a place of worship' become 'the treasures of the earth which were placed in my hand').

In accordance with this view that the whole earth was a place of worship, the very first mosque he founded – the one in Medina – was constructed at a site which because of accretions to Islam since then, in fact in large part due to what it has adopted of other religions, would leave our protagonists looking askance. Soon after his arrival in Medina the Prophet asked the Banu-An-Najjar to sell him a particular plot of land so that he may build a mosque on it. They would not accept a price for it saying they would seek it from Allah, and they turned the plot over to the Prophet. 'There were graves of pagans in it,' the *hadis* goes, 'and some of it was unlevelled and there were some date-palm trees in it. The Prophet ordered that the graves of the pagans be dug out and the unlevelled land be levelled and the date-palm trees be cut down....' All this was done and the mosque built in land which till that moment had contained the graves of pagans in it. The adherents today would regard such a site polluted, and yet that is where the Prophet himself constructed his mosque (*Sahih - Al-Bukhari*, The Book of Salat, tradition 420; also, *Sahih Muslim*, The Book of Salat, tradition 1068).

Conclusions

Our brief survey suggests three conclusions. Each of these strikes at the very root of the arguments which are being asserted by the Babri Masjid protagonists, and each does so in a different way:

❏ The latest argument – that no Muslim ruler destroyed any temple simply because doing so is against the Shariat – historians have themselves recorded about innumerable instances, but also because there seems to be no warrant for the rule in view of what the Prophet himself did;

❏ It is as difficult to prove the reasons for holding the most revered mosques sacred as it is to prove that Lord Ram was born at a particular place;

❏ The shifting of mosques is permissible not only in view of the practice to this day in the most orthodox Islamic countries, but also in view of the Prophet's acclamation that Allah had made the entire earth, that is each and every spot in it a place of worship.

These are conclusions which follow in regard to the immediate issue at hand. But I think an even more important lesson is implicit in the foregoing.

I have all too often seen persons lose patience as protagonists of the Babri Masjid shift their arguments, as they obfuscate what they had said earlier, as they adopt one set of criteria for one issue – to justify overturning the Shah Bano verdict for instance – and another set for another issue – in regard to adhering to the court verdict on some aspect of the Ayodhya issue for instance. But such exasperation must be eschewed. Instead, every assertion of the protagonists must be examined in detail. Every argument they advance must be examined logically and in the light of evidence.

Whatever be the outcome in regard to one structure, such an exercise – of treating the arguments seriously, of dealing with them rationally, of examining every statement thoroughly, of looking up the law, the history books – such an exercise will itself yield inestimable returns: instead of hurling calumny and threats at each other, we will learn to talk to each other; we will learn to settle issues rationally and by evidence; we – all of us, Muslims as much as others – will get to know these leaders and their politics ; most important, we will open up all parts of our heritage – Islam as much as Hinduism – and every aspect of each part to exhumation, and thus to discourse.

– 13 August 1992

When Communalism Becomes Terrorism

XXI

On Being Swept off by a Word

People often allow themselves to be persuaded by leaders that the way to restore their pride, to preserve their identity is to follow that leader and his parochial programme. We have had many such leaders and movements in the last few years. These years teach us to ask a question. The Shiv Sena for instance has come and gone. In what sense has it shielded Maharashtrian honour or interest, to say nothing of shielding the honour of the Hindus whom it later took to its heart? Did its pursuits – the exactions for instance – not turn out to be wholly trans-Maharashtrian, wholly secular?

The Akalis have always stoked the Sikhs in the name of Sikh honour and Sikh interests. When they were in power did they work for these or for their own pelf? Today also they shout in the name of the 'Qaum'. Does their bitterness towards each other testify to devotion to any cause higher than their own egos? Do they go on splitting because they have genuine differences about how the interests and identity of the Sikhs should be preserved or for that most secular and mundane of reasons – that they can't stand the thought of working with or under the other fellow?

The terrorists of course speak only in terms of preserving the Sikh identity. What iota of the tradition of the Gurus will survive them? The compassion and ecumenicism of Guru Nanak? The humility and gentleness of Guru Tegh Bahadur? The devotion to the innocent of Guru Gobind Singh?

Take Kashmir: there too the talk is of 'Kashmiriat', of Kashmiri identity and interests. The terrorists assert that the way to preserve these is to break away from India. Even the moderates talk of 'Kashmiriat' and assert that the way to preserve it is to have even more 'autonomy' from Delhi, to have even more powers and an even better fortified special status for Srinagar.

The youth are completely alienated, we are told, because

all elections, save the one in 1977, were rigged. They will have nothing of India, we are told, because, while Rs. one lakh crores were poured into the state ostensibly for development, no development took place, the funds were siphoned away by a corrupt handful.

But to blame Delhi is escapism. To look to breaking away or 'more powers to Srinagar' as a remedy is to swallow the wrong medicine. For: who rigged the elections? *Kashmiris.* Who gobbled up the one lakh crores? Mostly *Kashmiris.*

True, those who seek to replace these riggers and looters at the point of a gun will be different. But in only two ways: as their depredations – the rapes, kidnappings and murders, the looting and pillage – and those of their counterparts in Punjab show, they will be much more rapacious than the earlier corrupt oligarchy. Secondly, as they wield guns, there will be no way to check their depredations at all, save even more guns and even greater terror.

The claim that all this is being done to preserve some identity is even hollower than these examples suggest. The leaders who declaim about threatened identities, and even the people who are swept off their feet by them are not solicitous about the identities of others. The Kashmiri Muslims today say their identity is being smothered by Delhi. Have they lost any sleep sitting upon the Buddhists of Ladakh or the Hindus of Jammu? Similarly, those who have declaimed loudest 'Bengal is being discriminated against by Delhi', or Bihar for that matter, have not had a moment to spare for the tribals in Jharkhand when *they* have pleaded that *they* are being discriminated against and exploited by the non-tribals of those and other states.

The Cause Misconstrued

The first thing which every group which is stoked on the cry, 'Your identity is in danger,' should therefore remember is that to the leaders who are inflaming them that cry is just a device – a means by which to gain power for themselves. And that once in power, these leaders will use the same cry to go on appropriating more and more powers – witness what happened in Iran under Khomeini, witness what has been happening in Pakistan. And the 'identity' for the preservation of which the cry was first raised, and for which the people followed those leaders, will be smothered as nothing else: witness how first the Ahmediyas were pulverized in Pakistan, and witness what is being done now to the Muhajirs who had left India for Pakistan to preserve their 'identity' and further their interests.

Now, there *is* a sense in which identities are endangered: not because the majority has designs to swallow up the culture of the minorities, but because they are all – the culture of the majority as much as those of the minorities – being dissolved by the solvent of modernization. The influences to which people all over are being exposed – information about trends in the rest of the world for instance, whether the trend be the latest beat and decibel level in music or the latest cut in fashion – are the same, the aspirations of the people everywhere – for instance the hankering after consumer durables – are the same. This modernization is certainly dissolving identities – it is weaning adherents away from the traditional observances of religion for instance: the shedding of the *burqua* among Muslim women, the abandoning, indeed erasing from the mind of most observances by Hindus in North India. But it is modernization and the universal hankering after 'western' consumer patterns which is the cause – a hankering that is as common to the members of every minority as of every majority. To assail the 'majority' for this is wholly misplaced.

But even the best of intellectuals often do so, and, having done so, come to advocate the wrong remedy. By the 1960s for instance, Sikh youth had begun to get their hair cut, they had begun to smoke cigarettes, attendance at Gurudwaras had begun to fall, they had begun to learn and speak languages other than Punjabi in Gurumukhi script. These were exactly the sorts of things that were happening among the Hindu youth. But looking at these trends and seeing in the shedding of these externals a dissolution of the Sikh tradition, the best of Sikh intellectuals concluded that the trends were a reflection of Hinduism beginning to swallow up the Sikh tradition, and that the only way the tradition could be preserved was to forge a separate Sikh homeland. How much in error that inference was, how wrong the prescription was, is evident today.

Now, when modernization begins to wean away the people in this way evangelist-politicians inflame revivalist movements.

They compel the people to return to the externals: the *chaddar* in Khomeini's Iran, in Pakistan, the five Ks in Punjab today. Three things become evident at once.

The people were adopting more liberal ways, they are *forced* and *intimidated* into turning back by these evangelists. Thus even on the surface, these evangelist movements are anti-democratic.

They are anti-democratic in a much more basic sense also. They are an assertion by the leader that the people must follow his *diktat* in the most private elements of their lives and relationships, their demand is a proclamation that in no sphere shall the individual remain autonomous from the leader and his band. These movements in the name of identity are therefore truly totalitarian – they claim total power, they insist that the total life of every individual must yield to their sway: that the terrorists in Punjab should decree which words shall be used, what girls shall wear in schools, how marriages shall be conducted is typical, it is of the essence of a totalitarian movement.

Furthermore, while most of them – in Punjab for instance, in Kashmir – use the idiom of religion, they strike at what is the highest in the tradition – at the inner-directedness which the tradition has preached. By emphasizing the externals, they divert the people from the highest in each tradition, the spiritual.

This is not short of being ruinous because there is no tradition in which everything is worth preserving or resuscitating. The externals most certainly are not. And the externals are what the revivalist movement seeks to enforce. The consequences are inevitable: look at what has happened to the position of women in Iran and Pakistan, and to minorities – the Ahmediyas in Pakistan – in countries which have sought to re-establish their 'Islamic identity'.

In a word, while they set out on the cry of preserving 'identity', these movements and their champions obliterate it. The way to preserve that core which is worth preserving is for all to join hands across traditions to strengthen the ways and institutions which will keep us an open, plural society, a society in which we may all search for the core of all traditions and learn to live it.

That is the lesson those of us whose 'identity' leaders set out to protect should bear in mind. Those who control governments must bear the converse lesson in mind : Rulers must desist from

thc deceit and worse – the entirely 'secular' rigging of elections
etc. – which enabled the secessionists to inflame the people of
the Valley ; for there will always be persons who will see in
these malpractices an opportunity to establish their dominance by
frightening the people with the scare that their identity is in danger.

Further Lessons

There are further lessons. More often than not the people have
to be intimidated and beguiled into following such movements.
But intellectuals embrace them on their own. First, as I
mentioned in the case of Sikh intellectuals in the fifties and
sixties, they misconstrue the quarter from which the identity is
threatened, and thereby come to support the wrong remedy.
Second, often they are led to support these movements by
a blind regurgitation of the 'theories' of their idols: apart from
the presumption that doing so would garner them followers among
Muslims, it was the slavish adherence to a few sentences of
Stalin which led the communists to espouse the cause for Pakistan
in the 1940s. And there is fashion: it is progressive to be speaking
up for 'minorities', even when these in the regions in which they
are dominant are sitting upon others, and to be espousing ways
to preserve their 'identities'. And on top of all this is the
intellectual's presumptuousness – the confidence that the leaders
whose cause he is espousing will listen to him, and that thereby
he – i.e., the intellectual – will be able to moderate the excesses
to which the rhetoric of the movement would suggest it is headed.

There is yet another thing: the lack of experience in handling
practical affairs. The people in general, and intellectuals in
particular come too readily to conclude that the game is up, that
Kashmir, say, cannot now be saved ; and once they have concluded
this, their minds are quick to invent, or at the least to accept
rationalizations and justifications for its breaking away. You
would have noticed that the arguments for considering 'other
options', for giving even greater 'autonomy' to Kashmir reached
a crescendo in 1990 when it seemed that it had all but broken away.
We hear them less today.

But, not all crises are doomed to go on escalating. Most of
them abate. The identity-mongers in particular themselves
educate the people to their true intent and character. Often –

as has happened in Kashmir — it is enough to just hold on, deafening oneself to the discouraging counsel of the intellectuals.

Speaking in another context the other day Myron Wiener, the American specialist on Indian affairs, recalled that he had been visiting India since 1953. And each time he had come over, India was in the throes of, it seemed to be overwhelmed by a crisis. But over the years he began to notice that each time it was a *DIFFERENT* crisis! An important point, and an encouraging one!

— 18 April 1992

XXII

What if they were Judges?

Yet again newspapers report 'facts' on the authority of Mr. Bahauddin Farooqui, formerly Chief Justice of the Jammu and Kashmir High Court. Over the past two years, as the situation in Kashmir worsened, more and more 'facts' came to be stated on the authority of this gentleman. His statements and the reports of his 'fact-finding missions' have been circulated widely by Pakistani authorities in the UK and USA. Here just as he has been often citing the statements of Indian human rights organizations and bodies like the Naxalite oriented Indian People's Front to substantiate his assertions, his 'findings' and 'legal' arguments have often been used by activists to substantiate their assertions.

The fact that he was once the Chief Justice of the Jammu and Kashmir High Court is of course what has made all the difference. We continue to remain acutely conscious of status and the fact that a man once occupied high office always carries weight with us. And in a case such as this the gentleman has not occupied just some high office. He has been a Chief Justice. There is always the presumption on reading a statement from such a person that it is steeped in sobriety, that it is founded on a careful weighing of all available evidence. The presumption is even stronger in countries such as the USA and the UK than it is here for observers in those places are inclined to think that our Justices and Chief Justices are like theirs.

We should find out more about the person's premises and standpoint before we accept as 'facts' things certified by him. Farooqui heads the 'Jammu and Kashmir People's Basic Rights (Protection) Committee.' He is in fact the fount and soul of it. In April last year he filed a writ in the state's High Court asking for decisions on a vast array of matters. It gives a good clue to his premises and standpoint.

454   INDIAN CONTROVERSIES

He most emphatically rejects the Accession of the state to India. He believes that the Accession was in violation of the principles which were to guide such decisions – namely 'the wishes of the people, economic interests and geographical continguity of the states.' In his view of history, within a day of having acceded to India the Maharaja had to flee the Valley, not because of any marauders from Pakistan but 'under the pressure of mass upsurge.' That very day, he affirms in his writ, 'India airlifted its troops to Srinagar and deployed the same in other parts of the State,' not, mind you, to protect it from the raiders Pakistan had sent but 'to suppress the people's struggle for freedom.' 'Soon after the Indian Army landed in Kashmir,' he says, 'it mounted a powerful offensive on freedom fighters and imposed a reign of terror in the state with the help of Sheikh Muhammad Abdullah and his henchmen who became ready collaborators in the hands of manipulative India's leadership.'

The next step in his reconstruction is even more telling. 'Having regard to the righteousness of the cause and the determination of the people in Kashmir,' he affirms on oath, 'it became increasingly embarrassing and difficult for India in the eyes of world opinion to carry on the suppression unleashed by it to suppress the people and their will to freedom.' That accordingly, 'in an attempt to save their face and camouflage the aggression on the people of the state, the Government of India decided to put blame on Pakistan and carry the matter to the Security Council'!

And that is just the beginning of his presentation of facts and law. His 'two volume Report' about events in 1990 – KASHMIR AFLAME – follows the same pattern. In it Indian security forces are forever carrying liquor bottles in their hip pockets and burning houses, torturing Kashmiris, belabouring women and children, raping women, making their victims 'sip gutter water and lick fecal matter while they were herded together in vacant spaces during the course of such raids.'

No terrorist makes an appearance. No evil is ever done by them. On the other hand, innocent Kashmiris die helplessly. Sometimes of course – even though they are frail and 75 years old – they survive the terrible blows rained on them with rifle butts so as to live to tell their tales of woe to the Chief Justice. As in the following instance

'Mst. Rehima, 75 years,' the Chief Justice reports about his encountering her, 'was lazily walking with black circles around her eyes and jaws. She sustained rifle-butts' barrage and innumerable heavy fists. Her crimes were : (i) did not produce the women folk who had taken refuge in one of the big houses there; (ii) did not separate babies from their mothers to be molested; (iii) did not produce jewellery, golden ornaments or/and cash. In the bargain, a hard punch on her teeth deprived her of three teeth.'

The Chief Justice's prose is not merely arid judicialese: 'Our "forced-stay" at Hayan due to the imposition of curfew suddenly on 13 and 14 August, 1990,' he writes in the 'Second Volume' of his 'Report', deterred us to leave for Pazipora which had witnessed frenzy and uncontrolled passions of vengeance, brutal cruelty and barbarous behaviour of the once-disciplined Indian Army, and, had now attracted attention, and, ached the conscience of the world.

'On the 43rd anniversary of India's Independence when Kashmir was in a mournful state of mind due to excesses inflicted on common and innocent people, the team left Hayan in the morning, with local guides for Pazipora with heavy hearts. Winding way through thick paddy fields and, treading along running brooks, chirping birds and broody weeping-willows, the route was : Hari (Mohallah Rishi Pora) (to) Kenan (to) Posha Pora (to) Bali Pora (to) Pazi Pora.

'The lush green rice fields with unusual rich and bountiful (standing) crops offered a bemoaned welcome and their twirling plants seemed to convey the fearful twitter of peasants who, at this time of season were forced to remain indoors, would, otherwise, have been busy with cutting super fluous (sic.) grass and weeding out unwanted plants from the fields. The running brooks appeared to carry the mute notes of despair. An air of despondency loomed lazily large around (sic.). Birds hesitantly chirpped, and, haltingly called their mates. Hush of desert and silence of grave-yard seemed to have seized the fields, homes and hearths. The strains of elegy seemed to have gripped the hearts....'

His reconstruction of the crimes of the Indian Army is as graphic as his testimonial to their patriotism and attachment to the slogan 'Jai Hind' is definite :

'On the 10 and 11 August, 1990,' he writes 'the army soldiers, rank and file, hovering around Pazi Pora, Bali Pora, Kenan, etc., seem to have been overtaken by vengeance, greed, lust and revenge. They would shoot any one:- a passerbye; a farmer; a teenage boy; an aged man; an old woman or a youth busy with his vocation. The jawans were seen carrying bottles of liquor in pockets and guns in hands. More than a company descended on Pazi Pora and isolated forcibly women folk from children and men against the protests and weeping and wailing. Most of the women had run for safety to the forest, but still 20 to 30 women were lodged in a spacious house. The army jawans got a scent of their presence, and, pounced upon them like vultures. All of them were brought out from the hiding place and 10/15 robust, attractive and healthy women isolated between the age group of 7 yrs. and 50 years. One group of lusty soldiers tore their clothes to shreds and rendered them nude. A bon-fire was made of the dresses garments at the edge of a field of rice. The remnants of burnt clothes were found by the visiting members of the Committee even after a week. Another group gulping liquor from the bottles jumped over them and took them to the same hiding place wherefrom they were forced out and raped them one by one. The 7 year old girl was still bleeding after 5 days. The group then took their turn and after crying the slogans of 'Jai Hind' and so on ! What an opportune time for such slogans! The Indian soldiers' senseless acts of barbarity seem to be the behaviour of Occupation Forces such as Allies in Germany, Japanese in Burma, Americans in Korea and Nazis in Europe during the worst day of occupation after the 2nd World War.'

A Chief Justice! The first moral therefore is: do not believe a statement or a report – either on facts or law – merely because it comes over the name of a Justice or a Chief Justice. Assess it, cross-check it. As you would the statement or report of, say, a mere journalist!

Secession

The hue and cry which has been raised by editorialists and human rights organizations over the detention of Justice Ajit Singh Bains in Punjab illustrates the second point.

Supposing you or I addressed a gathering organized by militants, and, in support of the resolutions put out by them, told the crowd: 'We on behalf of the human rights organisations express our support to these resolutions passed here. We will give all support for the fulfillment of the objectives of these resolutions and whatever sacrifices we can make we should make for its achievement. A resolution was passed by the Muslim League in 1940. Many resolutions are not required for this resolve because of the historic boycott you organised. This historic boycott was, because we want Khalistan. In reality you are slaves today. You require a resolution of only 2-3 lines. In 1940 Muslim League passed a resolution, that "we do not want Hindustan, we want Pakistan," and they declared that they were prepared to make all sacrifices to achieve Pakistan. In the same manner, today the resolution should be of 2 lines, that "we want Khalistan and the people had given a verdict by joining the boycott." Then the slogan was "Britishers, Quit India," and today we should give a slogan, "Rulers of India, tyrants, killers, Quit our Punjab." Some demands (Shouts of *Bole So Nihal, Satsri Akal*). On this matter you do not need very detailed resolutions.'

Supposing you and I then went on to say how joyous we are at the fact that, at the call of the militants and others, vast numbers had boycotted the elections, and concluded, 'So Khalsa ji, this is people's verdict, the struggle was started by the militant organisations since '78, and the resolution was passed by the Sarbat Khalsa and it is a matter of great joy that these organisations also, by passing the resolution, have supported the struggle and we will cooperate with the militants for its achievement. There is no way left out for us now. We shall not remain slaves.'

Supposing you and I went on to affirm that the present rulers of India were far worse, far more tyrannical than the British, that Hindustan is not a nation at all, that it is just that the British named it one, that we are not extremists, or separatist or communal, that it is the government which is all these things and that therefore, 'We are now fighting the war of independence,' that 'Independence is our right,' that 'Genuine independence is our right' as 'It is written in the Declaration of Human Rights Act that those nations who want independence, they can get independence when they do not get justice,' and as our nation is most certainly not getting justice. . . .

If we said all this we would certainly open ourselves to being prosecuted on the charge of sedition. When, having said all this, we sought to buttress our claim by asserting that the killings of the Sikhs in Delhi in 1984 were worse than the massacre perpetrated by Nadir Shah, we would be opening ourselves to prosecution for inciting enmity between communities by wanton and deliberate exaggeration. When we sought to leaven all this with the protestation that our means would be peaceful, that would be dismissed as nothing but a careful, premeditated device to provide ourselves with an alibi were we to be proceeded against.

But the words are exactly the ones Justice Bains used in his speech at Anandpur Sahib on 18 March 1992, the speech for which he has been detained and is to be proceeded against. That not just you or me but a former Judge of the High Court of the state has delivered a speech of that kind makes it infinitely more, not less, consequential, and therefore more, not less worthy of being brought to the attention of the courts.

And yet there is hue and cry against his having been picked up. A former Judge, they say. A person senior in age, they say.

The lesson therefore is: our Constitution allows the State to restrict free speech in the interests, among other things, of the security and integrity of India; our laws make it mandatory for our governments to prosecute those who preach secession; these laws must be enforced irrespective of whether a person has been a Judge or not, irrespective of whether the person is old or young. In fact, as the more responsible the position a person has held or holds the more consequential his preaching secession is liable to be, the law must be enforced more promptly and more meticulously in his case than it would be ordinarily.

And there is another lesson too, common to the two cases of Justices Farooqui and Bains. The point is not only that former Judges read the facts and the law in this way. But that persons whose premises and perspectives, whose ability to assess facts is such came to be made Justices and Chief Justices of High Courts. Only in India could this have happened. Not because we are secular or tolerant, mind you. But because we are shoddy in the way we gather facts before we make such appointments and lunatic in the criteria by which we assess them.

— 27 June 1992

XXIII

Advantages to Build on

'Pakistan is implementing the final phase of its plan to break Kashmir from India,' a valiant person working among the refugees in Jammu was explaining. 'It had six initial objectives: to get the Muslims in the Valley to support the terrorists; to get Hindus out of the Valley; to blind the Government by shutting off all sources of intelligence; to confine the Administration to the Secretariat, to infiltrate it, and to put it in thrall of the terrorists; to undermine the will of the forces by making them feel that while the people of the Valley were against them, and therefore while their task was a thankless one, their own Government would not stand by them; finally, to render all moderate leadership totally powerless, totally illegitimate and totally irrelevant so that there would be no one around whom Delhi could seek to revive the political process. It has already achieved them.'

As he talked, and as the events in Kashmir began to seem even more ominous for they seemed to fit the pattern, the criminality of it all went home like a knife. How much more than Pakistan had our politicians and our own people contributed to the success the design had already achieved. The Hindus had moved out: and intellectuals and others were asserting that Jagmohan had given them trucks and buses to move out so that he could come down on the Muslims all the more harshly! Who had demoralised our defence forces more -- Pakistan or persons in our media and our civil liberties organisations who had broadcast horror stories against our forces without verifying the facts? Pakistan or the politicians who had compelled successive governments in Delhi to adopt its 'Stop-Go-Stop' policies? Who had kept trying to fabricate 'political solutions' around the old moderate leaders though they had not just lost all effectiveness and legitimacy in the Valley but had become the objects of ridicule and hatred there -- Pakistan or our leaders in Delhi?

'In this final phase, Pakistan is doing three things, ' the person continued. 'First, it is doing much more of the things it had done and which succeeded so well in the first phase. Second, it is destabilising Jammu so that the armed forces cannot continue to focus on the Valley alone and so that the refugees from Kashmir not only abandon all hope of returning to Kashmir, they disperse and move even further away from the Valley. And, third, it is moving to internationalise the issue so that when an interim government or a government in exile is constituted, there will be at least a few States which will recognise it swiftly. This it is doing by making the situation in Kashmir a human rights issue.'

The Other Side

One does not have to list the indications which lend even darker hues to what the gentleman was saying. They stare us in the face every day. The genuflections to the kidnappers and killers in Assam. The effort even at this late hour of one political party after another to score political points on Punjab -- for instance over the elections. The preoccupation with private pleasure and interest all across the country: we acknowledge that the country is in mortal danger, but is there one little demand we have foregone or even deferred, is their the slightest adjustment we have made as a consequence in the easy ways to which we have become accustomed? So, all these distressing signs are all around us.

And yet I feel that in spite of us many developments, or at least tendencies have surfaced which are positive and on which we can build.

The killings in Punjab continue of course. But the situation is a vast improvement over what it was five years ago. No one there entertains any illusions about the terrorists any longer: no one today feels that they are doing all this for the cause of religion, no one sees them as idealists. The terrorists have proven the contrary. I have not the slightest doubt that the same realisation will dawn in Kashmir. In fact, there are indications that the people of the Valley, subjected not just to the consequences of terrorist activity – the scarcities, the collapse of tourism etc. – but to the activities of the terrorists themselves – the extortions and worse – are already beginning to wince.

Second, while a year and a half ago the people of the Valley felt that 'Azadi' was just round the corner, today they see that terrorism has only resulted in the concentration of defence forces in even larger numbers in the area.

Third, there is definite disillusionment with Pakistan. Not many in Kashmir would ever have yearned to get under the heel of Pakistani governments. But in the heady days of December 1989 and January 1990, most expected Pakistan to come and 'complete the job'. That did not happen. Their hopes were fanned by stories that the major offensive would begin 'once the snows melt', and then 'once the snows set in and the Indian forces – the Madrasis – are bogged down in their bunkers', and then again 'once the snows melt', and now yet again 'once the snows set in'. True, the infiltration continues to be substantial. But the Kashmiri can see as well as any one that it is not going to fetch 'Azadi' at this rate. On the other side, he sees with every month that terrorism is crushing the old, easy, tolerant ways of the Valley, and these are being replaced by intolerance, by accusations of not being Islamic enough, by mutual suspicion.

The mood in the rest of India too has changed. Few heed the civil libertarians now. The people see the terrorists for what they are: the mercenaries of Pakistan. And are willing to see the Government do ANYTHING, to use ANY means to put them down. It is not just that the stories the civil libertarians put out have been shown to have been figments. It is that the terrorists have by their conduct closed the debate on civil liberties and humane ways.

Next, it is clear that, while the collapse of the Soviet Union has gravely reduced our defence capability, Pakistan too is in no position to launch a war against India. Its Government is beset with as many political uncertainties and problems as ours. Law and order have broken down as much in Karachi, in Sindh in general as in any part of India. It would also seem that the US, without which Pakistan cannot fight a full scale war for any length of time, is little inclined to help it launch into any adventure. Quite the contrary. Enough has become known about Pakistan's clandestine pursuit of atomic weapons, so that even the US Administration is not able to support it in the face of Congressional probing. The Administration has shifted its stand on Kashmir specifically, and done so in ways everyone would notice. We in India may well look upon these signals with skepticism -- too little, easily reversed, who knows what they will say next. But the Pakistan Government—were it to be making plans for an all-out war -- would certainly have to accord the greatest possible weight to them.

That leaves the Islamic countries. And there is no doubt that Saudi Arabia and Iran have been at the back of much of what has been happening. The Organisation of Islamic States has without the slightest examination once again dittoed Pakistan's assertions on Kashmir. So, Pakistan can count on this support.

But that is the crunch. The more it turns to this bloc, the more it makes its financing and training the terrorists a *jihad*, the more certain it can be that the West, in particular the United States, will turn off the tap. For, with the communist threat having collapsed, the West is bound to begin dealing with Islamic fundamentalism as the most imminent and substantial threat both to world peace and to the West. Pakistan will not also but notice that the more it gives these terrorists the colours of Islam, the more it solidifies opinion in India against them, the more it solidifies opinion in India for allying with and actively collaborating with countries such as Israel.

So, just as there are many difficulties, there are, after a long while, many positive things too. But they are just potentials, just opportunities. They are not going to deliver on their own. They have to be built upon.

Things to Do

'The problem is not so much in Jammu or Srinagar as it is in Delhi' -- that is how the one man who saved the Valley for the country last year, Jagmohan, puts it. His book, one of the most important to have been published in India, *My Frozen Turbulence in Kashmir*, provides a mountain of evidence which establishes that this precisely is the case.

We need clarity. The terrorists are not 'misguided youth' -- they are mercenaries. Their object is not a few more powers for states, a few more jobs. Their object is to break the country. What we are facing is not a little grenade throwing, a little sniping. We are facing an invasion by Pakistan -- in the form which is most cost-effective for it. Several things follow.

Neither Pakistan nor its mercenaries will desist until two things happen: until each is convinced that they will not succeed, and until each is made to bear costs it cannot tolerate. To think that the mercenaries can be weaned back by a few jobs, by a few more seats in IITs and medical colleges is to play the fool. To think — as Chandrashekhar made out earlier this year — that just because Nawaz Sharif is talking sweet on the telephone or because he is sending Special Emissaries, as he is always doing, Pakistan will desist is to play the even greater fool.

And it is not just a question of talking tough to Pakistan. 'We must tell the Pakistan government clearly, in so many words,' say many of us, 'that if it persists in aiding terrorists it is asking for war'. But that is exactly what Yakub Khan was told by I K Gujral last year. To what effect? Pakistan will not desist because of strong words. It will desist only if it is made to shoulder in return costs it cannot bear. We too must devise the most cost-effective methods of making Pakistan bleed for the way it is making our people bleed in Punjab and Kashmir.

Second, we must shed illusions. That a 'political solution' is possible, that the old National Conference leadership is the lever for it — these are mirages. No political solution is going to be possible until the mercenaries are defeated on the ground, and decisively and for long. Pundits talk glibly of Nagaland and Mizoram. 'When the insurgents could be brought into the mainstream there, and be defanged by being made ministers and chief ministers, why can that not happen in Kashmir and Punjab?,' they demand. But in Nagaland and Mizoram the 'political solution' came about after the insurgents had been completely defeated, after they had seen to the man that they would not prevail, after they had put down their arms. This quite apart from the manifest differences— in population, in the scale of foreign help. As Jagmohan's book shows, as the sad and terrible history of Punjab in the last ten years shows, till that moment arrives — when the terrorist and mercenary, exhausted and defeated gives up arms, when the people at large see that he shall not prevail — talk of 'political solutions' and the like serves only to weaken the defence forces. And this exhaustion cannot be achieved by a little swoop by the Army lasting all of fifteen days. As the campaigns in even those tiny pockets in the North-East showed, it can only be achieved by sustained, unremitting pressure applied for fifteen years.

To expect the National Conference leadership to turn the tide against the terrorists is equally suicidal. At the best of times this leadership has sustained itself on anti-Indian propaganda. There was one exception – the campaign of Farooq Abdullah in 1983-84. And that exception was snuffed out by Delhi. Today that leadership is not just the object of ridicule and hatred. To keep itself alive – not just politically, to keep itself alive even physically – this leadership will have to talk the language of the terrorists. We need do no more than look at what has happened to the Akalis in Punjab.

So, all talk of 'political solutions,' of ensconcing this moderate leader or that must be ended. As must all talk of 'restoring the democratic process'. No democracy is possible, no free and fair elections are possible under the gun of the terrorist. And today in the Valley it is the terrorist's gun which the people dread: he is the more effective in wielding it, and he is not restrained by laws or scruples or the admonitions of civil libertarians. Unless his spell is broken no democracy is possible. We should recognise this and acknowledge it and, I would say, proclaim it. The terrorists would then see that they are not going to be allowed to achieve indirectly – through 'elections' – what they are not going to be allowed to achieve directly. Those who at the risk of their lives and those of their families have to quell the terrorists would then not be unsettled every few months by the prospect of a government in the thrall of terrorists assuming office. And those few among the people who still sympathise with the terrorists would more clearly see the costs their empathy is visiting upon them as well as the people at large.

In fact, the costs must be made visible. For forty years the country has been subjected to potential blackmail – 'If you don't do such and thus we will go over to Pakistan'. In fear of this it has molly-coddled the people of the Valley. To think that by pumping in more funds, by buying up apples and carpets the gun of the terrorist will be stemmed is idiocy. The more politic way as well as the more honest one is to henceforth do absolutely nothing out of the ordinary for Kashmir and to let the full consequences of the activities of terrorists – disrupted supplies, foundering tourism – register themselves undiluted on the people.

A Qualitative Leap

But for all this we need a qualitative leap in our thinking. We are still mired in old cliches. We still sign documents and stake positions without going into the details. How many of the 200 odd MPs for instance who signed the memorandum last week asking the Government to stand firm on intellectual rights have examined the matter at all? And yet they sign, and thereby perpetuate an irritant. Should we be perpetuating animosities on such issues or should we be seeking ways to engage countries such as the US, the UK etc. to join us in curbing terrorism as well as fundamentalism'?

Ensuring such collaboration is essential to our survival today. But we cannot expect it if we are going to be picking a quarrel on every issue -- from the NPT to the level of tariffs to patents. Nor can we expect it if we are going to ourselves continue to do the opposite. Why should any one collaborate with us in fighting terrorism when they see us lionising Yasser Arafat and his crew? Why should any one collaborate with us in reining Islamic fundamentalism abroad when they see us pandering to it at home?

The position on matters nearer home is the same. It is evident that in Kashmir those who will break the country have acquired many pockets of influence in the state's administrative apparatus. Jagmohan's book gives chilling and specific evidence of the penetration of services by such elements. Even in normal circumstances weeding an undesirable man out of government service take decades -- thanks to our concepts of justice and law. In a situation like Kashmir it will take forever. Must summary procedures not be evolved so that the supporters of those who will break our country can be put out of harm's way? At the very least transferred to places distant from Kashmir, and put in the service of some other state government?

The way the name-calling on Article 370 has been going on and on, and the petty legalisms in which it has been conducted bears testimony to our unwillingness to face reality. Little shows the need for us to think in qualitatively different terms as this debate does.

That within Kashmir the Article has done nothing for the average Kashmiri, that it has only enabled a corrupt oligarchy to fatten itself, Jagmohan establishes conclusively. That outside Kashmir – in Mizoram, in Punjab, and now elsewhere – the Article has become a precedent for demanding changes which will dismember our country is manifest. And yet we go on with legalisms.

The Article was, as the very words of the Article in the Constitution state, a temporary provision. It was meant to enable the state to have some time in which to adapt to the laws and structures of the rest of the country. More than enough time has passed. Worse, the Article is being used as an impediment to integration. We should entertain it no more than we do the call for a plebiscite.

But that should just be the first step. Muslims in India are Indians. There is no doubt about that. But there is also no doubt that it has been possible to inflame the Valley in the name of Islam because such an overwhelming proportion of the population there consists of Muslims. We must therefore not just abolish Article 370. We must announce that every Jawan of the army, of the BSF and CRPF who today helps save the Valley for our country will not just be entitled to, he will be enabled to buy land and settle down in the Valley.

Hesitant, apologetic marginalism will not do. Unless we think in these qualitatively different ways, it is not just that we will not be able to build upon the opportunities which have opened up. We shall not survive.

– 23 September 1991

XXIV

We Must Reset the Sights

The next time Pakistan says 15,000 or 50,000 unarmed civilians are going to cross the border into India our response must be, as I hope it was this time, that in that case Indians will cross the border into Pakistan -- and thcy will not be just 15,000 or 50,000, and they will not be civilians, and they will certainly not be unarmed.

For years we have allowed ourselves to be put into what military men call the strategic defensive -- that is, even though a patrol of ours may havc takcn thc offcnsive in relation to a posse of terrorists, our overall aim has just been to hold on, to cope as best as we can with the depredations of the terrorists, to do what we can to combat the terrorists.

But the terrorists arc thc front men of Pakistan. They are its agents. It gives them sanctuary. It trains them. It arms them. It finances them. It uses them as bullets. And we try to run after these bullets after they have been fired from the gun.

The Pakistani Operation

Pakistan is committed to the dismemberment of India. Pakistani newspapers are full of anti-India venom. Defeating and breaking India is the object with which the Pakistani soldier is imbued. Each time they are in difficulty -- Benazir screaming before the crowds in 1990, her father before her, Nawaz Sharif now -- Pakistani leaders stoke the people against India. And this is what the 'moderates' do. The ruling establishment -- from Zia to Ishaq to the ISI -- are single-minded: their anti-Indianism is not a pose to be put on when they are in difficulty, it is the article of their faith, it is their singular objective.

In equipping and training terrorists Pakistan has found a costless way of achieving that objective. The advantages to it are manifest.

The lives that are expended are Indian.

As the terrorists can be projected to be 'freedom fighters', as what is happening can be projected to be a 'war of liberation', international opinion is not aroused against the operation. Quite the contrary, there is a presumption in favour of the terrorists – as there was for instance in India in favour of the PLO, in favour of the LTTE. And opinion within India is rent apart: recall how our civil liberties groups focused on the 'excesses' of the defence forces while not even tabulating, to say nothing of documenting the deeds of the terrorists, and recall too the prominence their admonitions received in our media.

Third, as the fight is thereby a struggle among Indians, India limits the force it deploys. The Government is always apologetic about the measures it takes. It limits the weapons it allows its forces to use. It feels compelled to relax the pressure from time to time – so that in effect its counter action is no more than a spurt, one that is called off within a month or two. Notice how apologetic we are about using the Army to combat the terrorists, how we limit its use to 'aid and assist civilian authority', how, before even a few weeks have passed, we feel compelled to withdraw it from an area.

Fourth, while a war, certainly a protracted war cannot be won without mobilizing the people as a whole, our governments hesitate to arouse them. For the terrorist 'is still an Indian,' 'he is our estranged brother' – the very words of three successive Prime Ministers of India. Far from arousing the people against the terrorist the instinct of the governments is to minimise the problem, to keep the people from awakening by putting out assurances that a breakthrough is just about to occur, that a group is just about to break away and come to a deal with the governments. Having fallen for the enemy's characterization of the affair as an internal difficulty, governments feel compelled to show that they are overcoming it – for what is a government which is not able to overcome a mere internal matter?

Worse still, advisors and social scientists are never wanting to goad our Government to busy itself dousing 'causes' which are not causes at all. 'Unemployment among the educated is at the root of tension in Punjab,' 'Cultural alienation is at the root of terrorism in Punjab' – remember all those analyses of the early eighties? So the Government works its head off to establish a coach factory in

Punjab, to establish a Cultural Centre in Patiala, to get Pepsi Cola to start a factory there. The same counsellors are analysing Kashmir now – 'More seats in IITs, in medical colleges.' The scarce organizational resources of the State are thus diverted. The sense of urgency is drained by the illusion that 'necessary steps are being taken.' The steps do not work even in generating jobs and winning loyalties in any case: the post-haste programmes to implement land reforms in insurgency affected areas, the enhanced central allocations in the North-East, the coach factory in Punjab, the Cultural Centre in Patiala – what has come of them? They become further proof of nepotism, of the State propping up 'stooges'. As they do not deal with the cause at all – with not even the terrorist, to say nothing of his patron – the depredations continue in spite of these measures. And so the measures end up not winning the people over, but making them more cynical about the State.

Nor is the diversion confined to coming up with measures of social and economic amelioration. By making the terrorist out to be the freedom fighter, the fight to be a 'war of liberation', the directors of the offensive – in this case Pakistan – and our political commentators put the authorities in India in the position of always having to come up with formulae to 'solve the problem', formulae which are for the terrorists to reject or approve. 'We promise to give Chandigarh', 'We promise to retain Article 370'. Each formula is rejected. And the only effect on the governments is that they strain to come up with an even more generous one. 'Everything can be discussed,' that is the chant now, 'provided it is within the framework of the Constitution.' It is an incantation to suicide, for the 'framework' is jelly, and the moment 'everything' is open for 'discussion', things will fly out of hand. But having been put in the position where they feel that it is *their* responsibility to come up with formulae, and having convinced themselves that the formulae will wean the terrorists, our governments – four successive ones – have been reduced to bleatiñg such things out.

Notice that the terrorist does not have to win any military victories. He certainly does not have to win any large pitched battle. Occasional murders and explosions are all he has to ensure. His aim is not to conquer territory. It is to exhaust the people, to make them weary, to convince them that the Government cannot save them from being murdered, to convince them that it is futile to go on, that the only way they can have peace is to come to terms with the terrorist. And his terms? They are the ones his patrons set. In this case, that Punjab and Kashmir be broken from India.

Notice also that it is infinitely easier for the terrorists to exhaust the people than it is for governments to exhaust the supply of terrorists. The technology of violence is now so compact and so lethal that even small numbers are enough to go on inflicting very large hardships on the people. And these few can always be secured -- if nothing else there are always in societies like ours enough criminally minded persons to man the operation.

Eventually of course sustained pressure will dissuade persons from joining up. But this it can do only if it convinces the would-be recruit that he shall not prevail, that on the contrary he personally shall meet a swift and cruel end. And even then, given the small numbers required for such disruption, even sustained pressure can do so only 'eventually' -- that is, over a very long period.

In the mean while, we should remember, attacking the terror-ist, to say nothing of just coping with his attacks, does not exhaust his directors. It does not even inconvenience them. On the contrary, it gets them larger budgets and caches of arms etc. to play around with. The ISI of Pakistan runs these terrorists. Through them it violates Indian territory and murders Indians. But as we still see this as an internal problem, Pakistan's territory remains inviolate. If as a consequence of the suffering that their agencies are inflicting on Indians the people of Pakistan were to suffer, they might stir to have their Government desist from such activities. Even in the normal course the degree of suffering to which they would have to be put for the purpose would be much harsher than in a society like India: anti-India poison has been poured into them for four decades; many of them are fired by Islamic fundamen-talism and Islamic milleniarism; most important, the real rulers -- the army, the ISI, Ishaq Khan -- are quite out of their reach. So, even if they were to be put to suffering, that would have to be of a very high order so that they may rise in numbers so large that their rulers would have to heed them. But that prospect just does not even arise for our response is purely defensive, it is to hold on in Punjab, in Kashmir, it is at best to combat the terrorist on Indian territory.

Once the victims -- in this case Indians -- are brought to the point of exhaustion, the killing of terrorists -- say the Kashmiri terrorists -- by Indian forces is not just something which will be of little consequence to their directors in Pakistan, it will *clear the way for them.* It will eliminate potential competition. The elimination of the Polish partisans in the Warsaw Uprising cleared the way for Moscow to set up a government entirely of its puppets; the elimination of the Viet Cong in the Tet offensive of 1968 cleared the way for North Viet Nam to acquire South Viet Nam wholesale. Assume that Kashmir is on the verge of being 'liberated'. If the terrorists are around after the 'liberation' they will form the government. They may want to have a Kashmir independent of both India and Pakistan. But if they are put up for the last lunge, they get decimated, their baton is taken up by Pakistani regulars, and the place falls. The government that would then come into being will consist solely of the puppets of Pakistan.

From the Pakistani directors' point of view therefore the best thing is not just that its war should be waged by Indians, which is how it is being waged; it is not just that those fighting India should sincerely believe that they are fighting to establish a country which will be completely independent, which is what several of the Kashmiris and Khalistanis have, I presume, been sincerely deluded into believing; it is that having all but attained their object, these terrorists should be killed by Indian forces in the penultimate lunge. Pakistani regulars need come in only at that time.

The Lessons

We must see what is going on: it is an invasion, a highly cost-effective invasion by Pakistan.

We must defeat the terrorists of course -- and that has to be done militarily, and there is no kind way of doing so, and it can only be done through unrelenting pressure sustained over a long period.

But even that will not be enough. The sights must be set on Pakistan -- we must break its ability and willingness to set these killers upon our people, we must break the illusion that many a terrorist is today fed, the illusion that there is a power behind them which will at the vital moment step in and 'complete the job'. These things can be ensured only by inflicting a cost on Pakistan

which it is not willing to bear. In fact, as the real rulers of
Pakistan are not readily accountable to the people, the cost that
has to be inflicted must be either so widespread and so intense
that the people there rise and overthrow these cliques, or it has
to be inflicted personally on the ones who are directing the
operations. In either event, we must reverse what Pakistan has
made the standard: Pakistan's territory should not be inviolate any
longer, ours should be made so again.

– 10 February 1992

XXV

Another Dangerous Cliche

'But you cannot win back the Kashmiris through the Army alone. The political process must be resumed.'

Now, that is the kind of meaningless cliche around which our discourse revolves. No one maintains that the Army and the para-military forces alone will be able to do all that needs to be done. But clearly until they have broken the back of the insurgency, until as a result of their operations the terrorists as much as the people are convinced that neither terrorism nor Pakistan shall succeed in breaking Kashmir away, nothing else can even get off the ground.

It is true of course that some other measures – some civilian measures – may have to taken to help the Army etc. prevail. But even in that sense two things are evident. First, at a time when the region is under terrorist assault, such civilian measures as are taken must be ancillary to military objectives, they must be wholly and solely in aid of the counter-insurgency operations. Thus, for instance, if it turns out, as the information marshalled by Mr. Jagmohan emphatically shows to be the case, that purchasing carpets, shawls etc. at inflated prices only results in the terrorists acquiring even larger resources, those sorts of measures to 'win over the local people' must never be undertaken. The second point is even more important, and the history of all counter-insurgency operations testifies to it : civilian, ameliorative measures have a very minor effect on the outcome. The thing which decides the outcome is who prevails militarily. More often than not, ameliorative measures become the subjects of ridicule, they only convince the people that the government is a sucker, they breed cynicism – it becomes a matter of pride to avail during the day of the goodies which the government is doling out and to help the insurgents at night.

The expression 'The political process must be resumed' of course means more than merely increasing the volume of ameliorative measures. At the most cynical it means that the subsidies and outlays, which with the dissolution of the elected government and Assembly are being handled by the bureaucracy alone, should once again be channeled through the conventional politicians. Now, there could be some point to this even in terms of combating insurgency if there was any prospect that the politicians would use the outlays to reactivate their patronage networks, and that these networks in time would muster a force against the terrorists. There is no prospect of that happening at the moment. The prospect of losing life and limb is so real at the moment that the overwhelming proportion of politicians have moved out of the Valley altogether – Farooq Abdullah with his lengthy sojourns in distant London symbolizes the state of affairs. And then there is the other difficulty: even before insurgency engulfed the Valley, these politicians were not known for letting the outlays slip past till the people; now that few of them remain and these few are at all moments confronted by the gun, were outlays etc. to be channeled through them, were contracts to be awarded on their recommendation these would end up being given to the nominees of the terrorists.

Normal political activity

There are three other things for which 'resumption of the political process' is a code word, and these warrant examination. The first is that normal political activity should resume – public meetings, seminars, leaders moving among the people, listening to them, educating them.

Now, no one is prohibiting the leaders from holding meetings, etc. – except the guns of the terrorists. Therefore, defanging the terrorists is a pre-requisite for resuming the political process in this sense.

There is of course one other thing which is holding up the resumption of political activity – and that is that the politicians are still continuing with their 'politics as usual'. Local Congressmen for instance are busier undermining each other than they are in attending to the terrorists. The jostling between the PCC-I President, Ghulam Rasool Kar, and the Gujar leader, Mian Bashir, is as intense and exactly of the same kind as among Congress leaders in any normal state. Congressmen at the Centre patronize one local faction to cut to size a rival at the Centre who derives strength from the fact

that the other local faction is in his camp. Thus, Ghulam Nabi Azad
has been patronizing the Gujar leader Mian Bashir, while the Gujar
leader at the Centre, Rajesh Pilot, has been patronizing Ghulam
Rasool Kar. Nor is the pattern any different in other parties.

In a word, the fact that what are our normal political processes
are unabated is what is hampering the resumption of normal
political activity in the Valley. That activity can be resumed only
by rising above these rivalries, it can be resumed only by all the
political parties working together. Two specific things can be done
in this direction.

The first is for the Prime Minister to rein in his colleagues.
That even persons in the second order of smalls – Rajesh Pilot and
Ghulam Nabi Azad – should go on exacerbating the problem with
their petty politics is nothing short of criminal. That Pilot should
be allowed to continue his forays in spite of the public protests of
the Home Minister is not short of that criminality either. That the
Home Minister should go on announcing that elections will be held
soon while the Governor goes on saying that the situation on the
ground is not such that elections can be held cannot but dishearten
everyone who is today risking his life in the Valley. So, the Prime
Minister should do at least his minimum duty – he should ensure
that members of his government are of one mind, that they speak
in one voice, and that they do not use a situation which is so very
perilous to advance their factional interests.

Second, while there is little that political parties can today do
in the Valley, there are things which they can do in the state. They
can together attend to the problems of the refugees in Jammu, to the
wails of the people in Ladakh, and they can together mobilize and
organize the people in Jammu to prevent terrorism from spreading
there too. Instead of berating the government or the Governor
therefore with the taunt, 'But what have you done to resume the
political process?,' political parties should take these tasks in hand
: thereby things which ought to be done would get done, and the
parties would learn to work together, in fact they would learn after
a long time to work.

Elections

The second thing which is meant by resuming the political
process is to hold elections. By now even the Prime Minister has

proclaimed that elections will be held soon in Kashmir. 'The skeptics opposed elections in Punjab,' the argument runs, 'And see the situation is so much better after the elections.'

Firstly, the situation in Kashmir is very different from what it has been in Punjab. At no point in the latter did the structure of governance – the civilian and police administration – evaporate the way it has in the Valley. In Kashmir today 'elections' will be what the terrorists, and that means the rulers of Pakistan, want them to be.

Should the terrorists decide to boycott the elections, and that boycott is effective, the non-participation will itself become a thunderclap. The avalanche in 1989 started with the elections that year: that just two percent of the votes could be polled even in crowded areas announced that the authority of India had evaporated, that 'Azadi' had all but come. The Valley nearly bolted out of the country's ambit. After enormous sacrifice, the presence of India has been re-established. It must be given time to consolidate.

Should the militants adopt the alternate route, things can prove just as troublesome. Assume that they do not boycott the elections, that instead they put up dummy candidates, that they exhort 'international observers' to come. Again, given the fact that we cannot provide security either to rival candidates or to voters, the elections will be made to go the dummies' way. Indeed, by exhorting 'international observers' to fly in, and by the content of the campaign they conduct, the terrorists can convert the elections into a referendum on 'Azadi.' Such a 'referendum' or, the alternate, a Lithuania-type resolution passed in the Assembly after the elections will become a horrendous set back.

In view of these prospects, elections must not be thought of until quite some time after we have been able to revive normal political activity in the state. Two good indicators of a semblance of security having returned would be that political parties have begun holding conventional public meetings, and that a good proportion of the refugees now in Jammu have returned to their homes.

Negotiations

The third thing for which 'resuming the political process' is a code word is to open negotiations with the militants. Every government fighting insurgency must always be alert to the opportunity of establishing contact with insurrectionists. Often such contacts must not just be established, they should be publicized : for instance, to sow confusion among rival groups, to foment suspicions and accusations among them that their rival has 'sold-out' to the government.

But such contacts can for a long time be no more than a tactic. It is only after the insurgents and the people of the area have become convinced that they shall not succeed that the time for 'a negotiated settlement' arrives. That time was twenty years a-coming in Nagaland and Mizoram. The people of Kashmir show signs of wearing out sooner, but the illusions of the terrorists, to say nothing of the designs of Pakistan, have not been broken as yet. Once all prospect of victory is gone, one or more groups will spontaneously arise with which it will be worthwhile to negotiate. But no group of this kind is in sight as yet. Moreover, when that moment comes, negotiations must be initiated in the closest coordination with the intelligence services and the defence forces. They must not be, as they became in the case of George Fernandez in 1989 and have been, if one is to believe what the men want us to believe, in the case of some central ministers now.

To persevere

The situation in Kashmir has improved in many ways :

❑ Militant groups have begun fighting each other with considerable cruelty; they have begun passing information about rival groups to the authorities with considerable regularity;

❑ The people of Kashmir are today much clearer than they were about the aims of Pakistan − that its object is to annex the Valley, that to it Kashmiri youth is just fodder. For a while Pakistan had adopted a tactical pretense. Nawaz Sharief, the Prime Minister, voiced it : We are for the third option, that is for Kashmir becoming independent, he said. The ferocity with which the Pakistani backed Hizbul Mujahideen have been attacking the JKLF gave the lie to that long ago. Now even Nawaz Sharief has abandoned the pentense: last week he led the public meeting in chanting, 'Kashmir shall be Pakistan.'

❑ The people of Kashmir are also much clearer about the char- acter of the terrorists − about their extortions of money and young

women – as well as about the consequences upon their day to day
life of the continuance of terrorism in the Valley – the drying up of
tourism, the cessation of development outlays, the shortage of
essential commodities; they also no longer entertain the illusion --
which they did in January 1990, and also in the aftermath of the
formation of the Central Asian Republics – that 'Azadi' is round
the corner;

❑ The government of Pakistan has also become enmeshed
in its own problems – the rivalries between the President, Prime
Minister and the Army; the troubles in Sindh; the uncertainties in
Afghanistan; the pressure, at least for the moment, from the USA
to cease and desist;

❑ Similarly, opinion within India as well as outside is less
inclined than it was three years ago to take the declamations of
human rights organizations at face value.

Now, these are real gains. But as the daily toll of lives as well
as the well-targetted attacks – on the Secretariat one day, on key
police officials the next -- show, they are just beginnings. A
moment's fool-hardiness shall jeopardize them all. This is not the
time therefore for reverting to the old politics in the name of
'resuming the political process'. It is the time to persevere: a
process *IS* at work, it is as political as any. We should see it through.

– *6 August 1992*

Facing the Future

XXVI

Two Potentials:
for Fundamentalism, for Reform

'All religions are in essence the same. All of them preach the Fatherhood of God and the Brotherhood of Man' — how often we are told that. Yet, when it is not an inane cliche, it is wishful thinking.

A proposition such as, 'All religions are in essence the same,' arises from looking at a few noble adherents of different religions, from looking at the spiritual quest and the saintly conduct of these few and noticing how similar these persons have been. But the conduct of these few, and the spiritual quest itself are just an element or two in each religion, and more often than not they are elements which have got buried under history, and priests, and the pursuit of power by adherents of that religion.

Two Potentials

Religions as we see them around us have little to do with the inner-directed spiritual quest. They are highly organized collective affairs. And between *these*, there are vast chasms. One of the chasms relates to what may be termed the fundamentalist potential in the respective religions, and the proclivity to fundamentalism. The position of the religion on factors such as the following determines this potential and proclivity.

Determining Factors

What is the ultimate point which that religion posits, the point of ultimate reference, what is its perception of ultimate reality? For the Advaitins, for instance, reality is one, undifferentiated, unchanging, formless entity. That is the point of ultimate reference.

By contrast, for the Old Testament, as for the Quran, the point of ultimate reference is God or Allah. Many attributes are ascribed to this ultimate entity, none as sternly as those of the 'Jealous God' -- the God whose principal concern is whether or not ycu and I acknowledge His supremacy, Who proclaims that He shall condone every transgression but not one -- namely, our failure to recognize and acclaim that He is supreme.

The second concerns the ultimate role model for the devout. Is it the compassionate Buddha or Jesus who turns the other cheek? Or is it Elisha who, upon being taunted by youngsters for being bald, cursed them, upon which 'two she-bears came out of the woods and tore forty-two of the boys'? That the Prophet is perceived as the keystone in the arch of Islam needs hardly be recalled : every few months the fundamentalists remind us of this. Every detail they state about the Prophet is true, they say, every act of his was true and glorious. Other prophets are honoured in the Quran, the liberals tell us every now and then. But neither the fundamentalists nor the Muslims are possessive about these prophets -- you can comment on whether there is evidence to corroborate some well known and widely believed events in the life of Jesus, for instance, who too is recognized as a prophet in the Quran, but you will not raise the hackles of the fundamentalists. On the other hand, should you cast doubt on any of the miracles attributed to the Prophet in or out of the Quran, you will ignite their ire. The uniqueness, the glory as well as the historicity of the Prophet are thus central to the religion. So one may entertain no doubt about anything the Prophet said or did. Nor may any one entertain any doubt about the account of any of the glorious or miraculous deeds which are part of the corpus. In this respect, the Messenger of Allah occupies a position more zealously shielded than that of Allah Himself. An atheist -- one who states there is no God or Allah -- for instance does not excite the anger which any one raising a doubt about some small deed of the Messenger of that very God or Allah is certain to do. And while you may honour other prophets-- which does not of course include letting any one else honour them so much that he takes to worshiping them or their representation-- you must venerate and believe and follow only Muhammed. Any return to 'the fundamentals' in this tradition therefore cannot but entail greater exclusivity, greater intolerance.

Contrast the attitude of a Vivekananda or a Gandhi to not just those who transmitted the doctrine — which is the pristine status of Muhammed — but to the Avataras themselves, that is to those who revealed the doctrine. The historicity or lack of it of Avataras is of no consequence at all, says Swami Vivekananda. Nor does the doctrine owe its greatness and truth to the fact that it was expounded by or revealed by them. On the contrary : the Vedas do not owe their authority to Krishna, Swami Vivekananda affirms repeatedly, Krishna derives his authority from the fact that he was the finest teacher of the Vedanta. 'Krishna of the Gita is perfection and right knowledge personified,' writes Gandhiji, 'but the picture is imaginary. That does not mean that Krishna, the adored of his people, never lived. But perfection is imagined. The idea of a perfect incarnation is an aftergrowth.' It is just that he performed extraordinary service for humanity, that he lived an extraordinarily religious life, says Gandhiji.

As this is the perspective, Swami Vivekananda says with the greatest naturalness : '...There is that most wonderful theory of *Ishta* which gives you the fullest and freest choice possible among these great religious personalities. You may take up any one of the prophets or teachers as your guide and the object of your special adoration; you are even allowed to think that he whom you have chosen is the greatest of the prophets, greatest of all the Avataras. There is no harm in that, but you must keep to a firm background of eternally true principles. The strange fact here is that the power of our incarnations has been holding good with us only so far as they are illustrations of the principles of the Vedas....' And the Vedas exclude nothing, indeed they include that Nothing too. The 'eternally true principles' Vivekananda is referring to are as non-sectarian, as non-denominational as, say, the Buddha's sermons on meditation. A return to fundamentals in this case cannot but spell tolerance and inclusiveness.

Next comes the attitude of the religion to The Book, the repository of that ultimate revelation. Is the Book just an aid — as the Upnishads are and the Suttas of the Buddhists — books that contain suggestions — of the greatest possible insight, pearls of great price, of course — as to how we may proceed, but books which themselves say that they must be transcended? Or is The Book itself an idol, one that, like the Quran, contains everything, one that must be believed in every particular because God sent it down, one that may never be questioned, one in which nothing will ever date, one to which nothing will ever need to be added? The contrast is as vivid as it is consequential. The *Gita* was mother to Gandhiji. But he does not ascribe divine origin to it, and questions about its literal inerrancy or otherwise he would regard as totally irrelevant. In fact, he maintains that neither the Gita nor the *Mahabharata* which contains it is a historical work at all. And the proof of this is exactly what in another tradition others would cite as proof of its divine origin, and therefore of its infallibility -- the accounts namely of supernatural powers and happenings. 'I do not regard the *Mahabharata* as a historical work in the accepted sense,' writes Gandhiji. 'The *Adiparva* contains powerful evidence in support of my opinion. By ascribing to the chief actors superhuman or subhuman origins, the great Vyasa made short work of the history of Kings and their people. The persons therein described may be historical, but the author of the *Mahabharata* has used them merely to drive home his religious theme.' The central event around which the epic is organized, the event on the morrow of which the Gita is expounded -- the war, the *Mahabharata*, between the cousins -- he says is not to be taken literally at all. The poet has merely used a physical illustration to drive home a spiritual truth, he has brought in the description of physical warfare merely to make the description of the real duel he is talking about more alluring, Gandhiji says. Vyasa is talking not about some particular war between cousins, Gandhiji says, but about the eternal war in the mind and heart of each of us between those other cousins, the two natures in us, the Good and the Evil. Duryodhana and his party are the baser impulses in man, Gandhiji says, Arjuna and his party the higher impulses, and Krishna is the Dweller within, ever whispering to a pure heart.

The view that the work is not historical, nor the origin divine, has far-reaching consequences. The Book is the work of a poet, says Gandhiji. And the poet does not exhaust the meaning of the words he uses, nor has he worked out the complete implications of the truths he expounds. Accordingly, it is up to us to work these out, Gandhiji says. And proceeds to do exactly that.

The orthodox often questioned the meanings he read into the

Gita, the inferences he deduced from it. What gives you the authority to say all this, they asked. The unremitting effort of thirty years to actually live the teaching of the Gita, was his reply.

The text as an aid. The centrality of direct experience. A return to fundamentals in such a tradition cannot but mean tolerance, it cannot but be struggle *against* the sectarian and absolutist lines which priests or politicians may try to lay down.

Next, what is the relationship of the individual to that ultimate reality, to that point of ultimate reference, to that Book ? Is he to traverse the way himself, verifying things for himself? Is the Book or the doctrine so complicated that, on the telling of the custodians themselves, the adherent cannot comprehend it on his own and must leave the decision of what is to be done to some intercessor – to the priest, as in medieval Christianity, or, as in Lenin, to the Party?

Finally, what is the nature of the quest which the religion prescribes for or recommends to the follower? Is it an inner-directed quest ? Or, to take one example, is his quest to be to make others acclaim the supremacy of that 'Jealous God'? Is the prescribed duty as it is in the *Dhammapada*, 'Irrigators guide water, arrowsmiths straighten arrows, carpenters bend wood, wise men shape themselves'? Or is it, as it is in *The Hedaya*, to convert the *Dar-ul-Harb* into the *Dar-ul-Islam*? Striving to live by the former cannot but lead to harmony, at the least because the focus is the self-regarding act. Striving to live by the latter cannot but lead to strife, at the least because the focus is the conduct of others, and because, as the episodes glorified by Islamic historians testify, the faithful is required to fulfil the duty by wielding the sword if necessary.

The two factors – What duty is prescribed for the adherent? And, by what means is he to fulfill it? – are closely related, and attitudes regarding them can in combination be lethal. If the follower, to use the phrase which was in currency till the other day, is to 'export the Revolution', and if he is to ensure that the Revolution/Revelation prevails by all possible means, then, naturally, aggression and violence and trampling others till they surrender become inevitable. From medieval Christian doctrinaires, to Islamic conquerors, to Lenin, to Mao – the premises on these two matters were, and therefore the consequences have been identical.

In brief, where the ultimate point of reference is an

undifferentiated reality; where this has to be experienced by the adherent for himself, and directly, face to face, as the word *darshan* signifies; where the corpus and role models of the tradition recognize and themselves acclaim that there are many paths to this experience, that it is for the individual, by unrelenting mindfulness, to determine which is most conducive for him; where it is acclaimed that the founders, and seers and teachers are no more than guides, that they are merely persons who have traversed that path before him and are for that reason liable to be helpful; where the Book is acclaimed because it contains the jottings and recommendations of these persons who have journeyed along that path, and is valuable for that reason alone, not because God or someone has given it; where the adherent is urged to concentrate all his energies on that inner-directed search rather than to set about to save souls, even those-- indeed, specially those – which do not want to be saved; where the monk or lay-follower is told that he may merely place the teaching before the person he wants to help, leaving the decision entirely to the latter, in contrast, for instance, to being told that he must offer the non-believer a choice between joining the faith or paying some extortionate tax, losing his rights and even his life; where such is the case, the tradition cannot be turned into an absolutist, fundamentalist creed. Where the case is the opposite, it cannot but end up as such a creed.

What it Means

Now, that does not mean of course that the Advaitin Hindu cannot be oppressive, nor that the Buddhist cannot be cruel : believing the same undifferentiated reality to suffuse everything and everyone the Advaitins, like the rest, for centuries shunned fellow beings as untouchables. The point is different : in one case the ultimate reference point in the tradition is one which the reformer can use to assail that oppression or cruelty; in the other it isn't. Thus when Gandhiji used these very notions of reality -- that it is a seamless One, that it is the same in one and all -- to assail untouchability, the orthodox had no answer. When the orthodox asserted that the scriptures sanctioned untouchability, Gandhiji did not just dare them to produce the text, he proclaimed that should the scriptures have done so they ought to be burnt, for a scripture contrary to conscience, to morality was to be shunned. Now, it is not just that a Muslim reformer could never take the latter sort of position *vis-a-vis* the Quran or the *Sunnah*. The point is that should he, to take just one instance, set out to combat an Islamic ruler's or cleric's division of the world into believers and non-believers and their insistence that the believers have such and such rights over non-believers; should he want to urge that the evidence given by a woman must count for as much as that given by a man and not one half as much as it does under *Shariat*, or that the share of a daughter should be as much as that of a son and not half as much, as it is under *Shariat*, there would be no comparable notion or authority which he could invoke; the basic notions, and texts, and examples of persons venerated in the tradition, would all be on the side of the ruler and the cleric, and of inequity in perpetuity. Similarly, as we have seen, Gandhiji could espouse his entirely novel interpretations of the Gita, he could advocate his completely heterodox inferences from it by maintaining that these were constructions which he had been led to by his own direct experience, that they were the result of his effort to live the teaching of the Gita in his own life for thirty years. No one could scotch his right to do so by appealing to the tradition: for in that tradition it was one's direct experience which mattered, and no authority -- no text, no interpreter, no collection of priests -- could over-ride that direct, immediate *darshan*. But where, as in Islam, the doors have been closed on interpretation centuries ago, where the right not just of an individual to decide by his direct experience but even the right of a wider body to decide by *ijma*, consensus, has been foreclosed, the reformer cannot rest his novel proposition on the text and the tradition.

It is in these senses that Hinduism and Buddhism are inherently liberal and catholic. And Islam inherently fundamentalist and absolutist. A return to, an appeal to the fundamentals in one case cannot but ensure freedom and autonomy for the individual. A return to, an appeal to the fundamentals in the other case cannot but become the ground for subjecting the individual to authority external to him. It is for this very reason that Ramakrishna Paramhamsa and Sri Aurobindo and Ramana Maharishi are of the very essence of Hinduism. And it is for the same reason that Sufis have so often been set upon in Islam.

Things to be Done

These contrasts suggest the first set of things which need to be done.

First, the mystic experience, as well as the lives and teachings of the mystics should be put at the heart of things. That is the way to the 'essential oneness of all religions' – for, irrespective of the traditions from which they come, the dispatches of mystics from the frontier are identical. It is also the way to liberate the adherents from the priest, The Book, the founder. For the mystic revels in his direct experience alone, he recognizes every one, every thing, every happening as an aid, as a teacher along the path, but no one and nothing as more.

Second, to liberate ourselves from The Book etc., we must have for each Book a core of specialists who can speak with authority on the claims made on its behalf to eternity, and to literal inerrancy. Nor do we need all that many for the job. Perhaps as few as fifty Europeans put together the view of Hinduism and of our history upon internalizing which we lost respect for our tradition. Just that many – dedicated, truthful, unstinting scholars – will be more than enough for us to be able to inform the country authoritatively about the points in different traditions, or about our history, which are liable to come up.

And the same goes for the founders and role-models of the tradition. We must examine every detail of their lives and deeds, on the touchstone of piety as well as for accuracy – as Christians have done in the case of Jesus over the last two hundred years. Nor should the faithful panic at this. Krishna has not suffered for all the caricatures of him, nor has the luminescence of the Buddha or Jesus been dimmed by all the scrutiny of accounts of their lives. If the accounts are reliable, and the faith of the adherents sound, where is the reason to shut out scrutiny?

– *July 1992*

XXVII

Islamic Fundamentalism:
Features, Consequences, Antidotes

At the heart of every fundamentalism are the millenarian presumptions : that there is one way, and one way alone to the Millennium; that that one way has been revealed to us, and to us alone; that should the rest follow it the world shall surely reach the Millennium; that therefore it is in the interest of the rest themselves that they should be shown the way and, if necessary, compelled to tread the way. These millenarian presumptions Islamic fundamentalism shares with all other fundamentalisms: 'Islam is the solution,' is its basic premise, as 'National Socialism is the solution' was that of Nazism, as 'Communism is the solution' was that of Lenin, Stalin and Mao.

Its Features

Of course the premise of fundamentalism is not just, 'Islam is the solution,' but that 'The solution is to return to the fundamentals of Islam.' There are many variations about what exactly constitute the fundamentals of Islam. These are not just the traditional 'Five pillars of Islam,' for instance. And we cannot expect the enumeration of fundamentals to be the same in Khomeini's Shiite Iran and Wahabi Saudi Arabia or even the more generally Sunni Pakistan. But there is a common trait : the focus is on the outward, visible symbols of conformity. Thus, having women don the *burqa*, the campaign against liquor and tobacco, decreeing Friday instead of Sunday to be the weekly holiday, breaking office work so as to enable everyone to say the *namaz* -- these are the hallmarks for which the fundamentalists strive.

Once in power, or once in a position to influence decisions, they require that the traditional law on punishments, on evidence, on inheritance and marriage be re-enacted. They require that Islamic taxes – the *zakat*, the contribution of a fixed proportion of one's wealth to charity, and the *ushr*, a levy on agricultural produce – be levied. There is also the singular concern with abolishing interest. All syncretistic practices – that is, ways which the local version of Islam has adopted from the time and place are naturally the special targets of these campaigns: as the object is to delineate the identity of Islam more sharply, every practice which fudges the demarcation between it and other faiths is sought to be resolutely stamped out. It is entirely natural therefore that the campaigners in Patna should want to scotch a more humane interpretation of the word '*Kafir*', that those in Bombay should have a Muslim organization give up plans to hold a workshop jointly with a non-Muslim organization.

Each of these concerns externals, it only tangentially touches the figure of faith that a religion aims to create. In spite of that, the campaigns for the return to the 'fundamentals' in regard to these externals are pursued with the greatest zeal. And for good reason. They establish three things. One that the fundamentals are what those leading the campaign say they are. Second, that these campaigners have the right, nay, the authority rooted in religion to dictate any and every aspect of life, even those aspects which relate to the purely private existence of an individual, even those which relate to the purely personal relations among individuals: the claim here is the familiar totalitarian claim – that is, the right of the authorities to dictate one's total life, that is to determine all aspects of one's life. Third, the severity with which the campaign is enforced brings home to everyone that those leading it have the wherewithal to ensure obedience.

To discuss the themes of the fundamentalist campaigns as things that touch only upon the superficial would thus be to miss the point altogether. They may concern the externals of a religion, but they reach to the very heart of power and governance : they settle who shall be obeyed, and on what, they settle who shall obey, and by what devices the former may make the latter obey. They settle what is to be the touchstone : as Islam, in particular Islam as the leaders proclaim it to be, is to be the determinant of which day of the week shall be a holiday, it shall be the determinant also of the position of women, of the position of non-believers in the new State, and so on. In a word, what seem to be campaigns about peripherals settle both – the possession of power as well as the character of the State.

Further Parallels

Islamic fundamentalism shares several other features with movements we have known recently, such as Marxism-Leninism.

Like them it places at the centre of things political power, in particular the acquisition of the State. There is similarity too in regard to the means by which this is to be gained. The Marxist-Leninists were convinced that they were the agents of History, that they were, as Lenin put it, merely giving History a helping hand. From that followed the conclusion that those who were opposing them were obstructing the march of History itself towards universal emancipation. And from that followed the conviction that the faithful were justified in using all means -- in particular intimidation, conspiracy, terror, violence -- to remove the obstructors. Exactly in the same way the conviction that they are merely executing God's Will leads Islamic fundamentalists to conclude that to be squeamish about using whatever means the situation requires is to be half-hearted about fulfilling Allah's Will.

The premise -- that they are merely fulfilling God's mandate -- and the inference -- that to do so they naturally must use whatever means are required -- reinforce each other. As Allah has assigned them the task, whoever opposes them for instance cannot be doing so for any good reason, he must be doing so out of an evil disposition, and it therefore becomes a part of the very task which Allah assigned them originally that the person standing in the way be put out of harm's way, by, if necessary, being put out altogether. That person is no longer just a person with a different view: he is a traitor to God's way, he is evil incarnate, and so the faithful are justified in using against him all means necessary.

Now, this line of reasoning has immediate consequences, and not just for the targets of the fundamentalists. As the fundamentalists are ever ready to use every possible device, they are convinced that their opponents too are going to do so. Dread and paranoia are the inevitable consequence -- the dread that everyone is conspiring against one, that none will stop at anything to do one in, that therefore one's life -- and with that the Allah assigned task -- itself is in peril.

This dread – that the others will stoop to anything to do one in – is reinforced by the earlier inference – namely, that the opponents are evil *per se*. As persons who are evil, they shall naturally not desist from evil devices.

Several consequences follow – and we saw them recently in the course of Khomeini's regime as vividly as we saw them in the regimes of Stalin and Mao. Indeed, as David Pryce-Jones' *The Closed Circle* shows, they stamp the politics of the Middle East as a whole. First, their stern, unruffled countenance notwithstanding, the leaders of these movements verge on paranoia. Every fundamentalist State has accordingly been a police State. Assassinations, purges, coups have been its hallmark, and each of these States has been in perpetual flux. Second, the leader does not just feel justified in adopting all means against his opponents, convinced that they shall stop at nothing; he turns to the extreme devices at the first go so to say. Disagreements immediately escalate into shouting and abuse and suspicions, and thence into conspiracy and violence. Moreover, non-believers are not the only ones who are in the leader's way – that is, in the way of his doing God's Will. To his eyes apostates, renegades, traitors abound within his own ranks too. Hence, the devices are deployed not just against non-believers, but against the leader's own comrades and co-conspirators; in actual fact, as he has more to do with the latter than with the former, they are deployed more frequently against his own than against the others.

The Islamic world, as the Communist, therefore abounds in conspiracies and conspiracy theories (to the point that the adversaries have begun to see that this proclivity to believe everything to be the result of conspiracies is something which can be put to good use : see for instance Daniel Pipes, 'Dealing with Middle Eastern Conspiracy Theories,' *Orbis*, Winter 1992). Moreover, in both cases each conspiracy is claimed and for a while believed to be the handiwork of The Great Conspirator: International Capitalism led by the US in the case of Communism, The Great Satan – i.e., the US – in the case of Islamic fundamentalism. This tracing back of conspiracies to some Great Evil Force serves two vital functions. As the Root Cause, as The Great Satan can not to be overcome for decades, the pattern of governance which the conspiracies have made necessary – the police State, the terror, the purges – naturally have to continue into the indefinite future. Second, the fact that the conspiracies are being master-minded by The Great Satan himself helps explain, if not exculpate setbacks and defeats. We could have slaughtered Israel, they then say, but what can we do, the damned fellows are being backed by The Great Satan. Our Saddam would have slaughtered the traitors in Saudi Arabia and Egypt and Israel, all together, say his backers, but, poor fellow, what can he do alone against The Great Satan....

The Violent Deed

Nor is it just the case that fundamentalist leaders and movements feel justified in using all possible means. They have great faith in the efficacy of intimidation and force, of terror and violence. This faith too has immediate consequences. The one who deploys these – intimidation, terror etc. – most diabolically is therefore not despised but admired. The one who takes the most intransigent stand – Arafat, Saddam – is the one who is idolised. The idolisation of intransigence goads the leaders: just as often they harangue in extreme and violent language, just as often they execute acts of terror and gore not to overpower the enemy but to establish their leadership of the faithful, to announce that they are the ones who shall 'go all out' to safeguard, or avenge as the case may be, the interests and honour of the community. That extreme rhetoric, that violent deed ties their hands for the future, as it ties the hands of their rivals. Compromise and peace become that much more difficult. The cycle leads the other side to be as intransigent, to put its faith just as much in violence, that is the tragic part. The farcical is seen in the way Saddam was lifted as the symbol of Islam one week – everyone having chosen to forget how 'secular' he had been for years in his murder and terror– and how the faithful did not know where to look the next. Just as often this appropriation of, this identification with the intransigent act, with that symbol of defiance is pathetic. Witness the exultation in the Middle East at the news that Saddam's Scuds had landed in Israel – even the troops from Saudi Arabia and Egypt which were taking part in the assault on Iraq were reported to have broken into cheers upon hearing broadcasts announcing that yet another Scud had landed in Israel. 'At least Saddam has hit Israel,' it was said, 'No other Arab ruler has been able to do even that much.' What a pathetic admission *that* was – for while the Scuds were a nuisance, they were no more; to have acclaimed and embraced Saddam for having hurled them any which way, to whatever point in Israel they could reach, was to acknowledge that nothing more than that futile thing could be done. But this embracing the one who makes himself out to be the most intransigent is not all pathos. Just as often the impulse to do *some*thing, *any*thing to 'avenge the honour' of the community or the faith has murderous consequences for innocents, persons whose only crime is that they just happen to be in the vicinity : as one cannot strike at the enemy, one hits out at some weak, helpless target nearby.

But I do not want to suggest that the faith fundamentalists place in violence and intimidation is all futility. True, in the long run it foments an alliance against them and invites greater violence. True, even before that consummation it results in a tyrannical and oppressive regime, and therefore an uncreative one at home. But the recent history of Communism and the entire history of Islam shows that intimidation and terror and violence enable the fundamentalists to prevail for long: the lightning conquests of Islam in the middle ages had as little to do with any intrinsic divinity or truth in Islam as the triumph of Communism over half the world had to do with any intrinsic truth in it. In both cases physical force and the technology of terror and violence, and the uninhibited zeal to use these are what prevailed: within but a hundred years of the Prophet's death Islamic theologians themselves lamented the fact that the people of the lands which had 'embraced Islam' – that is, yielded to its sword – knew not even the rudiments of the religion; this was one of the most powerful incentives, for instance, for codifying the *hadis*.

Further Features

On the premise that the Revelation is too complex and esoteric for the average adherent to grasp, and the presumption that the movement is surrounded on all sides by conspirators and enemies, Islamic fundamentalism, like Marxism-Leninism, is deeply anti-democratic. Like the latter it envisages a special role for, and therefore reposes overwhelming power in a select minority and its head. The 'theoreticians' of Islamic fundamentalism – from Shah Waliullah to Afghani to Maududi to Khomeini – are as unambiguous on this as Lenin or Stalin or Mao. To the credit of Maududi and Khomeini, they did not hide their aversion to democracy and its ways even in open and pluralist societies. But most others, like most Communists who have had to function in pluralist and open societies, have muffled their rhetoric on this matter. As they have, again exactly like the Communists, on the rights and position of non-believers in the society they are striving for. But once in power each has trampled the institutions and ways of democracy under foot, and each has reduced the non-adherents to the status in theory of second-class citizens, in practice to that of deprived and hunted animals. That has been so of course not just in the case of those who themselves claimed themselves to be non-adherents, but just as much in the case of those whom the regime declared to be non-adherents: Trotskyites in Stalin's Russia, Ahmediyas in Pakistan, non-Wahabis in Saudi Arabia, all have been subjected to the same heel.

And as emphatically as Marxism-Leninism, Islamic fundamentalism is internationalist. It scoffs at nationalism, as it does at every identity other than the Islamic one. This it calls its 'universalism'. 'Islam alone among religions treats everyone alike. It recognizes no distinction on the basis of caste, colour, or nationality' – that is how the matter is put. Except that it makes a profound distinction on the basis of religion – between believers and non-believers.

Even so, that means at the least that there is an over-arching bond between believers which over-rides boundaries of nations, States and the like. For that reason, for instance, it is held to be entirely legitimate for an Islamic organization in a country to receive money or other forms of assistance from abroad – indeed, it is held to be a natural consequence of the faith for it to do so. That again was exactly the case with the Communist parties and front organizations: for any organization in India to accept money from the US or UK was to be a tool of imperialism, but for the Communist parties to accept it from the USSR or China was but an aspect of their internationalism.

The same goes for the donors of course. Saudi Arabia, Kuwait, Iran, Libya have been financing fundamentalist groups in countries such as India, Pakistan, Sudan, Egypt and the like with the same zeal and on the same rationale as the Soviet Union and

China were doing so : to export the Revelation in one case, to export the Revolution in the other. And, exactly as happened in the case of the Soviet Union and China, the more oppressive and exploitative the regimes have become at home, the more, for instance, the members of the royal households of Saudi Arabia and Kuwait have taken to using the country's oil revenues as their private purse, the more they have taken to exporting the Revelation/Revolution.

There is finally, to use the current phrase, The Mother of All Similarities: fundamentalist Islam takes an instrumental view of everything, and everyone : the one, exclusive goal is to mould the world into the *Dar-ul-Islam*, a world in which peace shall reign and contention have ceased, and this naturally can only happen when everyone has accepted Islam. To bring this about, as we have seen, it does not only permit the believer to use all means, it enjoins on him the duty to do so. As is the fate of all ideologies that make an instrument of everyone and everything, Islam in the hands of fundamentalists itself becomes an instrument – a means to legitimise the absolute dictatorship of one man and his clique, to legitimise their brutality, their twists and turns. The fundamentalists wrest rulership on the claim that they are the ones who shall establish a State in accordance with the dictates of Allah. They perpetuate their rule on the claim that, as everything happens at Allah's Will, power would not have come to them, and they would not have been guided to act as they are acting had Allah not willed that to be so. That becomes their sole pillar of legitimacy. They hug it more and more tightly as their regimes become more and more corrupt and oppressive: witness the rising fervour with which Zia espoused Islamic goals as he postponed elections in Pakistan.

But an ideology that has itself become an instrument, a mere means of legitimising rulers and factions is emptied of all meaning – first in the eyes of those using it as a mere instrument, and eventually in the eyes of the laity. What meaning was left of Marxism-Leninism after it had been used to justify communization one day and the New Economic Policy the next, Kirov one day and the killing of Kirov the next, the Hitler-Ribbentrop Pact one day and its repudiation the next, the annointing of Lin Piao one day and his extermination the next, the Cultural Revolution one day and its repudiation the next.... In exactly the same way, what

meaning will be left to Islamic fundamentalism after it has been
used by Khomeini to set upon Saddam and the Great Satan, the
US, and then by Saddam, as the symbol of Islam to combat that
same Great Satan, by Saudi Arabia to combat Saddam, by Zia
ul Haq to perpetuate his rule and by his successors to erase it....
     As the core of these 'isms' is identical, the nemesis also will
be the same.

Consequences

Every regime professing itself to be founded on Islam is today
a dictatorship − of an individual and his cabal. It is a police State:
disappearances, torture, executions mark it. As David Pryce-Jones
remarks, governance in these countries remains what Richard
Burton had described it to be long, long ago: 'Despotism
tempered by assassination'. Since the death of Zia ul Haq, itself
a mystery, Pakistan is a bit of an exception − but with the Army
being so obviously the arbiter, and with agencies like the ISI
running States within the State, it is not clear how much of an
exception it is to the rule and, if an exception, how long it is liable
to remain one.
     Those of the economies of these countries which are doing
well owe their condition almost entirely to the revenues which
have fallen into the lap of these regimes since the oil-price hike
in 1973. Most of them − certainly those to the East of the Suez −
are kept going in no small measure by expatriate labour and
skills. A very large proportion of the oil revenues have been
squandered by the regimes in buying armaments − and thereby
enriching arms manufacturers and dealers in the same hateful
West the Islamic fundamentalists inveigh against. An equally
large proportion has been spent by the rulers, and their relatives and
associates on the sort of high living which would have been
anathema to the Prophet − in this too the regimes have enriched the
same hateful West. And a large proportion they are said to have
stashed, licitly and otherwise, in banks and havens − thereby again
enriching the same hateful West, and also thereby mortgaging their
fortunes to that Great Satan and his cohorts. By contrast, but a
fraction of the manna has been used by them to help each other,
or to alleviate poverty in other Islamic countries.

Quite the contrary. The regimes have been at each other: directly at war – as Iran and Iraq, and Iraq, Kuwait and Saudi Arabia; at war through proxies – as Iran and Syria have been in the Lebanon. If they are to be believed, several of them have been conspiring against and fomenting dissident groups in each of them. The same holds for the state of affairs within each country – Islamic groups within each of them have been as much at each other, and have found it as difficult to get along with each other as, say, our opposition groups. But with two differences. As these countries allow little open political activity, violence and intrigue have been the weapons of choice. And as each side has believed that it is doing God's work, it has sought to dispose of the other with staggering ferocity: the accounts from Khomeini's Iran, from Sudan today rival those from the most brutal regimes in recent memory. At the least, Islam has not disposed either Islamic side to deal with the other Islamic side more humanely: in the civil strife in Sudan today, for instance, it has not diluted the ferocity between tribes.

There is a sense in which adherents of Islam feel part of a trans-national community: witness the way millions across countries came to identify with Saddam – even in countries where the governments were equivocal, as in Pakistan, even where they were openly allied with the West, as in Saudi Arabia and Egypt, the people embraced Saddam as news came that his Scuds had landed in Israel. But just as clearly, there are limits to this feeling of oneness. While it has led them to applaud in unison when some object of hatred – in the case mentioned, Israel – was hit by some one – by Sadat for a few days in 1973, by Saddam for fewer still in 1991 – it has not enabled Muslims to do anything positive together: for instance, lifting food to the starving in Sudan or elsewhere, or getting help to Muslims blasted by a cyclone in Bangladesh. Similarly, the *inter se* hostilities among Muslim countries – have set against each other the very efforts which they made to spread the Revelation. Saudi Arabia, Iran, Iraq, Kuwait, for instance, had each been financing and patronizing Islamic organizations and groups in Pakistan. As tensions worsened in 1990-91 as a consequence of Iraq's usurpation of Kuwait, and specially once the strike on Iraq commenced, these different groups worked with much energy but at cross-purposes in Pakistan. Because the people themselves had been swept off their feet by the symbol Saddam had become, the groups which had been receiving aid from Iraq were naturally the more successful. That in turn became an embarrassment of the first order to the Pakistan Government: it could not afford to offend the US or Saudi Arabia. It had eventually to expel some Iraqi diplomats on the charge of fomenting demonstrations, inducing shop-keepers to put up posters of Saddam etc. (*Islamic Fundamentalisms and the Gulf Crisis*, James Piscatori, editor, The American Academy of Arts and Sciences, 1991, provides many glimpses of the diverse responses of governments, Islamic organizations and the people in Islamic countries). In a word, even short of the fact that adherence to Islam has not kept the countries from going to war with one other, nor groups within these countries from killing each other, some of the very things which have been done by each country to propagate that sense of transnational identity have disrupted that sense of commonality.

The Fate of Groups

Once Islamization has become real, the position of minorities has worsened. The persecution of Kurds – adherents of Islam, of course – in one Islamic country after another – Iran, Turkey, Iraq – is by now well known. Shias in Pakistan have had to take to the streets to stem the Sunni version of Islamic law enveloping them too. The position of Ahmediyas in that country of course is much worse, as they are far fewer and hence more defenceless: they have had to survive the clamour to prohibit them from using Muslim names and from calling their mosques 'mosques'; while applying for a passport they have been required to swear an oath repudiating their allegiance to the founder of their sect, and in effect declaring his claims to have been fraudulent.

Similarly, Islamization has meant a great setback to women in Pakistan. The Muslim Family Law Ordinance of 1961 issued during the time of President Ayub Khan substantially improved upon the Muslim Personal Law (Shariat) Application Act of 1937. Women's rights in divorce received some protection: the husband seeking to marry another wife was now obliged to obtain the written consent of his first wife, the rights to inheritance by grandchildren were recognised, and so on. The 1973 Constitution prohibited discrimination on the basis of sex. All this has received a setback with Islamization. Medieval conceptions regarding guilt in adultery, punishments, inheritance as well as the weight of evidence have once again been enacted into law. Women who have been raped have been pronounced guilty under the new laws. The most notorious case of course was that of a young blind woman who had been working as a maid, and had become pregnant after she was successively raped by a father and his son. The latter two were not punished, the father was discharged for lack of evidence and the son was let go by being given the benefit of doubt. The young blind helpless woman however was sentenced to 15 lashes for having been raped. The pregnancy itself was taken to amount to confession. The verdict was eventually reversed but only because a great storm had ensued. In other cases also while the women who had been raped or were held to be guilty of adultery received – 15 to 80 – lashes in public, the men were acquitted. The law of evidence was altered so that in most types of cases the evidence given by two women carried the weight of evidence given by one man. Another storm had to ensue and eventually as a compromise this unequal weight was limited to cases involving financial disputes; in regard to other types of cases the matter was left to the judge to decide. Similarly, the Council on Islamic Ideology decreed that the money to be received in compensation for the murder of a man shall be twice that for the murder of a woman. The official Commission which was appointed to review laws so as to ensure that they were in accord with Islamic tradition recommended that women be disqualified from ever becoming the Head of State, that in their case the minimum age for entering the legislature should be twice that for men, that they should be prohibited from travelling abroad without a male escort, and so on. (On these and related matters see the informative, *Islamic Reassertion in Pakistan*, Anita M. Weiss, editor, Vanguard, Lahore, 1987.)

Inevitable

Whenever attention is drawn to such facts – about the regimes in these countries being nothing but Police States, about the conditions in which their economies are, about the conditions to which groups like women and minorities have been reduced – the invariable response is, 'But real Islam has not been established in these countries'. That response is little more than a tautology: 'Real Islam' is defined as everything beneficent and beautiful and so by definition when that Islam comes to be established everything would naturally be good, true and just, just as whenever things fall short of being wholly and entirely good, just and true, that is because 'Real Islam has not been established in the country'. It is indeed ironic that on the telling of Islamic historians themselves during the 1400 years for which divine guidance – in the form of the Revelation – has been available to rulers, clerics as well as the millions who have embraced Islam, for only 30 years, that is during the reign of the first four Khalifas, has governance at all approximated these ideal conditions. Of course we know as little, in fact even less, about the real condition of the people in those few years than we do about the other distant societies which are idealized, whether that be Athens on the one hand, or the Paris Commune on the other. The other point is even more evident: the laws which have been enacted, in Pakistan for instance under Zia, as well as the laws which have been proposed by either the Council on Islamic Ideology or the Ansari Commission in that country, are in fact wholly in accord with traditional Islamic lore and law. The distinction between believers and non-believers, between men and women etc. is a part of the corpus itself. And when steps are taken to return to the fundamentals, these inequities cannot but get worsened. Nor would it escape the reader that the defence, 'But true Islam has not been established in Pakistan,' is exactly the defence which used to be given about every single Communist regime when facts about that regime could no longer be denied.

Yet the point to notice is that these results are not fortuitous. They are inevitable and follow from the tenets of the fundamentalist ideology itself.

We noticed, for instance, the deep anti-democracy strain in fundamentalism. This naturally results in a closed, absolutist State in which there is no room for contending opinions, in which dissent of all kinds is stamped under foot as is every attempt to bring facts about the rulers into the open, in which there are no devices – apart from assassinations and coups – for bringing rulers to book. Corruption, cruelty, nepotism fester and grow under absolutist regimes professing Islam as naturally and inevitably as they grow under absolutist regimes professing some other revelation.

The second set of difficulties arises from the fact that while fundamentalists insist, 'Everything is in The Book, and what is not in it is useless, if not harmful,' the fact is that when the corpus was frozen the society was a much simpler, in fact a fairly primitive affair. The fundamentalists insist that by looking up The Book or precedents of that time they will get not only the right guidance for administering the affairs of a modern, complex society, they insist that the guidance will be comprehensive and sufficient for the purpose. In actual fact the fundamentalists are themselves forced to dress up, on the one hand, what the regimes would ordinarily be doing by draping Islamic clothes over it, and, on the other, the regimes are forced to go through all sorts of contortions so as to legitimize what they cannot avoid doing.

A government levying a tax on non-agricultural wealth today, for instance, would be doing what many governments have done. But in a country professing Islam the measure gets to be shown as something which is taking the country closer to the Kingdom of God. In Pakistan a law was enacted requiring citizens to pay as tax differential proportions of the non-agricultural assets they owned. It was given the name 'Zakat' and proclaimed to be a tax which had been levied to institutionalize one of the Five Pillars of Islam. Similarly, were we ever to get around in India to levying a tax on agricultural produce or income, it would be regarded as being just that. In Pakistan a tax levied on agricultural produce with differential rates for unirrigated and irrigated land was given the name 'Ushr' and said to be again a tax which was a step towards Islamizing the country. The proceeds of these two taxes were set apart for meeting the needs of the indigent. Again, setting a proportion of the budget apart for social welfare objectives – for instance, for feeding the poor, housing the homeless, subsidizing the tuition fees of poor students etc. – is something which many governments do. Here it was given the hallow of Islam just as in the erstwhile Communist countries it would have been given the hallow of Marxism-Leninism. Nor is this just window-dressing. As has been pointed out by observers, making mandatory what was supposed to be voluntary acts of piety done in a spirit of compassion and surrender robbed them of much of their godliness. Making these an affair of government also meant bureaucratization of what were to be straightforward, transparent acts of charity and fellow feeling. But that is inevitably the result which follows from making religion a thing to be enforced by the State – but that latter is the very objective for which the fundamentalists strive.

The contortions that regimes have to go through are also well illustrated by what Pakistan has had to do while trying to conform with the injunctions of Allah and the Prophet against interest. The banks 'abolished' interest. Instead they began to 'buy' the goods which the borrower pledged to them as security against the loan, and simultaneously to 'resell' those very goods to that very borrower at a higher price. The difference in the 'buying' and 'selling' prices was of course only 'profit' and not 'interest'. It was just a coincidence that the margin always corresponded to what the rate of interest would have been had the interest been charged in the normal way! Once again the contortions which the Soviet planners went through to exterminate from their system the same hateful interest provide exact and comic parallels. The 'period of recoupment' and the other subterfuges which were invented so that the scarcity price of capital may be taken into account without using the word 'interest' occupied a prominent place over the decades in books on Soviet planning. They were in those days presented by the apologists and propagandists of Soviet planning as examples of innovation and lateral thinking of those planners. Today they strike us as little self-deceptions.

The difficulties do not end with subterfuges. The strain to which policy makers are put who have to harmonize the current compulsions for controlling population, for instance, with the *hadis* exhorting the young Muslim male to marry even as the greatest Muslim, the Prophet himself, had the largest number of wives, of policy makers who have to harmonize these current compulsions with the traditional lore to multiply the numbers of the faithful, do not have to be imagined.

Creativity Smothered

By insisting that the solution is to return to the fundamentals, that these fundamentals, although conceived at a time when society was so much simpler, contain all that is required, the fundamentalists ensure that, should such a society in fact be established – that is, a society which has been cabined into the straitjacket of these rudimentary fundamentals – it will be uncreative in the extreme. One part of the problem is that, even though some of the injunctions might have been progressive for the times when they were decreed, resurrecting them today certainly entails a regression. For instance, it may have been the case that restricting the number of wives to four was a great advance on the tribal practices as they prevailed 1400 years ago in a nomadic society. But to allow four wives today, to allow the husbands to discard any one or all of them by merely repeating one word thrice, is certainly to consign women, from among the alternatives available today, to a life of the gravest possible insecurity and terror. But that is just one set of problems. Creativity is smothered even more by the inevitably authoritarian character of the fundamentalist movement as well as of the State which such a movement spawns.

The basic premise itself of fundamentalism shuts out all examination. Everything that was necessary is said to have been revealed once and for ever. That Revelation is said to be complex and esoteric. Only a select few, and these few almost invariably allied to the rulers as they are in Saudi Arabia, are said to have the competence to comprehend the Revelation. The ordinary believer who dares to doubt any part of the corpus becomes by definition an apostate. To listen to him would be a crime. If the non-believer dares to raise a doubt, naturally what he says ought not to be listened to as he is a *kafir* whose impulse in raising the doubt cannot be anything but the evil predisposition on account of which he has not embraced the Faith in the first instance. The correspondence between this attitude and the attitude of the Communist theoretician-theologians needs no elaboration. Moreover, it is drilled into the laity that, as the religion as well as the State are surrounded by conspiracies on all sides, to question or criticize the ruler or the religion is to open the gates for the enemy. To displace any of the leaders is to leave ourselves leaderless and therefore vulnerable to the enemy. This line too ensures conformity.

The ignorance of the laity only compounds the matter. Having been led to believe that their religion or doctrine is synonymous with everything that is virtuous and beautiful, that the life and teachings of their founder are synonymous with compassion and justice and love, the lay follower just cannot conceive that any honest person could have any doubt about his Faith or lore. He is therefore predisposed to look upon as an enemy anyone who raises a doubt, or who shows up some evidence or fact which does not reinforce the image of his Faith which that follower at that moment believes and would like the world to believe. This is particularly the case as the lay follower has not only been taught to believe that his Faith is synonymous with everything that is good but in addition to believe that his Faith is in danger. To fortify their leadership the leaders of his Faith and State have instilled the insecurity in his mind. Confronted by an inconvenient fact, confronted by a doubt, therefore, the lay follower reacts immediately and violently. Once again, the consequences for creativity, for the out-of-the-way idea are fatal.

In India, since Independence, fundamentalism has had two further features which have compounded the harm to the community. The fate of Muslim Personal Law illustrates the matter. Even up to the mid-fifties steps were still being taken to reform and modernize that Law. Since then, as is well known, that law has been reformed and further humanized in several Muslim countries. But in India even that extremely slow process of reform has been completely frozen. When attention has been drawn to the changes which have been brought about, for instance in the law of marriage and divorce, in countries as diverse as Tunisia and Morocco, Turkey and Indonesia or even Ayub's Pakistan, the response has invariably been, 'But those are Muslim countries. They can decide to do those things. But India not being a Muslim country cannot legislate these changes.' That again exactly conforms to what used to be the standard Communist response when attention was drawn to the fact that while they were instigating demonstrations, and go-slows, and strikes in a country such as India, workers in Communist States did not have even the right to strike, they had not the slightest security in their jobs, their conditions of work and emoluments were what their employers decreed them to be, when attention was drawn to this contrast the response invariably used to be, 'But those are Workers' States. It is perfectly legitimate for them to do these things, because being Workers' States, they will in any case be looking after the workers' interests. As India is not a State of that kind, not only are these rights inalienable, the struggles must be waged on every front and on every occasion.' Regurgitating rationalisations of this kind, the fundamentalists have frozen Muslim Personal Law to what it was 40 years ago. They have frightened lay Muslims into believing that were anything to be done to bring those laws in conformity with the laws and practices of the world as it is today, their very existence itself would be in peril. The poor Muslims have thereby been driven into a ghetto of fear and apprehension.

At the base of that assertion – 'But those are Muslim countries' – has been the other one: 'Only Muslims can decide issues relating to Muslims.' But Muslim opinion has been in the grip of two sorts: politicians who have concluded that to be leaders of their community they must don fundamentalist clothes and keep the lay Muslim in a state of trepidation; and the controllers and products .of the theological seminaries at Deoband, Saharanpur, Lucknow etc. -- the syllabus of these latter, if nothing else, has kept them frozen in the middle ages.

There are liberals of course among Muslims as there are among other communities. Not only are they few, they have chosen to remain isolated. Barring a very small number, they have desisted from joining hands with reformers from other communities. In fact, they have been urging reformers from other communities *NOT* to address Islamic issues. 'How are we to answer the fundamentalists' accusation, "you are saying the same thing as that enemy of Islam'? In the event, reform, instead of becoming the common endeavour of citizens of all communities, is stalled. The Muslim reformers remain few, and are successively set upon by politicians and clerics. The ordinary Muslim as a result remains in the ghetto of fear and apprehension.

The final consequence of fundamentalism, of course, is that it foments and justifies fundamentalism in others. Bhindranwale in Punjab, the terrorists in Kashmir, as well as those who secured 'victories' for Islam in India in the last decade, have fomented fundamentalism among the Hindus. The consequences of this turn will soon be upon the Hindus of course, but they will be upon the Muslims and Sikhs sooner.

Antidotes

Putting the mystic experience at the centre of things, will go a long way in dissipating fundamentalisms. But in the Islamic case doing so can only be a beginning. For, as we have seen, the accounts of the life of the Prophet and the content of and affirmations about the Quran are only enabling circumstances: they are things which just enable the fundamentalist to ram his absolutist, evangelical programme. The fundamentalist movement is, and the appeal of that movement is essentially political. So, many things have to be done in that realm also.

The surest cure of course would be to help Islamic fundamentalists establish Islamic States: nothing so conclusively proved the case against those other fundamentalisms – Nazism and Communism – as the States that were founded on them; in fact these States closed the argument about those fundamentalisms. But that would be a very costly route. It will spell unspeakable torment for the millions who will come under the heel of such regimes of these countries – as Nazi Germany and the Communist States spelt for millions. And in these times, when the technology of violence has become so horrendous and so easily transferable, the establishment of such regimes will also spell death and suffering to millions outside the boundaries of these States. In a word: such movements should as far as possible be dissipated before they acquire States, but, if they do acquire a State, that State should be quarantined till there is evidence that this regime is going to be the exception – that, unlike every single fundamentalist regime which has come and gone, this one is going to be a humane one.

To prevent fundamentalist movements from acquiring States the best prophylactic is good governance. The corruption and venality and the cruelty of the Shah's regime turned the people to Khomeini, just as the subsequent loot by and heartlessness of the party which had once led the fight for freedom in Algeria has turned the people of that country to the Islamic Salvation Front. Soon enough such regimes open the eyes of the people, as Khomeini's did in Iran, but by then it is too late. By then the regime is so totally in control of the apparatus of violence and terror, and it is so uninhibited in using it, that the people can do nothing but try to survive it, by lying low, by going along, by telling on their friends and relatives.

It is just as necessary to reach information to the people in a country such as India about the record of such regimes. Our Urdu press, for instance, systematically plays down the corruption of

the rulers of Saudi Arabia, of Pakistan and the like. It shuts out
information both about the numerous ways in which so many of
these countries – Tunisia, Morocco, Egypt, Turkey, etc. – have
found it necessary to amend and on many matters replace the
Shariat – the very Islamic law which, it is forever proclaiming is
eternal and to change which in the slightest is to endanger Islam
itself. Simultaneously it shuts out information about the new laws
which have been passed in a country such as Pakistan to bring
affairs in line with *Shariat* and what a retrogression they have
meant for large groups – for instance for women, and for
minorities from Shias to Ahmediyas. It does not inform its
readers about mosques which have been demolished time and
again in Middle Eastern countries for all sorts of purposes. It does
not tell them that in Saudi Arabia the Government has demolished
tombs of the Companions of the Prophet himself. It does not
tell them that while the *Tablighi Jamaat* has full freedom to
preach the message of Islam throughout India, that while its work
has won the admiration of many here, the *Jamaat* is debarred
from Saudi Arabia. This shutting out must be compensated for
by providing information on these matters through other avenues.
Similarly, we should provide detailed data about the true state
of affairs in countries which have taken the fundamentalist route
– how every single one of them is an absolutist dictatorship, and
what the dictators there are doing. In a word, instead of wailing
against Shahabuddin's *Muslim India,* and its legitimizing fundamentalism, we should have *Muslim World*, a journal which gives the
true picture of the state of governance and of the people in countries
which have set up Islamic regimes.

And we must show how the state to which affairs in these
countries has been reduced is not fortuitous, how fundamentalism inevitably stamps out creativity – by insisting for instance,
that every word in The Book – the Quran today, Lenin yesterday
– is true, and eternally so, and everything not in The Book is
unnecessary and worse; how fundamentalism, and its inevitable
result absolutism, do so doubly by engendering a rigidly hierarchi-
cal and authoritarian set-up.

Information about the state of affairs nearer home also should
be made available in systematic form. Two things in particular
need to be documented in detail. The first of these is the fall-out
of fundamentalist politics in the last few years. Many Sikhs were

carried away by Bhindranwale and his band. What has been the consequence, in particular for the Sikhs? Many Muslims were elated by the 'victories' Shahabuddin and others brought them – by having the Supreme Court judgment on Shah Bano over turned, by having Rushdie's book banned. How do those victories look now – in the light, that is, of the reaction they have ignited among the Hindus? The second thing to document is the social practice of those who exploit religion for politics, who set themselves up as the Sole-spokesmen and protectors of religious communities. The cleansing of Hinduism was greatly assisted by the exposure of the kinds of lives the *mahants* were leading, of the way temples and their assets were being used. Documenting the alliances and associations of politicians and controllers of sacred places of other religions, documenting the mismanagement of Waqf Boards for instance, documenting what those who speak loudest in the name of religion have done to, say, the Aligarh Muslim University or are doing to the Jamia, will be just as liberating.

It is vital that such information – about the conditions in Islamic countries, about what consequences fundamentalist politics has brought down upon the Sikhs and is beginning to bring down upon Muslims – be made available to the average Muslim. It is just as important that it be reached to and be enabled to gain currency in the theological seminaries of Deoband, Saharanpur, Lucknow. The products of these seminaries have an enormous role in forming Muslim opinion. But their syllabi – by choice and conscious decision – have been frozen at what was conceived seventy five, even a hundred years ago. Not a ray of knowledge about what the actual results of Islamic rule have been in the Middle East or Pakistan, nor even an iota of information about the developments in science and technology, to say nothing of social sciences and history, has been allowed to filter into these syllabi. Yet the graduates of these institutions and their publications determine what is talked of, what is internalized in *madrasas*, in mosques. A special effort therefore must be made to get the information to these institutions.

One of the appeals of the fundamentalist doctrine is that it will give the adherents of a faith – sickened and made insecure by squabbles among themselves – an overarching identity, an identity that will subsume their differences, one that will lift them above these squabbles and weld them into a mighty host. It is necessary therefore to acquaint them with facts on this score also. Far from uniting the adherents, recourse to fundamentalism will result in – as it invariably has resulted in – a perpetual hunt for the impure, for the lax, for the renegades, for persons and groups who are in league with or, to recall the Leninist phrase, 'objectively' in league with the enemy – that is, for persons and groups who, though not allied to the enemy, are doing things which, 'objectively assessed', are helping the enemy, and this latter it turns out means everything short of full throated acclamation of whatever the fundamentalist leader is doing! Far from uniting, that is, fundamentalism splinters adherents.

One Islamic regime after another in the Middle East, as was noted above, has been at daggers drawn with its neighbour. Within each Islamic regime purges and assassinations and coups have been no less than they were in, say, that other fundamentalism which was to provide an over-arching identity – that is, Communism. Our neighbour, Pakistan, provides a ready example. It was founded on the premise that the Muslims are a separate – that is, one – nation. It declared itself to be an Islamic State in 1962. Did that prevent the West Pakistanis from butchering the East Pakistanis? It proclaimed Islam to be the State Religion in 1973. The Constitution prescribed that the State shall help Muslims to live in accordance with the fundamental principles of Islam, that Quranic instruction shall be compulsory for all Muslims. *Shariat* courts have been set up, as also an overarching Council of Islamic Ideology. Laws and judgments are being reviewed on the touchstone of Islam. Islamic taxes have been introduced. In a word, Islamization has been the *leitmotif* for almost two decades now. Does that today keep the Punjabis and Mohajirs and Sindhis from killing each other off?

These murderous rivalries apart, even the polemics between the regimes, between sects and ethnic groups will be an eye-opener. As is invariably the case in 'isms' which trace their legitimacy to some Book or founder etc., each rival uses the same texts, cites precedents from the same history, hurls the same 'concepts' and categories at all the others. We saw this in the debates which ensued between the Soviet and Chinese Communist parties after 1960, and as a consequence between different brands of communists and Marxist-Leninists in India. Reading these accusations and constructions, the lay follower gets an opportunity to assess whether

the texts are as solid as he has been led to believe they are, to assess
whether concepts and categories which he has internalized have
any meaning at all.   The resulting knowledge cannot but be a
liberating solvent.

Such information will be useful not just to Muslims, it will, as
I have suggested earlier in this book, help in another way : it
will dissipate the phobia Hindus have of Muslims. The Hindus
fear the Muslims, thinking them to be one granite block which
is going to roll down the hill and crush Hindus. When they see that
Islamic regimes are at each others' throats, that within Islamic
countries Muslims are as much at each other as we are, say in India,
their fears will abate.

A counrty like Israel of course has not bccn just studying thcsc
animosities and disseminating information about them. Made a
target of by regimes invoking Islam and the like, it has exploited
such animosities for its security. It has established working relationships with factions in every country which is instigating or
financing fundamentalist groups. Its example also shows that
being a non-Muslim country makes establishing relations with
factions in such countries a bit difficult – but only a bit. The
inter-se animosities between the factions arc so intcnsc – compounded as normal power rivalrics arc in their casc by thc
claim, and in many cases the belief, of each faction that it is doing
Allah's work and the other is obstructing that God-ordained work
– so intense are these rivalries that the factions eventually
establish   working relations with whomsoever, Muslim or non-
Muslim, they think can help them do in their immediate enemy.

Even if we cannot on our own establish working relations with
groups and factions in countries which fan or finance fundamentalist groups here, we must collaborate with other countries   which
are facing a threat from Islamic fundamentalism. We have so
much to learn from them – even in mere scholarship: the work
which scholars in these countries have done on the Quran, on
Islamic history, the knowledge they have garnered about political
movements and groups in Islamic countries will give us a head
start. But to be taken seriously in this venture, we have, at the very
least, to be consistent. We cannot – as our then Foreign Minister
did – laud Saddam Hussein as being one of the greatest statesmen
of the   world, we cannot confer   the   Award · for promoting
international understanding on Yasser Arafat, we cannot kow-tow

to fundamentalists at home on Shah Bano one day, on Rushdie the next, and expect France or Israel, Russia or China to take us seriously when we tell them that we want to join them in stemming Islamic fundamentalism.

Pre-requisites

But to do any of this we have first to clear up our minds and practice here at home.

We must look fundamentalism in the eye. Ever so often we fawn and cringe before a religious leader because of his age or supposed scholarship. Do we take care before doing so to examine what he has been preaching and teaching? How would we regard a person in whose view 'A religious order cannot be established unless religion comes to wield political power and the system of governance is based on Islamic foundations'? Who commends Iqbal's 'lofty idealism' and mature political outlook which, he says, 'lay at the base of the demand for Pakistan'? In whose view the Hindu, Greek, Roman, and pre-Islamic Arab civilizations are all now 'no better than ancient monuments'? Who has little but scorn for 'modernists of the Middle East' – from Ataturk to Nasser – and whose counsel to the King of Saudi Arabia is to hold fast to the ways of Orthodox Islam ? Who is on that King's *Rabitah al-Alam al Islami,* the organization which determines which Islamic organization will get what part of the Saudi funds for spreading Islamic orthodoxy ? But those are the views of the person everyone honours : Abdul Hasan Ali Nadwi, the Rector of the *Nadwat-ul-Ulama's Dar-ul-Ulum* at Lucknow. (And I have just picked a few sentences from the thumb-nail sketch given in the book most at hand: M S Agwani's informative, *Islamic Fundamentalism in India,* Twenty First Century India Society, New Delhi, 1986, pp. 29-39.) He is much sought after by politicians of all hues, he is the President of the Muslim Personal Law Board. He seldom speaks in public. But because of the deference everyone shows him, his influence is pervasive. Shahabuddin etc. are just foot-soldiers compared to him. And Ali Mian, as he is known, is much more circumspect in what he says, perhaps even in the views he holds than so many others whom we defer to because of their age, their 'standing in the community', because of the positions – in this instance, the headship of a theological seminary – they occupy. Surely, we should make it a point to study the books and speeches of persons before we laud them and turn to them to help sort out our problems.

Even such small things will go a long way. But naturally they are ancillary to the three basic things which need to be done, and to which attention has been drawn throughout this book.

The first of these is to purge our discourse, our way of looking at things of double-standards. Nothing has inflamed Hindu reaction as the way our pressmen and our politicians have been bending backwards to pander to the fundamentalists of other religions.

Nor has anything taught the Hindus that they too must pursue political power *per se*, that they too must organize themselves politically as Hindus, that they too must bend the State and strain at the courts as the success that fundamentalist Muslim politicians have had in doing each of these things. Other than disseminating information, therefore, the one way to thwart fundamentalism is to have a fair and firm State : a State that does not allow the adherents or organizations of one religion to do what it does not allow those of another religion to do, a State that does not allow an organisation wearing a religious garb to do what it does not allow a secular organisation to do, a State which enforces secular laws – from those regarding putting up loudspeakers to those regarding possession and storage of arms – strictly, a State which puts the requirements of peace and law and order always above contrivances like processions etc. in the name of religion, a State which gives absolutely no quarter to anyone who takes to the gun. Bending to one side to win votes because those who sway the opinion of that group have frightened the group that it is in danger or have cajoled its members into believing that by casting their votes *en bloc* one way they will secure special concessions, only impels others – in this case the Hindus – to organise themselves into a vote bank. Overturning judgments of the Supreme Court on the apprehension – to put the matter at the highest – that not doing so will cause the Muslims to go on a rampage only impels others – the Hindus – to work to create the same prospect when they find a judgment standing in their way. To compel the Archaeological Survey of India to condone the forced entry into and use of protected monuments by Muslim propagandists who assert that they must say their Friday prayers

in these monuments and in these alone, is to impel Hindus to brush
aside the argument that the Babri Masjid is a protected monument
under the jurisdiction of the same Archaeological Survey of India
and must therefore be left alone. Should the State bend to the
terrorists in Punjab and Kashmir, I have not the slightest doubt that
Hindus will conclude that they must rear terrorists of their own.

Finally, as Islamic fundamentalism is not just about acquiring
States but about power – the faith in intimidation and force
it can be stemmed only by thwarting might. It is because
of Islam's faith in power that Muslims the world over identified
with Saddam Hussein. When the US-led alliance was preparing to
confront him many a commentator warned, 'The entire Islamic
world will rise as one man' to defeat the alliance. But that symbol
of the power of Islam, of defiance crumbled. True, in the first
wave, Saddam's defeat intensified bitterness against the West,
against the US in particular. The self-pity into which Muslims
were plunged may also in a sense have sharpened their sense of
fellow-feeling, their sense of identity. But repeated failures will
in the end lead even the least reflective to re-examine the
premises.

In brief, information is the surest solvent, a fair and firm State
is the one dyke, but the determination and wherewithal to turn
back the physical might which fundamentalists muster is the
ultimate defence against fundamentalism.

– July 1992

INDEX